Seeing the Elephant

Related Titles from Potomac Books

Seeing the Elephant

The U.S. Role in Global Security

HANS BINNENDIJK

AND

RICHARD L. KUGLER

CENTER FOR TECHNOLOGY AND
NATIONAL SECURITY POLICY

NDU
Press

NATIONAL DEFENSE UNIVERSITY PRESS

POTOMAC BOOKS, INC.
WASHINGTON, D.C.

Library of Congress Cataloging-in-Publication Data
Binnendijk, Hans.
   Seeing the elephant : the U.S. role in global security / Hans Binnendijk and Richard L. Kugler. — 1st ed.
      p. cm.
   Includes bibliographical references.
   ISBN-13: 978-1-59797-099-0 (alk. paper)
   ISBN-10: 1-59797-099-9 (alk. paper)
   ISBN-13: 978-1-59797-100-3 (alk. paper)
   ISBN-10: 1-59797-100-6 (alk. paper)
   1. United States—Military policy. 2. National security—United States. 3. Security, International. 4. World politics—21st century. I. Kugler, Richard L. II. Title.
   UA23.B4985 2006
   355'.033573—dc22

                                           2006030145

Printed in the United States of America on acid-free paper that meets the American National Standards Institute Z39-48 Standard.

Available from:

Potomac Books, Inc.
22841 Quicksilver Drive
Dulles, Virginia 20166
800-775-2518

First Edition

10 9 8 7 6 5 4 3 2 1

Dedicated to Mary Locke and Sharon Stapleton

Contents

Illustrations

Preface

This book presents an intellectual history of national security thinking since the end of the Cold War. It is an attempt to see the evolving international system and America's role in it through the eyes of over 50 perceptive authors who have analyzed aspects of the unfolding post–Cold War drama. Its premise is that, like the blind men in the Buddhist fable who each feels a different part of the elephant, these authors and their assessments, taken together, can give us a better view of where the world is headed. In that fable, each blind man reported on a part of the elephant: its tusk, ear, leg, or tail. While the reports of the blind men were all different and none was particularly accurate, taken together they gave a better picture of the whole elephant. This book presents, not blind men, but some of the keenest observers of the international scene and of America's role in it. However, even these observers each tend to see only a part of the international system—only part of the elephant. By combining their observations into one picture, we hope to be able to see more of the whole elephant.

Seeing the elephant has another meaning. As used by soldiers of the Union Army during the Civil War,[1] the phrase referred to the rude awakening a raw recruit had when he first encountered the Confederate Army on the battlefield: when he first "saw the elephant." Seeing the elephant dispelled naïve illusions and replaced them with awareness of difficulty and danger. This did not mean paralysis and impotence; rather, it matured the soldiers and made them into professionals who could be effective at their jobs. The Union Army as a whole took several years to "see the elephant," but after it had done so, it won the war. In the early 21st century, the United States has had a similar rude awakening; it needs to respond with policies that are visionary, skillful, and constructive.

The primary audience for this book is the students of America's war colleges. During a year at the National War College, the Industrial College of the Armed Forces, or one of the four Service war colleges, officers who have excelled in military or diplomatic tactics and operations must become officers who are prepared to deal with strategy at the national and international level. We hope that this volume will show these students the best analysis available by introducing them to these important books, serving as a guide to further reading, and providing them with new insights. As these students become America's leaders, we hope that the lessons taught by the authors reviewed here will benefit our Nation. This book may also be useful to a broader audience, including Government officials, scholars, college students, and citizens interested in this crucial subject.

The books reviewed in this volume represent only a select few of the many excellent contributions made by scholars and practitioners during the past 15 years. We have chosen books representative of differing concepts and schools of thought concerning international relations since the end of the Cold War. We present only books and have not drawn upon the hundreds of important journal articles that have been written, nor have we reviewed many works by non-American authors. We limited the topics reviewed to a fairly traditional national security cluster; we do not talk much about environmental security, demographic vulnerabilities, or international pandemics. Although we comment on some of the authors' arguments, our purpose is not to deliver detailed critiques of these books. Rather, it is to present them in a logical fashion that will, we hope, further the reader's understanding of the new international system and America's place in it. We have not relied on existing schools of thought or theories of international affairs, such as realism, liberalism, constructivism, or institutionalism, although we discuss some of their concepts; instead, we have created our own scheme to organize the material that we review.

Chapters two, three, and four of this book examine the emerging new international system, both as it exists today and where it may be headed. Those chapters draw upon books published over the past 15 years that provide valuable conceptual lenses for interpreting today's complex realities. Chapter two examines books that provide what we call a *neo-Kantian* portrayal of world affairs: a relatively optimistic view arguing that the future will be shaped by growing democratization and economic prosperity. Chapter three examines books we categorize as *neo-Hobbesian*, which portray the future in more pessimistic terms, shaped primarily by stressful security affairs that often require military solutions. Chapter four examines books that explain how new technologies are giving rise to both new opportunities and new threats, including terrorism and the proliferation of weapons of mass destruction. This chapter shows how the empowerment of small groups by new technologies has amplified both neo-Kantian and neo-Hobbesian processes, trends that are so powerful that it leads us to suggest that we are in an "age of empowerment." Chapter five surveys books on American national security strategy as it has evolved in this new global system.

The changing global landscape discussed in chapters two, three, and four and the contending visions of America's global role discussed in chapter five provide a challenge to those making defense policy. In chapter six, therefore, we review several books that address American defense policy. A neo-Kantian world implies one in which defense spending can be trimmed, as was the case from 1989 to 1997. A neo-Hobbesian world calls for increased defense spending, and indeed such increases began around 1998. A world with empowered small groups that threaten the American homeland calls for accelerated defense spending, which the United States witnessed after September 2001. But the cost of war in Iraq and Afghanistan, plus increasing budget deficits, will put intense pressure on future defense budgets. New defense planning concepts may be needed to cope with this pressure.

In chapter seven, we offer our synthesis of what we believe to be the strengths of the views presented in the earlier chapters of this book. Such a synthesis should focus on developing cooperation among the world's major powers and adapting global institutions in a common effort to deal with what the U.S. Defense Department's 2006 *Quadrennial Defense Review* (*QDR*) calls the *Long War* against terrorism. This is a complex struggle, not really a war in the traditional sense, which requires American strength and fortitude. It cannot be won unilaterally or with military or hard power alone; it requires considerable soft or persuasive and diplomatic power, and an unprecedented degree of unity of effort among the great powers. This will require not only American leadership, but also an American willingness to consult with and adjust to accommodate the reasonable policies of its key partners.

Acknowledgments

We are grateful to each of the authors of the books that we have reviewed for their major intellectual contributions to this volume. We asked each to comment on our draft review of their books, and in many cases we adopted their suggestions so as to clarify their meaning and intent. We thank Gina Cordero for her research, for her help in assembling the material for this volume, and for her followup work with the authors reviewed. We thank Courtney Richardson for her work on the notes and for her very helpful suggestions. Thanks are also due to Charles Balck, Duncan Long, Timothy Lo, Cheryl Loeb, and Dennis Shorts for their research support. We owe a debt to Sean Kay and Frank Kramer for extremely helpful and thorough reviews of our manuscript. We especially thank Teresa J. Lawson for her outstanding editing of our manuscript and for her many constructive suggestions. And we thank Lisa Yambrick and the editors of National Defense University Press for their excellent work in bringing this volume to final publication.

Chapter One

Introduction

Even as its attention is riveted on Iraq and the war on terror, the United States must not lose sight of its larger role in world affairs and the new challenges arising there. Dealing with Iraq and al Qaeda is important, but they are merely parts of an unfolding global drama that will have an immense impact on the future. This drama pits the dynamics of peace and progress against those of chaos and turmoil, with an uncertain outcome. In his 2005 inaugural address, President George W. Bush emphasized the importance of spreading liberty and democracy around the world; other key issues and trends are potential sources of trouble as well as opportunity:

- the future of the world economy and the global imbalance in the distribution of wealth
- the fragile unity of the transatlantic alliance and the global democratic community
- troubled relations among some of the world's major powers
- strategic conditions along the so-called southern arc of instability whose danger is exacerbated by the proliferation of weapons of mass destruction (WMD)
- the impact on security and the environment of the scramble for hydrocarbon resources as growing Asian economies seek secure energy sources
- the disruptive impact of cross-border and health issues such as conflict over riparian rights, transnational disease, natural disasters, and population movements
- the search for values and identity around the world, pitting democracy, capitalism, and community-building against radical religious fundamentalism, ethnic nationalism, and other premodern ideologies and belief systems

- the impact of new technologies both on states within the Westphalian state system and on newly empowered nonstate actors
- the ability of the United States to act wisely and effectively in the face of these great challenges and uncertainties.

Failure to pay proper attention to similar undercurrents caused trouble in Europe at the start of the 20th century. In 1910, many Europeans thought their continent was headed toward perpetual peace. Indeed, in a popular book of the time, Norman Angell declared that war in Europe had become impossible because of growing economic interdependence and modern cultural values.[1] Only four years later, however, Europeans found themselves plunged into a devastating world war. It might have been foreseen and prevented, had people understood more clearly the trends silently taking shape. Nobody wants to be caught by similar surprises in the 21st century, yet many recent events—good and ill—have been so surprising that they caught even experts flatfooted. This should warn us that today's world is not understood as well as it should be.

The answers to key questions are uncertain. For example, what is the current state of the global security system, and where is it headed? What challenges and opportunities are arising, and what dangers are emerging, silently or otherwise? How will the various regions of the world be affected? How should the United States act to help shape the future, while protecting its security, interests, and values? How can it deal with the threats of terrorism and WMD that could menace its homeland or allies? How can it keep allies by its side and opponents at a safe distance? These essential questions are addressed in this book, not to answer all of them definitively, but to help craft an intellectual framework by which readers can think usefully about them.

The time is ripe for an overall assessment of the U.S. role in world affairs. The end of the Cold War and the early 1990s ushered in a welcome but temporary international system, often referred to as the post–Cold War era. This period, in the eyes of many observers, was the beginning of an enduring era of tranquility and harmony that would be overseen by an American superpower. Grounds for this optimism came from Europe's progress toward peace and unity, an unprecedented degree of stability in relations among the great powers, and the spread of democracy and capitalism into many new regions, including Asia and Latin America. Ethnic violence in such areas as the Balkans and sub-Saharan Africa seemed to be marginal problems along the road to progress.

The terrorist attacks of September 11, 2001, shattered this hopeful vision and ended the post–Cold War era. It became impossible to ignore the fact that the greater Middle East had become a seething cauldron of chaos and violence, capable of directly damaging the United States and other wealthy democracies. The dynamics of globalization and spreading information technologies were drawing the world closer together at an accelerating pace. While these trends were beneficial in many respects, they also magnified new and previously unseen dangers, and they elevated the importance of regions that had not previously been considered central to global order. Today, the greater Middle East and the war on terrorism are focal points of international security affairs. But it is not at all clear that the global system of 10 or 20 years from now will closely resemble that of today. If the pace of change over the next decade or two is as fast as that of previous years, entirely different regions, problems, and challenges are likely to demand the world's attention.

Current world trends are mixed. The sense of optimism bequeathed by the 1990s should not entirely yield to pessimism. Progress can be made if the United States and others commit themselves to the pursuit of global security, human liberty, and economic prosperity, and if difficult problems can be managed efficiently so that existing opportunities can be developed. Much depends upon how multiple countries and other actors decide to behave. Actively seeking to recognize how global trends are evolving, to understand them, and to devise ways to deal with them is vital if the United States is to lead wisely. Because today's world is complex and changing rapidly, knowledge and self-awareness are crucial to shaping the future rather than being shaped by it.

Scope and Method

This book deals not only with how the world is evolving, but also with America's perceptions of the world: the images, concepts, and theories in the minds of its government and people. It examines these perceptions by surveying how a large number of scholars and writers have portrayed world affairs and U.S. national security strategy over the past 15 years. In today's world, understanding world affairs is essential, and it is equally essential to be able to judge how to attain national purposes. Knowledge and wisdom are needed not only by the U.S. Government, but also by the community of academicians, consultants, journalists, and writers who think and write about modern world affairs. Because the United States is a democracy with open debate, their work informs the public dialogue and influences how the Government sees the world. The national security attitudes and the performance of all Presidential administrations since the end of the Cold War, including the Clinton and Bush administrations, have been affected—for good and ill—by this literature. This undoubtedly will remain true for future administrations. To the extent this literature provides wise analyses and advice, U.S. national security policy will be strengthened; to the extent it is misguided, the United States may suffer. This literature also provides a measure of how American perceptions of world affairs and U.S. global strategy have been evolving during the astonishing changes of the past 15 years.

A stock-taking book would have been impossible to write even five years ago, because too little was certain about the post–Cold War world and the U.S. role in it. Since then, the security system of the 21st century has begun to show itself more clearly. The United States has accumulated experience—successful and otherwise—in dealing with it. This book endeavors to draw upon this growing knowledge and experience to put forth judgments that are less hypothetical, and more concrete, than would have been possible even a few years ago.

This volume endeavors, therefore, to see the elephant by surveying more than 60 books, describing them and examining them for their implications, strengths, and shortcomings. These books assess contemporary world affairs as well as U.S. national security policies: thus, the elephant we are attempting to portray is both the world scene and the U.S. role in it.

Organization of the Chapters

The immediate post–Cold War period was dominated by relatively optimistic neo-Kantian writers such as Francis Fukuyama and Samuel Huntington, who focused primarily on democratic successes in Eurasia and Latin America. We talk about these in chapter two. Later in the decade, national security analysts such as Zbigniew Brzezinski, William Pfaff, and Robert Kaplan presented decidedly more neo-Hobbesian analyses, focusing on troubles in the Balkans, the greater Middle East, and Africa. We talk about this approach in chapter three. During the decade, Huntington shifted his focus from the unifying theme of democracy to the dividing theme of clashing civilizations, which reflected the changing state of world events and also affected the changing policies adopted by successive U.S. administrations.

A third wave of analysis, emerging more recently, emphasized that the technology of the globalized world empowers individuals and small groups, giving them some statelike attributes that can either enhance or, as on September 11, 2001, threaten American interests. Thomas L. Friedman, for example, focuses on the positive side of empowerment, while Graham Allison concentrates on one of its dangers, the increased risk of nuclear terrorism. The result for international affairs is a mosaic that is much more complex than the Cold War and that holds both new opportunities and new challenges for the United States. This powerful dynamic shapes what we call, in chapter four, a new *age of empowerment.* Empowerment has the effect of amplifying the existing neo-Kantian and neo-Hobbesian views of the world, because now it is not just states, but even small groups of individuals, that could dramatically affect world events for good or ill.

Several schools of strategic thought have presented alternative visions of America's engagement in this complex world, as we detail in chapter five. Those whom we classify as *traditional conservatives* focus on maintaining great-power equilibrium through an array of diplomatic and military tools. Their approach was successful in managing the termination of the Cold War in the late 1980s and early 1990s. The *progressive multilateralists* tend toward a neo-Kantian view of the world, and they prefer the use of soft or nonmilitary persuasive power when possible; their views dominated the policies of the mid- to late 1990s. The *assertive interventionists* rose to prominence in 2000–2001 as a darker neo-Hobbesian view of the world was reinforced by acts of global terrorism. They tend to favor military and sometimes unilateral solutions to global problems. More recently, a fourth school is entering the debate in reaction to the assertive interventionists; these *offshore balancers* would significantly reduce America's overseas military presence and rely much more on local partners to keep the peace.

It was relatively easy during the Cold War to categorize individual analysts along a linear spectrum from left to right based solely on their views on a single topic, the Soviet Union. Today, this linear approach would not be useful. Instead, it is easier to explain these four schools using a matrix that describes their policy motivations and their inclination toward instruments of power, as we explain in chapter five. For example, both the progressive multilateralists and the assertive interventionists favor building democratic institutions (as Kant did), while both traditional conservatives and offshore balancers look to power relationships as the dominant factor in their policies (as Hobbes did). Traditional conservatives and assertive interventionists tend to stress the use of military force, while progressive multilateralists and offshore balancers focus more on soft power as the primary instrument to be used by the United States. Thus, a progressive multilateralist who changes a few assumptions about the need to use force can become an assertive interventionist.

All of these strategic views have weaknesses as well as strengths. Traditional conservatives have not paid adequate attention to transnational threats; progressive multilateralists have shied away from the use of military force; assertive interventionists have tended to disregard the limits of American power; and offshore balancers generally support large reductions in forward-deployed troops, which could further destabilize places like Iraq and Afghanistan.

In chapter six, we review recent transformations of defense policy, both in theory and in practice. A revolution in information technology has profoundly affected the way in which the United States fights. America's military dominated the high-intensity combat in Kosovo, Afghanistan, and Iraq using these new technologies and concepts of warfare. An unintended consequence of these rapid successes has been that the United States was unprepared for postconflict operations. The U.S. military is now adapting to meet these postconflict challenges, but if defense resources become tight, critical priorities will need to be set. As we argue in chapter seven, a synthesis of the best of the strategies presented in preceding chapters could overcome the weaknesses of each.

Hobbes and Kant

The picture that emerges from the next three chapters of this book is one of considerable dynamism, intellectual ferment, and change. In the early to middle 1990s, many observers of the post–Cold War scene were responding to encouraging trends. Perhaps initially they were simplistic in some respects, but in the years that followed, writers developed increasingly sophisticated theories of how the new global security system was taking shape. Along the way, the literature on world affairs evolved from mainly neo-Kantian interpretations to include a growing number of neo-Hobbesian books as numerous writers became more skeptical about prospects for enduring harmony and democratic solutions. As they grew more worried about the dangers ahead, many tilted toward solutions emphasizing the use of assertive power rather than multilateral community-building. The division of this complex, multifaceted literature into what we have called neo-Kantian and neo-Hobbesian camps illustrates a basic trend in the literature. The existence of two bodies of literature, each offering different interpretations of contemporary trends, means that a better understanding of modern world politics can emerge, provided that both bodies of literature are seen for what they are worth and both are explored in search of common insights.

Our distinction between neo-Kantian and neo-Hobbesian interpretations requires a brief explanation. Both Thomas Hobbes and Immanuel Kant were modernists who endeavored to create approaches to orchestrating government and society that would be more practical and realistic than the utopian schemes of the ancient Greeks. Cognizant that human relations, in their natural state, may descend into anarchy and violence, both sought ways to create order and peace so that stable societies could be built and progress achieved. Where they differed was in the political philosophies each articulated to achieve this end. Whereas Hobbes sought solutions through state power, Kant sought them through moral conduct and law. The result was two different approaches not only to building modern states, but also to orchestrating international relations. In today's world, Hobbes is often portrayed as a conservative or a realist, and Kant as a liberal or an idealist. However, if they were alive today, both probably would shun these labels and would point out that they were writing about conditions prevailing centuries ago. Their names are invoked here not to suggest that their respective philosophies can be directly applied to today's world, but to provide a convenient frame of reference for loosely grouping the attitudes and perspectives of modern-day writers into the two camps we call neo-Hobbesian and neo-Kantian.

Thomas Hobbes (1588–1679)

British philosopher Hobbes is commonly regarded as pessimistic about human nature.[2] He described the natural state as: "No arts; no letters; no society; and which is worst of all, continual fear, and danger of violent death; and the life of man, solitary, poor, nasty, brutish, and short."[3] Many of Hobbes' views were formed by the bloody civil wars fought in Britain and by the Thirty Years' War that tore Northern Europe apart. Hobbes viewed humans as naturally prone to struggle and violence as a result of fear as well as competition over wealth. Yet he believed that humans had a capacity to reason and to make intelligent collective decisions aimed at advancing the common good. His goal was to define a social contract whereby men could live together within a strong state that would keep the peace. Under this contract, people would exchange some of their rights and freedoms to gain security. He thought government's proper role was to create a Leviathan of centralized power and order that would be capable of enforcing this contract, thereby providing security and preventing civil war. In his view, government must hold sovereign authority over its citizens and be capable of withstanding challenges to its rule. While he was not indifferent to the rights and liberties of citizens, he was favorably inclined to monarchies capable of wielding absolute power in order to prevent anarchy. His philosophy helped create legitimacy for monarchical rule in Britain (which became democratic only long after his death). Across Europe as a whole, Hobbes' philosophy helped establish a foundation for the modern commonwealth or nation-state, which sought to safeguard peace and stability within its borders and to protect itself against foreign invasion.

Hobbes viewed interstate relations as inherently conflict-ridden and regulated, if at all, by power: "wherein men live without other security, than what their own strength and their own invention shall furnish them."[4] The absence of a central Leviathan or a world government meant that the international system was highly anarchical. In this system, states commonly acted out of fear of each other or engaged in predatory conduct toward each other. States, as a result, were prone to assemble military power and to use it to conquer other states when they could. The implication of Hobbes' view for Britain was that it must maintain a strong navy capable of defending its island, and an army capable of influencing Europe's wars in order to prevent threats to British ascent. At the time, Britain was mostly worried about France and Spain, against whom it engaged in frequent wars. Yet Hobbes was also aware that diplomacy could be an effective tool for regulating international conflict and preventing war. During his lifetime, the Peace of Westphalia ended a long period of European religious wars and made the modern nation-state legitimate. European politics began to shift from religious rivalries to contests between monarchical states over territorial and economic interests and power.

Immanuel Kant (1724–1804)

Kant, a Prussian moral and political philosopher, was well aware of human propensities toward conflict and violence. But he also believed optimistically that over time, mankind could be rendered more peaceful and humane through commitment to moral conduct and common law.[5] His moral philosophy was anchored in what he called the Categorical Imperative, a form of the golden rule calling upon people to treat each other as they would want to be treated themselves. He believed that people should enjoy freedom and liberty, including freedom from government repression. But he also argued that individual autonomy could be enjoyed only if people made a rational and enduring commitment to proper moral conduct, public duty, and respect for law, which constrained their capacity to victimize each other. To Kant, this sense of duty, obligation, and law could hold a society together, thus lessening the need for a governmental Leviathan as envisioned by Hobbes.

Drawing upon the work of John Milton, John Locke, and others, Kant argued in favor of anchoring government on the rule of law for the common benefit of citizens. He favored republican government as the best guarantee of a lawful society. Thus, he was an early architect of concepts of representative government and democracy. Emerging political conditions in Europe may have encouraged Kant to be more optimistic and liberal than Hobbes could have been during the 17th century. When Kant wrote in the 18th century, absolute monarchy was giving way to constitutional monarchy, nascent parliaments, and even democracy. Indeed, Kant lived to see the American Revolution of 1776 and the French Revolution of 1789.

However, even if Kant was swimming with the tides of domestic government in Europe, he was swimming against the tides of interstate politics, which remained decidedly war-prone during his life. The 18th century witnessed a lengthy succession of wars brought about by struggles for supremacy among Britain, France, Prussia, Austria, Russia, Spain, and others. To help solve this problem, Kant proposed the application of humane principles and moral conduct to guide interstate relations. He argued in favor of creating a federation of republics or a community of liberal democracies, anchored in commerce and cooperative diplomacy in order to prevent war and preserve peace. In his 1795 book *Perpetual Peace*, Kant declared that even though war was the natural state of international relations, countries could take deliberate steps to establish a state of peace.[6] He said that this required them to reduce their standing armies, to agree not to try to dominate each other or to interfere with each other's internal affairs, to establish international law to govern their relations, and to enter a "league of peace" to end all wars. He argued that if statesmen heeded philosophers, they could achieve an international federation of independent republics whose conduct would be governed by codes of universal law and hospitality. In a sense, he sketched a forerunner of the modern United Nations. He would have been pleased at the peace established by the Congress of Vienna in 1814–1815, but he would have remained aware nonetheless that it was anchored mainly on agreement of monarchies to respect pragmatic rules of geopolitical conduct, rather than on moral commitment to republican governments and international law.

There is no way of knowing how Hobbes and Kant would view today's world, but with some simplification, their differing philosophies can help characterize writers on contemporary issues. As we see it, modern-day neo-Kantians embrace similar attitudes: optimism about opportunities for global peace and progress; belief that democracy can effectively displace dictatorships, militarism, and nationalism; confidence that traditional competitive geopolitics can give way to cooperative economics anchored in free trade and global integration; and faith that international law and multilateral institutions, properly organized, can expand zones of peace and prosperity. While many neo-Kantians acknowledge that power remains important on the world scene, they tend to discount the need for a modern-day Leviathan, and they argue that the United States should not try to play this role unilaterally.

Modern-day neo-Hobbesians are generally more pessimistic. They do not believe that democracy is triumphing, noting that dictatorships, authoritarian governments, and fanatical anti-Western ideologies remain entrenched in many regions. They do not believe that traditional geopolitics is disappearing, and they dispute the idea that the globalizing world economy will bring about peaceful integration. They see mounting chaos, anarchy, and violence in the Middle East and other unstable regions. They doubt the efficacy of international law and multilateral governing bodies in dealing with those challenges. They fear that such emerging threats as terrorism, WMD proliferation, and ethnic mass murder are likely to get worse. Like Hobbes, they judge that order and stability would require the presence of a powerful, assertive modern-day international Leviathan, and they believe that the United States and its close allies must play this role.

Some authors are difficult to catalogue definitely. Indeed, we have placed writings of at least one prominent author in both camps: we consider Samuel Huntington's book, *The Third Wave*, to be neo-Kantian, while we categorize his later book, *The Clash of Civilizations,* as neo-Hobbesian.

A related analytical problem arose as we sought to categorize these books, involving whether the author's ideas are descriptive or prescriptive. Often the categories are the same either way: Francis Fukuyama's volume, for example, is neo-Kantian in both description and prescription, and John Mearsheimer's book offers both neo-Hobbesian description and neo-Hobbesian prescription. In some cases, however, a book's descriptive or predictive assessment of world affairs is more neo-Hobbesian, but its prescriptive recommendations are neo-Kantian. Examples include works by Robert Gilpin, Ronald Asmus, and Samantha Power. Categorizing each book based on the overall weight of its arguments, we put Gilpin and Asmus in the neo-Kantian group, and Power in the neo-Hobbesian group, but an argument could be made for putting each into either group.

With these caveats, we summarize key postulates of the two schools of thought in table 1–1.

Where Is the World Headed: Kant or Hobbes?

During the early to mid-1990s, the neo-Kantian literature presented in chapter two held center stage. Some neo-Hobbesian books were appearing, but they were mostly at the margins of the prevailing consensus. At the time, the world seemed fairly peaceful and headed toward progress. By the middle to late 1990s, however, a growing body of neo-Hobbesian literature (presented in chapter three) began appearing in response to the acceleration of worrisome trends in world affairs. After the terrorist attacks of September 11, 2001, neo-Hobbesian books increasingly gained center stage and public attention, while neo-Kantian books fell from favor in many quarters. This trend does not necessarily mean that the neo-Hobbesians have permanently triumphed over the neo-Kantians. The global reality is that while dangers and threats abound in today's world, hopeful dynamics have not totally faded from the scene, and indeed remain potent in some places. For example, Europe continues to make strides toward peace and unity, and the world economy continues to grow. Because a global clash between hopeful trends and dangerous trends is raging today, both bodies of literature are worthy of serious attention, and each sheds light on the trends toward empowerment of small groups outlined in chapter four.

Often the truth is best perceived not by clinging rigidly to a single theory, but by taking two competing theories and searching for their common ground. Such is the case for seeing the elephant of international affairs. Both the neo-Kantians and the neo-Hobbesians are partly correct, because each group sees part of the elephant of modern world affairs. Both are partly wrong because neither sees the entire elephant.

Taken together, both schools of thought expect the early 21st century to be considerably different from the late 20th century, because globalization and other dynamics are altering how the global security system operates. Neo-Kantian observers in the early to middle 1990s noted that the end of the Cold War

Table 1–1. Key Postulates of Neo-Kantian and Neo-Hobbesian Books		
	Neo-Kantian	**Neo-Hobbesian**
Modern world affairs are driven mainly by:	Democratization and economic growth	Stressful security affairs
The primary instrument is:	Democratic institutions and economic instruments	Military power
The geographic focus is on:	Europe, Asia, and Latin America	Greater Middle East
The main goals of foreign policy should be:	Democracy and economic growth	Stable security affairs
The future is:	Optimistic	Pessimistic
Treaties, alliances, and international institutions merit:	Strong support	Less faith
Interdependence creates:	Opportunities for cooperation	Vulnerabilities
Best chance of success in world affairs comes from:	Liberal democracies working together multilaterally	United States often acting unilaterally as a Leviathan

washed away the dangerous ideological confrontation, nuclear standoff, and bipolar rivalry between the United States and the Soviet Union. In its wake, they point out, came positive developments: the spread of democracy into Eastern Europe and Latin America, the promise of accelerated growth in the economies of many countries and regions, and the quick dissemination of information and knowledge around the world by means of the Internet and other communications systems. Seeing this, some neo-Kantian writers were so optimistic as to predict an enduring era of peace, freedom, and prosperity everywhere.

Beginning in the mid-1990s, events dashed such high hopes and led to the appearance of pessimistic neo-Hobbesian views. The collapse of bipolarity exposed the dangerous heterogeneity of such regions as the Middle East and South Asia, as well as the crippling poverty of Africa. It also revealed troubling new forces, including violent ethnic nationalism in the Balkans, radical Islamic fundamentalism in the Middle East, brutal rogue tyrants, WMD proliferation, and a volatile world economy capable of damaging many regions with its sudden contractions. The world began to appear chaotic and dangerous, and the future seemed uncertain and worrisome.

Neo-Kantians thus tend to be more optimistic about world affairs than neo-Hobbesians. The two groups also disagree on related issues, such as the roles of power and law in world affairs, and the roles of large multinational institutions (such as the United Nations), ad hoc coalitions of the willing, and the desirability of the United States acting alone. But there may be a degree of convergence between the two camps. In recent years, many neo-Kantians have become more worried about the future, and few of them would now say that a positive outcome is assured. For their part, neo-Hobbesians focus on worrisome trends, but many acknowledge important positive developments unfolding across the world. The conceptual gap between them remains large, but it is potentially bridgeable. When the intersection of the two schools is examined, a common theme stands out: most members of both camps agree that a worldwide struggle is taking place, pitting the dynamics of peace and progress against those of chaos and turmoil. They also agree that the outcome is uncertain and that much will depend upon how key countries behave in trying to guide this struggle toward a successful outcome. Because both schools seem to agree on this basic proposition, even though they disagree on many particulars, it provides a basis for forming strategic judgments that draw upon the best research and writing from both schools.

Later in the post–Cold War period, a third group of authors wrote about the effects of technology and empowerment on transnational challenges. These authors, presented in chapter four, stressed a trend of decline in the Westphalian state-centric system and a resulting loss of state sovereignty. As nuclear, biological, and information technologies enhance the power of nonstate actors, they increase the complexity of the international system. The result is an amplification of both the neo-Kantian and the neo-Hobbesian views of the world. On the neo-Kantian side, several authors emphasize that technology can enhance the power of states if properly harnessed, pointing to ways in which technology and sound strategy can topple dictators and make room for democracy. Other writers stress the darker, neo-Hobbesian side of globalization, which was underlined on September 11, 2001. These books link together new threats from terrorism, rogue states, and WMD, influencing perceptions of threat.

Unlike the Cold War, whose bipolar structure was virtually frozen solid, today's complex security system is highly fluid. The new technologies of the information age are accelerating the pace of change while giving rise to new opportunities and threats: the global spread of information networks empowers the integration of the world economy and enables democracy movements to challenge authoritarian rule in many countries, but at the same time, they make it possible for terrorist groups to create far-flung organizations capable of striking with great destructive power almost anywhere in the world.

Thus, a great deal of turbulence and strife could lie ahead if events are not managed properly, while if events are handled wisely and effectively, positive dynamics could take hold. Much depends on whether the United States acts with wisdom and courage. This, in turn, may depend on whether we are able to collaborate in seeing the elephant.

In writing this book, therefore, our aim has been to help readers see the elephant of modern world affairs in its entirety. To the extent we succeed, it is because we have been able to draw upon so many excellent books written by world-class authors. All of these books were selected because they were superbly done; each of them makes a contribution individually. Their strengths stand out even more when they are brought together and evaluated with their collective messages in mind, as we have attempted to do here. The enduring lesson is that if contemporary world affairs are to be understood, the combined efforts of many people will be needed.

Chapter Two

A Neo-Kantian World of Progress

I n this chapter, we review 11 key books of what we call the neo-Kantian genre to capture its main themes: a relatively optimistic view of democracy's condition and of the ability of democratic institutions to manage global affairs. Four of these books emerged early in the 1990s; the remainder were written later, but they reflect upon the lessons of that decade. Although these books were not blind to emerging troubles in the post–Cold War era, their main emphasis was on the opportunities for progress arising from positive trends in global politics and economics.

This chapter begins with four books that examine global political trends:

- Francis Fukuyama, *The End of History and the Last Man* (1992)
- Samuel P. Huntington, *The Third Wave: Democratization in the Late Twentieth Century* (1991)
- Charles Lipson, *Reliable Partners: How Democracies Have Made a Separate Peace* (2003)
- Thomas L. Friedman, *The Lexus and the Olive Tree: Understanding Globalization* (1999).

The chapter then discusses three books on U.S. alliances and great-power relations of the emerging post–Cold war era:

- Jeffrey E. Garten, *A Cold Peace: America, Japan, Germany, and the Struggle for Supremacy* (1992)
- Ronald D. Asmus, *Opening NATO's Door: How the Alliance Remade Itself for a New Era* (2002)
- Charles W. Kegley, Jr., and Gregory A. Raymond, *A Multipolar Peace? Great-Power Politics in the Twenty-first Century* (1994).

The chapter concludes with two books on global economics and two books on global governance:

- Daniel Yergin and Joseph Stanislaw, *The Commanding Heights: The Battle Between Government and the Marketplace that is Remaking the Modern World* (1998)
- Robert Gilpin, *The Challenge of Global Capitalism: The World Economy in the 21st Century* (2000)
- Robert O. Keohane, *Power and Governance in a Partially Globalized World* (2002)
- Anne-Marie Slaughter, *A New World Order* (2004).

We start with one of the most famous books of the neo-Kantian genre.

Francis Fukuyama: Democracy Triumphant

Fukuyama's *The End of History and the Last Man* captured much attention and acclaim when it was published in 1992.[1] The book heralded the imminent triumph of democracy over tyranny, reaching this hopeful conclusion through a combination of logical reasoning and futurist extrapolation of general trends, rather than in-depth empirical studies of specific regions. Drawing upon the evolution of Western political philosophy during the 18th and 19th centuries, Fukuyama examined the role of ideas in shaping social action (see table 2–1.) He paid special attention to Georg Hegel and Friedrich Nietzsche, political philosophers who emphasized the impact of ideas on political life and human behavior. Fukuyama noted that people of all historical eras have pursued not only material satisfaction, but also prestige (*thymos*), often by trying to dominate each other; thus, he was not oblivious to humanity's failings. Nor was he indifferent to the disruptive effects of social conflict or the risks of continued turbulence in the decades ahead. His central assertion, nevertheless, was that the great ideological struggle between the two modern forms of government—democracy and totalitarianism—had at last been settled with democracy's victory in the Cold War.

It is in the arena of political ideology, Fukuyama argued, that history has come to an end. Because democracy has won out over its competitors, the contemporary era is witnessing the end of the age-old debate over the best form of government. This development, he believed, justified the resurrection of 19th-century optimism, which had been dealt cruel blows by the wars of the 20th century. Fukuyama did not predict the imminent arrival of utopia, but he did conclude that in the political realm, the final stage of Hegel's dialectical process of thesis, antithesis, and synthesis had been reached, with liberal democracy as the synthesis—hence, the end of history.

Table 2-1. Political Ideologies and Philosophical Origins According to Fukuyama	
Ideologies	Contributing Philosophers
Monarchy, Authoritarianism	Hobbes
Nazism, Totalitarianism, Fascism	Nietzsche
Communist Totalitarianism	Marx, Engels
Liberal Democracy	Locke, Kant, Jefferson

Fukuyama portrayed the ideological struggle between democracy and tyranny in historical terms. He found the origins of the idea of democracy in the Enlightenment, the 18th-century European philosophical movement that put faith in science, progress, and the perfectibility of man through human liberty and freedom. Monarchy was the main form of government across Europe as the century began, but democracy gradually evolved from a theoretical idea to a real-world agenda. As Fukuyama wrote, by the early 19th century, democracy was becoming established in the United States, Britain, and France. However, it encountered opposition from monarchies in Central Europe. The failure of revolutions in the 1830s and 1840s left monarchies in power. Germany's unification meant that conservative Prussia controlled Europe's biggest industrial power. Even Germany slowly pursued constitutional reforms and welfare policies, but the liberalizing impulse did not extend further eastward: autocratic Russia continued to be ruled by the tsars, and the Austro-Hungarian Empire remained monarchical. During the latter half of the 19th century, Europe's traditional regimes and balance-of-power rivalries stalled further democratic enlargement. Even as industrialization made the continent as a whole steadily wealthier, it bred discontent among the working poor who saw themselves left behind.

World War I quickly became a grueling attrition war that left the continent devastated and destroyed Europe's sense of ongoing progress, as Fukuyama wrote. However, the victory over Germany and Austria-Hungary in 1918 briefly seemed to set the stage for further democratization, embodied in President Woodrow Wilson's Four Freedoms, the destruction of the old Central European Empires, the concept of self-determination for oppressed nations, and the League of Nations. These soaring hopes were quickly dashed in the late 1920s and 1930s, as Fukuyama wrote: the Great Depression, with its accompanying social strains, spawned tyrannical and totalitarian modern ideologies. With these challenges to democracy, the League of Nations collapsed, ending hopes for collective security. The United States reverted to isolationism; Britain sought appeasement.

From the political right, with its philosophical origins in Nietzsche's writings, came fascism in Italy and Nazism in Germany. Both ideologies were anchored in corporatist political values that suppressed human liberty in order to mobilize society against the extremist impulses of Marxism and class warfare that were seen coming from the left. Nazism was the more xenophobic of the two, with its emphasis on totalitarianism, racism, and military aggression. From the political left came Marxist communism, which took hold in the Soviet Union after World War I. Under Stalin's brutal rule, communism established itself as a savage single-party dictatorship that snuffed out human liberty and capitalism, treating the individual as a tool of the state in order to pursue forced industrialization. As Fukuyama explained, the stage was thus set for a colossal struggle among democracy, fascism and Nazism, and communism.

Fukuyama viewed the six decades from 1930 to 1990 as an enactment of Hegel's dialectic of competing political ideologies, with liberal democracy as the victor. World War II resulted in the crushing defeat of fascism and Nazism. The Cold War in turn defeated the Soviet Union and European communism. Although, as Fukuyama acknowledged, these victories over totalitarianism were partly due to the military and industrial strength of the Western powers, they got their real strength, he said, from the enduring appeal of democracy over dictatorship. Democracy's decisive victory in Europe, Fukuyama reasoned, set the stage for its consolidation and expansion elsewhere. It seemed destined to sweep aside lingering forms of authoritarianism and oppression because it is not just a superior form of government, but the best possible model for organizing human society, economics, and politics: the apex of political ideas, reflecting the best of the Enlightenment's optimism.

Fukuyama thus identified compelling reasons that liberal democracy emerged from centuries of turmoil to have widespread appeal in today's world.

In the political arena, it provides elections and constitutional rights, and also recognition of each citizen's moral worth. In the economic arena, it protects private property and permits creation of wealth, laying the foundation for market capitalism and its benefits. No other system or ideology, he wrote, provides both of these critical benefits, which work together to create stable, prosperous societies. Fukuyama claimed that while authoritarian governments might try to create capitalist economies, they quash political freedom in ways that tend to dampen economic initiative and responsibility. Liberal democracy, he concluded, is triumphing because it makes the most sense for organizing political and economic life.

Fukuyama's book argued that liberal democracy will benefit countries that are newly adopting this system, partly because market capitalism generates greater prosperity than command economies, but more importantly, because liberal democracy provides for personal freedom and a civic culture. Beyond this, such developments increase the odds for international peace because, as he noted, democracies typically do not wage war against each other. To the extent this continues to hold true, he asserted, interstate military rivalry and war will give way to growing community. With liberal democracy prevailing in more and more of the world, peaceful cooperation among nations will become more the rule than the exception. The desire for material rewards and prestige will be channeled elsewhere than to interstate aggression; the principal challenge will be for human beings to learn to find self-fulfillment in peace. Provided this can be achieved, Fukuyama concluded, the *Last Man* of his title will not be a military man or even a man of strategic affairs and world politics: these preoccupations will diminish dramatically. Instead, the Last Man will be Economic Man, seeking prestige through material wealth and related activities, and content to live within a liberal democratic order that perpetuates peace, justice, and equal opportunity.

Fukuyama's book was met with considerable approval by readers who shared his optimism after the sudden collapse of European communism in the early 1990s. His optimistic themes were reflected in the foreign policy of the Clinton administration during its first term, when hopeful trends seemed to outweigh worrisome ones. However, Fukuyama's book also triggered skepticism among those who foresaw a future with new sorts of international trouble after the Cold War, and who doubted that democracy could be adopted everywhere. The book undoubtedly made a good case for why democracy *should* be adopted everywhere: it safeguards liberties and usually is better at economic management than totalitarianism is, by fostering private property and market capitalism. But whether democracy actually *will* be adopted everywhere, overcoming all the roadblocks along the way, is an issue that Fukuyama did not fully resolve.

In retrospect, Fukuyama's book was important because it called attention to the role that ideas play in political life, and because it pointed out that ideas are not fixed but constantly in flux, capable of bursting out of periods of temporary stagnation to propel sweeping change. He set the modern-day struggle over ideas in historical perspective, showing that totalitarian ideologies of the 20th century were transient phenomena, not permanent conditions that would always prevent human political and economic progress.

The book was a corrective to literature of the 1950s and 1960s that had praised communism because of its alleged superiority at using forced industrialization and command economies to achieve sustained economic growth, even if at the expense of human liberty. Fukuyama was correct in assessing that rather than being the wave of the future, communism and other totalitarian ideologies would be mostly relegated to the ash can of history. He thus accurately portrayed the central ideological drama of the 20th century. He also correctly predicted the further spread of democracy across Europe, as well as parts of Asia, that would take place as the Soviet Empire receded and communism lost its appeal. Events during 1995–2005 would show, however, that Fukuyama had underestimated the enduring appeal of Islam across the Middle East and adjoining regions. Islam's resistance to modern Western ideas hardened the cultural and religious impediments to the spread of liberal democracy into those regions.

Fukuyama's thesis thus can be judged as partly right, especially with respect to Europe; however, it was stretched too far to regions where it was not applicable, such as the Middle East. Fukuyama relied too much on normative political philosophy, and not enough on empirical political science and sociology, in his predictions of a rosy future for democracy everywhere. He apparently neglected a sizable literature generated by political scientists and sociologists as far back as the early 1960s, addressing the causal foundations of democratization and of failure to democratize, such as the book by Barrington Moore, Jr., called *Social Origins of Dictatorship and Democracy: Lord and Peasant in the Making of the Modern World.*[2] Moore concluded that democracy tends to become established where the middle class becomes dominant over the upper and lower classes, rather than where either extreme wins the class struggle. Moore was hardly alone in this view; a frequent theme of the democratization literature is that democracy does not necessarily prevail simply because it is a good idea or that it is, in theory, better than dictatorship. It tends to prevail only when a set of important conditions is in place, including a stable integrated society, a civic culture, private property, and a middle class that operates businesses in the marketplace. Had Fukuyama anchored his analysis more firmly in this literature, he might have concluded that, despite the downfall of communist totalitarianism in Europe, democracy would not necessarily take root everywhere, because many places lacked the necessary ingredients.

Fukuyama wrote subsequent books that addressed his critics and modified his conclusions. In his 1995 book, *Trust: The Social Virtues and the Creation of Prosperity*, Fukuyama put limits on his earlier optimistic conclusions by noting that economic markets and democracy take hold best in societies that are capable of forming "associational relationships" rather than relying on kinship, clan, and ethnic ties.[3] In his 2006 critique of neoconservative support for the Iraq war, entitled *America at the Crossroads*,[4] Fukuyama argued that it was not people's hunger for liberty that would lead them to liberal democracy, but their desire to live in a modern economic society, which in turn would lead to demands for political participation. He thus broke with the Bush administration's neoconservatives not over long-term goals, but over the means and pace of change, specifically as it applied to Iraq. He also made clear that his belief in democracy's inevitable triumph did not necessarily mean the sudden arrival of permanent peace. In *America at the Crossroads*, Fukuyama called for a policy of "realistic Wilsonianism," which would include both more effective forms of American soft power and new "horizontal" international institutions capable of dealing with the new challenges. In that sense, Fukuyama modified his neo-Kantianism somewhat in this 2006 book by suggesting a slower pace of democratic progress and a need to reform both the instruments and institutions often associated with a Kantian approach.

Samuel Huntington: Complex Sources of Democratization

In 1991, Huntington, who would later emerge as a major proponent of neo-Hobbesian thinking, published a book on global democratization that was mainly neo-Kantian.[5] *The Third Wave: Democratization in the Late Twentieth Century* set out to explain the wave of democratization that, during 1974–1990, brought 30 countries of Eastern Europe, Latin America, and Asia into the democratic camp. The march of democracy into Eastern Europe during this period is well known, but less often realized is the extent to which democracy also swept over Latin America, as authoritarian and military regimes were replaced by various types of democracies. Democracy also made progress in Asia, installing itself in South Korea, Taiwan, the Philippines, and elsewhere. Huntington set out to explain why a gradual process that had started years earlier culminated in such a rapid transition in so many regions during this decade and a half.

Huntington defined *democracy* as a system in which public elections are used to choose government leaders. He concluded that the third wave of democratization was a product of both traditional sources and new factors. Traditional factors included the spread of liberal values into these countries, the rise of the middle class, economic development, urbanization, industrialization, and political modernization. New factors included the collapse of communism and Soviet power in Eastern Europe, the widespread failure of authoritarian regimes to achieve effective economic growth, the emergence in several countries of a modernizing political leadership, exposure to global communications, the pro-democracy activities of the United States and its European allies, and the leadership of the Catholic Church. In addition to these factors, Huntington said, there were "bandwagon effects" in a number of countries that saw where the future was headed and decided to come along for the ride.

In gauging the impact of the third wave of democratization on global affairs, Huntington concluded that it enhanced prospects for peace and international cooperation in the regions he was examining. This was not, he said, because democracies are inherently peace-loving; indeed, some of them have had well-deserved reputations for being warlike. But democracies seldom go to war with each other, as he noted; moreover, modern democracies have incentives to participate in global trade regimes and other multilateral entities. The main threat to peace, according to Huntington, arises where democracy appears on the borders of a tyrannical dictatorship and, by its example, threatens to undermine the latter's domestic legitimacy. In reaction, the dictator may take aggressive steps aimed at quashing the neighbor's democratic tendencies.

Huntington stopped short of proclaiming that democracy was now permanently established in all of those countries where it was newly adopted. Indeed, he predicted that some reversals might occur, due to military coups or to failure of weak democratic regimes to consolidate their power or to achieve economic growth. He also did not predict that there would be a fourth wave of democratic expansion into regions that had previously been resistant to democratization; he believed that Confucian cultures in Asia would tend to resist democracy, as would Islamic cultures of the greater Middle East and parts of Africa, due to the relative unimportance placed on individual freedom and the fusion of church and state. He did not rule out democratic gains in these regions, but predicted that progress would be slow. Much, he said, would depend upon further economic growth, the rise of a middle class, and a decline in the legitimacy of authoritarian governments. His guarded appraisal of prospects for democratization in unreceptive regions presaged the emphasis he would place on looming cultural clashes in his later books.

Huntington's book contrasted with popular literature that forecast democratization everywhere simply because communism had fallen by the wayside. A scholarly study, it took account of the large body of literature that had been published on the many causes and sources of democracy-building. His book explained how multiple trends interacted to produce the third wave, and further, that these causal trends were deeply rooted in the societies, economies, governments, and cultural values of these countries. His book thus provided some comfort in its conclusion that, apart from some backsliding, the third wave was not vulnerable to wholesale reversals, but it also illuminated the reasons why democracy might not soon spread to other countries and regions lacking the factors that had produced the third wave.

Huntington's book also had the virtue of focusing attention on strategies for achieving democratization. Whereas Fukuyama's book had seemed to imply that democracy would win the struggle against competitors merely because it was a superior value system, Huntington's careful analysis showed that its successful adoption was not guaranteed, and that much depended upon the nature of the efforts made to establish it. In Eastern Europe, toppling authoritarian government and replacing it with democracy in one fell swoop had proved feasible because of the fertile terrain there. In Asia, by contrast, democracy was pursued in a slower, incremental manner. In South Korea and Taiwan, modern governmental administrations and market economies were first created; then, democratic elections were carried out at the local level, followed by national elections that resulted in popularly chosen governments. Some observers criticized this Asian model as too slow, but it proved successful, and it confirmed Huntington's pragmatic assessment that the transition to democracy can follow different paths.

Viewed in retrospect, Huntington's hopeful but guarded 1991 assessment of democracy's future seems on target. During the decade after his book was published, democracy made impressive gains in Eastern Europe. Communist regimes were swept aside and replaced with democratic governments that, even as they struggled to find their bearings, were generally moving to expand human liberty and market economies. Democracy also began to take root in Russia and elsewhere in the former Soviet Union, although without inspiring full confidence of enduring success. In Asia, democracy was consolidated in South Korea, Taiwan, and elsewhere, but it did not spread to China. In Latin America, it continued to be the norm in most countries, although some backsliding occurred in Venezuela and elsewhere. In Africa, it made checkered progress, while in the Middle East, it made little progress at all, remaining confined, when Huntington wrote, to Israel and Turkey. Although this mixed pattern may have disappointed optimists while not confirming the worst fears of pessimists, it seemed in keeping with Huntington's nuanced analysis.

If Huntington's book could be criticized, perhaps it might be for defining democracy too narrowly and, as a result, underestimating the demands likely to be placed on it as it expands into new regions in the 21st century. Huntington defined democracy in terms of the popular election of leaders. Other theorists point out that democracy must, in addition, safeguard constitutional liberties and human freedoms after elections are held. In this regard, a country is not truly democratic if the majority elects leaders who then trample the rights of minorities. Beyond this, new democratic governments generally will be judged by whether they produce effective policies that promote the common good, including economic growth and prosperity for their citizens; if newly installed democracies are to survive, they must demonstrate effective leadership in politics and economics.

Huntington warned of backsliding and reversals, and this observation seems salient today. Some of the backsliding seen in recent years—Russia and Venezuela are examples—has stemmed from popular doubts about the capacity of these new democracies to provide effective political and economic leadership. History has seen democracies fail: Germany's Weimar Republic of the 1930s is a sobering example. In the early 21st century, practical performance may be the test that determines the long-term survival of democracy where its legitimacy cannot yet be taken for granted. Although the United States successfully transplanted democracy to Germany and Japan after World War II, its ability to do so in Afghanistan and Iraq remains uncertain. Moreover, recent events in Venezuela, Iran, and Palestine show that democratic elections do not necessarily mean that governmental leaders will respect and foster the other elements of democracy such as minority rights, private property, and a free press.

Charles Lipson: Democratic Peace Theory

The books by Fukuyama and Huntington can be seen as part of a broader category of neo-Kantian literature that deals with the *democratic peace theory*: as a general rule, democracies do not go to war with each other (exceptions may be weak democracies that morph into more aggressive forms of government, such as Weimar Germany, or secessionist movements within democratic countries, such as the Confederacy in the American Civil War). This theory has had a profound impact on policymakers during both the Clinton administration and the subsequent Bush administration. For over 25 years, the democratic peace theory has been one of the most closely studied and debated issues in the fields of political science and international relations. Kant himself accepted this theory and argued that it held both because citizens of a democracy are reluctant to bear the costs of war, and because shared values tend to defuse hostilities between democracies. Others have argued that it is the unique institutional arrangements in democracies that restrain elected leaders from going to war. Michael Doyle, writing in the early 1980s, determined that democracies had not engaged in wars against one another since 1815.[6] Doyle's research led him to identify, as causes of the "democratic peace," the constitutional restraints found in a democracy along with respect for the moral autonomy of citizens including freedom of speech, commerce, and the right to vote.

A new explanation for democratic peace emerged in a 2003 book by Charles Lipson. *Reliable Partners: How Democracies Have Made a Separate Peace* expands on existing explanations of democratic peace.[7] Examining decades of research and speculation on the theory, Charles Lipson concluded that established democracies do not go to war against each other because they have a unique ability to settle disputes with one another by creating reliable agreements: "Because democracies have unique 'contracting advantages,' they can usually avert or settle conflicts with each other by reliable, forward-looking agreements that minimize the dead-weight costs of direct military engagement."[8] Lipson found that relationships among established democracies can be expected to involve fewer military threats, displays of force, skirmishes and low-level conflicts, and outright wars.

Lipson used several historical case studies to illustrate how democracies have kept the peace during crisis situations. His argument is that democracies avoid fighting one another because their domestic institutions enhance their ability to enter into and keep durable agreements. He found that established democracies have several traits in common that make this possible: transparency of democratic societies, high audience costs (promises made to a mass electorate), and ability to make durable commitments that extend beyond the term of a particular leader.

Democratic states, Lipson says, are not easily able to bluff, deceive, or launch surprise attacks on other democratic nations. Attributes of stable democracies, such as transparency, allow for more effective bargaining between democracies. Leaders of democratic nations are constrained by constitutional rules, the independence of officials, and the political costs of abandoning public commitments. Thus, when democracies contemplate breaking their agreements, their open debate gives partners advance warning to renegotiate agreements and commitments; in the worst-case scenarios, it gives them a chance to protect themselves.

Lipson's contracting theory, drawing upon research conducted by Lars-Erik Cederman, asserts that "contracting among democracies grows stronger and more reliable as they draw on their experience working together and forge better mechanisms for governing their relationships."[9] These attributes appear to operate most strongly in mature democracies. A pertinent question for U.S. policymakers is whether they can rely on such contracting advantages in dealing with newly formed, unstable, or illiberal democracies, or whether instead the mutability and lack of transparency in new democracies will make peace a less predictable outcome.

Thomas Friedman: Globalization's Dynamics

Friedman's book, *The Lexus and the Olive Tree: Understanding Globalization*, appeared in 2000, but the term *globalization* had first appeared in the 1980s.[10] President Clinton's National Security Strategy of 1997 had identified globalization as a new dynamic that was influencing world affairs and U.S. foreign policy.[11] Meanwhile, scholars were turning out a growing number of journal articles and books about globalization.[12] Friedman, however, probably did more than anybody else to popularize the concept of globalization and introduce it to the general public. He achieved this by means of a journalistic rather than an academic style that, although criticized by some as too sweeping and simplistic, succeeded in conveying important concepts to a wide audience. His book said that globalization is a powerful force for worldwide economic and political progress, and it is thus decidedly neo-Kantian. Whereas Fukuyama and Huntington celebrated democratization as a trend fueled by its own appeal, Friedman portrays democratization, along with a great many other modern trends, as a consequence of globalization.

While many observers have pointed to globalization as an important dynamic on the world stage, Friedman portrayed it as the single most important force, so powerful that it provides an overarching framework for all other forces. As such, he said, it is the essence of the new international system. Friedman did not offer a formal definition of globalization, but he implicitly characterized it as a dynamic process involving the integration of economic markets, nation-states, and technologies to a far higher degree than the world has ever experienced before. Essentially defining globalization in economic terms, he measured it by the growth in cross-border flows of trade, investments, and finances and other economic activity. The initial form of globalization, a century ago, was propelled by growing transportation assets, such as big cargo ships, and shrinking costs for using them. By contrast, he said, today's globalization is being propelled by the growing volume and shrinking costs of information flows, which are bonding all countries, markets, and actors in a web of fast-paced communications and commerce. Moreover, globalization is altering how the old nation-state system operates: it is increasing the prominence of multinational corporations, nongovernmental organizations, information networks, and super-powerful individuals that operate across national borders.

Friedman's treatment of globalization would have been far less provocative had he confined its implications to the world of trade and finance. After all, a world economy had already existed for decades, and globalization is simply increasing the share of national economies devoted to foreign activity. Friedman, however, put forth a bolder proposition: that the almost irresistible pressure to participate competitively in today's world economy is compelling countries everywhere to adopt democratic governments and market-capitalist economies. Friedman stopped short of saying that globalization would have a totally homogenizing effect around the world, but he did assert that countries and governments could not profit in the world economy unless they followed globalization's dictates for organizing their domestic arrangements. Likewise, Friedman stopped short of saying that globalization is destined to dissolve state-centered geopolitics and war; indeed, he explicitly said that the future would be a blend of the old and the new. But he made clear his belief that in today's world, economic performance in global markets is a driving imperative, and that all other goals—security, strategic domination, and ideology—would become secondary considerations for most countries. Friedman argued that the logical consequence of such an economic focus is peace, because peace is necessary to create the conditions for profitable interstate commerce.

The great strengths of Friedman's book were its focus on the increasingly important role of global economics in shaping world politics and its highlighting of the fact that globalization means that modern-day international economics are radically different from the old. By quantitative measures, Friedman was correct in judging that economic globalization would become a dominant force. During the 1990s, foreign trade in the form of exports and imports, foreign investments and capital flows, and currency flows leaped upward across much of the world. By the end of the decade, the United States, Europe, and Japan found that 25–30 percent or more of their economies depended on international commerce. Other countries and regions were less involved in the global economy, but their roles in it were steadily expanding. Only desperately poor countries remained disengaged from global commerce, mostly due to circumstance rather than choice. By 2000, a world economy truly had a life of its own, and it was far more than a collection of self-contained national economies. In this sense, those trumpeting a future of globalization proved prophetic.

The events of the 1990s may have confirmed the globalization hypothesis of an emerging world economy, but they also revealed that this economy was not going to be homogenous. Indeed, the globalizing world economy revealed itself as distinctly bifurcated. For the most part, the wealthy democracies were already trading nations, enmeshed in a web of exports and imports, and as a result they profited from globalization. So did some other countries, such as the Asian tigers, that proved adept at marketing exports and encouraging foreign investments on their home soil. In contrast, many underdeveloped countries that lacked such assets found themselves bypassed by globalization. As a result, the gap between rich and poor countries did not diminish during the 1990s; at best, it narrowed just a bit. By the end of the decade, meetings of the Group of Seven (G–7) and the World Bank faced angry protesters who decried globalization as a conspiracy to rob from the poor and give to the rich. This charge may have been off-target, but it illustrated one of globalization's troubling features: the unevenness with which its gains are distributed. To his credit, Friedman warned against such a backlash. Indeed, the olive tree of his title stood for traditional cultures such as Islam that seemed likely to react negatively to the modernist and Western values underlying globalization. In this, he has been proven prescient.

Friedman's book is, perhaps, overenthusiastic about globalization in places. Its arguments can also be criticized as verging on economic determinism, while paying insufficient attention to other factors that might be more influential than global economics. Friedman seemed to be saying that the globalizing world economy is the most powerful independent variable, pressuring many countries to adopt the version of business-oriented democracy and information era capitalism it dictates, and to behave peacefully in their foreign policies lest they sacrifice their prospects for economic growth. To critics, this argument carried a partly valid point beyond the outer limits of plausibility. Yet even sober-minded theorists of international politics and economics acknowledge that globalization is a very powerful force that is changing how global security affairs and the world economy operate in the early 21st century. Whether, however, the consequence is to strengthen prospects for peace, or instead to increase the likelihood of conflict and war, is an open question. In his book, Friedman recognized that globalization is provoking a backlash in some places. The attacks on the Pentagon and the World Trade Center showed that this backlash is not limited to protests at G–7 (now G–8) summits or at meetings of the World Bank.

After September 11, 2001, Friedman acknowledged globalization's downside, including the way it has inflamed radical Islamic fundamentalism against the United States and other democracies. His book can best be seen as a product of a period in which the dangers of the early 21st century had not yet fully manifested themselves. At the time, globalization seemed relatively benign in strategic terms, or at least unlikely to contribute to conflict and war. Since then, however, the world has seen more of the dark side of globalization. Nonetheless, if Friedman's book is judged in relation to its time of publication, it gets high grades because of its success at alerting the general public to a new, complex, and important trend.

Friedman's book was not the only study of globalization. For example, David Held and his colleagues produced a lengthy book in 1999 entitled *Global Transformations: Politics, Economics, and Culture*.[13] In 2001, the National Defense University published a two-volume study entitled *The Global Century: Globalization and National Security*.[14] Economic textbooks of the 1990s provided a set of theories and models to help explain the growth of world commerce, such as *International Economics: Theory and Practice* by Paul R. Krugman and Maurice Obstfeld.[15] Such studies assessed globalization's troublesome features as well as its positive impacts. Taken together, they confirmed one of Friedman's core postulates: that globalization undeniably is an important dynamic, capable of altering how the world economy and the global security system operate. (Friedman himself published another book on globalization in 2005; its arguments are addressed in chapter four.)[16]

Jeffrey Garten: Preserving and Reforming Alliances

In contrast to Fukuyama's optimism about prospects for global democratization, some writers worried about the health of the key democratic alliances that connected the United States to Europe and Asia. These alliances had emerged from the Cold War as the strongest ties in the neo-Kantian world envisioned by Fukuyama and others who shared his optimism. Jeffrey Garten's 1992 book, *A Cold Peace: America, Japan, Germany, and the Struggle for Supremacy*, was a leading example of this literature.[17] Unlike books that examined Europe or Asia independently, Garten's book focused on both regions by addressing America's relations with its biggest alliance partners in each: Germany and Japan. He argued that maintaining and strengthening these relationships is key to future world stability. But he also found a great deal to be worried about; he feared that new-era trends were slowly but surely pulling both alliances apart. Although Garten was not the only writer to put a finger on these problems, his book did so in a particularly comprehensive way. He addressed root causes and also helped identify a constructive agenda. We call his book neo-Kantian because it suggested that these alliances could be reinvigorated by sensible policies in security affairs and economics. He proved to be correct in noticing the differences that began to divide the democratic partners early in the post–Cold War era, but he was not correct in predicting that power would shift to Germany and Japan, nor that they would become political allies and economic rivals of the United States. Nonetheless, his policy recommendations, which focused on preserving, consolidating, and reforming these alliance ties, proved apt, and helped shape some of the Clinton administration's most noteworthy accomplishments, such as North Atlantic Treaty Organization (NATO) enlargement.

Unlike some writers of the time, Garten did not portray Germany and Japan as bent on ambitious economic agendas at the expense of the United States. But he did conclude that the end of the Cold War had removed a critical reason for the preservation of these alliances, by eliminating the Soviet military threat to Europe and Northeast Asia. Outside of Europe, he said, the United States was taking the main responsibility for defending shared Western interests, such as in the Persian Gulf, while neither Germany nor Japan did much to share this burden. In this setting, all three nations were focusing on international economic agendas of profits and growth through trade and foreign investments; this created considerable economic competition among them. In addition, Garten pointed out, the economies of Germany and Japan were not growing fast and were still highly protectionist, and both countries continued to embrace domestic policies that reduced the competitiveness of their economies. The effect was to make it hard for the United States to export its products to European and Asian markets, or to count upon Germany and Japan to stimulate global economic growth and to carry security burdens.

To Garten, these trends pointed to trouble ahead. While he expressed some concern that Germany and Japan would seek to loosen their security ties to the United States, his greater worry was that the United States, tiring of its Cold War allies, would begin to pull away from them. Garten feared that the governments of all three countries would be so focused on domestic priorities that they would be oblivious to the negative dynamics taking place in their most important alliances. The widespread consequence would be diminishing cooperation in security affairs and economics. Indeed, this dynamic manifested itself in a lack of responsiveness to ethnic warfare in the Balkans and little progress in global trade negotiations.

Rather than abandon hope for these alliances, however, Garten proposed a constructive agenda for change aimed at reinvigorating these alliances by making them responsive to new-era challenges. He called for Germany and Japan to improve their economic performance, to open their borders to more trade, and to carry more security burdens in partnership with the United States.

He acknowledged that Germany and Japan would pursue reforms only slowly, but he called upon the United States to play a strong leadership role to reassert alliance cooperation in security affairs and global economic management. He pointed to this agenda as the highest priority facing U.S. foreign policy in the 1990s. When Garten wrote a new introduction for the second edition, released in 1993, he noted that the Clinton administration had begun to heed his call.

Whether the Clinton administration did enough is a subject for debate, but it unquestionably made alliance reform a key part of its foreign policy agenda during 1993–2000. The biggest efforts, and the biggest gains, were made in Europe. U.S. support for NATO reform helped cement closer transatlantic ties in security affairs as NATO set aside its Cold War stance of defending only its borders in favor of a new strategic concept aimed at bringing stability and progress to all of Europe and adjoining regions. By the mid-1990s, NATO was pursuing a Partnership for Peace aimed at establishing cooperative security ties with countries of the former Soviet bloc. In 1999, NATO admitted three new members from Eastern Europe: Poland, Hungary, and the Czech Republic. The ink was barely dry on the treaty when additional countries began clamoring for admission as well. In 2002, 7 new members, including the 3 Baltic states, were admitted, enlarging NATO to fully 26 countries throughout Europe, apart from the troubled Balkans. Meanwhile, the European Union (EU) began expanding as well, ultimately growing to 25 countries and covering nearly all of Europe.

The Clinton administration did not pursue alliance reform to a comparable degree in Asia, but it did retain the system of bilateral alliances that it had inherited from the Cold War. The U.S.-Japanese alliance remained the cornerstone of the U.S. alliance system in Asia, and Japan agreed to take responsibility for a larger zone of maritime affairs beyond its borders. The U.S.-South Korean alliance continued to provide deterrence and defense on the Korean Peninsula. America's alliances with Australia and other Pacific-Asian countries remained largely unchanged, even though the United States withdrew its military forces from the Philippines. In the greater Middle East, alliance cooperation did not increase, but the United States maintained its existing collaborative relations with several countries, including Israel, Egypt, Jordan, Saudi Arabia, and the Gulf Cooperation Council states of the Persian Gulf.

Among the achievements of efforts to preserve and reform alliances during the 1990s, the main strategic effect was to foster unity in Europe and to preserve stability in Northeast Asia. For the most part, however, these alliances did not reform themselves to the point of pursuing new security roles and missions in other, distant regions. The Clinton administration did not try to push its Northeast Asian alliances along this road, but it did try to nudge NATO to start considering how it could handle security affairs in North Africa, the Middle East, and the Persian Gulf. Progress was slow, at best. Indeed, France largely withdrew from the Persian Gulf, leaving the security mission to the United States and Great Britain, and no other European countries acted to fill the void. NATO adopted a Mediterranean Dialogue of diplomatic outreach to North African countries, with few positive effects.

Throughout the 1990s, a key impediment facing NATO was the incapacity of European countries other than Britain and France to project military power to the Middle East or elsewhere outside Europe's borders. With defense budgets falling, their militaries lacked the investment funds for pursuing new initiatives. However, signs of progress began to emerge at NATO's Washington Summit of 1999, where NATO adopted a new Strategic Concept that addressed the possibility of security missions outside Europe. NATO had also created the Defense Capability Initiative (DCI), a multiyear effort aimed at reducing the wide disparity between the U.S. and European capacities for power projection missions. Over the first 3 years, the DCI made little headway, but in late 2002, the Prague Summit took a major step in creating a new NATO Response Force and establishing the so-called Prague Capabilities Commitment to reenergize force improvements. A bitter debate over the U.S. invasion of Iraq in 2003 left the alliance badly divided about Middle East policy, but behind the scenes, military progress was starting to take shape.

During the 1990s, the U.S. economy grew so fast that the sluggish economic performance of Germany and Japan went largely unnoticed in Washington. Predictions that America's security alliances would fall apart under the pressure of mounting economic competition did not come true. In most regions, the fading of Cold War threats did not result in the dissolution of alliances, mainly because most members had come to value the well-established patterns of alliance security collaboration, and most were also worried about what fresh dangers the new era might bring. It can be argued that these alliances did not reform fast enough to adapt to the new era. But the mere fact that they survived intact and pursued some reforms put to rest the arguments that alliances would not survive if external threats no longer cemented them. As the 1990s showed, the new bonds were common goals and the perceived benefits of multilateral collaboration.

In retrospect, Garten's book should get high marks not only because it identified a key problem of the new era, but also because it put forth sound policy advice; many of its recommendations were adopted to good effect. Garten did better with Germany and Europe than with Japan and Asia; his conclusions and recommendations about how to deal with the Atlantic

Alliance proved prescient. Garten was not the only writer to reach provocative conclusions about the future of democratic alliances from the perspective of the early 1990s. For example, Lester Thurow had forecast growing economic competition in his influential book, *Head to Head: The Coming Economic Battle Among Japan, Europe, and America*.[18] However, such worried forecasts did not come true during the 1990s. Instead, NATO showed signs of renewed life as it enlarged eastward; the Pacific alliances remained intact, even though they did not pursue reforms to a comparable degree; and economic competition failed to erode the security ties that were still valued everywhere. Yet this literature was correct in pointing out that if democratic alliances were to contribute to a neo-Kantian world as the industrial age gave way to the information age, they would need to respond to the times by reforming their policies and practices, not clinging to the status quo.

Ronald Asmus: Unifying Europe

Although the 1990s are often viewed as a time of frustrated hopes for the views of Fukuyama and other neo-Kantians, in one region these hopes were largely fulfilled. In Europe, the consolidation of security and democracy was achieved by means of the enlargement of NATO and its strategic reorientation. During the 1990s, NATO not only grew into Eastern Europe, but also became involved in the Balkans as part of U.S.-European efforts to halt the ethnic warfare pitting Serbia against Bosnia and Kosovo. *Opening NATO's Door: How the Alliance Remade Itself for a New Era*, by Ronald Asmus, told the story of how enlargement unfolded.[19] Unlike most of the other books discussed in this volume, which are works of prediction and prescription, Asmus' book is a work of description—a diplomatic history—reflecting upon the events of 1993–2000. We have included it as a neo-Kantian book because it emphasizes the importance of a community of liberal democracies, in this case NATO, as an instrument for producing positive change.

During most of the 20th century, Europe was the cockpit of global calamity, producing two world wars and then the Cold War, which held the threat of nuclear holocaust over mankind for 40 years. Even when the threat of nuclear war receded with the end of the Cold War, it did not guarantee that Europe would emerge as peaceful. It resulted in the withdrawal of the Soviet army from Eastern Europe and the dismantlement of communist regimes there. But this created a security vacuum and left multiple countries without established governments in a region in which multiple wars had started in earlier times, many of them triggered by rivalry between Germany and Russia. In the early 1990s, many thoughtful observers feared the potential for new instabilities and turmoil. Yet the outcome was instead the eastward march of NATO and the EU, without major opposition from Russia, as more of Europe came under the flag of democracy. By 2000, Europe was emerging as the global exemplar of unity, peace, and progress. The story of how this transition took place was a vindication of neo-Kantian theory even though it applied only in one region, not across the entire world.

Opening NATO's Door told this story from the perspective of NATO enlargement, but it illuminated other underlying strategic dynamics. As Asmus explained, the Soviet Union's abrupt decision to withdraw from Eastern Europe in 1989–1990 created many uncertainties about how the future of Europe would take shape. Foremost was the question of Germany. The decision to see Germany reunified was reached quickly in Western capitals, but it was not a foregone conclusion that a unified Germany would remain within NATO. Initially, the Soviet Union insisted that Germany must leave NATO, but it was rebuffed by Western opposition. The Soviet government then insisted that Eastern Europe must become a neutral zone, with Poland and other territories separating Germany from the Soviet Union. In the ensuing "2 + 4" negotiations with NATO countries (the two German governments and those of the four victorious World War II powers), the Soviet Union was granted this request, at least temporarily. The subsequent collapse of the Soviet Union, leaving Russia and a host of other independent countries on former Soviet territory, altered the strategic conditions that gave rise to the 2 + 4 agreement. From this arose a quest for a new strategic concept.

At the time that the idea of NATO enlargement began germinating, Asmus reported, many observers had become deeply worried about Europe's future. Ethnic violence was erupting in the Balkans; Eastern Europe was in disarray and potentially headed toward crisis. The sudden collapse of communist rule left these countries without viable governments and with outmoded command economies that were yielding deepening poverty. A widespread consensus in favor of adopting democracy and market economies had emerged in almost all of these countries. But exactly how were they to be created in countries that lacked any vestige of either? How could they be made effective so that they actually brought about freedom and prosperity? The answers to these questions were anything but obvious, leaving these countries to progress by trial and error. Complicating this situation was the reality that all of these countries lacked security guarantees against external dangers: all of them felt vulnerable to each other, to renewed Russian assertiveness, and to reappearance of the competitive geopolitical dynamics that had devastated Europe in previous eras. Many Eastern Europeans worried that in a setting of chronic insecurity, they would be unable to adopt democracy and capitalism or to make a success of them.

As Asmus wrote, the Western response was to pursue NATO enlargement into Eastern Europe, followed by EU enlargement. Coming to this bold decision for dual enlargement, which redrew the political and military map of Europe, was anything but easy. As detailed research by Asmus revealed, it involved three distinct phases for NATO: first, development of the strategic theory of enlargement; then, formation of an alliance-wide consensus to admit, initially, three new members to NATO, to be followed by more later; and then, negotiating Russian acquiescence to NATO enlargement, in exchange for close consultations and partnership relations in matters pertaining to Europe's future security affairs.

Acting in response to Eastern European pleas and its own analysis of Western strategic interests, the Clinton administration developed a plan for NATO enlargement during 1993–1995. The theoretical underpinnings of this plan—a unique creation of the post–Cold War era—cut across previous ideological divides and forged a synthesis of neo-Hobbesian and neo-Kantian thinking. The theory was neo-Hobbesian in the sense that it aimed to head off a new era of instability in Eastern Europe arising from local rivalries and from competition between Germany and Russia over control of Poland and other countries. It was neo-Kantian in the sense that it endeavored to establish a foundation of security upon which democracy, market capitalism, and community relations could be built. If President Clinton was the neo-Kantian proponent of this plan, Senator Jesse Helms (R–NC) was its neo-Hobbesian champion. Only when both schools pressed for the policy did it achieve real traction and begin moving forward.

The theory of NATO enlargement was to pursue military security not only as an end in itself, but also as a means to a larger end. NATO enlargement became a way to render Eastern European countries more secure, which would allow them the luxury of building democratic governments, establishing market economies, and joining a unified continent. NATO and the European Union would enlarge eastward in parallel, with NATO creating the foundation of security, and the EU building the superstructure of economic and political relationships. The outcome of this bold theory would be a new Europe that was democratic, peaceful, whole, and free.

Because this theory was new and revolutionary, Asmus said, forming a political consensus on its behalf was initially difficult. East European countries badly wanted to join NATO and were frustrated when they were initially offered instead only the more limited Partnership for Peace, which gave them no security guarantees. The impediment was doubt, in Western quarters, about the wisdom of the enterprise. Conservatives feared that enlargement eastward would overextend the alliance and weaken its internal cohesion.

Liberals feared a confrontation with Russia. Questions also arose about technical details of the enterprise, including military requirements, budget costs, and program priorities. Fortunately, the Clinton administration was successful in creating a bipartisan consensus in the United States, reflected in a decisive Senate vote in favor of enlargement. Similar success was achieved in Europe as the German, French, and British governments helped sell the idea to the rest of the alliance. The decision was to admit just three new members at first (Poland, the Czech Republic, and Hungary) and to leave the door open to other applicants. This pleased alliance members who wanted NATO and the EU to enlarge not just to Central Europe, but the Baltic region and the Balkans as well.

The hardest sell was convincing Russia to accept NATO enlargement. The task became far harder as, in 1993 and 1994, Russian foreign policy shifted from its earlier emphasis on Atlanticism to a new assertion of traditional state interests. As Asmus explained, the new Russia was loath to cede control over historical invasion corridors to a NATO alliance that the Soviet Union had viewed as a mortal enemy. The Clinton administration endeavored to persuade Russia that its legitimate interests would be respected. Russia initially resisted, with President Boris Yeltsin threatening a "cold peace" of animosity, but eventually began showing flexibility. Moscow evidently decided, Asmus wrote, that it lacked the strength to block NATO enlargement, that it did not want to sever ties with the Western democracies, and that it therefore needed to make the best of the situation. After prolonged negotiations, NATO and Russia finally reached accord. The NATO-Russia Founding Act called for close NATO-Russian consultations on future security matters, and a permanent Russian representative at NATO headquarters in Brussels. The stage thus set, the three new members were admitted in 1999. Russia would later acquiesce quietly to the admission of additional members as NATO continued its enlargement.

The idea of NATO enlargement initially had been highly controversial; in retrospect, however, it stands out as a wise strategic choice that has brought enormous dividends to Europe, helping insulate it from a dangerous world elsewhere. In his book, Asmus documents the complex intellectual gymnastics necessary to create this theory, and the equally complex political gymnastics required to get it adopted by the United States, the rest of the NATO alliance, Eastern Europe, and Russia. Seldom in modern peacetime history has a policy so vast been attempted, and succeeded so well.

The positive experience of NATO and EU enlargement shows that neo-Kantianism is more than wishful thinking when it is accompanied by an effective strategy and action agenda for accomplishing its goals. If such transformational steps are possible in a region as historically troubled as Europe, they may be possible elsewhere. Yet the difficulties encountered along the way suggest that NATO enlargement may remain a unique achievement: the necessary preconditions could be found only in Europe and no other regions. The idea of establishing a security foundation as the basis for a superstructure of democracy and capitalism can, in theory, be applied elsewhere, including the Middle East. As Asmus' book suggests, however, this may not be an easy task.

Charles Kegley and Gregory Raymond: Stable Multipolarity

A Multipolar Peace? Great-Power Politics in the Twenty-first Century, by Charles Kegley and Gregory Raymond, did not get as much public attention as books by Fukuyama and some other neo-Kantians, but it addressed a critical issue in the post–Cold War world with a scholarly analysis and hypotheses about the future of relations among the great powers, especially the United States, Russia, and China.[20] During the early 1990s, some neo-Kantian observers dismissed the idea of a renewed great power rivalry as anachronistic thinking. In other quarters, however, the end of the bipolar Cold War structure gave rise to concern that a new multipolar system would emerge that would be inherently unstable, like the European balance of power of the early 20th century, and prone to crisis and war. While agreeing that a multipolar system might lie ahead, Kegley and Raymond employed a combination of logical reasoning and historical evaluation to rebut the idea that it would inevitably be unstable. Their notion that a new multipolar system could be stable and could help establish a foundation for global progress turned a neo-Hobbesian concept on its head and made it neo-Kantian.

As Kegley and Raymond wrote, a multipolar system is one in which physical power is distributed among a number of independent countries that are not bound together in multilateral institutions; each is thus free to maneuver against the others on the world stage. They argued that when a multipolar system exists, its stability depends upon its composition and dynamics, such as whether the pursuit of principal actors' incompatible interests and goals produces polarization and competition. They acknowledged that multipolar systems can be unstable when big powers try to take advantage of opportunities to assert their interests at the expense of other big powers. But they also argued that when the major powers embrace common values and are not pursuing goals that menace each other's vital interests, a multipolar system could be quite stable; indeed, it could be more stable than a bipolar system anchored in military alliances opposed to each other.

Kegley and Raymond suggested that the Concert of Europe of the early 1800s provides a classic model of a stable multipolar system, and that history shows other examples of such stability. They concluded that, while the early

21st century might produce a new multipolar system, this should not necessarily be cause for despair. Instead, wise policies by the big powers could manage this system for stability. If a foundation of stability could be established, they argued, a new multipolar system could produce desirable advances toward peace, prosperity, and progress. Instead of wishing away new geopolitical realities, they endeavored to work out how to harness and tame them.

This interpretation of European history differed from that of many realists. Kegley and Raymond rejected the idea that bipolar systems are inherently stable because they are anchored in an equal, unchanging balance of power. They asserted that in the years before Europe spiraled downward into World War I, it had essentially moved from multipolarity to bipolarity anchored in a highly unstable military balance that created strong incentives for rapid mobilization and offensive actions in a crisis. They also dismissed the view that the Cold War's bipolar standoff in Europe had been stable: even though it did not erupt into war, they said, its structure of two nuclear-armed military alliances created perpetual conditions for a big explosion. By contrast, they wrote, the Concert of Europe fashioned at the Congress of Vienna, after Napoleon's downfall, had created conditions of multipolar stability that endured from 1815 to 1848 and beyond. Europe was stable because the major powers had agreed, in essence, to respect one another's vital interests and to honor "rules of the geopolitical game," which prevented big wars aimed at redrawing the map of Europe.

Crafted by such famous diplomats as Prince Klemens Metternich, Talleyrand, and Lord Castlereagh, the Concert's consensus on values, goals, and codes of conduct helped produce a peaceful continent for several decades. Kegley and Raymond concede that it eventually unraveled when, from 1850 onward, Otto von Bismarck started throwing Prussia's weight around, seeking to unify Germany. But even after the Franco-Prussian War of 1870, Europe's new multipolar system remained stable for a considerable period. Only after Bismarck was dismissed by Kaiser Wilhelm in the early 1890s did Europe begin its slide into constant multipolar tension and then the explosive bipolarity that, in 1914, flared into the First World War.

When it was published in 1994, the book by Kegley and Raymond offered renewed grounds for optimism about how the United States and its allies could handle future relations with Russia and China. Only a few years earlier, many observers had judged that Russia and China were on the path to becoming democracies and could eventually be admitted to the Western democratic community as full-fledged members. By the mid-1990s, however, this hope was fading: Russia's democratic experiment was starting to falter, and China was becoming a country with an authoritarian government and a capitalist economy. Moreover, each country was pursuing foreign policies anchored in its own pragmatic national interests, not in partnership with the United States or membership in the democratic community. Responding to these circumstances, Kegley and Raymond accepted the likelihood that the world was headed toward a new multipolar system and offered policy advice on how this situation could be handled.

Kegley and Raymond argued against U.S. unilateralism and called upon the United States to preserve its existing alliances to maintain future global stability. They urged the United States to use its power to help create a stable multipolar system. Special bilateral relationships and multilateral security organizations such as NATO could contribute if they followed appropriate policies and, like the Concert of Europe, focused on creating an equilibrium of interests and a stable balance of power. In retrospect, their policy prescriptions seem sensible, but it is still unclear whether these authors were correct in their prediction of a new multipolar system and their diagnosis that it might be managed safely. The world of 2006 is not multipolar, but if big-power relations deteriorate, it could become so. The United States and other countries would then face the challenge of keeping the new system stable, at the risk otherwise of sliding into a dangerous new bipolar order.

The hopeful perspective reflected in the work of Kegley and Raymond and some others was reflected in Clinton administration policies throughout the 1990s. In particular, the Clinton administration strove to establish a close partnership with Russia during its first term in office. The administration's hope was that it could encourage Russia's successful democratization and its adoption of cooperative relations with the United States and its European allies. This effort initially seemed fruitful as Russia, under President Yeltsin, took steps to establish a democratic government and to pursue a foreign policy oriented toward and across the Atlantic. However, optimism faded as the Russian government began to mix central rule with democracy and to focus its foreign policy increasingly on assertion of its state interests rather than partnership with the United States and Europe. NATO enlargement into Eastern Europe put new strains on relations with Russia, although an accommodation was eventually reached. As the 1990s ended, U.S.-Russian relations were not as close as optimists had originally envisioned, but they were on an even keel—an achievement in itself.

In Asia, U.S. relations with China underwent ups and downs during the 1990s. The Clinton administration initially criticized China's failure to democratize. But when tensions with China rose and alarmed much of Asia, the administration moderated its rhetoric and focused on trying to establish calmer relations with China. For the most part, China reciprocated by toning down its hostility toward Taiwan, urging stability on the Korean Peninsula, and taking steps to enter the Asian economic system in order to promote its own economic progress through exports, imports, and foreign investments on its own soil. Even so, some aspects of a competitive U.S.-China relationship emerged in relations over Taiwan and over such economic issues as tariffs and exchange rates. The 1990s ended with U.S.-Chinese relations in a status that mostly confirmed the postulates of Kegley and Raymond, rather than the fears of those who had predicted a new cold war of big-power rivalry with China and Russia.

What subsequent decades will hold remains to be seen. During the first years of the 21st century, the Bush administration endeavored to keep relations with Russia and China calm. U.S. relations with Russia remained largely cordial, but were strained by President Vladimir Putin's drift away from democracy and the Bush administration's invasion of Iraq. Although U.S. relations with China initially seemed to be moving toward greater hostility, they improved in the aftermath of September 11, 2001; however, Taiwan, trade frictions, and uncertainty about China's long-range strategic intentions in the Asia-Pacific region remain sources of potential trouble.

Daniel Yergin and Joseph Stanislaw: From Governments to Markets

Some of the globalization literature of the 1990s, such as the book by Thomas Friedman, portrayed the world economy as a powerful force unto itself that dictates how countries should and will behave. This portrayal tended to ignore the role of nations as independent actors able to influence the evolution of the world economy. The world economy would not even exist if countries did not have capitalist economies, or if their governments chose to prevent free trade—exports, imports, foreign investments, and other cross-border flows of finance and capital—as, prior to the 1980s, governments often did. The globalizing world economy sprang to life over the past two decades because many governments changed their ways, choosing to embrace market economies and foreign trade. In their landmark 1998 book, *The Commanding Heights*, Daniel Yergin and Joseph Stanislaw provided a compelling account of how and why this important transition took place.[21]

Yergin and Stanislaw began by pointing out that prior to the late 1970s, in many countries and regions, governments held the "commanding heights" of their economies; that is, they controlled the strategic parts of their economies. Totalitarian communist governments owned and operated virtually all of their economies, banning private property and markets almost entirely, and planning economic development themselves. While democratic governments provided safeguards for private property, they too typically practiced, to some degree, public ownership, regulation, national planning, and control of outputs and growth. This was especially true of Western Europe, whose mainly mixed economies were anchored strongly in social welfare, but it was also true to a lesser degree of the United States, where the Federal Government practiced strong regulatory policies. Many governments around the world erected protectionist trade barriers, hoping that sustained economic growth could be achieved through a combination of government management and insulation of markets from the outside world. The United States was a major trading country. While some countries were moving toward greater trade and global commerce, less developed regions had not yet begun to try to use trade to propel their growth.

Why was there such a widespread consensus in favor of government control and against open markets? Yergin and Stanislaw pointed out that it stemmed from experience going back to the Great Depression of the 1930s. At that time, unfettered capitalism was seen as a cause of global economic disaster, and governments had lacked the policy levers to fix it. Typically, they withdrew into economic isolationism to try to ward off its effects, but this step only compounded the problem. Governments everywhere embarked upon efforts to control their economies as the 1930s gave way to the 1940s, and even more after World War II. Seeking to mitigate the destructive features of capitalism, restore growth, and pursue redistribution to foster social welfare for the lower economic classes, they were inspired by Keynesian economics, which heralded the benefits of government management. The common effect, however, was to dampen capitalism and markets and thus to alter how national economies operated. Yergin and Stanislaw wrote that this great experiment endured because it produced positive results: especially in the United States and Western Europe, many countries, having endured the Great Depression and World War II, recovered afterward to experience three decades of remarkable growth, bringing benefits to all social classes and surmounting periodic recessions and business-cycle fluctuations.

By the mid-1970s, however, these practices were reaching the end of their usefulness and becoming counterproductive. The 1970s saw a host of serious problems arise in the wealthy democracies: major unemployment, inflation, stagnant growth, high interest rates, and recessions. In certain quarters, led by conservative political leaders and professional economists of similar beliefs, a consensus arose that government economic management had not only failed to provide a viable solution, but also was a large part of the problem, imposing barriers to economic revival. They sought a major change of direction: a step back from government management, coupled with reinvigoration of capitalism, markets, and open trade. At first these ideas were dismissed as reactionary, but within a few years, they took hold and ultimately produced a global economic revolution. As Yergin and Stanislaw wrote, "The decamping of the state from the commanding heights marks a great divide between the 20th and 21st centuries."[22]

The first leaders of this revolution were Great Britain and the United States. Under Prime Minister Margaret Thatcher, who was influenced by economist Keith Joseph, Britain took major steps to privatize its government-owned economy, to reduce the power of unions and the scope of social welfare policies, and to restore market competition among capitalist entrepreneurs. In the United States, President Ronald Reagan began deregulating the economy; he used deficit financing to stimulate recovery and high interest rates to stifle inflation. As the British and American economies picked up, market reforms spread elsewhere. Most European countries did not privatize and deregulate to such a degree, but they did seek to lower trade barriers, expanding the Common Market into a continent-wide European Economic Community and moving toward a common European currency. Japan and other Asian countries continued to cling to corporatist economies, but they also poured great effort into increasing their exports. Within a few years, exports were powering sustained economic growth in many Asian countries, including China. In South Asia, India's decades of government planning gave way to markets and capitalism. In Latin America, many countries abandoned authoritarian governments and *dependéncia* economic policies to embrace democracy along with capitalism, markets, and trade. In Eastern Europe and the Soviet Union, communism collapsed and was replaced by widespread efforts to establish democracy, private property, and market capitalism. Globally, the combined effect was to shift possession of the commanding heights from government to markets, both in the United States and abroad.

Yergin and Stanislaw wrote that this revolutionary change in favor of markets and trade liberalization is what produced today's globalizing world economy, not the other way around. They mostly applauded this trend toward competition, privatization, and deregulation. Their book criticized as systems of economic management not only communism but also modern-day socialism, with its mixture of government ownership and market capitalism. It questioned the socialist practices of several Western European countries as well as the socialist models previously followed by many countries in Africa and elsewhere. It argued that most countries could best achieve sustained economic growth by lowering trade barriers and by participating in the world economy. But it also made the point that countries could participate profitably in the world economy only if they first put their domestic economies and governments in order.

Yergin and Stanislaw also identified potential problems with globalization. One danger, they said, was the globally contagious effects of financial shocks caused by abrupt shifts in currencies, capital flows, and investments. For example, in 1997, a sudden depreciation of the Thai *baht* and subsequent capital flight sent shock waves around the world, causing a big slowdown in growth. Other questions included whether market economies could continue to produce sustained growth, ensure fairness, uphold national identities, prevent environmental degradation, cope with demographic changes, or provide prosperity to countries that lack the necessary ingredients for competing in the world economy. Yergin and Stanislaw concluded that, because governments produced globalization by embracing markets, they could also diminish it by reversing course and restoring public economic management and trade barriers. Their book suggested that governments will still have an important role in economic management, for example, by helping encourage investments in national infrastructure, scientific innovations, and workforces that are skilled, productive, and adaptable. Thus, the move of markets to the commanding heights may not signal the end of economic history, much less political history.

Robert Gilpin: Toward Global Economic Management

Gilpin's 2000 book, *The Challenge of Global Capitalism: The World Economy in the 21st Century*, raised even greater concerns about unfettered global capitalism than Yergin and Stanislaw had done, but it also offered policies for managing the challenge.[23] Gilpin's diagnosis may be seen as neo-Hobbesian, his prescriptions as neo-Kantian. We have chosen to include Gilpin, a renowned political economist, in the neo-Kantian category because of his belief that stable political systems can be achieved that will support strong economic systems.

Gilpin argued that economic globalization is less extensive than commonly thought, occurring mostly in the United States, Europe, Japan, and East Asia. Elsewhere, its impact is less pronounced: most national economies are still driven mainly by traditional dynamics. He expressed strong doubt that globalization would produce a homogenous world any time soon. Globalization is likely to spread, he wrote, but not always robustly; nor is it destined to have a healthy impact everywhere. Global economic integration and resultant growth cannot be taken for granted, said Gilpin, who portrayed the globalizing world economy as fragile and threatened by multiple dangers.

Gilpin's main theme was that the globalizing world economy requires a foundation, and that foundation is the international political system, composed of individual sovereign nations, not multilateral governing bodies. To the extent that this political system fosters multilateral collaboration, economic globalization can succeed. But if it becomes mired in competition and rivalry, wrote Gilpin, globalization cannot deliver on its promises, and the world economy might even disintegrate, as it did during World War I and the Great Depression. Unlike some emerging critics of globalization, he did not predict another Great Depression; his stance was one of optimism, albeit cautious and guarded optimism. But he did forecast a future of struggle and difficulty in which multilateral political cooperation would be crucial.

Gilpin's view thus differs from those of Friedman or Yergin and Stanislaw. Friedman argued, in essence, that globalization itself can be relied upon to propel the world economy toward growth and prosperity. Yergin and Stanislaw argued that the ascension of markets to the commanding heights, where they displaced governmental management, was the main engine of growth. Gilpin was not persuaded that either globalization or markets are all-powerful engines. His book emphasized the importance of deliberate collaboration by governments to create the political conditions that allow globalization and markets to achieve their beneficial effects. His declaration that such cooperative policies are possible marks his book as prescriptively neo-Kantian, but he warned that great damage could be done if the neo-Hobbesian dynamics he described are allowed to rule the world economy. He especially emphasized the importance of cooperation among the wealthy democracies, but he pointed out that other countries and regions also would need to participate responsibly in global economic management.

Gilpin portrayed globalization as fueled by capitalist markets, trade liberalization, and the expansion of multinational corporations, foreign direct investment, modern information systems, and other new technologies. He identified the main engines of global growth as the economies of the United States, Europe, and Japan. Provided these three economies grow, he said, the world economy will grow as well. But if they falter, so too will the world economy. Gilpin pointed out that global capitalism is a competitive exercise in profit-seeking: not every country enjoys a competitive advantage that would give it a market niche for profit and growth. Instead, he said, globalization tends to produce a hierarchy of countries: winners, losers, and those at the margins struggling to improve. Moreover, Gilpin noted, globalization threatens many traditional social values, beliefs, and institutions. The countries that most readily adapt to it are those that are already comfortable with democracy, markets, capitalism, private property, skilled workforces, work ethics, and entrepreneurial behavior. Elsewhere, it compels difficult adjustments, or leaves angry and frustrated losers, who may blame global capitalism and the wealthy democracies for their troubles. Gilpin did not specify here the greater Middle East and Islamic countries, but many of them have been on the losing side of globalization.

Beyond this, there are challenges for globalization itself, such as fostering a stable monetary system, stable financial flows, free trade, and aid to underdeveloped regions. Gilpin identified serious problems in all of these areas. The stability of the monetary system, he said, is affected by floating currency exchange rates, which allow currencies to appreciate or depreciate in response to market dynamics. Sharp falls in exchange rates—such as those caused by the sudden devaluations of 1997—can trigger major effects elsewhere. The difficulty of fostering stable financial flows is even more problematic because of their enormous volume and the mobility of capital that can abruptly depart endangered regions in search of better markets. Gilpin noted that free trade and open competition can be hindered in a variety of ways: countries may provide governmental support for industries or engage in other neomercantilist behavior, raise protectionist barriers, or form regional trading blocs.

Gilpin called for multilateral governmental cooperation to help resolve these problems. While acknowledging the contributions of the G–7, the World Trade Organization (WTO), World Bank, and the International Monetary Fund (IMF), he urged the development of stronger institutions capable of establishing binding consensual rules for managing currency exchange rates and global financial flows. He also called for major efforts to ensure that regional trading blocs such as the EU, North American Free Trade Agreement (NAFTA), Association of South East Asian Nations (ASEAN), and Asia Pacific Economic Cooperation (APEC) become stepping stones to global integration, rather than impeding it by putting up trade barriers. He also urged stronger efforts to provide constructive aid to regions that are poverty-stricken or otherwise at the margins. Gilpin argued that although capitalism and markets have reclaimed dominant roles in the past two decades, they should not be allowed to rule unmanaged in the years ahead, because they could fail, backfire, or cause disastrous unintended consequences. His proposed solution was the restoration of governmental leadership and management by the United States and others, not to stifle capitalism and markets, but to guide them to further success.

A great strength of Gilpin's book was its emphasis on the important role to be played by governments and multilateral institutions in guiding the future evolution of the globalizing world economy. Gilpin was not the only writer making this claim; a host of writers put forth global economic management theories, some of them mutually inconsistent. They may not have been unanimous in telling governments unambiguously what theories to adopt, but at least governments saw that they had options at their disposal and became better informed about how to evaluate them. Since Gilpin's book was published in 2000, there has been no repeat of the financial contagion of 1997; the global economy has returned to growth, and some important steps have been taken to strengthen the policies of the World Bank, IMF, and WTO. Additional steps may lie ahead, such as further reductions of protectionist trade barriers. While this progress seems to have improved the stability and predictability of the world economy, it thus far has done little to remedy the deep-seated problems facing the Middle East and other regions left behind by globalization.

While success at guiding the world economy on the path of steady growth will be one important goal for multilateral governance, another will be elevating poor countries out of poverty. Gilpin did not focus particularly on this challenge, but a host of other writers have done so, and it has become an issue of mounting concern to wealthy governments in recent years. The United States and the United Nations have embraced such visionary goals as doubling the gross domestic products (GDPs) of poor nations and cutting their poverty levels in half during the coming decade. Crafting effective development strategies for poor countries is crucial; many of them cannot achieve prosperity simply by joining the world economy, because they lack products to export abroad, and they have trouble attracting foreign investments.

A few years ago, many observers felt that economic progress required compelling poor countries to undergo painful reforms in such areas as fiscal and monetary policy, banking practices, legal systems, currency stability, and cutbacks in welfare expenditures. This theory then faded. A new theory called for reduction of protectionist trade policies, targeted aid strategies, a switch from loans to grants, improved infrastructures, better educational systems, and productive workforces. Whether this approach will work is to be seen. Success at making poor countries wealthier will be a critical factor in determining not only whether the growing world economy brings widespread benefits, but also whether democracy and peace can take hold in poverty-stricken regions. As Gilpin wisely observed, this is a job for both markets and governments, working together.

Robert Keohane: Prospects for Building International Institutions

Keohane has been a highly influential political scientist and theorist of international relations since the 1970s. Early in his career, he focused on the growing interdependence of nation-states in response to changes in security affairs and the world economy. In his book, *Power and Governance in a Partially Globalized World*, he broadened this perspective to take account of the process of globalization and to examine prospects for building international institutions and governance in the coming years.[24] Published in 2002, his book contained a set of essays he wrote during the previous decade both as sole author and with colleagues, including Celeste Wallander and Joseph Nye. The book reveals Keohane's intellectual evolution during this critical decade, during which neo-Hobbesian expectations jostled with and even replaced neo-Kantian expectations. Keohane's book grappled with the prospects and limits of international institution-building in an era of diminishing hopes for inexorable progress in world affairs and mounting worry about gathering dangers. Yet his stance was moderately hopeful.

In proclaiming himself an institutionalist, Keohane set himself apart from both idealism and realism, two major schools of international relations theory. Idealism, Keohane said, is of value in its commitments to utopian beliefs and goals, but it lacks a sense of how inevitable real-world dynamics create conflicts and power struggles among nations. Such struggles, he said, cannot be resolved by wishing them away or by presuming that the spread of democratic values and humanitarian beliefs will fundamentally change the self-interest of nations in dealing with others. Yet realist theories, Keohane said, presume that nation-states, intent on preserving their sovereignty and advancing their pragmatic interests, will always fall into power struggles, competitive rivalries, and conflict leading to war. In contrast to both schools, Keohane asserted that nations pursuing their individual interests can sometimes find common cause, setting aside their competing sovereign interests to negotiate arrangements that allow them to cooperate on the world stage in functional arenas where they have mutual goals. This process of pragmatic negotiating, bargaining, and multilateral consensus-building, he said, provides hope that effective multilateral institutions can be created to deal with at least some global governance problems.

Keohane argued that globalization is increasing the incentives for such institution-building because it is fundamentally altering how world affairs operate. He portrayed globalization as a process of growing cross-border flows, drawing countries and regions closer together in complex webs of ties and increasing interactions and interdependencies among them. He argued that the modern world is becoming "partially globalized." That is, the wealthy democracies and some other countries and regions are being drawn together, while other places such as the Middle East are not experiencing similar effects. This dynamic is dividing the world into separate zones of peace and conflict. Institution-building, in Keohane's view, will continue to encounter major difficulties in the zone of conflict, but it has positive prospects in the zone of peace.

Why would nation-states, pursuing their self-interest in a world of potential dangers, willingly sacrifice their sovereignty in order to create international organizations such as the United Nations, the World Trade Organization, and the Nuclear Non-Proliferation Treaty regime? The answer, Keohane said, lies in their recognition that the standard neo-Hobbesian solution—establishing strong governments at home while accepting international anarchy abroad—permits strife and war that can damage a state's own prosperity and safety. Even a powerful country risks being damaged, both because the costs of constantly defeating adversaries are formidably high, and because a coalition of adversaries could gang up and conquer it. For all countries, joining an international organization can entail painful losses of sovereignty plus the costs of membership and the risks of entangling commitments. Even so, membership in such institutions can provide compensating benefits, such as reliable information regarding how other countries are behaving, codes of conduct and rules of restraint that limit menacing behavior from others, and cooperative relationships that enable countries to achieve their goals at lower costs or more effectively than otherwise might be possible. International institutions bring countries together to create formalized collaborative relationships. Forming such relationships often requires negotiation, bargaining, and mutual reciprocity, but when the process is complete, the gains may well exceed the losses for all participating countries. As a result, Keohane wrote, nation-states operating purely on the basis of calculated rationality can still reach the conclusion that, for pragmatic, self-interested reasons, institution-building makes sense.

Although Keohane focused much of his book on the role of international law and the creation of institutions for managing the world economy, he devoted a chapter to security affairs and NATO's transformation. He noted that, contrary to some realists' prediction of NATO's demise after Cold War military threats disappeared, the alliance has persisted, grown in size, and taken on new missions beyond protecting its borders. Asking why this is the case, Keohane found the answer in how NATO differs from most previous alliances: it is highly institutionalized and legitimized. Threat-based alliances typically fall apart, said Keohane, because they are premised solely on defense against particular threats. When those threats disappear, the rationale for alliance members to continue collaborating disappears as well. By contrast, said Keohane, NATO is anchored in broader and deeper fundamentals. It reflects a common consensus among its members, plus a set of negotiated agreements and bargained relationships, to pursue common democratic values, to prevent Europe from sliding back into its history of geopolitical competition, and to provide collective defense and security against all types of external menaces, not just the threat of Soviet military aggression. The reality is that all of its members view NATO as a positive commitment: the returns it provides in security gains and budgetary savings outweigh its costs in lessened sovereignty, entangling obligations, and monetary expenses. Moreover, said Keohane, NATO's elaborate institutional structure of civilian and military staffs gives it added effectiveness, legitimacy, and durability.

It is for these reasons, Keohane wrote, that NATO is adapting and reforming, not fading away. It is enlarging by admitting new members from Eastern Europe. It is configuring itself to handle new security challenges arising outside Europe. As a result, NATO is mutating: no longer an old-style collective-defense alliance, it is becoming a new alliance focused on new risks and on management of general, not specific, threats to security. In order to complete this transformation, NATO will need to adapt by creating new capabilities and new decisionmaking procedures. Provided it does so, its prospects are good for continued viability and important strategic functions. Regardless of its exact future, Keohane concluded, NATO validates the proposition that even in the security realm, international institutions can have a meaning and life that reflect more than the individual activities and intentions of its member nation-states.

Keohane brought a similar political perspective to assessing the role of international law in handling world affairs. He noted that international laws are not, like laws within states, typically crafted by courts or legislatures acting according to ideals or abstract principles, but instead are created by nation-states that are seeking to advance their pragmatic interests. When a widespread multilateral consensus mobilizes around some principle for governing behavior, it can become a commonly accepted international law, and it often will be granted legitimacy by the global community. Keohane argued further that international laws often also acquire a normative dimension by codifying acceptable conduct; this code then influences how countries evaluate their own interests and behavior. Regardless of the mix of practical and normative considerations that give rise to such laws, said Keohane, they help govern contemporary world affairs in many critical areas. Moreover, he said, such laws form the foundation for many contemporary international institutions and diplomatic treaties that help regulate and adjudicate state conduct, such as the European Court of Justice, the International Criminal Court, the World Intellectual Property Organization, the World Health Organization, and the World Trade Organization. The future of such institutions, Keohane said, will depend upon the politics affecting them, but to the extent they continue to multiply and grow, they improve the prospects for achieving governance in a partially globalized world.

Keohane emphasized the extent to which globalization is altering how the world economy operates, increasing the need for global governance. Globalization, moreover, is occurring in many areas beyond economics: military, environmental, social, and cultural. He contrasts it with the term *globalism*, which he uses to refer to the extent to which global interaction and interdependence have already become established. He uses the term *globalization* to refer to the ongoing process of change, which could increase or decrease the extent of globalism. Keohane declared that while the process of globalization is nothing new, its present-day manifestations are greatly increasing the level of globalism around the world. The response to economic globalization has been creation of a variety of international institutions, with varying degrees of power and impact, such as the WTO, G–7 (now the G–8), World Bank, IMF, and regional institutions. Whether these institutions perform effectively or not, they do form an increasingly elaborate network that aspires to global governance. Such international institutions, Keohane explained, typically operate on the basis of a club model, in which technical experts and cabinet ministers meet behind closed doors to make decisions on the basis of functional criteria. The club model has had positive effects in enhancing global cooperation, he said, but its downside has been a "democratic deficit": some observers fear that key decisions are being made by players who do not represent the people of participating countries. A challenge facing such institutions, Keohane said, will be to increase their democratic legitimacy without sacrificing their technical expertise.

Keohane ended his book not by endorsing the type of global government that might be exercised by a super-empowered United Nations, but instead by envisioning a future in which growing networks of institutions perform an increasing range of governance functions. Such institutional pluralism, with nation-states still exercising their sovereignty, offers a plausible hope for global governance of the sort needed in areas such as trade relations, climate control, and nonproliferation. Globalization makes creation of such a network a necessity and a possibility. Yet, as Keohane acknowledged, globalization and information networking have downsides: among other dangers, they are empowering global terrorist groups intent on destroying prospects for global governance of the type sought by wealthy Western democracies.

To his credit, Keohane identified interdependence and globalization long before many observers saw them coming, much less crafted theories for explaining them. Keohane's writing style may be too academic and theoretical for some readers, but many of his ideas and insights have undeniable explanatory insight. His theory of institutions stands as a powerful and appealing mid-point between the extremes of idealism and realism. Likewise, his recognition that global institutions are slowly emerging and that they can greatly aid the important task of global governance is both hopeful and accurate. In this sense, Keohane deserves credit for being a practical-minded, politically aware, and progress-oriented neo-Kantian.

The shortcoming of Keohane's theory of institution-building and global governance is that, as he acknowledges, it applies only to one part of a "partially globalized world": mainly the wealthy democracies and other countries striving to join their communities, the *zone of peace*. But it is of little help to the *zone of conflict*: the large, endangered part of the world, including the Middle East, that is not benefiting from globalization and that faces chaos, turmoil, and conflict. These may be the regions most in need of multilateral institution-building and governance, yet they are least able to achieve these objectives. Institutions and governance can apparently best be achieved in regions populated by democratic countries that are already prosperous and that have the requisite cultures and histories that would allow them to forge binding agreements and undertake sustained cooperation with others. Countries lacking these qualities have far greater trouble working together. To the extent that these regions cannot achieve what is needed for them to survive and prosper, the benefits of institutions, governance, and neo-Kantian politics may be beyond their reach. If so, the task for these regions will be to create the fundamental conditions in which institutions and governance can take hold.

Anne-Marie Slaughter: Networks of Government Officials

The final neo-Kantian author we reviewed published *A New World Order* in 2004, but as she had been working on the project for over a decade, her volume displayed some of the optimism of the early 1990s.[25] Anne-Marie Slaughter began with an idea that Keohane introduced in his book: the notion of a growing network of international institutions that perform governance functions. She looked at the "horizontal and vertical" networks of government officials that increasingly shape policies in the globalized world. As she noted, terrorists, arms dealers, money launderers, drug dealers, and other international criminals all operate through global networks; so, increasingly, do governments. In fact, for governments to deal effectively with networked international terrorists and criminals, those governments themselves must be well networked. She argued that the importance of such networks—of police investigators, financial regulators, judges, legislators, and others—is underappreciated and underused, and that with the appropriate set of norms, these governmental networks could form an increasingly important stabilizing element in international relations.

As Slaughter wrote, these networks exist widely today, and each has specific aims and activities. For example, after the events of September 11, 2001, the Bush administration relied on informal networks to freeze terrorist assets, share law enforcement information, and cooperate on intelligence. During the East Asian financial crises of 1997, networks of finance ministers coordinated both policies and public responses. Within the NAFTA countries, environmental officials have formed networks to deal with cross-border environmental issues. Judges of many nations influence each other through conferences, judicial organizations, and information shared on the Internet; judicial rulings increasingly cite cases in other countries as informative, if not dispositive. Legislators are developing transnational ties through international parliamentary organizations such as the NATO Parliamentary Assembly. National officials in the European Union have a highly developed array of transgovernmental networks. Most of the existing networks are horizontal, between domestic officials of different nation-states. Some are vertical, between officials of nation-states and those of supranational organizations.

Such networks, Slaughter argues, expand the international reach of participants, build trust among officials, and allow for information-sharing and technical cooperation. They are most effectively built where they can be based on existing alliances; they work less well as ad hoc coalitions established for specific missions. Together, she argues, they constitute a new form of global governance.

Slaughter writes that a conceptual shift is needed to understand the power and consequence of these governmental networks. Rather than unitary state actors that react predictably to one another like "billiard balls," or traditional international organizations such as the UN or the WTO, states can be seen as "disaggregated," with elements of each state connected to elements of other states through these networks. For example, law enforcement officials in one country may work closely with law enforcement officials in other countries. These powerful connections, she argues, are less likely than top-down global governance to engender resentment. They operate primarily based on *soft power*, to use Joseph Nye's term for "the ability to get what you want through attraction rather than coercion" by military or economic might. Such networks help solve what Slaughter calls a *tri-lemma*: "We need global rules without centralized power but with government actors who can be held to account."[26]

Slaughter's book assesses both the contributions of these trans-governmental networks and some criticisms of them. They can create policy convergence; improve compliance with international rules; and increase the scope, nature, and quality of international cooperation. On the other hand, they may hand excessive power to unelected technocrats, or magnify asymmetries in power within the international system. Slaughter presents several suggestions to enhance the contributions and address the criticisms, including making government networks more visible and creating global norms to regulate these networks.

In its emphasis on multinational and legal solutions, Slaughter's work revives concepts presented by the neo-Kantian authors of the early 1990s. But Slaughter has adapted those concepts to address the new realities and threats of the 21st century. In doing so, she uncovers part of the elephant that has been little noticed, and she also presents a strong case for the current importance and future potential of these governmental networks. However, they may have only limited impact in the troubled parts of the world described by the neo-Hobbesian authors in the next chapter. True, the networks formed to fight terrorism and international crime are critical for dealing successfully with those problems, but most of these networks are found in the globalized world. Expanding them to penetrate and incorporate government officials from what Thomas Barnett calls the "unconnected world" would significantly strengthen the potential that Slaughter champions.

Taking Stock of the Neo-Kantian Literature

The books surveyed by this chapter, seen collectively, offer a composite portrayal of world affairs, a sense of emerging opportunities, and key policy recommendations:

- Fukuyama and Huntington called attention to the prospects for expansion of democracy into new regions
- Lipson sought to identify the reasons why democracies seldom go to war with each other
- Friedman pointed to the opportunities created by accelerating globalization
- Garten and Asmus both highlighted the need for alliance reform and the possibilities of doing so
- Kegley and Raymond identified the hopeful prospects for management of great power relations
- Keohane emphasized the importance of interlocking networks of institutions to manage relations among nations

- Slaughter noted that the new world order already encompasses networks of government officials that could be a force for stability
- Yergin and Stanislaw called attention to the positive economic impact of relying upon markets, rather than governments, for management of domestic economies
- Gilpin pointed to the need for governments to cooperate in guiding the evolution of the world economy.

Taken together, these books and others like them helped provide a powerful theoretical paradigm for understanding the democratized and globalized portion of the post–Cold War world. A new paradigm was badly needed after the end of the Cold War and the Soviet threat suddenly left an intellectual vacuum. The neo-Kantian literature offered not only valuable descriptive and explanatory propositions about emerging world affairs, but also substantive policy prescriptions for capitalizing on opportunities. In this sense, it certainly passed the tests of insight, relevance, and originality. While not all of its propositions have been proven valid, the neo-Kantian literature helped educate many readers and triggered many constructive debates.

Another test of important literature is whether it had an impact on public opinion and government policy. The neo-Kantian literature passed this test with flying colors. Throughout much of the 1990s, it was the focus of considerable attention. A main reason for its popularity was that, apart from appearing to assess world events accurately, its hopeful messages were appealing. Because the early 1990s were a period of exhaustion from the Cold War, many readers welcomed reassurances of optimistic times ahead, and many observable contemporary trends suggested that such times had already arrived. As a consequence, many governments embraced the central tenets of the neo-Kantian literature. They viewed such disturbing events as the genocide in Rwanda as unhappy exceptions to the march of global progress. In the United States, the Clinton administration issued national security strategy statements during 1993–1996 that emphasized global democratic enlargement and a flourishing world economy, rather than impending dangers and threats. Governments in Europe and elsewhere reacted in similar ways. The neo-Kantian literature not only reflected this viewpoint, but also helped nourish it.

Today, critics often point out that many of the core hypotheses of the neo-Kantian literature have not continued to be borne out. In the post–September 11 world, nobody speaks of history coming to an end, or democracy sweeping over the entire world, or globalization elevating all poor countries out of poverty while making the rich still wealthier, or countries everywhere joining together to create world peace. Because of the sobering events of recent years, globalization's sharpest critics would move the neo-Kantian literature to the same bookshelf as Norman Angell's 1910 book predicting an end to major war.

With hindsight, the deficiencies of the early neo-Kantian literature seem obvious. Neo-Kantians who predicted swift global democratization brushed aside the impediments to this outcome in traditional regions, especially the Middle East. Similarly, the proponents of globalization ignored the full complexity of international economics.

Dismissing the neo-Kantian literature, however, would be a mistake. Some of its arguments may have been too sweeping, but other parts were more scholarly and took account of the world's complexity and unpredictability. In addressing democracy's future, there were big differences between Fukuyama and Huntington. In addressing globalization, there were big differences between Friedman and Gilpin. Garten was not naïve about alliance relationships; Asmus showed how neo-Kantian policies succeeded in Europe; Kegley and Raymond were not blind to the potential troubles facing big power relations; Yergin and Stanislaw were cognizant of the difficulties and dilemmas of switching from government-run to market-dominated economies. While some writers in the neo-Kantian literature did suggest that global progress was inevitable, and that governments did not have to do anything special to bring it about, others made it clear that progress could occur only if governments had the will and the wisdom to make it happen. Some of the most recent neo-Kantian writing, by Keohane and Slaughter, for example, stresses the importance of positive actions by institutions and government networks in bringing about desired change. Distinctions must be made in evaluating this literature; each part of it should be judged on its own merits.

Equally important, it should be remembered that neo-Kantian trends remain alive and thriving in key parts of the world. The democratic community is a living demonstration of the validity of neo-Kantian thought. Europe continues toward democracy, peace, prosperity, and unity; large parts of Asia are making democratic progress; Latin America is now mostly democratic (albeit with some backsliding). Although neo-Hobbesian trends mark much of the Middle East and adjoining regions, neo-Kantian trends are at work even there. The current era represents a struggle between neo-Hobbesian and neo-Kantian trends, not a permanent triumph of the former over the latter.

In both its strengths and deficiencies, the early neo-Kantian literature must be seen as a product of its times. It reflected the fact that in the early 1990s, the world had undeniably become less threatening than during the Cold War, and contemporary trends seemed genuinely to be moving toward peace and prosperity. The problems—the Balkans, North Korea, Iraq—seemed local and isolated. At the time, the Middle East was relatively quiet, Islamic fundamentalists were not characterizing globalization as a new Western crusade, terrorists were not on a global rampage, and WMD proliferation was not accelerating: indeed, nuclear weapons were being removed from South Africa and from former Soviet Republics in Central Asia. To many observers, the isolated troubles of the early 1990s could be seen as fading leftovers of the past, rather than harbingers of future trouble. If some of the early neo-Kantian literature failed to identify deeper dangers in the emerging geostrategic order, this was because a dense fog of uncertainty concealed these dangers and their underlying causes. The lesson here is that at times of great uncertainty, many things are not only unknown, but inherently unknowable as well.

Perhaps the accusation can be made that the neo-Kantian literature created conceptual lenses though which reality was selectively perceived and distorted, and it thereby perpetuated blindness to future events that otherwise could have been foreseen. This criticism seems most apt with respect to the greater Middle East, where much of the neo-Kantian literature, along with U.S. policy, failed to perceive the gathering dangers of Islamic fundamentalism and global terrorism until the storm broke with unmistakable fury in 2001. Greater awareness, earlier, might have alleviated this danger, or at least made the United States and its allies better able to handle it.

Yet it is equally true that the neo-Kantian literature helped contribute to many sensible government policies that helped consolidate Cold War victories and take advantage of the new era's opportunities. Neo-Kantianism helped produce NATO enlargement into Eastern Europe, U.S. efforts to build cooperative relations with Russia and China, and the Oslo Peace Process in the Middle East, and it accelerated world trade negotiations. These policies took hold in varying degrees, and while they did not bring permanent peace, they helped make the world more peaceful and better able to absorb the shocks that began on September 11, 2001.

If the neo-Kantian period of the 1990s produced one unmistakable strategic change for the good, it was that of rendering Europe peaceful and united. This alone was a huge strategic accomplishment: earlier in the 20th century, Europe had been a constant source of political conflict and war. Peace in Europe enabled the United States and its allies to turn their attentions to regions that were still unstable, including the greater Middle East, and gave them greater flexibility to concentrate their resources there. To the extent that the neo-Kantian literature helped bring about this vital strategic change, it deserves high marks for relevance and impact. More fundamentally, the neo-Kantian literature helped encourage the U.S. Government to see the world as a whole, rather than as a collection of separate regions, and to perceive democratization and the globalizing economy as powerful factors influencing security affairs. These were important contributions, the positive effects of which continue.

The neo-Kantian literature saw part of the elephant of world affairs, but not the whole elephant. It correctly saw the most important parts of its time, but in general it failed to foresee the troubled times just ahead. The lesson is that when complex systems are being examined, all of their major variables should be studied, and none should be neglected. Underlying dynamics must be examined, because surface manifestations can be misleading. The neo-Kantian literature was undeniably optimistic, but it was not, in that, entirely wrong. It correctly identified factors in world affairs that still have the potential to make the next decades a time of opportunity. The neo-Kantian literature may have inflated the importance and power of these factors and failed to note other trends pulling in the opposite direction. But these positive factors are still influential forces that can help push the world toward peace and prosperity.

Chapter Three

A Neo-Hobbesian World of Turmoil

To illuminate the neo-Hobbesian literature and its main themes, we review 14 key books and note several others along the way. Some appeared in the early 1990s, but most were published since 1995, as the troubles of the new era started manifesting themselves. Although most of these books recognized some future opportunities, their main emphasis was on challenges, problems, dangers, and threats. Together, they reveal a general theory of chaos and turmoil arising from multiple sources: they give a view of the dark side of the elephant.

This chapter begins by focusing on three books that provide a holistic theory of the stresses of global politics and a fourth that assesses the role of China as an emerging empire:

- Zbigniew K. Brzezinski, *Out of Control: Global Turmoil on the Eve of the Twenty-first Century* (1993)
- Samuel P. Huntington, *The Clash of Civilizations and the Remaking of World Order* (1996)
- John J. Mearsheimer, *The Tragedy of Great Power Politics* (2001)
- Ross Terrill, *The New Chinese Empire: And What It Means for the United States* (2003).

Next, five books that explore the issue of ethnic antagonisms, anarchy, genocide, and chaos in Africa and other poor regions are examined:

- Liah Greenfeld, *Five Roads to Modernity* (1992)
- Daniel Patrick Moynihan, *Pandaemonium: Ethnicity in International Politics* (1993)
- William Pfaff, *The Wrath of Nations: Civilization and the Furies of Nationalism* (1993)

- Robert D. Kaplan, *The Coming Anarchy: Shattering the Dreams of the Post Cold War* (2000)
- Samantha Power, *A Problem from Hell: America and the Age of Genocide* (2002).

The chapter concludes by reviewing several books on radical Islamic fundamentalism and on the greater Middle East and its rogue states:

- Bernard Lewis, *The Middle East: A Brief History of the Last 2,000 Years* (1996); *What Went Wrong? The Clash Between Islam and Modernity in the Middle East* (2002); and *The Crisis of Islam: Holy War and Unholy Terror* (2003)
- Kenneth M. Pollack, *The Threatening Storm: The Case for Invading Iraq* (2002); and *The Persian Puzzle: The Conflict Between Iran and America* (2004).

We start with one of the first high-profile books to counter the optimistic predictions of neo-Kantianism.

Zbigniew Brzezinski: A New Era of Turmoil and Chaos

Brzezinski's 1993 book, *Out of Control: Global Turmoil on the Eve of the Twenty-first Century*, was one of the first statements to dash the optimism of neo-Kantianism, instead forecasting increasing anarchy and chaos in the early 21st century.[1] While granting that the end of the Cold War might yet produce a global community, Brzezinski asserted that unless contemporary trends were reversed, worldwide disorder would be more likely.

Brzezinski, who had served as National Security Advisor under President Jimmy Carter, agreed with Francis Fukuyama that political ideas, along with their associated beliefs and value systems, play a critical role in determining how the future will evolve. Unlike Fukuyama, however, he did not presume that liberal democracy is destined to be adopted everywhere merely because it is a theoretically superior value system. Brzezinski pointed to the importance of seeing whether and how old and new values actually are being embraced in the post–Cold War era, not just how democratic philosophers thought they should be embraced. He reasoned that, whereas common values can lay a foundation for global cooperation, dissimilar values can lead to conflict. In his view, global trends were in the direction of dissimilarity, not commonality. Predicting discontinuities ahead, he forecast a world of accelerating change, with the future arriving in a rush: "History has not ended, but has become compressed."[2]

Viewing the future through the lens of history, Brzezinski pointed out that the 19th century had given rise to political ideologies and mass politics, as well as to nationalism, idealism, and rationalism. The result, he said, was a 20th century in which totalitarianism's attempt to create coercive utopias spawned instead mass murder, repression, and world wars. The coming era represented, to Brzezinski, a sharp reaction against this disastrous experience, but not necessarily a global embrace of Western liberal democracy or of its European philosophical foundations. Instead, he saw the world entering a "post-utopian" phase, in which all millennial ideologies have lost their appeal, leaving social groups to fall back on their own interests and experiences for identity and meaning. With major changes taking place at ever-faster rates amid mounting economic interpenetration and social upheaval, the result is a global "crisis of spirit" that reflects a lack of common values.

Brzezinski urged that preservation of global order required assertive trilateral leadership by the United States, Western Europe, and Japan. Unlike some pessimists, Brzezinski did not greatly fear that the United States might fall back into geopolitical rivalry with its principal Cold War partners. But he concluded that strong leadership from the three traditional allies was not likely to be achieved unless all three changed policies. Brzezinski noted that the United States remains a peerless military power but today is so identified globally by its materialist culture—the "permissive cornucopia"—that it cannot serve as a moral beacon or provide central authority to the rest of the world. Western Europe and Japan, also economic powerhouses, are so introspective and self-centered that they cannot play the role of global leader either. Brzezinski's central policy recommendation was that all three must overcome this paralysis in order to forge the necessary trilateral leadership to handle a world that otherwise might drift toward anarchy and chaos.

Even if such leadership were offered, Brzezinski acknowledged, its effectiveness would hinge on whether it was accepted as legitimate across the globe. Successful efforts by the wealthy Western democracies to alter global perceptions of their self-absorption in materialism would be crucial. Otherwise, this legitimacy might not be granted because in many quarters, these countries are not regarded as models worthy of emulation. In Brzezinski's view, communism collapsed in Europe not because markets and democracy were overwhelmingly preferred, but because communism had become a grotesque political-economic failure and was therefore cast aside by countries and ethnic groups seeking their own national identities. Self-determination, he said, is the dominating imperative. The strains of transitioning to capitalism do not, however, foster the moderate political climate needed for democracy to take hold. As a result, he predicted, Europe was unlikely to see a progressive march eastward of democracy and capitalism. Instead, it was more likely to be divided in two, with a diffuse European Union to the west and a turbulent zone of undemocratic countries to the east.

Elsewhere, Brzezinski asserted, the world is witnessing a political awakening defined in material and psychological terms. As the gap between expectations and realities enlarges, starving spectators in poor countries look with anger at wealthy democratic countries whose insatiable consumers appear to lack moral legitimacy. Thus, he said, there is no universal consensus in support of common Western values that would foster multilateral cooperation and community-building.

Many countries resist the idea of falling under the West's tutelage, Brzezinski observed, and some are even reluctant to cooperate with their neighbors in anything beyond basic trade. The trend is toward a dangerous divergence of outlooks as different cultures and economic contexts are brought into more contact by modern communications. What is needed, Brzezinski said, is a global confederal culture, but instead the world might get an uncoordinated assemblage. Regional conflicts, economic strife, xenophobia, new ideological conflicts, nuclear proliferation, power contests, and mounting dissatisfaction, anger, and frustration could mean a descent toward anarchy.

Looking at Europe, Brzezinski expressed doubt that the EU or NATO could permanently tame this long-turbulent continent. He said that although the EU might continue evolving slowly toward integration, it would be tangled in too many contradictions to unify all of Europe. In Eastern Europe, Brzezinski forecast that continued efforts to install democracy and markets would encounter considerable difficulty and limited success. In Russia and the former Soviet Union, he foresaw a geopolitical black hole of great political instability and upheaval. The transition away from communism had only just begun when he was writing in 1993; Brzezinski expressed doubt that Russia would emerge as a democracy any time soon. At best, he said, Russia might be able to follow the Asian model, using strong government control to establish a capitalist economy. Equally likely, however, would be some new kind of authoritarian statist nationalism or even outright fascism and a determination to restore an empire beyond Russia's borders. Russia was likely, in his view, to be surrounded by a cluster of unstable nations caught up in ethnic ambitions, raw nationalism, and mutual hatred. As Russia began to gain more autonomy, he predicted that it might challenge Germany for domination of Eastern Europe in a reappearance of the geopolitical rivalry that had often destabilized Europe in the past.

In Brzezinski's view, regional stability in East Asia would depend largely on how relations among the big powers played out. He expected that Japan would continue to be America's closest partner, but that U.S.-Japanese trade frictions could cause political trouble; however, he discounted any serious risk of a Japanese descent into mercantilism, nationalism, or militarism. He concluded that its history and limited policy horizons would keep Japan from playing the role of a constructive regional leader. He thus forecast that the Asian region would not integrate, but would instead be dominated by fluid multipolarity.

Brzezinski expressed hope that China would emerge as a constructive partner of the Western democracies, but thought it more likely that a future China would be a power-seeker in Asia and an authoritarian but capitalist leader of the Third World, offering an alternative to Western models. The result would be an Asian region dominated economically by Japan but rendered tense by growing Chinese strategic assertiveness and the absence of a collective security structure. A stronger role by China, he warned, might even trigger Japanese rearmament, creating a security standoff between these two powers.

In South Asia, Brzezinski forecast Indian hegemony. In the greater Middle East, he predicted an impoverished, shapeless Islamic cluster that, although permeated with anger at the West, would lack sufficient cohesion either to lift itself into modernity or to strike back forcefully at the West. The result, he predicted, would be a vast region of chronic instability, caught between the competing impulses of traditionalism and modernism. He did not forecast terrorist strikes against the United States, or another war with Iraq, but he did see clearly that the greater Middle East would remain tense, not because of rivalry among the great powers, but because of turmoil within the region itself. In this region, he said, "American supremacy is built quite literally on sand."[3]

In light of his survey of the global strategic terrain, Brzezinski offered his recommendations for U.S. national security strategy. He called upon the United States to remain engaged abroad and to reject any return to isolationism or premature withdrawal out of false optimism that the world would be stable merely because the Cold War had ended. He urged the United States to remain militarily strong, to employ the other elements of power and diplomacy at its disposal, and to work closely with allies in order to gain the benefits of multilateralism. He predicted that the United States would face troubles in the coming years, not because a new peer rival would arise to replace the Soviet Union, but because the global security system is structurally unstable and prone to widespread tension. He warned that the United States and its allies must be prepared for major and often unpredictable changes. His most important point was that the United States must be able to supplement its physical powers with an appealing political message to other countries, anchored in shared values. Otherwise, he said, the United States might suffer an erosion of its influence abroad, even as the absence of common values produced further fragmentation and discord.

Because Brzezinski's book was one of the first of what would become a wave of neo-Hobbesian literature, it served as an early corrective to the excessive optimism of the neo-Kantian literature. In pointing to the lack of common political values and identities in the post–Cold War era, it rebutted the neo-Kantian hope that Western democratic values would sweep over the entire world. In contrast to a vision of global affairs ruled by democracy and economic interests, Brzezinski put forth a different yet equally coherent theory of resurgent geopolitics involving a great deal of anarchy, chaos, and turmoil. A strength of his theory is that it included many key variables that are visible on the world stage today, including the actions of the United States and its allies, relations among the major powers, trends in troubled regions and the underdeveloped world, the role of political ideas and values, and the impact of modern communications systems. His book showed that a knowledgeable observer, viewing the same world as the neo-Kantians, could draw from it a much different synthesis.

Seen in retrospect, Brzezinski seems to have come closer to the truth in many areas than did proponents of the extreme versions of neo-Kantianism. Yet critics could judge his analysis as too dismissive of positive trends and too pessimistic in some areas. For example, despite setbacks for the EU constitution, Europe has made greater strides toward unity and democracy since 1993 than Brzezinski predicted. Overall, however, Brzezinski seems to have judged correctly in forecasting a future of slow, troubled progress for Russia and the former Soviet Union, and a murky evolution in Asia driven by economics and new-era geopolitics centered on the interaction between China and Japan.

About the greater Middle East, Brzezinski was not pessimistic enough. Whereas he predicted continued tensions but no great crises, the decade after he wrote saw renewed Israeli-Palestinian violence, global terrorism by radical Islamic fundamentalists, another U.S. war with Iraq and one with Afghanistan, and mounting troubles with an Iran trying to acquire nuclear weapons. Brzezinski was, of course, hardly alone in this: while many neo-Hobbesians of the 1990s fretted about potential trouble with Russia and China, few saw the greater Middle East as the hot zone of the next decade. In this sense, the neo-Hobbesians and neo-Kantians equally failed to predict the future in an era of contradictory trends and silent underlying developments.

Samuel Huntington: A World of Cultural Antagonisms

After Samuel Huntington's 1991 neo-Kantian book, which we surveyed in chapter two, his 1996 book showed him moving to the neo-Hobbesian school.[4] In *The Clash of Civilizations and the Remaking of World Order*, Huntington, like Brzezinski, rejected the neo-Kantian notion that the end of the Cold War had opened the door for the adoption all over the world of Western liberal ideals such as democracy and capitalism. He agreed with Brzezinski that in the new era, nations would renew their search for identity defined in local terms, rather than in the millennial political and economic ideologies of the past. Unlike Brzezinski, he did not predict growing fragmentation and chaos brought about by the inability of large groups to create unifying identities. Instead, he said, in the new era, groups of people would define their identities in terms of culture, shaped by tribal ancestry, language, religion, and social values. The result would be a future of considerable heterogeneity, with struggle, conflict, and large-scale culture clashes as globalization and interdependence drew the world closer together. In particular, he expected conflict between the Western democratic community and two principal antagonists, Islam in the Middle East and Chinese Sinic culture in Asia. This bleak forecast of a "clash of civilizations" placed Huntington squarely in the camp of neo-Hobbesians who forecast great trouble ahead.

Huntington's central thesis was that Western belief in the universality of its culture had three major flaws: it is false, it is immoral, and it is dangerous. It is false, he said, because the assumption of universality is not accepted by other cultures; it is immoral because it wrongly tries to impose alien views on others; and it is dangerous because it inflames already stressful cultural antagonisms. Huntington sketched a competition of dissimilar cultures as a new paradigm for analyzing world politics in the early 21ˢᵗ century. In his view, the world was divided into different cultures, each in a distinct geographic locale. These main civilizations are:

- the Western culture of North America, Europe, and Australia
- the Hispanic culture of Latin America
- the African culture of sub-Saharan Africa
- the Islamic culture of the greater Middle East, North Africa, South Asia, and Indonesia
- the Hindu culture of India
- the Orthodox culture of Russia, the former Soviet Union, and the Balkans
- the Sinic culture of China and Korea
- the Buddhist culture of Southeast Asia
- the Japanese culture of Japan.

Huntington said that each of these civilizations brings unique cognitive frameworks, moral values, affective ties, and expectations to the task of organizing its societies, economies, and governments. As a result of this diversity, he said, the 21st century will produce not a single global civilization, but multiple strong civilizations that bump up against each other as they endeavor to establish their identities and enhance their power. Huntington did not claim to predict the specific outcome, but he made clear his expectation that great turmoil would be brought about by this clash of civilizations. The challenge for the Western democracies, he warned, would be to manage this diversity and turmoil in an era when their own relative power would be declining and their values were not globally accepted. On the surface, this book might seem to contradict Huntington's earlier book on democratization, but closer inspection shows the harmony between them. Huntington's earlier book recorded the spread of democracy mostly among Western cultures. *Clash of Civilizations,* by contrast, mainly focused on how other cultures are reacting to the modern world and the accelerating spread of Western influence.

Implicitly rejecting Fukuyama's "end of history" thesis, Huntington dismissed predictions that liberal democracy will be universally adopted as resulting from cultural blindness and arrogance. Modernization and Westernization, he pointed out, are not the same thing: the pursuit of modernization does not necessarily lead foreign cultures to embrace Westernization. The rest of the world does not especially admire the secular materialism and individualism of the United States and Europe, as he noted, and it has no intention of adopting their approaches to politics, economics, and society. Indeed, he said, political power and moral authority are slipping away from the Western democracies as other cultures become more vigorous and as economic gains give them more strategic power to assert their place in world politics. Moreover, modern communications are bringing cultures into closer contact and making their borders more permeable, exacerbating the risks of cultural conflict.

Huntington also did not agree, however, with those who forecast global chaos and anarchy. The world will have central organizing principles, he said, but they will be anchored in clashing cultures. The rise of culture as an organizing principle did not mean the end of the nation-state model as a foundation for future world politics. Most cultures would, he predicted, be led by dominant nation-states, with lesser states, cultural groups, and diaspora populations in concentric orbits. Thus, in his paradigm, nation-states would continue to play major roles in shaping world politics, mostly as leaders of great multinational cultures rather than as individual actors solely in pursuit of their own interests.

Huntington also downplayed an earlier hypothesis, advanced in his 1993 *Foreign Affairs* article, that "the West versus the rest" would dominate world politics.[5] He expected the West to encounter stiff resistance from other cultures in such areas as human rights, nuclear proliferation, and immigration policies, but his 1996 book did not predict an organized global coalition against the West. Nonetheless, he expected a future of difficulty and struggle as leadership by the Western democracies began to recede in the face of other cultures' growing power and assertiveness. He predicted wars and other armed struggles, especially at locations where major cultures meet and create friction points and fault lines. He gave as an example the Balkans, with fault lines where Christian, Orthodox, and Islamic cultures intersect. He did not, however, predict unremitting struggle among all cultures, nor a zero-sum game in which the gains of some were inevitably losses for others. Instead, a complex world with mixed, shifting patterns of conflict and consensus could make things easier for the Western democracies in some respects, but more difficult in others.

For example, Huntington predicted that the West would have closer and more harmonious relations with Latin America and Africa, mostly positive relations with Orthodox Russia, and still cooperative, if frayed, ties with Japan and Hindu India. The West's most significant conflictual relations would, he said, be with an angry Islamic Middle East and an assertive China. He predicted a significant realignment involving growing ties between China and Islam, not because of cultural affinity, but rather because of the strategic advantages provided by mutual association. In the paradigm of the future that he sketched, the West would cooperate with Russia, and Russia would cooperate with India. Arrayed against this loose strategic cluster would be China and Islam teamed together, with Islam dominating the Middle East and North Africa, while a powerful China gained domination over Asia to the point where Japan would loosen its ties to the United States so it could reach accommodation with China.

In addressing the role of Islam as a powerful cultural force in the Middle East, Huntington pointed out that Islam is organized around local tribes and religious faith rather than nation-states. The result, he said, is a region of "tribes with flags" where no single country has been a dominant power since the collapse of the Ottoman Turkish Empire after World War I. A development of recent decades that he found significant has been the resurgence of Islamic identity in response to the collapse of pan-Arab nationalism and socialism. Huntington judged that the lack of a dominant country makes it harder for the Islamic culture to pursue either unified diplomacy or military confrontation in dealing with other countries and cultures, including the Western democracies, Russia, and India. As a result of this strategic ineffectiveness, coupled with the failure of Arab governments to achieve economic prosperity, a great deal of anger and frustration is directed outward, toward Western cultures that are blamed by Islam for material secularism and imperial exploitation of the Middle East. Out of this anger, he concluded, would grow a future of radical Islamic fundamentalism, terrorism, and military clashes with the United States and Europe, Russia, and India. Because Islam will remain strategically weak, however, military clashes will take place largely on the geographic periphery where Islam meets other cultures, rather than in the form of organized Islamic military aggression of the sort that occurred in past centuries.

Huntington portrayed Islam as strategically feeble for years to come, but he saw China as quite different. He observed that China not only is emerging as a huge nation-state anchored in a dominant Han culture, but also is acquiring great strategic and military power because of its booming economic expansion. China's culture of collective rather than individual values and of authoritarian political leadership, said Huntington, made it unlikely to become a liberal democracy, even as it embraced capitalism of a sort. A more powerful China was, he said, likely to seek to dominate Asia, not militarily so much as politically and economically, by creating a web of relationships that would draw other Asian countries into its orbit. Many Asian countries would thus face the dilemma of choosing between China and the United States, which would continue to provide them valuable military security. Japan and other countries, he predicted, would seek to accommodate China to the extent they could do so without completely severing their ties to the United States. This mixture of bandwagoning and balancing, said Huntington, would result in growing strategic rivalry between the United States and China that could produce war, a scenario to which he devoted the last chapter of his book.

Huntington's overall thesis posited several challenges for the United States. He expressed concern that "multiculturalists" in the United States were challenging central elements of the American creed and rejecting the American culture; he warned that this trend, if left unchecked, could undermine Western civilization. He also predicted that the United States would find it difficult to shape a policy that took account of the fact that, as he said, the great beneficiaries of the war of civilizations would be those who abstain from those wars.

Huntington offered strategic guidelines for the United States and its European allies in dealing with this future of ethnic conflicts and clashing civilizations. Rather than imposing their cultures on the rest of the world, the Western democracies are entering a period of declining power; they should, therefore, endeavor to protect and renew their own civilization. He urged U.S. and European policies aimed at:

- achieving greater Western political, economic, and military integration, in order to preclude other states and civilizations from exploiting differences among them
- unifying Europe under the flags of NATO and the EU
- encouraging Westernization of Latin America, and close alignment of Latin America with the West
- restraining the development of the conventional and unconventional military power of the Islamic countries and of China
- slowing the drift of Japan away from the West and toward accommodation with China
- accepting Russia as a leader of the Orthodox culture and a major regional power with legitimate security interests along its southern border
- maintaining Western technological and military superiority over other civilizations
- most importantly, recognizing that Western intervention in the affairs of other civilizations is probably the single most dangerous source of instability and potential global conflict in a multi-civilizational world.

Since Huntington's controversial book was published in 1996, it has had both admirers and critics. Any fair evaluation of it would conclude that Huntington was on solid ground in pointing out that the world is divided into multiple cultures, each with its own beliefs, values, and standards of behavior. Moreover, Huntington was undoubtedly correct in concluding that, in a world of great cultural diversity, Western ideals are unlikely to be adopted so rapidly and widely as forecast by some neo-Kantians. His prediction that clashing cultures would create new fault lines of global politics seems to have been borne out by events in the Balkans, the greater Middle East, and Africa.

Whether this world of diverse cultures will, as he saw it, produce a future in which great cultural antagonisms are the central organizing principle of world politics, however, is another matter. The great wars of the 20th century were produced by clashes among universalist political ideologies and nationalist imperatives, not the cultural antagonisms that Huntington points to as the dangers of the future. Cultural and religious wars have not been a major shaper of world politics since Islam's attack on Europe was rebuffed four centuries ago and Europe's religious wars were settled in the late 1500s.

Cultural antagonisms are indeed on the rise again: renewed Islamic anger and violence are a prime example. Yet the rise of China, a principal fear expressed by Huntington, seems dictated more by nationalism and its strategic imperatives than by Chinese culture, which has not tended to be imperial or assertive. Many of today's potential strategic frictions—the emerging struggles among Europe, Russia, India, China, Japan, and the United States—may reflect a renewal of traditional great power rivalries rather than deep cultural feuds; these countries might be jostling for power even if they all shared the same culture. After all, Germany, France, and Britain have had similar cultures for centuries, and this did not stop them from repeated wars against each other.

To this extent, Huntington's paradigm has not been borne out. Beyond this, the neo-Kantians were correct in noting that the modern era creates incentives for countries everywhere to adopt some form of capitalism and democracy. There are also incentives for countries to become integrated into the world economy, and to join multilateral political institutions that can help manage stressful security affairs. None of these incentives mean that the future will produce a homogenous world, but they may be compelling enough to induce cooperation, even by diverse cultures. This, at least, is the hope of pragmatic neo-Kantians who realize that although a peaceful future may not be inevitable, it may be achieved through wise governmental policies.

Whereas some neo-Kantians may have been too optimistic, *Clash of Civilizations* may have been too pessimistic. However, Huntington was right about some fundamentals. In an era of accelerating globalization that is bringing regions into closer contact and interdependence, the world is still full of chaos and conflict. Differences in culture mean that countries will view the future in dissimilar ways, and thus they may have trouble finding common ground for cooperation. Cultures regarding each other in antagonistic terms may raise the risk of interstate conflict, terrorism, proliferation of weapons of mass destruction, and war. Huntington accurately fingered this as a principal danger ahead.

Huntington offered policy recommendations similar to those offered by other neo-Hobbesians, but his differ in a key respect. He strongly urged the United States and its European allies to refrain from intervening crudely in the affairs of other cultures, especially in the Islamic Middle East. Such interventions, he said, even if mounted in the name of Western democratic ideals, will backfire and inflame cultural hatreds, not lessen them. In this regard, Huntington's book stands out as sending a strong cautionary note that the United States would have done well to heed.

John Mearsheimer: A Future of Renewed Great Power Rivalry

Mearsheimer, a political scientist at the University of Chicago, published a provocative book in 2001 that built on his 1990 *International Security* article entitled "Back to the Future," and stimulated the ever-raging academic debates over international relations theory.[6] Mearsheimer's book, *The Tragedy of Great Power Politics*, shook the neo-Kantian literature's optimistic forecast to its foundations. Because the neo-Kantian literature was partly anchored in idealist theory, it portrayed a future of stable, cooperative relations either because the end of the Cold War made this outcome more likely, or because, as Kegley and Raymond argued, modern great powers could wield the mature diplomacy to achieve it. Mearsheimer poured cold water on this comforting notion. He drew on the theory of realism originally developed by such writers as Hans Morgenthau and Kenneth Waltz and applied it emphatically to the early 21st century.[7] His key argument was that because great power relations are inherently conflictual, a new era of major rivalry likely lies ahead: maybe not tomorrow, but definitely over the next two decades or so. The United States, he concluded, needs to react accordingly by striving to ensure that it will have the capacity to master the challenges of the future.

Mearsheimer's theory of great power relations, which he dubbed *offensive realism*, is distinctly neo-Hobbesian. It starts from the premise that states cannot be certain of the benign intentions of other states and that therefore "great powers have aggressive intentions."[8] Great powers, he wrote, fall into rivalry not because their intentions are necessarily aggressive, but because the nature of the international system creates a dynamic that inevitably leads them to behave competitively toward each other. The international system, as he points out, is inherently anarchical in the sense that there is no world government that can establish and enforce laws and codes of conduct. As a result, every country is left on its own; each must protect its security and interests largely through its own devices and must constantly fear being attacked by others. This situation, Mearsheimer said, compels great powers to seek to maximize their strength—that is, the physical assets of military forces and economic strength at their disposal. Moreover, he said, great powers must view power not just in absolute terms, but in relative terms as well: they must compare their physical power to that of potential rivals and seek a competitive advantage. The logic of such power politics, Mearsheimer said, is that great powers will strive to become hegemons: they desire to become so much stronger than potential rivals that they can dominate them. This constant search for physical security and hegemony produces continuing rivalry and competition among great powers irrespective of their ideologies and value systems. In other words, the law of the jungle prevails in international politics. This has been the case in the past, and it will, he said, hold true in the future; the competitive, beggar-thy-neighbor nature of world politics has not changed, because the international system is still anarchic. Mearsheimer acknowledged that great powers can also dissuade and deter each other through balance-of-power mechanisms, but such stability is anchored in underlying principles of competitive rivalry, and these create the setting for perpetual trouble.

Mearsheimer turned to history to find support for his key propositions. He noted that the past four centuries of European and global history have been a constant tale of great power rivalries that, despite changing shape from one era to the next, never lost their central character. Thus, the struggles among Britain, France, and Spain for supremacy in the 17th and 18th centuries were followed by the Napoleonic wars of the early 19th century, to German unification under Bismarck during 1862–1870, and then to Europe's balance-of-power system, which exploded into world war in 1914. In the early 1930s, the Treaty of Versailles ending World War I collapsed, giving way to a new rivalry as Nazi Germany, fascist Italy, and imperialist Japan strove for domination of Europe and the rest of the globe, triggering World War II. The end of that war, in turn, set the stage for the Cold War, with a global rivalry between the United States and the Soviet Union, and the prospect of nuclear war as a constant threat for more than four decades.

Mearsheimer dismissed any neo-Kantian notion that a new era of idealism, democratic peace, and economic globalization had relegated geopolitics to the ash can of history. Because today's international system remains one of nation-states amidst anarchy, he reasoned, a new era of rivalry among the major powers was all but inevitable. Mearsheimer stopped short of saying that the great powers can never collaborate to produce alliances, collective defense pacts, and stability. But he viewed such actions as transient and eventually doomed to unravel under the pressure of fundamental dynamics that lead the great powers to view each other distrustfully and to compete with each other for supremacy. He portrayed the tranquil decade of the 1990s as a temporary interlude that eventually would be superseded by a new era of menacing rivalry. Indeed, he saw signs of such geopolitical behavior already in NATO's enlargement into Eastern Europe, Russia's emerging nationalist foreign policy, China's bullying of Taiwan, and India's assertive conduct toward Pakistan.

Mearsheimer did not say that all great power rivalries are identical or are destined to produce disastrous consequences, instead asserting that these rivalries can produce different types of international systems having differing degrees of instability. He wrote that bipolar systems—in which the great powers organize into two similarly strong blocs—tend to be stable because neither bloc can hope to gain enough strength to overpower the other. He viewed multipolar systems of three or more power blocs as inherently less stable. He allowed for the possibility that balanced multipolar systems could be relatively stable if none of the great powers had plausible prospects for gaining ascendancy over the others. However, unbalanced multipolar systems would be highly unstable, especially if a potential hegemon was actively striving to dominate the system. This, he said, would result in severe competition because all participants would be striving to master a fluid situation of great change, uncertainty, and danger. Wars could easily erupt: the would-be hegemon might perceive an opportunity to weaken rivals by attacking them, or other countries might decide to attack the potential hegemon before it became too strong to defeat.

Mearsheimer dismissed the idea that the current international system is unipolar even though the United States may have hegemonic superiority over all potential rivals. He said that the United States possesses true hegemony only in the Western hemisphere, where it easily dominates all other countries. But he does not view the United States as a hegemon outside the Western hemisphere, because it is separated from other regions by two huge oceans that are significant barriers to the assertion of its military power, especially its land power. Moreover, he observed, the military and economic power of the United States is so divided among the regions of Europe, the greater Middle East, and Asia that it lacks preponderant strength in any of them. Thus, in his view, the U.S. role is similar to that of Britain in the 19th century: it is an offshore balancer in multiple regions, but a true hegemon in none. The central challenge facing the United States, he said, is to act as a power balancer in all of these regions in order to prevent hegemons from rising in any of them, and to prevent dangerous great power rivalries from taking shape.

Looking into the future beyond 2020, Mearsheimer expressed pessimism because he does not believe that today's stable regional balances are sustainable. If Europe is stable today, he said, it is because the United States is still present with sizable military strength to dampen tendencies toward renewed geopolitical maneuvering. However, the United States and Europe are gradually being pulled apart by post–Cold War political and economic dynamics. Sooner or later, he wrote, the United States can be expected to withdraw all of its military forces from Europe and downgrade its leadership role in the NATO alliance, resulting in Germany's emergence as the head of a new European power bloc under an EU flag. He warned that this would also increase the likelihood of a renewed rivalry between Germany and Russia over control of the zone that separates them. Rivalry between these two traditional opponents could, he concluded, give rise to intense security competition in Europe, leading to renewed multipolar dynamics of the sort that convulsed Europe into the 20th century.

While Mearsheimer's warnings about Europe were nuanced and conditional, his warnings about Asia were distinct and emphatic. Like Huntington, he expected China to emerge soon as a potential hegemon intent on acquiring enough military, economic, and political muscle to intimidate other Asian countries and to diminish the U.S. leadership role in the region. This, he said, would compel many Asian countries to seek U.S. protection, develop sufficient national powers to protect themselves, or both. Mearsheimer saw Japan as an especially important influence on the new Asian strategic architecture. It could be provoked by China's emergence as a potential hegemon to depart from its earlier low-profile pacifism into acquiring nuclear weapons and building additional ground, naval, and air forces. The outcome, Mearsheimer said, could be an Asia of intensifying great power rivalries in an unstable multipolar setting, with the risk of crises and even war.

Mearsheimer's book offered advice on how, given the future he forecast, the United States should shape its national security policy and defense strategy. He argued that the United States should dispense with illusions of idealism and instead embrace the postulates of realism. It should, he said, remain physically strong and maneuver carefully on the world scene to preserve its privileged position and to contain emerging instabilities brought about by emerging dynamics. Urging the United States to remain powerfully present in Europe for as long as possible, he hammered even harder on the U.S. need to gird for an intensified great power rivalry with China. Instead of inviting China to join the world economy in order to gain prosperity and democracy, he said, the United States should try to keep China weak. This effort would not succeed forever, but for a time, it would be the only way to prevent rivalry between a headstrong China and a nervous Japan from causing big trouble in Asia. These prescriptions might postpone trouble in key regions, but they would not spare the United States, as a central player in a new era of great power struggles, from what Mearsheimer called the tragedy of great power politics.

To its credit, Mearsheimer's book offered a reasoned theory of global politics, developed an integrated set of clear postulates, and then applied them logically to generate coherent descriptions, explanations, and predictions. It thus passes academic muster with flying colors. Likewise, while its theory of offensive realism may be anchored in conjectural propositions rather than iron laws of politics, it undeniably squares with a great deal of historical experience over past centuries. As such, it offers a healthy intellectual antidote to idealist theories, including those of some contemporary neo-Kantians, which often imply that major powers will have an easy time establishing warm, cooperative relations if only they abandon old-style geopolitical thinking and commit themselves to democracy and peace. Mearsheimer and other realists are correct in pointing out that the problems affecting great power relations are not so easily remedied.

At the same time, Mearsheimer and other realists can be criticized for deterministic thinking that results in overly pessimistic forecasts. To say that relations among the great powers are affected by competitive dynamics is not to prove that these dynamics are all-powerful nor that the result—always and necessarily—is a dangerous and downward-spiraling rivalry. Likewise, to say that great powers often evaluate their relations in terms of amassing physical power against each other is not to prove that—always and necessarily—this is their primary calculation. Great powers, like most countries, pursue a wide spectrum of foreign policy goals, ranging from physical security to economic prosperity and peace abroad. While they are capable of struggling for power with each other, they also are capable of recognizing good reasons for cooperating. In addition, where the great power rivalries of the past were often anchored in competition over control of territory, raw materials, and natural resources, most of these resources can now be acquired more cheaply through market mechanisms than by militarism and imperialism. This trend does not mean that future great power rivalries are impossible, but it does mean that a principal source of historical rivalries is losing its force.

The key issue is whether Mearsheimer's troubling forecasts accurately gauge trends during the early 21st century. While current events suggest that his prediction of German-Russian rivalry in Europe may be improbable, his prediction of impending trouble with China might still come true if events are allowed to slide downhill. In Asia, the conditions for descent into great power rivalry are taking shape, while the incentives for collaboration may not be adequately mitigating, and there are no collective defense or security institutions to moderate states' propensity for geopolitical maneuvering. As a result, Mearsheimer may eventually be proven right in Asia, if not in Europe and elsewhere. Regardless of the outcome, his book performs a valuable function. Just as idealist theory illuminates the path to peace, realist theory illuminates the path to war. Realist theory also helps show how rivalry and war might be avoided, if countries avoid being blindly naïve, and instead act to manage stressful geopolitics with the goal of stability and peace. To the extent that Mearsheimer's insightful book performs this valuable function, it will have made a worthy contribution not only to neo-Hobbesian thinking, but also to the larger subject of managing great power relations.

Ross Terrill: The Red Empire

While John Mearsheimer predicted that the dynamics of the current international system would pit China against the United States based on his application of realist logic, Ross Terrill assessed the China-U.S. relationship from the perspective of Chinese history and politics. Terrill characterized China as relatively weak, an unstable "steppe empire" with a desire for an expanded naval empire. He described the Chinese regime as having legitimacy problems that lead to it being a "rhetorical enemy" of the United States. He did not predict military conflict between the United States and China, but his description of China's situation and policies certainly suggest the potential for conflict. Therefore, Terrill's 2003 book, *The New Chinese Empire: And What It Means for the United States*, might be described as neo-Hobbesian with Chinese characteristics.[9]

Terrill pointed out that despite the demise of the dynastic system in 1911, the seizure of power by the Communists in 1949, and China's recent emergence as a leader in the global economy, it has been unable to escape its heritage of empire and authoritarian political systems. Although Sun Yat-sen and Chiang Kai-shek were hailed as China's new "republican" rulers, they tossed aside the ideal of a federal and democratic China in favor of top-down control more reminiscent of China's imperial past. Mao Tse Tung ruled as a "neo-emperor," issuing life-and-death edicts from above and accepting homage from the nation's workers. The death of Mao did not bring an end to centralized rule; instead, imperialism became even more necessary as regime preservation remained the top priority of Deng Xiaoping and his successors. So while China has been "hurtling down one road in economics," it is "limping down a different road in politics." China will not reach its full potential, Terrill posited, until it sheds its empire status and embraces political liberalization.

Much of the book is a history of China's major dynasties and of the modern period. Terrill offered three reasons why China still is an empire and not truly a nation. First, he pointed out that the 3 largest of China's 30 provinces are in territories that historically were not Han Chinese at all: Tibet, Xinjiang (the Muslim area in the west), and the southern part of Mongolia. These territories have historically been, for long periods, independent regimes that dealt as one state to another with the ruling courts of China. During the Tang Dynasty of the 7th and 8th centuries, Terrill notes, Tibet was an equal of the Chinese polity and defeated it militarily. The Mongols conquered and ruled China for a couple of centuries. The atmosphere in these territories today is semicolonial, and so in this sense, China is still more of an empire than a nation-state.

A second reason for viewing China as an empire is that, as Terrill wrote, China is now the only major power with unsatisfied territorial demands. It seeks to acquire substantial additional territories, including Taiwan and some islands in the South China Sea. As Terrill described it, there is little to support Beijing's claims over Taiwan; he dismissed China's "Taiwan Problem" as Beijing's dissatisfaction with the status quo. Terrill concluded that Beijing hopes to take these areas when it has the capacity to do so.

Third, Terrill described what he identified as imperial traits in the Beijing polity. One of these traits is that China historically had no boundaries. The jurisdiction of the Chinese Emperor, who was called "the Son of Heaven," extended to everything under heaven, and thus it was not lines on a map, but rather culture and a way of life that set China apart from its neighbors. The Chinese believed that there was only one civilization, and it was theirs. Non-Chinese were simply barbarians. Another historical trait of the Chinese state was its sense of superiority, coupled with external passivity: the Chinese emperors tended to view the barbarians as not even worth fighting or conquering. While arrogant in its viewpoint, Terrill wrote, it also had an "aspect of modesty or defensiveness." The People's Republic of China perpetuates this dualism. For example, it shows contempt toward Taiwan, hurling insults at its president, Chen Shui-bian. But although Chen has made close to a declaration of Taiwan's independence, Beijing has done little about it. However, China's presumption over Taiwan continues, even as its practical actions are essentially passive.

Terrill also identified the rewriting of history, as perpetrated by the "red empire," as an imperial characteristic. He cited several examples. In the 1960s, when Mao was defying the Soviet Union and the United States alike and quickly lost the two close friends it did have, Albania and Vietnam, the slogan went up in Beijing: "We have friends all over the world." In preparation for Jiang Zemin's 1998 visit to Hong Kong to mark the first anniversary of the end of British rule, Jiang's advance party leased 4 empty stores along his route and, for a 3-week period, stocked them with commodities to make the stores look prosperous. In classic Potemkin-village fashion, they thus dismissed reality from view.

Terrill then asked, "Can China evolve from its autocratic state, or must the polity crash, as the imperial system crashed in 1911–1912?" He suggested that the chances of a crash loom large, pointing to conditions that had played pivotal roles in the demise of earlier dynasties: diminishing leadership qualities, corruption, and succession struggles. Farmer uprisings, especially in the peripheral provinces, and the leadership's misjudgment of the power of outsiders, inherent in an empire's condescension toward other nations, are other potential causes Terrill identified for a crash. The crux of his argument, however, is that Beijing's instinct to put the maintenance of communist power at the center of its calculation will eventually be its undoing.

Terrill reviewed a list of incidents in U.S.-Chinese relations that indicate they will remain difficult, including China's objections to former Taiwanese president Lee Teng-hui's 1995 visit to Cornell University; the May 1999 NATO bombing of the Chinese Embassy in Belgrade; and U.S. protests at the Chinese government's persecution of the Falun Gong sect. Terrill does not believe that China could, as some fear, eclipse the United States if it continues to maintain its authoritarian system. Nor is he alarmed by China's current strength, postulating that, while China is an ambitious power, it is constrained in a number of ways. In his view, China treats the United States as a rhetorical enemy so that the communist regime can use anti-American propaganda to buttress its own legitimacy.

Perhaps because he sees China as both fairly aggressive and relatively impotent, Terrill was critical of the unwillingness of successive American governments to challenge China's human rights record for fear of angering Beijing. The United States should, he urged, remain noncommittal about the final outcome of issues that arise on the periphery of the Chinese Empire, such as those involving Taiwan, Tibet, and Xinjiang, but it should nevertheless seek to maximize opportunities for obtaining the consent of the local populations.

The community of China watchers in the United States is deeply divided on the issue of U.S. policy toward China. In contrast to Terrill's view, which urges greater political confrontation with China, is Ernest H. Preeg's 2005 book, *The Emerging Chinese Advanced Technology Superstate.*[10] Preeg argued that the paramount U.S.-Chinese relationship is about economics, that the national security interests of the two superstates are converging, and that the two nations have an ethnic and cultural affinity for one another. Meanwhile, technological advances and China's 1997–1999 military reforms are significantly strengthening its military capabilities. Unlike Terrill, Preeg sees the U.S.-China relationship as "positive-sum" and urges greater partnership in most areas, including dealing with terrorism.

Liah Greenfeld, Daniel Patrick Moynihan, and William Pfaff: Ethnic Politics and the Reemergence of Nationalism

Early in the 20th century, nationalism was the subject of a great deal of writing and analysis, as it played a major role in shaping global security affairs and balance-of-power politics and triggering both world wars. The study of nationalism declined during the Cold War, a conflict driven mainly by the ideological conflict between democracy and communism. As Zbigniew Brzezinski and other neo-Hobbesians pointed out, the end of the Cold War's ideological confrontation reopened the door for nationalism to reappear. A new nationalist literature began to emerge in the early to mid-1990s, as nationalism became more prominent in world affairs and especially as brutal ethnic politics in the Balkans threatened to spread elsewhere.

An early study of modern nationalism was written by Liah Greenfeld; her book, *Nationalism: Five Roads to Modernity*, appeared in 1992.[11] Stripping nationalism of its negative connotations, Greenfeld portrayed it as a system of beliefs and values that shape identity, psychological satisfaction, and motivation for nations, societies, and ethnic groups. Her book was a historical account showing how nationalism took shape and helped drive modernization in vastly different ways in England, France, Russia, Germany, and the United States. Her conclusion was that nationalism is not necessarily a good or an evil force; much depends upon how it is manifested. It can give rise to peaceful democracy and capitalism or to fascism, imperialism, and aggression. At the end of her lengthy history, she concluded that nationalism remains a powerful force in today's world, one that seemed likely to reemerge as the ideological conflicts of the Cold War faded.

Greenfeld was correct in portraying nationalism as multifaceted; its initial manifestation in the 1990s in the Balkans showed its ugly side. Yugoslavia, which had previously been held together by Marshall Tito's communist government, unraveled in 1992 and 1993, spinning off countries with distinct ethnic identities in a region whose violent politics had triggered World War I. Slovenia squirmed free, but when Croatia and Bosnia also sought separation, a vicious ethnic war broke out between its Muslim and Serbian groups, with neighboring Serbia supporting its ethnic cousins. The mounting violence in Bosnia presented Western governments with a new challenge vastly different from their Cold War experience.

Events in Bosnia also prompted a growing neo-Hobbesian literature about the troubles posed by volatile combinations of ethnic politics, nationalism, and mass violence. Among these was Senator Daniel Patrick Moynihan's 1993 book, *Pandaemonium: Ethnicity in International Politics*.[12] It predicted that ethnicity was on the verge of exploding into a major force capable of causing great disorder in the Balkans and elsewhere. The future, Moynihan predicted, involved not a reassertion of rivalries among the major powers, but a fracturing of many existing nation-states. Civil wars and tribal conflicts would result as smaller and smaller fragments would claim the right to self-determination.

These fragmentary states would themselves encompass minority groups that would, in turn, assert their own rights. Macroconflict, he wrote, would thus lead to a growing number of microconflicts, and a chaos of their own. Moynihan cited many danger zones, including the Balkans, the Caucasus, Central Asia, Indonesia, and Iraq.

Moynihan wrote that the United States has a poor record of understanding ethnicity and developing policy toward it. He traced the problem to World War I and President Woodrow Wilson, who endorsed the principle of universal self-determination without understanding how many and how varied were the nationalities that might claim this right. One who foresaw the trouble was Wilson's Secretary of State, Robert Lansing; he regarded *self-determination* as a phrase that would cause trouble in the future because its meaning and application had not been thought out. Lansing recognized that the First World War's destruction of the Hapsburg, Ottoman, and Romanov Empires was a mixed blessing, because disorder might spread in its wake. Moynihan and similar-minded neo-Hobbesians viewed the unraveling of the Soviet Empire in the 1990s in the same light. Moynihan said that America's failure to grasp ethnicity's importance accounted for its initial clumsiness in calling for the preservation of the Soviet Union and Yugoslavia, even after ethnic forces had fixed their hopes on dismantlement.

The ethnic genie was now out of the bottle, Moynihan wrote, and it could not be forced back in, nor, in many cases, should it be. Offering no simple remedies, he saw the challenge as making the world safe both for ethnicity and from it. The U.S. aim should be to abate ethnicity's deleterious effects. Thus, Moynihan recommended that the United States strengthen its efforts to understand ethnicity, including cases where its negative forces were successfully contained and its potential for violence controlled, such as in the South Tyrol between Austria and Italy, and Catalonia in Spain. Western military intervention should become more frequent, preferably under the UN flag. The key to success, he concluded, would be to use military force in ways that would produce political settlements among social groups whose hatreds run deep, in the Balkans, in Africa, and in other regions.

Other writers, too, were concerned about violence in the Balkans and elsewhere. In 1993, William Pfaff wrote an important book entitled *The Wrath of Nations: Civilization and the Furies of Nationalism.*[13] Pfaff portrayed ethnic warfare as a subset of a larger problem, malignant nationalism, then threatening to reappear on the world stage. Pfaff defined nationalism as an affective tie to one's community based upon deep emotions. It is marked, he said, not by identification with borders or governmental institutions, but by kinship loyalty, common history, defining myths, and images of shared destiny. Pfaff saw nationalism as the dominant force of the 20th century, and he believed it would dominate the 21st century as well. In some ways, he said, nationalism can be a positive force: it can form the bonds that keep a society together. But when it is defined in exclusionary terms and incites nation-states to pursue aggressive policies, it can become very destructive and bring about great turmoil.

Pfaff argued that nationalism was initially a 19th-century European reaction against the rationalism, universalism, and internationalism of the French Enlightenment. He found the roots of nationalism in romanticism, a philosophy that stresses the primacy of emotion over reason, of history over the modern and the future, of action over thought, and of the individual and group over the ideological. Acknowledging that nationalism had been tainted by its association with the blame for World War I and World War II, Pfaff pointed out that it had earlier been regarded as a progressive force, and that it had played a key role in bringing down the tradition-bound Hapsburg and Ottoman Empires; defeating Napoleon, Nazism, and Soviet communism; and protecting Europe from many types of totalitarianism in the name of millennial ideologies. But in the hands of demagogues and other power-seekers, he said, nationalism could become malignant, and extreme nationalism had frequently propelled countries to invade their neighbors. Moreover, he said, nationalism can mutate to become nativist, populist, exclusionary, and xenophobic. By promoting ethnic hatred, it creates fertile ground for ethnosocial mobilization by a leader who offers war as a romantic expression of virility and a way to recapture a lost historical utopia.

Pfaff argued that U.S. observers are so imbued with Enlightenment values that they fail to perceive how strongly nationalist values are held, even by the intelligentsia, in many parts of the world, especially in the Balkans. Not only the Yalta accord of 1945, which determined many postwar borders, but also the Versailles accord of 1919, which had tried to bring order to the remains of the collapsed Hapsburg and Ottoman Empires, had been swept away by the downfall of the Soviet Union and the Warsaw Pact. This, he said, liberated long-suppressed nationalism in societies increasingly angered by the strains of adjusting to new economic and political conditions. He saw this sudden upsurge of angry nationalism as a principal cause of the violence sweeping over the former Yugoslavia, pitting Serbs, Bosnians, and Croats against each other.

Pfaff warned of surging nationalism as a potentially global phenomenon and thought Russia, too, was liable to succumb to nationalist impulses as it struggled with its loss of power and empire. He saw nationalism on the upswing in Asia, expecting that the foreign policies of Japan and China might be increasingly shaped by nationalist agendas in the coming years. In the Middle East, he wrote, nationalism rose as a reaction against the West's secular materialism and colonial heritage; its value system, together with that of

Islamic fundamentalism, resulted in increased hostility toward the United States and its European allies. Pfaff portrayed nationalism elsewhere as a force by which some countries had cast off Western imperialism in past years, or that allowed them to define themselves in opposition to the United States and the Western democracies today.

Pfaff warned the United States to become aware of nationalism's growing primacy in the Balkans and elsewhere. Writing in 1993, he decried the failure of the United States and its European allies to intervene forcefully to stop the killing in Bosnia and to oppose virulent Serbian nationalism in the Balkans. Beyond this, he said, the United States should abandon the neo-Kantian illusion then prevalent, that liberal internationalism was the wave of the future and that most nations would be willing to help carry out Washington's designs. He urged that the United States replace its naïve faith in progress with a skeptical pessimism capable of recognizing the potential for reversal, disaster, and tragedy. Although global chaos was not the inevitable consequence of nationalism, he warned of this danger if nationalism was not carefully controlled by the United States and its allies.

These neo-Hobbesian writers were largely proven right by events in the Balkans. Serbians continued to murder Bosnians and Croats, even in the presence of UN peacekeepers, until the Bosnians and Croats finally acquired the military power to fight back. The violence ended only when the Dayton Accords of 1995 imposed an uneasy peace and inserted NATO military forces to keep the antagonists apart. Violence then flared in Kosovo, where Serbian military forces embarked upon ethnic cleansing of Kosovar Albanians in late 1998. This time, NATO intervened with airpower; a prolonged bombardment campaign forced Serbian dictator Slobodan Milosevic to withdraw his force from Kosovo. NATO ground forces then entered Kosovo to bring peace to the province, where they remain indefinitely.

Since 1999, the Balkans have been relatively calm, but this tranquility is due largely to the presence in Bosnia and Kosovo of NATO troops (and more recently in Bosnia of an EU force). An international protectorate keeps ethnic groups from fighting in both countries. Milosevic is gone from Serbia, but his country's commitment to democracy and its abandonment of angry nationalism remain uncertain. Balkan nationalism seems unlikely to abate until the region makes major strides toward economic progress and democracy but, in a vicious cycle, this progress will be hard to achieve until the poisonous hatreds of nationalism diminish.

Ethnic and religious violence have also appeared in Africa, with particularly devastating effect in Rwanda, Somalia, and Sudan. Nationalism reared its head in South Asia, where India and Pakistan nearly went to war a few years ago over rival claims to Kashmir. Elsewhere, it has the potential to create strains in relations among multiple countries. Thus far, nationalism has not shown signs of infecting the big powers, but neo-Hobbesian observers worry that it may begin to influence the foreign policies of China, Russia, or India. In the years since the war on terror erupted in late 2001, nationalism has receded from the headlines as religious fundamentalism has come to be seen as more of a threat. Yet it continues to lurk in the background as one variable in the complex equation of modern neo-Hobbesian security affairs.

Robert Kaplan: Global Anarchy and Violence

A writer of travelogue journalism, Robert Kaplan had gained prominence in 1994 with a book that traced the roots of ethnic violence in the Balkans to centuries-old struggles among the Orthodox, Christian, and Muslim religions.[14] In 2000, he published *The Coming Anarchy: Shattering the Dreams of the Post Cold War.*[15] Dismissing predictions of worldwide peace and progress as naïve, his theme was neo-Hobbesian to an extreme. Indeed, he quoted Hobbes in the book's epigraph. Seeing positive trends almost nowhere, he offered little hope for substantial reversal of the negative trends he saw almost everywhere.

Kaplan put forth three key propositions. The first dealt with the emerging global scene of chaos and anarchy in underdeveloped regions outside the democratic community, where he identified governmental leadership, social change, economic dynamics, and mass politics as the problem rather than the solution. The second proposition asserted that it was unlikely that democracy could take hold in many troubled regions, much less guide them out of chaos. The third urged the United States to adopt a foreign policy of power-asserting realism, rather than a policy of promoting democracy, economic globalization, and other facets of neo-Kantian idealism. He called for the United States and its democratic partners to do their best to cope with spreading global troubles, but not to expect too much in a future that represented the rebirth of history, including its darkest Hobbesian aspects, rather than, as Fukuyama had predicted, its end.

Kaplan began his book by describing a world divided between wealthy democracies and the rest; he portrayed the remaining 70 percent of the world as deeply troubled and becoming worse by the day. He blamed this mainly on failed states, which he portrayed as both producers and victims of wider trends. His core thesis was that overpopulation, poverty, urbanized ghettos, social stresses, environmental decay, crime, tribal violence, and incompetent governments leave teeming, ungovernable masses in settings of chaos and anarchy where national borders have little meaning. Kaplan began his narrative with Sierra Leone in West Africa, where he described a failed government leading an unruly army, a corrupt and ineffectual bureaucracy, renegade armed commanders aligned with tribal chiefs, unchecked spread of disease, deforestation, and environmental destruction, and mounting violence. He portrayed similar trends in the Ivory Coast, Guinea, and elsewhere in Africa: illegitimate regimes propped up by militaries, urban shantytowns, declining economies, widespread malaria and human immunodeficiency virus, hopeless despair, and illiterate teenage gangs inflicting unbridled violence in societies marked by incessant tribal rivalry. Whereas poverty is not necessarily crippling in rural societies that live off the land and cling to traditional values, he wrote, it threatens the breakdown of societies where people are massed in urban slums lacking food, housing, and arable land, and where intolerant religious beliefs increase the divisions in society.

Turning to the Middle East, Kaplan found less anarchy and chaos, but plenty to worry about nonetheless. Democratic Turkey has a great deal of poverty, but its urban slums are held together, Kaplan wrote, by a sense of community and culture reinforced by faith in Islam. Elsewhere in the region, however, the situation was worse; apart from Turkey, almost none of the Middle East benefited from the Enlightenment and modernism. In most Arab countries, he wrote, autocratic and incompetent governments preside over exploding populations, shrinking economies, and escalating conflicts over water and other natural resources. Because nationalism is now seen as a failed ideology, Arab masses are turning to Islam to find identity. In many places, however, Islam is becoming a vehicle for expressing anger and violence rather than tolerance and peace. Kaplan explained that many young Islamic fundamentalists turn to militant violence because such a life is more psychologically liberating than resignation, acceptance, and despair. He predicted political, social, and religious upheaval in Egypt that would leave it with a fundamental Islamic government.

Kaplan blamed similar trends for producing in Iran a mullah-led regime of religious extremism intent on returning the country to the past rather than addressing the challenges of secularism and modernism. In South Asia, Kaplan found less religious extremism but predicted that Pakistan and India are both headed toward breakdown and fragmentation because of mounting social tensions, exacerbated by overpopulation, stagnant economies, and ineffective governments. A similar dynamic, he said, applies to other parts of Asia, South Asia, and Central Asia that are not benefiting from the globalizing world economy. Even in China, Kaplan saw major troubles ahead, as the economic gains of the coastal regions leave the interior of the country behind in poverty.

Surveying this bleak global scene, Kaplan portrayed the world as headed to a "postmodern" era that will mostly be dominated not by Fukuyama's "Last Man," but instead by the "First Man," the Hobbesian prototype. Where man lives in "continual fear and danger of violent death," to use Hobbes' words, governments must serve as Hobbes' Leviathan to control social violence. The future, as Kaplan saw it, therefore will increasingly be dominated by fascist and tyrannical governments, dysfunctional cultures, impoverished masses falling back upon angry ethnicity and religion for their identity, and social groups violently contesting control of scarce resources and economic goods. Nor did Kaplan exempt the United States from this depressing portrait: here, he foresaw a country dominated by multinational corporations, disconnected cultural elites, and wealthy citizens in gated communities oblivious to mounting social tensions within their own country, much less those in the rest of the world.

Kaplan dismissed the belief of neo-Kantians that democratization would be a solution to the problems of the underdeveloped world. He argued that democracy was adopted and has succeeded in the United States and other Western nations only because it was established on the foundations of a literate middle class, a civic culture, effective governmental institutions, and a productive economy. Absent these conditions, he wrote, democracy is unlikely to be adopted or, if it is, unlikely to succeed in protecting human freedom or bringing economic prosperity. To think otherwise, Kaplan wrote, is to indulge in blind determinism and ethnocentrism.

Kaplan argued that the essential preconditions of democracy are mainly absent throughout most of the underdeveloped world. He approved of democratic enlargement into Eastern Europe, which he portrayed as able to adopt democracy and make it work. But elsewhere, he saw regions dominated by unstable societies, illiterate lower classes, violent tribalism, weak governmental institutions, and sinking economies. When popular elections are held in such places, he wrote, either ineffective governments will make matters worse, or populist dictators will hijack lower-class support into new tyrannies that snuff out minority rights without bringing any of the gains they promised their supporters.

Kaplan wrote that effective democratic rule can normally be established only through an incremental process from tyranny to popular rule. This process, he said, normally requires the emergence of a well-established middle class with enough strength to overthrow an authoritarian government and establish a true, functional democracy in its place. He cited with approval Hobbes' observation that in the period before this transition is accomplished, enlightened despotism may often be preferable to democracy because it protects the masses from themselves. He did not endorse such Leviathan governments for the 21st century, but he did endorse hybrid regimes that occupied the space between democratic anarchy and military tyranny, because the former typically leads to the latter. Such hybrid regimes, he wrote, could provide the robust, well-balanced combination of democratic and authoritarian rule needed to help establish a foundation for eventual democratization. He found such regimes in Turkey, Pakistan, and Peru, and singled out Singapore, where Lee Kuan Yew's authoritarian government had transformed abject poverty into prosperity by fostering the growth of market economics, foreign investment, and a wealthy middle class.

Kaplan's views on U.S. foreign policy reflected his premise that idealism cannot stop mass murder. He rejected the theory that the United States and its wealthy allies can cure the underdeveloped world's problems by employing moral sloganeering to establish democracy, self-determination, globalized economies, and other indicators of Western-style progress. He called for a realist foreign policy anchored in the assertion of strategic power to create a balance of power and stable security affairs. This foreign policy, he said, would reflect the thinking of Henry Kissinger and such 19th-century realists as Austria's Metternich, who rejected idealistic visions in favor of using geopolitical balancing to avert tragedy. He also endorsed the conservative thinking of British politician and philosopher Edmund Burke, who valued stability as essential to gradual progress, and who opposed revolutions because, in the name of establishing democracy, they more often resulted in mass murder and tyranny.

Kaplan did not urge the United States to remain aloof from the Third World. Instead, he urged a policy of proportional realism that, although it might be distasteful to moral and ideological purists, was anchored in common sense. The United States needed to recognize that although some underdeveloped countries had made end-runs around history, they are the exception. Russia's transition to democracy is likely to be more typical: long, faltering, and uncertain. He urged a U.S. policy toward foreign aid that would devote limited funds to specific targets where investments in economic infrastructure and other foundation-builders could nudge selected countries along the slow path to progress. In such regions, he wrote, the United States would need to accept a certain amount of evil, such as authoritarian but progressive governments, in order to achieve a greater common good. He urged a U.S. involvement that is engaged but not overreaching. He conceded that U.S. military interventions might sometimes be needed, but urged caution: the fewer the better.

Kaplan's book challenged many neo-Kantian assumptions and helped alert readers to coming dangers that were not strongly apparent at the time of its publication in 2000. Yet the doubt it cast upon an opposing theory does not mean that its own theory is valid. Its relentless and pessimistic neo-Hobbesian views may have exaggerated the troubles facing the underdeveloped world. There are exceptions that undercut his predictions. If the political future is so bleak, how can democratic successes in Eastern Europe, Latin America, and parts of Asia and Africa be explained? If the economic future is so bleak, how can the steady gains in China, Asia, and parts of South Asia be explained? Kaplan's book does not provide satisfactory answers to these questions. The reality is that the underdeveloped world presents a complex checkerboard, and failures in some places are offset by encouraging successes in others. In Latin America, for example, democratic success has become more common in recent years, and populist tyrannies more the exception. In focusing mainly on failures, Kaplan may have been blinded by his pessimism to the reasons for optimism in key places.

Whether Kaplan's dark view of the future is accurate remains unknown. When he wrote, the attacks of September 11, 2001, had not yet occurred, and the war on terror had not yet erupted, but neither had democratic elections in Afghanistan, Iraq, Ukraine, or Georgia taken place. The more pressing issue is whether his proposed policy of proportional realism makes sense in today's world. Modern-day idealists would probably reject this stance. The architects of the Bush administration's foreign policy seem also to have done so for reasons of their own, opting for a major U.S. military intervention in the Persian Gulf and calling for a global pursuit of democracy and human freedom.[16] This ambitious effort presumes the invalidity of Kaplan's pessimism about what is realistically possible. Kaplan's book made an important contribution to the ongoing debate between neo-Kantian and neo-Hobbesian theories of the 21st century. For this reason alone, it deserves high marks.

Samantha Power: Dealing with Intrastate Genocide

Because public attention today is mainly focused on the war on terror, it may be easy to forget that the 1990s were dominated by a different threat: genocide within failed and authoritarian states. Where a malevolent government, backed by a powerful social group, endeavors to wipe out a minority through mass murder, this is genocide. It was especially extreme in Bosnia during 1992–1995, when Serbians killed 200,000 Bosnians with support from the Serbian government, and in Rwanda in 1994, when Hutus killed 800,000 Tutsis in only 10 weeks.

In 1993, Secretary of State Warren Christopher called the Balkans a "problem from hell," implying that its intractability meant that the United Stated could not achieve much and therefore should not intervene. Samantha

Power picked up Christopher's words as the title of her 2002 book, in which she sought to prove that American engagement in such cases could help and that therefore the United States should act to stop genocide. Power's book, *A Problem from Hell: America and the Age of Genocide*, provides a journalistic history of genocide in the 20th century and seeks to uncover why the United States has so often failed to respond effectively in time to prevent genocide. It issues a call for stronger, earlier intervention in future cases of threatened genocide.

Most recent genocides have utilized relatively low-technology weapons such as guns and knives. However, technology, too, has sometimes facilitated mass killing, with such examples as gas chambers or hate radio. A chilling prospect is that as modern information systems proliferate, they will strengthen the capacity of autocratic governments to commit more rapid and devastating high-tech genocide. Thus, genocide may be an increasingly serious threat in the early 21st century.

In her book, Power provided a distinctly neo-Hobbesian analysis of one important dimension of contemporary world affairs.[17] As she wrote, 20th-century genocide appeared in 1915, when Turkey set about to eradicate all Armenians within its borders. Britain and France were preoccupied with fighting World War I against Germany, Austria-Hungary, and Turkey, and so they did little to halt this genocide. The military invasion of Turkey at Gallipoli, which might have interrupted the genocide, collapsed in failure. The United States, attempting to stay out of World War I, chose to sit on the sidelines. It debated denouncing Turkish policies against the Armenians and pressuring Turkey's German allies to act, but in the end the Wilson administration did nothing more than express regrets while declining to take any significant actions to stop the massacres.

As Power observed, genocide exploded into public consciousness after Hitler's Germany slaughtered Jews and other ethnic groups in concentration camps. Because this genocide was undertaken as Hitler tried to conquer all of Europe and the Soviet Union, it triggered an international reaction after Germany was defeated. Soon after the war, German leaders were prosecuted for their crimes against humanity. In late 1948, the United Nations issued a "Convention on the Prevention and Punishment of the Crime of Genocide,"[18] which defined as genocide not only mass murder, but also efforts to relocate victimized groups to places where they could not survive and efforts to prevent births in those groups. It portrayed genocide as a serious violation of international law and authorized UN member states to take action to prevent or suppress it. This convention entered into force in 1951 after a sufficient number of UN members had ratified it. President Harry Truman urged the U.S. Senate to ratify the convention but, Power wrote, domestic opposition and preoccupation with the Cold War kept the United States from joining it until 1986.

During the Cold War, genocide was manifested in Bangladesh's 1971 efforts to gain autonomy from West Pakistan, when tens of thousands or even hundreds of thousands of Bengalis were murdered. In another case, during the mid-1970s, Pol Pot's Khmer Rouge regime killed more than two million Cambodians as it tried to impose a revolutionary Maoist order. The United States had only recently withdrawn from the Vietnam War and was loath to become entangled in another Southeast Asian crisis. The United Nations also largely ignored the situation, belatedly condemning the genocide in 1978 but doing little of practical consequence. The genocide was finally halted in late 1978 by a Vietnamese invasion that toppled the Pol Pot regime. Vietnam claimed to have acted for humanitarian reasons, although it also saw the Khmer Rouge as a threat to its own security. The United States opposed Vietnam's action, wrote Power, on the grounds that interstate aggression by a communist regime constituted a greater harm than mass murder inside a state.

In the 1980s, Saddam Hussein's brutal regime in Iraq employed mass violence and even poison gas to try to suppress its Kurdish minority. Power noted that the United States and Europe did little to protest Saddam Hussein's action, because Iraq was then at war against Iran, an object of intense Western dislike. Indeed, the United States provided financial and intelligence assistance to Iraq. A few years later, in 1990–1991, the United States led a large multinational coalition to eject Iraq from Kuwait, but the United States and its coalition partners chose to allow Saddam Hussein to remain in power afterward. When Saddam Hussein then brutally repressed uprisings by Kurds and Shi'ites, the UN coalition established a safe zone in northern Iraq to protect the Kurds, but until after 2003, no one in the Iraqi government was held legally accountable for genocide against the Kurds.

In the 1990s, Power recounts, genocides occurred both in sub-Saharan Africa and in the Balkans amid failed states and explosive ethnic warfare. A genocidal campaign of staggering size unfolded in Rwanda in 1994, when in a political crisis the Hutus were encouraged to slaughter their Tutsi neighbors. The United States, having withdrawn from Somalia only a year before after 18 American soldiers were killed, was disinclined to undertake a military intervention in Rwanda, and neither were European countries. The United Nations provided some humanitarian relief in refugee camps in neighboring states, but it did not send military forces to restore peace. Nearly one million Rwandans were killed in 1994.

In 1992, Yugoslavia began to fall apart. Slovenia seceded in relative calm, but the Serbian government in Belgrade tried to prevent Croatia from seeking to do the same, igniting a war that killed 10,000 people within 7 months. As Croatia gradually escaped the control of Serbian dictator Milosevic, ethnic fighting soon spread to Bosnia, whose population was a mixture of Muslims (43 percent), Orthodox Serbs (35 percent), and Roman Catholic Croats (18 percent). Initially, wrote Power, the local Serbs held the upper hand militarily and used their strength to murder 200,000 or more Muslims over a period of 3 years. The United States and its European allies protested Serbia's conduct and imposed economic sanctions but initially did little to intervene forcefully. They dispatched UN peacekeepers but did not authorize them to use significant force to end the violence. They also imposed an arms blockade on Bosnia, which failed to constrain the well-armed Serbs while depriving the Bosnian Muslims of the capacity to arm themselves.

More than 3 years after the ethnic war had erupted, the United States and its European allies began to act strongly in 1995, shortly after the brutal massacre at Srebrenica. By this time it was clear that the future of the NATO alliance would be threatened if it did not respond. In 1995, Bosnian and Croatian forces were finally receiving enough arms to fight effectively against the Serbs, who had overextended themselves as they conquered more territory. With Western governments under increasing domestic pressure to stop the massacres, and with the UN peacekeeping missions on the ground ineffective, NATO began conducting airstrikes against the Serbs. Progress on the battlefield helped set the stage for political negotiations, which produced the Dayton Accord of late 1995, orchestrated by the United States. The accord ended the fighting and introduced NATO peacekeepers into Bosnia. The accord also created a multiethnic Bosnian government but left the Serbs with much of the land. A tenuous peace took hold, owing largely to the presence of NATO forces, which had the numbers, arms, and rules of engagement necessary to keep the warring parties separate.

Balkan violence next erupted in 1998 when Milosevic began a new campaign of ethnic cleansing in Kosovo. This time, wrote Power, NATO reacted more promptly and forcefully. Against the prospect of permitting a government to commit crimes against humanity, it rejected the once-sacrosanct idea that a sovereign government was free to orchestrate its internal affairs without outside intervention. After negotiations failed, NATO began bombing not only Serb military forces in Kosovo, but also Serbia itself, including Belgrade. The bombing campaign was launched in March 1999; after several months, together with political pressure from Russia, it convinced Milosevic to withdraw Serbian forces from Kosovo. NATO ground forces then entered the province and imposed peace.

Power presented this checkered history as a searing indictment of repeated U.S. failure to intervene to halt genocide in Asia, the Middle East, Africa, and the Balkans. She attributed this failure to several reasons: the outmoded Westphalian doctrine of respecting state sovereignty even in the face of genocide, a belief that genocide elsewhere did not put vital national interests at stake, initial blindness to the impending scope of genocidal crises, and reluctance to become entangled diplomatically or militarily in crises deemed unsolvable and likely to result in the death of U.S. soldiers. Above all, she said, the United States has suffered from a lack of political willpower, allowing rationalizations to justify inaction. Power concluded her book with a ringing call for corrective action. The United States and Europe should, she wrote, join together to muster both the will and the capacity, including military force, to intervene in future genocides before they attain explosive energy. She notes that the toolbox needed to deal with genocide includes not just military force but also an array of diplomatic and economic tools; there is thus an element of neo-Kantianism in her prescription. But there is a neo-Hobbesian note in the doubts she expressed about whether the current Western preoccupation with the war on terror would allow such steps.

Power's book identified a crucial problem that may have been pushed off the front pages of newspapers by the war on terror and the invasion of Iraq, but nevertheless remains acute in places such as Darfur in Sudan. Rather than providing a theory that explains the outbreak of genocide in various places, her detailed catalogue of recent cases underscored her judgment that genocide is not an isolated event or one of merely local concern. Power also correctly dissected many of the reasons—both justifiable and otherwise—that have constrained Western countries from promptly intervening to halt genocide. Her book is highly critical of U.S. action and inaction. Power set out to focus on U.S. policy, and thus her book might be criticized for not expanding this analysis to other nations. However, it clearly demonstrates that genocide is a problem that will not go away, but will require much closer attention and much greater political will.

Bernard Lewis: The Middle East and Angry Islam

The Middle East has become a focal point of neo-Hobbesian writers and a source of despair for neo-Kantians. Among the many analysts of the Middle East, Professor Bernard Lewis stands out as especially insightful. A widely recognized historian at Princeton University, Lewis has written 21 books on the Middle East during his long career; many have won awards, and all are well regarded. Since 1996, he has published three best-selling books that have addressed the violent turmoil erupting in this complex region, and the growing role of resurgent, angry Islamic fundamentalism in triggering it. They have helped explain trends and troubles that have caught many Western observers by surprise. Radical Islam poses a threat to the United States and other Western democracies, and to progress in the Middle East as well, Lewis has argued, both because it employs terrorism and it opposes what the Middle East needs to cure its ills: modernization, economic prosperity, and democratization.

Lewis explained the current era from a historical perspective in his 1996 book, *The Middle East: A Brief History of the Last 2,000 Years.*[19] This volume documented the rise of the Islamic Middle East to become the world's premier civilization from the time of Muhammad (571–632) through its apex in the 17th century, and its calamitous descent afterward. Four trends stand out during the period of the Islamic Middle East's flowering. The first is the extent to which Middle Eastern history was dominated by the Turks for almost 1,000 years, beginning in the 10th century. Initially, the Islamic Middle East was largely centered in Baghdad; power was distributed among several regions, where caliphs provided religious leadership and sultans were political leaders. But eventually Turkey, under its Ottoman sultan, grew predominant, and only Morocco, Iran, and Arabia preserved a measure of independence.

The second trend is the extent to which Islam encompassed the diverse societies of the Middle East to create a unified religious civilization. Islam, Lewis wrote, imposed a religious orthodoxy not through a church hierarchy, but through a widespread consensus that Islam should spread elsewhere and should overcome all nonbelievers, infidels, heretics, and apostates along the way. The third trend is the extent to which religious and political authority was fused in the Middle East: monarchies and autocracies were charged with protecting the Islamic faith by means of central control, military defense, and foreign conquest.

The fourth trend is the extent to which the Islamic Middle East failed to make economic progress from the 1600s onward, a trend that had multiple causes, including weak government leadership and the failure of agricultural societies to embrace trade, technological innovation, and industrialization. The high-water mark of the Islamic Middle East was reached in 1683, Lewis wrote, when the second Turkish siege of Vienna failed. From there, the Ottoman Turks were steadily pushed back, losing their foothold in Central Europe and the Balkans. Meanwhile, the Russian Empire expanded into Central Asia and the Caucasus, dominating the Muslim regimes in these regions. Turkey, which had been a feared military power, gradually became the "sick man of Europe," noted for its economic backwardness. Its decline sent ripple effects across the Middle East. In the early 1800s, France invaded Egypt with a small army and easily defeated Muslim opposition. Napoleon was then pushed out not by Muslim armies, Lewis wrote, but by the British navy, whose blockade strangled his source of supplies. The Ottoman Empire was caught between imperial pincers from Russia and Europe; it survived for a century partly because it was shored up by Britain and France, which opposed Russian imperialism. But when World War I ended, the Ottoman Empire collapsed, leaving a fractured Middle East, where traditional Islam still ruled a civilization that had lost its vitality and self-confidence. The stage was set for further decline during the 20th century, which produced the turbulent situation of today.

In Lewis' 2002 book, *What Went Wrong? The Clash Between Islam and Modernity in the Middle East*, he set out to explain in greater detail why the Middle East had fallen from its dominant perch to its sad position of today.[20] He began by noting that in Europe's medieval era, the Islamic Middle East was rightly regarded as the world's premier civilization not only because of its formidable military power, but also because of its advanced standing in the arts and sciences and its humane tolerance of minorities. In these it was far and away ahead of Europe, Asia, and other civilizations. That it fell so far and so fast, losing in two centuries what had taken a thousand years to achieve, Lewis attributed partly to Europe's growing supremacy in military power, especially naval power, and to commercial trade, in which the Middle East was at a competitive disadvantage. But the more fundamental reason, Lewis said, was that the Islamic Middle East failed even to respond to modernity, much less take advantage of it as Europe did.

Lewis pointed out that from the Middle Ages onward, Europe was a modernizing continent: it underwent a succession of profound revolutions that transformed its politics, economics, and society. These revolutions included the Renaissance, the Reformation, the age of discovery, the Enlightenment, the scientific revolution, industrialization, and democratization. Their effects were to shake Europe out of the Dark Ages, separate church from state, create competent secular governments, explore the rest of the world and establish colonial empires, promote a cultural commitment to intellectual advance, make many scientific discoveries, create new technologies, establish communications systems, achieve fast economic progress, and, ultimately, produce the democratic countries of today. Along the way, Europe experienced great turbulence and many wars, but the effect was to create a modern, wealthy, democratic continent that today lives in peace and prosperity.

By contrast, Lewis argued, the Middle East missed almost all of these profound changes. A main reason was a self-preoccupied culture and inward-looking mentality brought about by the Middle East's politics, economics, society, and religion. Indeed, wrote Lewis, the Middle East was largely ignorant of Europe's changes, making little effort to establish intimate contact with a civilization that it regarded as backward and barbaric. When European military power appeared at its borders to threaten the Middle East and deny Islam further conquests, governments of the region did try to modernize their military forces, but they failed to pursue modernity in more comprehensive ways. The one exception was Turkey after the fall of the Ottoman Empire; Kemal Ataturk launched a determined effort to pursue secularization and modernization. Elsewhere, however, Middle Eastern countries remained largely anchored in the past throughout the 19th and 20th centuries.

The Middle East, wrote Lewis, was not entirely oblivious to modernization: newspapers, for example, appeared there in the 19th century. In some ways, the arrival of the modern era enabled autocratic governments to strengthen their hold over their societies, but they did not develop the administrative and managerial competence needed to achieve economic progress. The Middle East failed to develop modern universities, scientific research, or widespread literacy. Technological innovation did not occur, and industrialization had little impact; Middle Eastern economies remained dominated largely by agriculture and small artisans. Although the Persian Gulf benefited from its oil, other Middle Eastern countries failed to develop the marketable products and commercial ties that would allow them to profit from export and import. Meanwhile, Middle Eastern societies continued to embrace traditional Islam rather than adopt the secular values that might have allowed modernity to penetrate more deeply into their cultures. Indeed, Islam mostly reacted to the challenges of Westernization and modernization by deepening its commitment to traditional values. Thus, its leaders could blame the Middle East's fall from prominence on a departure from Islam rather than on failure to modernize. The result, said Lewis, is the Middle East of today: deeply frustrated by its failures and prone to blame Western interference rather than its own shortcomings.

In 2003, with *The Crisis of Islam: Holy War and Unholy Terror*, Lewis set out to explain the hostility that Islamic fundamentalists feel today toward the United States and why they direct terror at it.[21] Lewis was careful to state that the Islamic Middle East is not of one mind on this subject: traditional regimes in power in many countries still want to carry out normal relations with the United States, even while regarding it with some wariness. In parts of the Middle East, modernizers want to embrace some aspects of Western economic and political values, including democracy. They are, he wrote, very different from radical Islamic fundamentalists, who view the United States as a dire enemy that must be fought to the fullest, even by jihad and terrorism against innocent people. They hate the United States not only because they genuinely fear it, wrote Lewis, but also because they need an enemy to explain the failures of Islam in the modern world and to help support their agenda of restoring traditional Islam across the Middle East.

Lewis argued that the antipathy toward the United States, and Western culture as a whole, originates in the historical experience of Islam going back a millennium and more. Centuries ago, the Islamic world viewed itself as culturally superior to Europe, he said, and as charged by God to use jihad—a combination of moral exertion and war—to spread Islam across the world, including to Europe. The Europeans, however, rebuffed this effort. From the late 17th century onward, Islam was on the strategic defensive, and jihad came to be defined in these terms. By the 19th century, the Turkish Ottoman Empire in the east was crumbling. To the west, meanwhile, European imperialism made major inroads into North Africa and the Middle East: by 1900, France occupied Algeria, Tunisia, and Morocco, while Britain occupied Egypt and Sudan. The collapse of the Ottoman Empire after World War I resulted in League of Nations mandates by which France was to create modern states in Syria and Lebanon, and Britain to do so in Iraq, Palestine, and Jordan. In the Middle East, only Turkey, Iran, and Arabia escaped the humiliation of colonial occupation.

Lewis wrote that this colonial occupation had some positive effects, promoting economic modernization by building roads and other infrastructure, and creating educational systems that fostered literacy. But in politics, the effort backfired. The original goal was for Britain and France to create democratic regimes in the occupied countries. But their occupation was viewed as colonialism, and the democracy they proffered was rejected. The results were semimodern states led by single parties and autocratic rulers, many of whom oppressed their people. Much of the Middle East blamed Europe for this result. The end of World War II was a victory over authoritarian government, but it did not result in a new European effort to democratize the Middle East. Instead, the main initiative was the UN decision to create a Jewish state. Israel, however, was viewed as an alien presence by virtually all Arab countries. The creation of Israel triggered wars in 1948, 1956, 1967, and 1973 that all resulted in defeat of the Arabs and thus further humiliation.

Initially, wrote Lewis, Islamic countries in the Middle East paid little attention to the United States. But this began to change in the 1950s and 1960s, when the Europeans departed and the United States came in. At the time, the United States was focused mainly on the Cold War against the Soviet Union; it therefore sided with those Arab regimes, including autocrats, who were prepared to support its geopolitical agenda. Other Arab countries, especially Egypt and Syria, embraced anti-Western pan-Arabism and sided with the Soviet Union; this created a widespread sense that Arab interests were not aligned with U.S. interests. Meanwhile, the United States increasingly backed Israel, in part as an alternative to Arab ties, and sought a Middle Eastern peace that preserved Israel's existence. It supported the dictatorial Shah of Iran, and for that reason, when he fell from power in the late 1970s, the theocratic regime that took his place adamantly opposed the United States. The end of the Cold War washed away the Soviet Union, leaving room for a growing U.S. presence in the Middle East, especially in the Persian Gulf. There the United States was initially intent on protecting Western access to oil. After it led a massive military campaign to eject Iraq from Kuwait, the United States maintained a sizable military presence in Saudi Arabia in order to contain Saddam Hussein; in the eyes of Islamic fundamentalists, this was viewed as a colonial occupation of sacred Muslim territory.

By the late 1990s, wrote Lewis, Islamic fundamentalists hated the United States for several reasons. It was seen as a purveyor of economic globalization, which exposed the Middle East's backwardness, and it was blamed for victimizing the region and keeping it locked in poverty. A second reason was cultural: to Islamic fundamentalists, the United States is a morally corrupt society that embraces materialism and sexual licentiousness at the expense of religious piety. The United States is believed to be guilty of the worst possible heresy: the separation of church and state and the maintenance of a secular society. Its degenerate values attract some Middle Easterners, leading them into heresy and apostasy. The United States is called the "Great Satan," wrote Lewis, not because it threatens military aggression and a new colonialism, but because it is capable of being a great seducer and destroyer of Islam's moral purity. Another reason for the hatred of the United States is its support of Israel, which is viewed as an alien, infidel regime and an outpost of a new Western crusade against Islam. A fourth reason was the belief that U.S. geopolitical policy in the region seeks to maintain autocratic, apostate regimes that are intent on oppressing Islamic fundamentalists.

The central theme of Lewis' 2003 book was that hostility in parts of the Islamic world toward the United States is both psychological and political. Unwilling to blame the Middle East's decline on its failure to modernize, fundamentalist Islamists had to assign blame elsewhere, and the United States and Israel were convenient targets. Islamic fundamentalists also, he said, fan hatred of the United States in order to mobilize Arab masses to support their political agenda in the Middle East. They want to expel the United States, extinguish Israel, and overthrow apostate Arab regimes, so they can install theocratic regimes that would restore the entire Middle East to Islamic purity. Their agenda thus is holistic and reactionary: a rejection of modernity by restoring fundamentalist Islam to rule, with all of the attendant consequences for Middle Eastern politics, economics, and society.

Lewis attributed the upsurge of terrorism by al Qaeda, Hamas, Hezbollah, and other terrorist groups in recent years to this alienated, frustrated psychology and its reactionary religious agenda. It also reflects a cyclical surge in violence against infidels, which has occurred periodically in past centuries. In addition, it signaled, at least prior to the U.S. invasions of Afghanistan and Iraq, contempt for United States and its willpower, and a belief that it could be defeated just as the Soviets were beaten in Afghanistan. Lewis held out little hope that reason could persuade terrorists to halt their killing, nor even attacks against innocent people, which are not sanctioned by traditional Islamic values. Unlike some observers who believe that a lower U.S. profile in the Middle East and more restraint in the use of military power would help, Lewis expressed support for the U.S. war on terror and called for victory in the U.S. occupations of Iraq and Afghanistan. But he cast this stance in terms of a much larger U.S. agenda. The ultimate cure for what ails the Middle East, he said, is modernity and democracy. Lewis held out hope that this agenda is feasible but acknowledged that it would take years and decades of patient effort. The importance of this agenda and the disastrous consequences of failing to achieve it, he concluded, make it imperative.

A great strength of Lewis' framework is that it is comprehensive and anchored in a deep understanding of history. This enables him to explain root causes of today's troubles, not merely describe recent trends. He combines profound sympathy for the Middle East with cogent criticisms of it. Recently, Lewis has influenced the thinking of U.S. neoconservatives, but his work long precedes this ideology, and he is a historian of the Middle East, not a global strategist. His portrayal of the Middle East as a region that resists progress as well as outside intervention raises questions about whether the United States can hope to transform it any time soon; if the Middle East is to be transformed, its people may well have to do most of the work.

Some historians will debate whether Lewis is correct about all the particulars, but the larger issue is whether he accurately identifies the core dynamics of the Middle East and Islam in today's world. Although he faults U.S. and European policy in many respects, especially the colonialism of earlier days and the more recent support for dictators, he finds the sources of many of the Middle East's problems in the region itself, deriving from its culture, economics, and politics. Most observers would be persuaded that Lewis may be correct in finding the rejection of modernity at the heart of the Middle East's problems. Likewise, he may be correct in judging that the region can be rescued through modernity, some degree of democracy, and a rejection of tyranny, including that of Islamic fundamentalism. Precisely how this agenda can best be promoted by Western countries, which are accused of colonialism and subversion when they try to advocate democracy and capitalism there, is unclear. While Lewis does not resolve this difficult conundrum, as a historian he is permitted to leave it in the hands of policymakers, who must try to do so.

Kenneth Pollack: Rogue States in the Middle East

For over a decade, neo-Hobbesian analysts have seen a major danger to peace and prosperity from rogue states: those dangerous, medium-size countries that are animated by menacing strategic ambitions that lie outside the boundaries of acceptable international conduct and normal diplomatic persuasion and that have the strength and aggressiveness to pose serious threats within their regions. During the 1990s, Serbia was often portrayed as a rogue state of the Balkans. Today in Northeast Asia, North Korea is called a rogue state because of its tyrannical and unpredictable government, threatening stance toward South Korea, and pursuit of nuclear weapons. The largest concentration of rogue states since the Cold War ended has been in the greater Middle East, including Iraq, Iran, Syria, and Libya. Two recent books by Kenneth Pollack, the first on Saddam Hussein's Iraq and the second on current-day Iran, provide rich analytical insights on the political character of rogue states in the Middle East and the challenges they pose to U.S. national security policy.

Originally a Central Intelligence Agency and National Defense University analyst and later a member of the Clinton administration's National Security Council (NSC) staff, Pollack first gained public recognition when *The Threatening Storm: The Case for Invading Iraq* was published in 2002 during the debate over whether to invade.[22] By urging invasion to achieve regime change, Pollack anticipated and encouraged the actions taken by the Bush administration in 2003. His book is of continuing interest because of its comprehensive portrayal of the Saddam Hussein regime and its insightful analysis of why the U.S. policy of containment, carried out during the 1990s, gradually eroded to the point where the option of invasion rose to prominence.

While the UN debate of fall 2002 focused specifically on allegations that Iraq possessed weapons of mass destruction, Pollack's book offered a broader strategic appraisal of Iraq's role in the Persian Gulf. Since Saddam Hussein's elevation to power in the late 1970s, Pollack wrote, his regime had been malignant in virtually all respects. The neo-fascist Ba'ath Party had established a brutal, tyrannical dictatorship that employed mass violence to oppress the Kurds and Shi'ites who made up the majority of Iraq's population.

Acknowledging that Saddam Hussein was a secularist rather than an ally of Islamic fundamentalism, Pollack charged that he was a regular sponsor of terrorism, especially against Israel. He was also, Pollack wrote, a geopolitical dictator who aimed to dominate the Persian Gulf, a violator of many UN Security Council resolutions, a repeat aggressor against neighboring Kuwait and Iran, and a mass murderer with a demonstrated willingness to use chemical and biological weapons against his own people as well as Iran. Pollack asserted that military power was the main vehicle by which Saddam Hussein pursued his regional ambitions. Although Operation *Desert Storm* and the aftermath had badly damaged Iraq's army, Pollack wrote, it still fielded enough divisions and weapons to reinvade Kuwait and the northern Saudi oilfields if the United States did not react. It was in this context that Iraq's industrial capacity to produce chemical and biological weapons, and its potential ability to build or acquire nuclear weapons, were most worrisome. Iraq's physical possession of these weapons might enable it to pursue malevolent external policies that would pose grave threats to U.S. interests, to close allies, and to regional peace.

Pollack favored invasion of Iraq mainly because he believed that the decade-long U.S. policy of containment had failed. A prevalent view among Western intelligence agencies was that Saddam Hussein was reconstituting his nuclear weapons programs to prepare for a new round of assertiveness and threats. Pollack presented a lengthy historical analysis of containment: how it was adopted shortly after the 1991 war and gradually unraveled under the pressure of persistent Iraqi scheming, feckless support from France and Russia, the failure of UN sanctions, and U.S. reluctance to apply adequate firmness and consistency. He reasoned that containment could not be restored and that a new strategy of military deterrence was too difficult and dangerous to sustain over a period of years. He also dismissed as infeasible a policy of fostering internal revolution in Iraq or using an approach like the successful U.S. invasion of Afghanistan, which had relied mainly on limited U.S. airpower and the efforts on the ground of internal opponents to the Taliban regime. His reluctant conclusion was that, because none of these options could succeed, invasion was the only viable choice, and that it would only become more difficult if delayed.

With the U.S. invasion of Iraq in 2003, Pollack's recommendation became policy and was thus open to evaluation in the light of history. After postinvasion problems surfaced and no weapons of mass destruction were found, Pollack acknowledged that while his book had accurately forecast that U.S. military forces could easily overpower the Iraqi army, the absence of those weapons, coupled with the difficulty of rebuilding Iraq afterward, called into question the ultimate value of the invasion.[23] Whether Pollack's advocacy of invasion will stand up well in the eyes of history is to be seen, but the troubles that the United States encountered in Iraq may have made him more cautious about urging military solutions when he wrote his next book, on Iran.

Pollack published *The Persian Puzzle: The Conflict Between Iran and America* in 2004, as U.S. debate over Iran's alleged pursuit of nuclear weapons was heating up.[24] Once again, he offered an in-depth historical and strategic assessment of a rogue state in the Middle East. He portrayed a country that was menacing, but for different reasons. Saddam Hussein was a secular dictator, but Iran is led by a radical Islamic fundamentalist regime. The result is a different type of threat to the Persian Gulf and Middle East. Here, too, Pollack soberly weighed the difficult policy choices facing the United States, but this time he reached a different conclusion. He argued against invading Iran or otherwise carrying out military strikes against it. His preferred policy was a triple track approach of diplomatic outreach, use of carrots and sticks, and preparation of a new containment regime.

Pollack's 2004 book deftly portrayed the tangled history of U.S. relations with Iran during the Cold War and afterward. As the Cold War heated up in the early 1950s, the Eisenhower administration had viewed a friendly Iran as a bulwark against Soviet expansion into the Persian Gulf. But Iran's political leadership under Mohammed Reza Shah Pahlavi was unstable and its government ineffective. Owing to complex circumstances, the Eisenhower administration was complicit in the overthrow of Prime Minister Mohammad Mosaddeq in late 1953. Mosaddeq had been an ineffective leader who was driving Iran toward chaos. His removal restored full power to the Shah. U.S.-Iranian relations quickly improved and the Shah succeeded in stabilizing Iran, but U.S. involvement in the coup left lasting resentment among Iranians.

The Shah remained in power until the late 1970s. Pollack wrote that although the United States had less influence over the Shah than is widely supposed, he generally acted as a strategic ally of the United States in the Persian Gulf, and thus was viewed with favor by administrations from Eisenhower through Carter. Internally, however, he was a tyrant who used police power to consolidate his hold over Iran's turbulent body politic. He tried to use oil revenues to modernize the country, but his efforts largely failed, resulting in a corrupt government, bloated special interests, a malfunctioning economy, and a deeply alienated public. His ouster in 1979 set the stage for a takeover of the government by Ayatollah Ruhollah Khomeini. He and his mullah-led regime of Islamic fundamentalists were animated by a combination of religious fervor and paranoid hatred of the United States, which they portrayed as the prop for the Shah's long regime and his despised policies.

Iran's seizure of American hostages in late 1979, Pollack wrote, began over 20 years of deep alienation in U.S.-Iranian relations. Throughout most of the 1980s, the United States openly backed Iraq in its war with Iran, providing military and economic aid. That conflict resulted in massive bloodshed. The war began when Iraq invaded Iran, but Iran counterattacked and seized Iraqi territory. In the final stage, Iraq reorganized its army and pushed back into Iran. The war finally ended on terms that basically restored the territorial status quo ante. The Persian Gulf War of 1991 made Iraq an enemy of the United States, but this did not result in any U.S.-Iranian rapprochement. Iran's fundamentalist Islamic government, wrote Pollack, fanned public fear of the United States in order to consolidate its internal hold on power. Meanwhile, the Clinton administration imposed a "dual containment" regime on both Iraq and Iran, imposing stiff economic sanctions against Iran. By the late 1990s, there were indicators that Iran was liberalizing at home with the elevation of Mohammad Khatami to the presidency and growing public disaffection with mullah rule. But Khatami failed to consolidate his power, and the religious conservatives under Ayatollah Ali Khamenei regained control, quashing hopes for internal reforms or rapprochement with the United States.

Pollack draws distinctions between the current Iranian government and Saddam Hussein's regime. Whereas Saddam Hussein was a secular dictator bent on military conquest of his neighbors, Iran's regime is dominated by the religious agenda of Islamic fundamentalism. This difference does not, Pollack said, mean that Iran is significantly less dangerous to U.S. interests or to Persian Gulf security. Pollack charged that Iran's government is a sponsor of terrorism, a proponent of Islamic revolutions across the Middle East, a foe of Israel, and a determined advocate of reducing U.S. influence in the region. Pollack expressed special worry about Iran's pursuit of nuclear weapons and delivery systems because they might embolden Iran to support more aggressive terrorist operations and to subvert governments friendly to the United States. Pollack warned that the United States faced a dangerous race against time: the question is whether Iran might acquire nuclear weapons before its Islamic fundamentalist government is overthrown by a disgruntled population.

In reviewing the potential U.S. policy options, Pollack dismissed military strikes against Iran's nuclear facilities as unlikely to succeed. He reached the same conclusion about invading Iran, a country three times bigger than Iraq that would be even harder to occupy. He also discounted the feasibility of orchestrating a revolution within Iran, or of reaching a grand strategic bargain with the mullahs, whose hatred of the United States is thought to be implacable. Pollack instead recommended a triple track strategy: the first two tracks would hold out the distant prospect of a broad diplomatic settlement, while in the interim using carrots and sticks to try to temper Iran's pursuit of nuclear weapons and its other menacing strategic policies. The third track would be focused on efforts to create a robust, multilateral containment regime of economic sanctions, diplomatic opposition, and military presence in the Persian Gulf if Iran did acquire nuclear weapons. Pollack made no claim that this triple track strategy would be likely to alter Iran's behavior in the absence of an internal revolution. But, he reasoned, it offered the prospect of keeping a deteriorating situation within bounds, and he argued that it was the best of the options available to the United States.

Both of Pollack's books are well researched and logically reasoned. Both rely on thoughtful strategic assessments and careful reviews of U.S. policy options. Both are controversial because of their policy recommendations— the first recommending invasion of Iraq, the second urging diplomatic restraint in handling Iran. Hawks and doves thus will find reasons for favoring one book and not the other, but neither faction is likely to approve of both. The ultimate value of these two books may lie not in their controversial policy appraisals, but in their appraisals of rogue states. Pollack's books correctly view both prewar Iraq and Iran as rogues, yet his books also show clearly that rogue states differ, and each must be addressed according to its specific characteristics. Rogue states must be handled with policies that are individually tailored to them, rather than by a single strategic doctrine that treats all of them as cut from the same cloth. The U.S. Government followed Pollack's advice on Iraq and may be following it on Iran. Whether the wisdom of these policies will be borne out by future events, only time will tell.

Taking Stock of the Neo-Hobbesian Literature

The neo-Hobbesian literature surveyed in this chapter shows that there are numerous reasons to be concerned about global security affairs today and tomorrow. Brzezinski, Huntington, and Mearsheimer pointed to fundamental problems potentially affecting the entire world: lack of common values, clashing cultures, and great power rivalries. Moynihan, Pfaff, Kaplan, and Power pointed to dangers that mostly affect the underdeveloped world: ethnic rivalries, renewed nationalism, failed states, chaos, and genocide. Terrill warned of an unstable emerging Chinese Empire with naval ambitions. Lewis and Pollack identified the greater Middle East and nearby regions as a hot zone of turmoil roiled by Islamic fundamentalism, terrorism, rogue states, and other troubles.

These problems are not necessarily mutually exclusive; indeed, they may reinforce each other. Thus, the various dangers of the neo-Hobbesian literature should be examined not separately, but together. A central question is whether the neo-Hobbesian literature captures the essence of contemporary world politics: does it see the elephant? A fair answer is that, like the neo-Kantian literature, it sees part of the elephant, but not the whole elephant. Whereas the neo-Kantian literature sees primarily the elephant's bright side, the neo-Hobbesian literature sees primarily the elephant's dark side.

Clearly, the literature reflects the temper of the times. Just as the neo-Kantian literature expounded the seemingly favorable trends of the early to mid-1990s, the neo-Hobbesian literature responded to the troubles that have arisen since then. The neo-Kantian literature saw a future of great opportunities for global peace and progress under the mantle of Western liberal ideals and multinational cooperation, but the neo-Hobbesian literature outlined a future of great problems and dangers in which nations not only have trouble collaborating, but also are often in confrontation with each other. Taken as a whole, the neo-Hobbesian literature creates a sense of overwhelming dangers that could swamp opportunities for progress, making the future very worrisome. Recent trends may suggest that the neo-Hobbesian literature is closer to the truth than the neo-Kantian literature, yet it, too, has its limits.

The neo-Hobbesian literature provides valuable conceptual lenses for viewing the future. Each of the books reviewed here provides a partial theory of how the world works that illuminates some trends and causal dynamics. The strength of the neo-Hobbesian literature becomes apparent when all of these books are seen together and their separate themes are integrated into a comprehensive view of the sources of danger in the early 21st century. These multiple, deep-seated, and persistent troubles do not necessarily mean that the entire world will go up in flames. Indeed, the Western hemisphere is mostly free of these dangers: Europe appears to be headed toward enduring peace, and Western relations with Russia do not seem destined for inevitable confrontation. This alone is cause for celebration. Where the neo-Hobbesian literature warned of trouble ahead, it mostly pointed toward the greater Middle East because of angry Islamic fundamentalism, toward Africa because of deep poverty and chaos, and toward Asia because of China's rising power and assertiveness. These are major problems, but they do not yet amount to the risk of global cataclysm that erupted into World War II, nor do they threaten nuclear holocaust of the sort that constantly shadowed the Cold War. A sense of perspective is needed here that is lacking in some parts of the neo-Hobbesian literature.

The neo-Hobbesian literature offered some worthy policy advice to the United States and its democratic partners: if the world's dangers are to be contained, the United States must be active in troubled regions. Although some neo-Hobbesians are unilateralists, most of the writers surveyed in this chapter tend toward multilateralism, favoring alliance cooperation to address emerging problems. Because the United States is not capable of handling the world's problems on its own, these writers call for the United States to work multilaterally with its allies in Europe, Asia, and elsewhere.

Some of the neo-Hobbesian literature's most relentless pessimism, such as that found in Kaplan's books, may be exaggerated because valid reasons for optimism are discounted. The greater Middle East is beset by angry Islamic fundamentalism, as Lewis wrote, but nevertheless, signs of democracy and economic markets are emerging in some places. Africa faces problems of poverty, social chaos, and weak governments, as Kaplan wrote, but nevertheless, democracy is taking root in some places, and multilateral cooperation is growing. China poses potential problems in Asia, as both Mearsheimer and Terrill wrote, but it is currently behaving responsibly in many areas, and there can be hope of integrating it into a stable multilateral order that respects Western interests. In all of these regions, the future is a variable, and it is not predestined but can, to a significant degree, be molded, created, and guided in the direction of progress rather than turmoil.

The neo-Hobbesian literature is good at seeing the dangers ahead, but much of it is not as good at seeing how to use all of the tools at America's disposal to handle these dangers. By contrast, the neo-Kantian literature tended to discount these dangers, but it suggested how the use of multilateral engagement by the community of liberal democracies could provide a way of coping with future challenges. Whereas the neo-Kantian literature may have been too transfixed by the hopeful trends and policy challenges of the early to mid-1990s, the neo-Hobbesian literature may be so preoccupied with the challenges of the current decade that it loses sight of the bigger picture. The conceptual lenses of both the neo-Kantian and neo-Hobbesian literature may grant a kind of stereo vision that gives a more in-depth and revealing view than either by itself.

Chapter Four

A New Age of Empowerment

The future will be shaped not only by the broad political and strategic trends discussed in chapters two and three, but also by new
opportunities and threats. Many of these are enhanced by new technologies such as information networks. New technologies help multiply and
diversify actors on the world scene, empower them, magnify their impact,
and project them around the world. In this sense, although these new technologies will not necessarily alter the balance between the neo-Kantian and
neo-Hobbesian dynamics under way in the world, they will tend to intensify
both and to complicate international affairs by putting power into the hands
of new actors on the global scene. Thus, to help us see the elephant in full, in
this chapter we review the work of a number of writers who have examined
these questions.

During much of the 20th century, nation-states were the main actors in
world politics and almost the sole actors of significant consequence. In the
early 21st century, nation-states retain much of their original power and are
still the principal building blocks of world politics, and their number has
considerably grown over the past decades. Yet a potent new trend has been
the emergence of new types of actors, including multinational governmental
bodies such as the United Nations and the WTO, and multinational businesses and multinational nongovernmental organizations (NGOs). Social
bodies such as ethnic groups and terrorist organizations, often cutting across
national and regional borders, have become more salient in international
politics. Even individuals or small groups can now become powerful actors
because of their access to the Internet. These trends toward empowerment
were silently gaining force during the 1990s, and they have become manifest
in the post–September 11 world. They are so potentially influential that we
may be entering a new age of empowerment.

This diffusion of power does not necessarily mean that all nation-states
are losing their importance. Some are actually becoming more powerful

because their economic strength, military capability, and access to new technologies are also growing. Owing to the worldwide diffusion of power, however, other actors are also growing in number and variety and are becoming more able to act effectively on the world stage, thereby helping shape the future. In many cases, new technologies are critical causes of this growing empowerment, enabling all actors to magnify their leverage significantly in crucial areas. A key accompanying trend is that, whereas these actors originally were confined to their home regions, now they can project their impact far wider, even around the world. A terrorist leader can destroy skyscrapers in New York or trains in Madrid. A newspaper editor in Denmark can print cartoons depicting the Prophet Muhammed, which, seen worldwide on the Internet, provoke massive and sometimes violent demonstrations in protest. A Serbian opposition leader can use communications technologies to train dissidents in Ukraine. Information networking and other new technologies help multiply, empower, and magnify new actors and help them to project their power. These are truly revolutionary features of the modern world.

New opportunities also arise with the emergence of new information systems and other technologies, global economic interactions, and democratizing political pressures, all of which can contribute to greater security, prosperity, and representative government. These new opportunities are seldom discussed on the front pages of newspapers, but as several of the books reviewed in this chapter show, they are silently at work behind the scenes, often as powerful tools for good. Expanding opportunities for the creation of wealth and representative government, which have their roots in the empowerment of individuals, have the potential to alter world politics at its roots. The global dissemination of new technologies has many beneficial consequences. Information networks contribute to faster growth rates for the world economy. New biological and chemical research is helping produce many new commercial products and medicines. Yet new information systems and other military technologies also help empower and magnify threats that menace global progress as well as U.S. interests. New threats are a product of such strategic factors as chaotic security affairs, fanatical ideologies, and the ambitions of threatening actors, including rogue states and terrorists. Technologies—old and new—contribute significantly to these opportunities and threats. Examples are the proliferation of weapons of mass destruction and the capacity of terrorist organizations to use the Internet to enhance their global reach.

In reviewing 12 key books, this chapter discusses these new opportunities and threats and how they are affected by technologies. The first book assesses how the role of the nation-state is changing, and perhaps declining, in the era of globalization and information networking:

- Martin van Creveld, *The Rise and Decline of the Nation-State* (1999).

The next four books are neo-Kantian in the sense that they explain how current trends can fuel opportunities in world affairs. They address the impact on military forces, the growing use of space, the acceleration of economic globalization, and the upsurge of democratic nonviolent protest movements against authoritarian governments:

- Alvin and Heidi Toffler, *War and Anti-War: Survival at the Dawn of the 21st Century* (1993)
- Michael O'Hanlon, *Neither Star Wars nor Sanctuary: Constraining the Military Uses of Space* (2004)
- Thomas L. Friedman, *The World Is Flat: A Brief History of the Twenty-first Century* (2005)
- Peter Ackerman and Jack DuVall, *A Force More Powerful: A Century of Nonviolent Conflict* (2000).

The other seven books are primarily neo-Hobbesian: they focus on new-era threats and dangers, and how they are being magnified and projected by new technologies in ways that threaten their immediate locales and even the United States and the rest of the democratic community. These books address the Asian region, genocidal practices, terrorism and religious militants, America's new vulnerability, biological warfare, nuclear proliferation, and international crime:

- Kent E. Calder, *Pacific Defense: Arms, Energy, and America's Future in Asia* (1996)
- Jessica Stern, *Terror in the Name of God: Why Religious Militants Kill* (2003)
- Robert A. Pape, *Dying to Win* (2005)
- Stephen Flynn, *America the Vulnerable* (2004)
- Judith Miller, Stephen Engelberg, and William Broad, *Germs: Biological Weapons and America's Secret War* (2002)
- Graham Allison, *Nuclear Terrorism: The Ultimate Preventable Catastrophe* (2004)
- Moisés Naím, *Illicit: How Smugglers, Traffickers, and Copycats are Hijacking the Global Economy* (2005).

The chapter starts with a book that assesses the role of the nation-state in world affairs, and how that role is changing.

Martin van Creveld: The Changing Role of the State

The idea that the nation-state provides a main building block of the modern international political system is so commonplace that it is taken for granted in most quarters. But the role of the nation-state may be changing. In his 1999 book, *The Rise and Decline of the State*, Martin van Creveld, a widely published historian at the Hebrew University in Jerusalem, examined the past, present, and future role of the *state*, defined as the organizational corporation that governs nations, exercises sovereignty over them, and determines their foreign and domestic policies.[1] Seen through the lens of history, the state reached its apogee in recent decades, argued van Creveld; it now is in a process of decline.

He offers many reasons for this important trend, and one is modern technology, which makes new actors—multinational, transnational, and domestic—capable of functions once exclusive to states, such as access to satellite photography and massive Internet databases, global communications, and control of military power and even WMD. As states, all around the world, are being supplemented by a host of new actors, this trend will have a profound impact on future international affairs. Van Creveld did not argue that this trend would be wholly good or wholly bad; its impact is likely to be mixed. The key point, he said, is that one of the pillars of modern world affairs is changing rapidly.

Van Creveld began his book by pointing out that the modern state has not always existed: it is a product of Europe's historical evolution over the past six or seven centuries. In particular, it grew out of Europe's politics and society as the Middle Ages gave way to the modern era, and as such trends as the Renaissance, the Reformation, the Enlightenment, and industrialization swept over Europe. The European state first began emerging between 1300 and 1648, as monarchs consolidated their power over France, Britain, Spain, the Netherlands, Prussia, Russia, and other key countries and geographical regions. These monarchs successfully brushed aside rivals including the Catholic Church, the Holy Roman Empire, the feudal nobility, and local towns and communities. This historical process, said van Creveld, culminated when the Peace of Westphalia was signed in 1648. This treaty not only ended the Thirty Years' War, in which multiple religious wars had devastated Europe; it also created a new Europe organized into nation-states, most of which were under the control of monarchs who claimed hereditary right to rule.

The emergence of countries led by monarchs, said van Creveld, was a step toward modern states, with their full bureaucratic apparatus, which would evolve during the next 130 years, from 1648 to 1789. Bureaucratization of the state, he wrote, came about because monarchs discovered that they could not govern their nations by means of the existing structure of feudal lords, townships, and local communities. It was inadequate to allow them to raise modern armies, guard their borders, enforce law, quell domestic crime and violence, raise taxes, control their currencies, regulate trade and commerce, create an economic infrastructure, or guide their economies and societies toward growth. In order to perform these vital functions, an administrative structure was needed. As such structures were gradually built in multiple countries, van Creveld said, "the state" acquired an abstract identity of its own, separate both from monarchs and from civil society. With the emergence of this bureaucratic structure, new political theories celebrated the state as an entity at the centerpiece of European politics and economics. Van Creveld credited Thomas Hobbes as the main creator of the theory of the modern state, but he also cited such political philosophers as John Locke, Baron de Montesquieu, David Hume, and Jeremy Bentham. Many viewed the state not only as an instrument of security, internal sovereignty, and control, but also as an institution for helping build and protect a civil society. From these theories were to come a variety of governments, ranging from democracy to traditional monarchies to absolutism, but they held in common an acceptance of the state as the key structure for governing nations and for managing Europe's diplomacy and security affairs.

The period from 1789 to 1945, wrote van Creveld, saw the flowering of the state as a moral and strategic ideal. Prior to the French Revolution, states had mostly been viewed in instrumental and pragmatic terms, that is, in terms of their ability to perform governmental functions, but not in terms of inspiring the moral loyalties and enthusiasm of their citizens. Although states had raised armies and waged wars, the actual fighting had mostly been carried out by professional militaries or mercenaries; while average citizens were required to pay taxes to finance these endeavors, they were usually insulated from the full savagery of war. The French Revolution and its aftermath changed this. After the *ancien régime* was overthrown, a republican government appeared, which soon fell under the control of Napoleon Bonaparte. Facing the prospect of wars against neighboring monarchs determined to stamp out republicanism, Napoleon not only mobilized the entire country to create a large national army, but also infused French society with an aroused spirit of patriotism and emotional fervor. The age of nationalism had thus begun, wrote van Creveld, and this "great transformation" changed not only European interstate politics, but how states themselves were viewed. From that point forward, states were seen not just in instrumental and pragmatic terms, but as focal points, symbols, and repositories of the emotional loyalties, cultural identities, and ethical qualities of their societies and nations.

After Napoleon was defeated at Waterloo in 1815, Europe's security affairs were managed by the Concert of Europe, which was essentially a club of aristocratic monarchies determined to prevent the spread of republicanism and democracy. Even so, wrote van Creveld, the remaining decades of the 19th century witnessed both the further development of the modern state and growing nationalism across the continent. Regardless of whether national governments were democracies, constitutional monarchies, or autocracies, virtually all of them acquired steadily growing powers over their economies and societies. The state became the main institution determining how each nation would evolve. With industrialization and technological advances, states also acquired vastly greater military power. Huge armies were made possible by mass conscription, modern weapons, and other technologies, for example, to transport and feed them. Large navies also appeared, with heavily armed battleships and cruisers. Europe came to resemble an armed military camp, marked by competitive nationalisms and offensive militaries that were capable of quickly striking and sometimes conquering their neighbors.

Van Creveld attributed the rise of the modern nation-state to many underlying political, economic, and social forces, but he argued that technologies played a major role. Modern communications systems, including the printing press and the telegraph, were especially important to the modern state by helping it to gather and distribute information. He also cited the importance of modern transport—roads, rail lines, and waterways—as key to economic development and the strength of the state. Industrialization created goods and services that gave rise to modern economies, and produced the resulting need for states to manage currencies, commerce, and trade. The need for an educated workforce to populate an industrial and high-technology economy compelled states to develop national education and healthcare systems. Among all of these technological changes, wrote van Creveld, the key was the emergence of modern militaries with modern weapons such as artillery and machine guns, backed by railroads and telegraphs, making states the unquestioned masters of the means of violence. As the 19th century unfolded, European states defined their identities increasingly in terms of their military power, their monopoly on organized violence, and their ability to intimidate each other.

The European system of nationalist states and huge armies exploded into World War I in 1914, killing 10 million people before peace was restored in 1918. The subsequent Versailles Treaty dismantled old empires and gave rise to new states in Eastern Europe and the Middle East. In the aftermath of World War I and the Depression of the 1930s, wrote van Creveld, came a new version of state virulence: extremist ideologies and totalitarian governments in Nazi Germany and the Soviet Union. Nazism was defeated in World War II, but totalitarian governments persisted in the communist world. Meanwhile, democratic states in Europe and North America continued to expand their powers by taking command of their economies, creating large welfare systems and, in some cases, nationalizing industries. Elsewhere, the century-long increase in the number of states accelerated, sweeping over Asia, Africa, and Latin America. Many of these new states did not perform as well as modern democracies, but they were states all the same.

Thus, van Creveld concluded, the state reached its apogee in the mid-20th century, then began to decline about 1975. He argued that this trend has accelerated since the end of the Cold War. One reason he gave for the decline of states is that the long period of major interstate warfare has come to an end, as nuclear weapons have made such wars too costly and calamitous. While modern states remain willing to fight conventional wars, modern technology has produced a steady decline in the size of military forces, thereby shrinking one key area of the state's former predominance. Beyond this, he said, modern international law and norms have swung decidedly against cross-border aggression, invasions, and colonial imperialism, which had helped give states their power and preeminence a century ago.

In addition, van Creveld said, states are no longer seen as effective architects of economic prosperity. Communist states have been discarded because their command economies suffocated economic growth. Democracies have also swung away from state economic management, and instead are now embracing more capitalism and free markets. The resulting privatization, decrease in welfare systems, and deregulation strip away state powers.

In an equally important trend, said van Creveld, modern states are increasingly being joined by international organizations and nonstate institutions. This trend, he said, started late in the 19th century, when new global technologies created a need for international coordinating and standards bodies such as the International Telegraph Union, the International Postal Union, and the International Bureau of Weights and Measures. In the 20th century, the League of Nations and then the United Nations each established many subsidiary bodies for regulation and coordination of interstate relations. The rise of the modern global economy, with its explosive growth of trade, financial flows, and foreign investments, has given rise to multiple economic bodies, including the G–7/G–8, the WTO, and regional economic groups, such as NAFTA. Among the biggest manifestations of multilateralism identified by van Creveld is the European Union, whose steady growth could eventually result in a unified Europe in which old-style states will lose their identities and sovereignty.

In addition, new information systems and other technologies are empowering business corporations, NGOs, social groups, and individuals. The effect, said van Creveld, is to enable these entities to act on the world stage independently of state governments, and sometimes even in defiance of them.

Many of these developments have had positive effects, but some negative developments have also emerged. For example, wrote van Creveld, international terrorism has been empowered by modern information networks, communications, and easy global travel, and terrorists can now conduct violent strikes almost anywhere in the world. Van Creveld penned these prescient observations about terrorism in 1998 and 1999, well before the calamitous strikes of September 11, 2001, in Washington and New York, those of March 11, 2004, in Madrid, and those of July 7, 2005, in London.

Skeptics may challenge elements of van Creveld's thesis that the state is now in decline on several grounds. First, the number of states on the world scene has been growing, not shrinking, and now stands at about 200, the largest number in history. The idea that states are losing military power seems questionable; information warfare and smart munitions permit smaller forces to generate vastly greater conventional combat capability than their larger predecessors. The fact that totalitarian ideologies have been discredited does not mean that all states have been equally discredited, or that nationalism and patriotism are permanently dead. Nor does dwindling support for welfare states and central economic planning imply that governments are abandoning all forms of involvement in regulating capitalism or providing social safety nets. Likewise, the growth of international institutions does not imply that states are losing most of their sovereign powers. The travails of the EU in seeking to adopt a constitution suggest that multinational integration may have limits where states, nations, and national cultures are well entrenched. Nor do other regions, such as Asia and the Middle East, seem likely to experience such integration any time soon. In these regions, the state system endures, even if it does not perform with the effectiveness and efficiency sought by its critics.

Statistics for the United States since 1975 show a more complex picture than portrayed by van Creveld. It is true that total Federal employment declined between 1975 (when it was 5 million) and 2005 (when it was 4.2 million), but the change is more than accounted for by a decline of 1 million in the Department of Defense, largely owing to the end of the Cold War. The nondefense Federal workforce grew in this period from 1.9 million to 2.1 million. Total public-sector employment from Federal, state, and local government (apart from defense) rose from 14.2 million to 21.1 million, or about a 50 percent increase, roughly comparable to growth in the U.S. population and private-sector workforce. Over these three decades, Federal spending fell from 23 percent of GDP to 20 percent, but this is a relatively small decline, not a signal of a sea change in national policy. Meanwhile, the size of the U.S. Federal budget mushroomed during this period from $1 trillion to $2.2 trillion in constant dollars.[2] The percentage of GDP spent by the Federal Government declined slightly because the national economy grew somewhat faster than the Federal budget, but both grew. These figures do not suggest a major decline in the importance of government in the United States. For the United States and perhaps for other wealthy democracies as well, the rate of rapid expansion experienced by the state in past decades may now have leveled off. Perhaps domestic economies are now growing faster than the state, but this trend is incremental rather than radical. In these countries, the state is not withering away, and in some key respects—budgets and manpower—it is even growing in absolute terms, although it may be declining somewhat in relative terms.

If the state is in decline, as van Creveld asserts, it is so only in some respects, and not necessarily the most important ones. States will continue to be the main building blocks of human affairs for the foreseeable future, for the simple reason that they continue to perform highly important functions for their societies. Democratic states that are capable of providing good governance will remain essential for the emergence of civil societies and prosperous capitalist economies. International institutions cannot be relied upon to perform all of the many functions needed to govern modern countries. The fact that the modern state has declined somewhat from its earlier apogee does not mean that it is doomed to shrink into irrelevancy in either domestic affairs or international relations.

Yet van Creveld is clearly correct in pointing out that states are being joined by new and diverse actors, both small and large, on the world scene. These actors are emerging partly because of new technologies, and partly because they can perform some functions better than state governments can. As van Creveld notes, some of these new actors may abet the cause of world peace and prosperity, while others may damage it. The future international system will be considerably more complex than the state-centric system of the 20th century. In pointing this out, van Creveld's book makes an important contribution to the literature and to the task of seeing the elephant.

Alvin and Heidi Toffler: New Forms of War

Authors of such futurist best sellers as *Future Shock* in 1971 and *The Third*

Wave in 1980, Alvin and Heidi Toffler set out in their 1993 book to assess how new forms of warfare will develop in the early 21st century.[3] The basic premise of *War and Anti-War: Survival at the Dawn of the Twenty-first Century* is that military forces and the wars they fight are a reflection of how economies operate and the technologies they produce.[4] Thus, the agricultural age produced what the Tofflers called *first wave war* among armies armed with primitive weapons. The industrial era of the 19th and 20th centuries produced what they called *second wave war*, marked by huge armies, mass production of modern weapons, and mass destruction. Among today's wealthy countries, as industrial-era economies give way to information-era economies powered by computers, networks, and the wide diffusion of knowledge, this change is destined to sweep over modern militaries as well. As a result, the Tofflers asserted, modern military forces will operate on the basis of networks and information, and *third wave war* will be heavily knowledge-based: the combat power and battlefield effectiveness of modern military forces will come from their mastery of information and knowledge, rather than their sheer size or the lethality of their weapons.

A main implication, argued the Tofflers, is that information networking has great potential to empower military personnel of all types. This begins with individual troops, manifests itself in small units such as army platoons and companies, and becomes increasingly important in larger units. They can fuse together information networks, smart munitions, and modern weapons to create a far greater degree of combat power than ever before. An army brigade becomes capable of covering more terrain, maneuvering more adeptly, and striking a greater number of targets more lethally. A fighter wing or a naval surface action group will experience similar expansions of capability. Equally important, information networks permit the fusing of ground, air, and naval forces into joint operations for integrated battlefield campaigns. The enhancement of elements of state power thus predicted by the Tofflers provides a contrasting view to those of van Creveld.

Writing shortly after the Persian Gulf War of 1991, the Tofflers predicted that the transition to knowledge-based warfare would sweep first over the U.S. military but would later also affect other military establishments. The Tofflers found the start of this transition in the early 1980s, when U.S. Army generals, including Donn Starry, William DePuy, Don Morelli, and others, called for the Army to adopt new doctrines of warfare and weapons aimed at replacing warfare based on attrition, firepower, and linear defense with a wholly new emphasis on information networks, sensors, smart munitions, and use of maneuver warfare. The Army began implementing such changes, and the U.S. Air Force and Navy pursued parallel innovations. The result was the capacity for the decisive U.S. victory over Iraqi forces in 1991, which displayed the power of the new type of warfare to the rest of the world.

The Tofflers declared, however, that *Desert Storm* was not the culmination of these changes, but rather their debut. They predicted that over the next decade and beyond, the transition of the U.S. military toward third wave warfare would steadily accelerate. Increasingly advanced information systems, sensors, smart munitions, and weapons would be introduced and integrated with new doctrines, training patterns, and sophisticated military skills. They predicted the emergence of joint forces anchored in knowledge-based operations, space systems, robots, and other new technologies. As a result, they said, the U.S. military would temporarily achieve preponderance over most other militaries, whose reforms would be slower. The U.S. victory over Iraqi forces in 2003 proved them correct in this arena. But the Tofflers also correctly judged that this preponderance would begin to diminish as other militaries, including those of adversaries, began to pursue modern, knowledge-based warfare. Here, too, recent events confirm this prediction, as China and other foreign militaries begin to adopt information-age military systems.[5]

Notwithstanding their optimism that new technologies would make the global economy wealthier, the Tofflers' forecast of future global politics and security affairs was grimmer, differing markedly from writers such as Thomas Friedman (whose 2005 book is discussed below), who forecast positive results from economic globalization. The modern world, the Tofflers said, is increasingly becoming divided between those countries and regions that are profiting from the globalizing economy, and those that are being left behind in poverty because they are unable to compete and grow. In these regions, new dangers are erupting: failed states, organized crime, terrorism, and nuclear proliferation. Nor are even prosperous countries necessarily destined to form peaceful communities of commerce. They might instead fall into new forms of geopolitical rivalry: the Tofflers pointed, for example, to Chinese rivalry with the United States and Japan as likely. The world will see a great deal more political conflict and strife, they predicted, and perhaps a growing number of wars fought with military forces that are made more destructive to some degree by the new technologies of the information age.

The Tofflers forecast that the U.S. military eventually will confront big-power rivals such as China that have also armed themselves with modern information systems, sensors, space systems, and smart munitions. Less powerful adversaries from unstable, poverty-stricken regions will also acquire some elements of these modern technologies. Terrorist groups might use systems of knowledge-based warfare to amplify their capacity to spread violence to the four corners of the world. Accordingly, the Tofflers warned the U.S. military not to take its newfound superiority for granted. They also called for new forms of multilateral political cooperation to create dynamics of *antiwar*, the capacity to prevent new wars from erupting.

If written today, the Tofflers' book might seem like nothing new, but seen from the perspective of 1993, it comes across as prescient even if it did not probe all of its various topics in scholarly depth. It accurately identified emerging trends not only in international politics and economics, but in new-era military forces as well. The notion that modern warfare would be knowledge-based may be commonplace now, but it was new then. The Tofflers oversimplified their treatment of some complex defense issues, but the transformation path followed by the U.S. military since 1993 closely parallels the vision they presented. During the 1990s, U.S. military forces shrank about 25 percent from their Cold War size. Although procurement budgets declined, slowing the upgrading of weapons systems, enough money was available to permit important progress in information networking, acquisition of smart munitions, and development of joint operations. As the Tofflers had suggested, U.S. military forces also began performing peacetime engagement missions abroad, helping build ties with new friends and partners in regions that previously were outside the U.S. geostrategic perimeter. By the arrival of the new decade in 2000, the U.S. military had increased its predominance in capabilities over virtually all other military establishments.

As the Tofflers said, the growth of U.S. combat capabilities was partly due to information systems and smart munitions, but also to new weapons systems that permitted new operational doctrines. For example, prior to development of the Abrams tank, Army tanks had lacked adequate cross-country speed, defensive armor, and firepower; tactical combat aircraft had shown deficiencies in air-to-air dogfighting and striking targets on the ground; naval cruisers and destroyers did not have adequate systems for air defense and for the antisubmarine warfare needed to protect carriers from attack. The new weapons procured during the late 1970s to the early and mid-1990s addressed these deficiencies. The new Army tanks (M–1 Abrams) and infantry fighting vehicles (M–2 Bradleys) could maneuver adeptly on the modern battlefield and thus win close engagements. The new F–15 and F–16 fighter aircraft could sweep the skies clean of enemy aircraft and destroy a wide spectrum of ground targets. New Aegis cruisers and destroyers could protect carriers, and the new aircraft flying from carrier decks were better able to perform their missions. Most of these new weapons were acquired to strengthen the defensive capabilities of U.S. forces, but when they were fitted with new information systems and smart munitions, they also greatly enhanced the U.S.

military's offensive capabilities. As a result, the Armed Forces became better at swift and lethal power projection in expeditionary missions, especially against the adversaries of the 1990s, which lacked the military strength of the Soviet Union during the Cold War.

A disappointment of the 1990s was that most European and other allied militaries did not much improve their forces and capabilities for expeditionary operations outside their borders and other new missions. The Persian Gulf War of 1991 exposed the inability of European militaries, apart from the British and French, to swiftly project power to distant regions. In the following years, low European defense budgets continued to constrain improvement efforts. By 2000, several European militaries were beginning to acquire new information systems and smart munitions, but they still lacked the command structures, mobility systems, and logistic support to deploy rapidly and fight effectively outside NATO's borders. This failure to reform became noticeable when NATO intervened in Kosovo in 1999, and it helped set the stage for NATO's struggles over how to respond to the invasions of Afghanistan and Iraq when the war on terror got under way in 2001. In 2002, NATO began pursuing defense reforms by creating the NATO Response Force and a new Allied Transformation Command.

In the years since 1993, potential adversaries of the United States and other countries may not yet have made rapid progress in acquiring new information systems, smart munitions, or other modern warfighting assets, but recent trends suggest that they are moving in the direction described by the Tofflers. China's military modernization is becoming noticeable, and terrorist groups in Afghanistan and Iraq employ cellular and satellite phones, encryption technologies, and other modern technologies to increase their lethality. Thus, the Tofflers were correct in predicting major strides for the U.S. military and, to a lesser degree, its allies. They also were correct in predicting the emergence of new threats employing new technologies of the information age. The future of warfare will be partly determined by how these competing trends interact.

Michael O'Hanlon: Military Uses of Space

One of the principal manifestations of the information age and modern technology is the number of satellites that now orbit the Earth at low, medium, and high altitudes. The United States and the Soviet Union were the first to enter space with a few satellites beginning in the late 1950s. Over the past three decades, an explosion of space activity has taken place. Today, there are about 3,000 satellites in orbit (although not all of these are still functional). About 100 new satellites are sent into orbit each year, placed by

40 different countries and many private enterprises. Satellites are now used for communications, navigation, weather forecasting, scientific research, observing developments on Earth, and many other purposes, both commercial and military.

A main effect has been to empower states that have adequate wealth and resources to take advantage of space for military, commercial, and other purposes. Currently, the United States enjoys a major advantage over other countries in the use of space, and its military spending on space has been increasing. Over the long term, other countries are also likely to make growing use of space, narrowing the gap with the United States. Future activity in space can help stimulate global economic growth and scientific knowledge, but it also will have an impact on military relationships and geopolitical crosscurrents.

Michael O'Hanlon's 2004 book, *Neither Star Wars Nor Sanctuary: Constraining the Military Uses of Space*, aimed to survey trends in the militarization of space, assess the controversies regarding its potential weaponization (placing actual weapons there, not just satellites of military usefulness), and offer policy guidance to the United States.[6]

O'Hanlon observed that the United States dominates other countries in using space for military purposes. It operates a host of satellites for military communications, navigation aids, early warning and tracking of missile launches, and intelligence gathering on foreign countries through a variety of technical means such as optical sensors, radar imaging, and signals intelligence. The United States is developing space-based radars to help operate the new missile defense interceptors it is deploying in Alaska and California.

The United States has begun using its space systems not only for strategic purposes, but also to aid tactical military operations in wartime. In *Desert Storm* of 1991, wrote O'Hanlon, the U.S. military used 16 military satellites to transmit information to its deployed forces at the rate of 200 million bits per second (equal to 40,000 simultaneous telephone calls). During the Kosovo war of 1991, twice as much capacity was available. By the time of the invasions of Afghanistan in 2001 and Iraq in 2003, communications bandwidth had increased to five times the level of 1991. Fifty satellites, both military and commercial, were used in the invasion of Iraq. Navigational data from global positioning system (GPS) satellites enabled U.S. warplanes to drop joint direct attack munitions bombs with unprecedented accuracy and permitted ground forces to maneuver effectively on trackless deserts in blinding sandstorms. To an important degree, said O'Hanlon, the United States owes its battlefield superiority over opponents not only to its high-technology weapons and trained military forces, but also to the immense and varied advantages offered by its space-based systems.

Other countries are now moving into space for military purposes, as O'Hanlon noted. Despite its economic troubles, Russia remains the world's second-largest space power, continuing to launch 25 satellites per year, some of which are used for military intelligence and communications. Europe and Japan are operating many satellites, some for military use. Thus far, adversaries of the United States have not exploited space to any major degree: Iraq, Iran, and North Korea, for example, do not have military satellites. But China, a potential rival, is becoming a space power, with 3 launch sites, a half-dozen launches per year, and about 30 satellites in orbit. O'Hanlon warned that China and other potential adversaries will be acquiring more satellites (or gaining greater access to them) as well as other space systems that can be used for military purposes. This, said O'Hanlon, will challenge U.S. primacy in certain areas and pose a set of specific military threats to the United States and its forces.

Surveying these future threats, O'Hanlon wrote that although adversaries will be unable to rival the U.S. military in physical capability, they are likely to acquire a growing capacity to use satellites to communicate with their forces, provide battlefield intelligence and navigational data, and support wartime targeting. Adversaries may also develop improved capabilities to interfere with U.S. satellites by jamming or destroying them. Antisatellite (ASAT) capabilities, O'Hanlon said, could come in the form of sophisticated jamming technologies, ground-launched missiles capable of striking satellites, high-energy lasers, nuclear detonations in space, or microwave weapons, which could threaten U.S. satellites and other space systems. O'Hanlon dismissed alarmist fears of a "space Pearl Harbor" that would leave U.S. forces blind and unable to communicate with each other. But he agreed with warnings that such threats could impede U.S. force operations in varying degrees and diminish their effectiveness enough to make a difference in the outcome of battles or even wars.

To illuminate his forecast of credible future threats, O'Hanlon presented a scenario showing how a future U.S.-China confrontation over Taiwan, circa 2015, might be affected by Chinese space systems. The Chinese, he said, could use high-energy lasers, nuclear-armed missiles, and microsatellites to blind or destroy U.S. satellites that provide broadband communications, battlespace intelligence, and real-time targeting data. The Chinese might be able to use their own intelligence satellites to provide real-time information on the location of U.S. Navy carriers and other warships, so that China could target them with cruise missiles and ballistic missiles. O'Hanlon wrote that it was unlikely that such measures could prevent U.S. forces from defending Taiwan or inflicting a crushing defeat on Chinese forces if they attempted to invade Taiwan. But they could enable China to impose higher losses on U.S. and Taiwanese forces.

On the question of what the United States should do in response to these potential space threats, O'Hanlon rejected arguments for a ban on all forms of militarizing space. He portrayed such an arms-control effort as politically infeasible, given the onward march of technology and competing national interests. He also disagreed that the United States should unilaterally forswear space technologies and capabilities that might someday be important to national security. O'Hanlon dismissed, as premature and not cost-effective, U.S. efforts to militarize space with antisatellite capabilities and space-based weapons. For example, he explained that strike systems based in space would offer no advantages over cheaper military ground-based systems, such as tactical aircraft and missiles. He judged that future adversaries would not be launching so many satellites in the next few years that the U.S. military must quickly acquire high-tech weapons for shooting them down. Instead, O'Hanlon endorsed a moderate, gradual effort to preserve U.S. space domination as long as possible and to shore up U.S. military capabilities in specific areas where threats are imminent, while delaying the militarization of space as long as possible. He favored relatively inexpensive steps to harden U.S. satellites and communications systems against jamming and electronic attack, and to provide a reserve capacity so that replacement satellites could be launched quickly if some were destroyed. He endorsed a hedging strategy of research and development on ASAT systems, so that the United States could deploy them quickly should they become necessary. He favored limited arms control agreements in such specific areas as controlling the pace of ASAT development and policing debris in space.

Advocates of arms control may disagree with O'Hanlon's rejection of sweeping proposals for preventing militarization of space. Advocates of major increases in U.S. spending for space may disagree with his appeals for moderation and gradualism in pursuing new space technologies and weapons, including ASAT systems. O'Hanlon's arguments are most likely to find greatest acceptance at the center of the political spectrum, where participants typically try to balance pragmatic approaches to defense preparedness and arms control. Regardless of how O'Hanlon's specific assessments and recommendations are appraised, his book does a good job of highlighting an emerging area where new technologies and new threats create new imperatives to make hard decisions regarding U.S. defense goals and spending priorities.

O'Hanlon's book focuses on the military uses of space, but he recognizes that the proliferation of many other types of satellites into space has been accelerating the information revolution as well as globalization. This trend is drawing previously remote regions of the world closer together and greatly increasing the global reservoir of scientific and technical knowledge about weather, navigation, natural resources, climate, and other key issues. In this larger sense, the use of space is a neo-Kantian activity that helps promote global progress and economic prosperity, even if the growing presence of military activities in space poses problems of its own.

Thomas Friedman: Accelerating Economic Globalization

In 2005, Thomas Friedman updated his earlier look at globalization (*The Lexus and the Olive Tree*) with a new book that addressed how economic globalization had been accelerating and spreading into new regions as a result of burgeoning commercial business activities that cut across national and continental boundaries.[7] In *The World Is Flat: A Brief History of the Twenty-first Century*, Friedman declared that although public attention since 2001 has been focused on the war on terror and Iraq, an important dynamic that has mostly escaped public notice is the flowering of economic globalization via new information-age business practices.[8] Economic globalization, Friedman said, is entering a new and exciting third stage that he called "Globalization 3.0." Whereas earlier stages were manifested by growing trade and telecommunications, the new stage is propelled by the Internet and the new forms of international business activities it makes possible.

Focusing on economic changes in China and India, Friedman nonetheless claimed global importance for his thesis. Where other writers have viewed economic globalization as mainly confined to trade and investment among wealthy countries, Friedman argued that it is now spreading to underdeveloped countries such as China and India, thereby providing them growing opportunities to profit by using their comparative advantages to compete in the world economy. The world is now "flat," Friedman said, because accelerating globalization has allowed many new producers and exporters to enter the global marketplace; thus, the old hierarchical world economy is giving way to an increasingly level playing field. New countries as well as multinational corporations have a growing capacity to produce, market, sell, and buy valuable products. Individuals are now using information networks and related software to act as business entities on their own. International commerce is thus sweeping over the world economy, driving it in new directions that have economic, political, and strategic impact.

Friedman states his provocative thesis as follows:

We are entering a phase where we are going to see the digitization, virtualization, and automation of almost everything. The gains in productivity will be staggering for those countries, companies, and individuals who can absorb the new technological tools. . . . [M]ore people than ever before in the history of the world are going to have access to these tools—as innovators, as collaborators, and alas, even as terrorists. . . . [T]he real information revolution is about to begin. . . . [T]his new era of globalization will prove to be such a difference of degree that it will be seen, in time, as a difference in kind. . . . Everywhere you turn, hierarchies are being challenged from below or transforming themselves from top-down structures into more horizontal and collaborative ones.[9]

Forecasting that new political, social, and business models will emerge at a faster pace than ever before, Friedman ascribed this sweeping, disruptive new era of globalization to several causes. For example, he writes, the collapse of communism and other command economies was partly triggered by the appearance of computers, communications systems, and information networks. The appearance of fiber optics, the Internet, the World Wide Web, and popular, easy-to-use commercial browsers such as Netscape gave people the ability to surf the Internet and to gather and share documents, files, and information of all kinds, even with distant parties. The development of high-speed interoperable work-flow software enabled businesses to integrate performance of multiple functions on computers, permitted multinational businesses in widely separated areas to collaborate, and facilitated global research that increased scientific progress. Self-organizing collaborative communities have been enabled by use of open-source software, where the source code—the underlying programming instructions that make a piece of software work—is made publicly and freely available so that anyone might test it, use it, and improve it. Another cause of the new era of globalization, wrote Friedman, has been the practice of offshoring, or moving major integrated functions to another country to take advantage of lower labor and healthcare costs, lower taxes, subsidized energy, and other advantages.

Friedman argued that these forces have facilitated a convergence of new economic players, a new playing field, and new processes and habits of horizontal collaboration, and thus brought about a new global economy. Because the world economy is now increasingly anchored in information and knowledge, people possessing education, skills, and connectivity are positioned to succeed and to increase their wealth. Those lacking these assets, warned Friedman, will face trouble. Friedman singled out China and India as active participants in the globalizing world economy through creation of skilled workforces, foreign investments, insourcing, outsourcing, offshoring, exports, imports, and related activities. While Friedman acknowledged that only small portions of the populations and economies of these two countries are as yet affected, he predicted continuing and substantial growth for both China and India because they have become skilled players in the globalizing, information-age world economy.

In the second part of his book, Friedman addressed the implications of these accelerating trends in global business practices. A connected and collaborative global economy will, he argued, bring major changes to economics, government, and politics. A major consequence will be what he called "multiple identity disorders," as new economic dynamics disrupt old allegiances, cultural values, ties to nation-states, and reliance upon governmental policies. Many countries will face pressures to alter how their governments and economies operate, even as they also discover incentives to regulate the global economic dynamics that affect their destinies. As a consequence, domestic politics may change, pitting new political parties that favor free trade and openness against those opposing it.

Friedman was relatively optimistic about the United States, provided it continues to embrace free trade and does not revert to protectionism. While he acknowledged that outsourcing, offshoring, and importing result in some job losses, he argued that these losses are offset by their benefits, including a growing world economy, profitable U.S. investments overseas, job-creating foreign investments on U.S. soil, increased exports, and new foreign markets in countries whose growing wealth enables them to buy American-made products. The United States can feel confident, he said, because its economy is vigorous, its workforce is productive, and its laws foster capitalism. The key to success will be a focus on retaining U.S. comparative advantages in creating knowledge-based products, but he warned that the United States nevertheless faces serious challenges. One challenge is to provide continuing education and retraining for its blue-collar workforce, which will need to possess technical skills suited to the new economy. It must increase its emphasis on research and development in science and technology, and educate greater numbers of mathematicians, engineers, and scientists. These are areas in which, he warned, growing troubles could result in loss of the U.S. competitive edge.

Friedman offered a mixed appraisal of the prospects facing underdeveloped countries. Countries that are creating modern governments and market economies and that are open to involvement in the world economy would, he predicted, mostly prosper in a flat world; these include China, India, South Korea, Singapore, and Russia. Poor countries that cling to traditionalism and resist the imperatives of change will likely remain poor, and might even see their prosperity decline as their export markets are taken over by rivals—such as, for example, China, which threatens to displace Mexico from much of the export market in the United States. The Middle East faces critical difficulties because its authoritarian politics and traditional religious values do not suit it well for the changing global economy, and Latin America is also struggling, although it has made some progress toward democracy and market economies in recent decades. Friedman had little to say about impoverished Africa, where information-age business practices have not yet made much of an appearance.

In surveying the implications for geopolitics, Friedman predicted that accelerating globalization and a flattening world economy will tend to promote peace and stability, because many countries will need to preserve peace in order to maintain the complex supply chains upon which their economic growth depends. In addition, he said, as more countries become middle class in wealth, they will be more satisfied and less prone to challenge the status quo: wealth breeds contentment, which yields peace. Friedman did not offer this as inevitable: several developments could partly or wholly derail globalization, including protectionism in Western countries, radical Islamic fundamentalism that rejects economic modernization, depressions and recessions, or wars involving many countries and regions. His book closed with a call for governments to make the necessary internal changes, and also to collaborate with one another so that the benefits of a flattening, globalizing world economy could be broadly realized. He urged governmental efforts to soften the negative humanitarian impacts of globalization, and he called upon the antiglobalization movement to focus on measures aimed at channeling globalization in constructive directions, rather than hoping to derail it entirely.

One of the strengths of Friedman's book is that it reintroduces globalization and international business practices into the public debate, adding a measure of neo-Kantian optimism to help counterbalance growing worry arising from the war on terror and other geopolitical stresses of recent years. Friedman seems correct in arguing that the world economy is mostly performing well in today's world, showing solid overall growth and no recent recessions or financial shocks to parallel those of the late 1990s. His arguments seem sound when he asserts that expanding information networks, communications, multinational business collaborations, interlocking trade and investment patterns, international supply chains, and other trends play important roles in propelling this global growth. In offering many details on new business relationships, Friedman's book helps illuminate this subject for a broad audience.

Critics are likely to fault Friedman, however, for oversimplifying and exaggerating in his tendency to portray China and India as leaders of economic globalization. China and India may be important economic players, but globalization still has by far its largest impact on the world's wealthy economies, including the United States, Europe, and Japan. Together, China and India account for only about 15 percent of global GDP and, despite booming economic growth in coastal areas, both have huge populations that are still mostly poor. Even if they could sustain rapid growth rates until 2020, their per capita GDP would still be likely to fall short of that of middle-class countries (about $5,000 annually), and they might not attain that status for another 20 years afterward. Judged on a per capita basis, some other underdeveloped countries are making as much progress as China and India.

Both also face major challenges in reforming their governments so as to realize the benefits of globalization for their entire societies. China remains an authoritarian country with a communist government and an economy that is still mostly state-run. India is a democracy, but its governmental bureaucracy remains inefficient in many areas. The economic growth of these two countries will not necessarily transform them into guardians of stable cooperative geopolitical relationships. Friedman says little about China's assertive stance toward Taiwan and East Asian security affairs, nor about India's struggles with Pakistan as well as China. He implies that their greater prosperity in the flattening world economy will constrain both countries, and others like them, from transgressing in the geopolitical arena. History shows, however, that economics does not govern geopolitics, and sometimes economics produces wars of its own. China's growing dependence on imported oil, natural gas, and other resources could, for example, cause it to act as a menace in the region from the Persian Gulf to East Asia. If it tries to support oil-producing dictatorships in the Persian Gulf, or to seize physical control of the Straits of Malacca and the Taiwan Strait, the result could be trouble for the United States and many democratic partners.

At times, Friedman seems to imply that growing commercial business collaboration is a natural development sustained by its own dynamic, but in fact this is possible only if governmental policies permit it. Friedman devotes little attention to how the WTO and regional trade bodies have helped encourage these trends, or how new policies by the World Bank, IMF, and other multilateral bodies could contribute. Nor does Friedman discuss the growing backlash to globalization, markets, and democratization evident in Venezuela and elsewhere. The great black hole of Friedman's optimistic portrayal is the Middle East and surrounding regions, where economic globalization is not working the wonders he describes and is not even an important dynamic. Instead, key parts of several Arab cultures seem to regard globalization as an alien menace created by decadent Western countries to undermine Islamic values and social order. Many countries of these regions are locked into political authoritarianism, ineffective governments, unproductive workforces, stagnant economies, and frustrated populations. Several are breeding grounds for terrorism. While these countries are not, perhaps, being victimized by globalization, they clearly are not benefiting from it either. As Friedman acknowledges, globalization and a flattening world economy do not seem likely to provide a source of salvation for the Middle East and the Islamic world any time soon. If the Middle East remains a festering source of terrorism, WMD proliferation, and other dangers, the world will become less flat, or at least less peaceful, than Friedman's predictions suggest.

Peter Ackerman and Jack DuVall: The Politics of Nonviolent Struggle

In their 2000 book, *A Force More Powerful: A Century of Nonviolent Conflict*, Ackerman and DuVall examined an important political instrument that could help dissolve oppressive governments and usher in democracy and human rights in the 21st century.[10] They offered an in-depth examination of how 20th-century civic resistance movements used nonviolent tactics—such as strikes, boycotts, civil disobedience, and mass protests—to put pressure on repressive rulers, and in some cases compelled them to reform or even toppled them entirely. Ackerman and DuVall did not portray nonviolent movements as the cure for undemocratic rule everywhere, but they did show how and when these efforts have succeeded by employing pragmatic strategies aimed at achievable political goals. They also made a strong case that modern communications and information systems are empowering and magnifying the capacity of nonviolent movements to bring coercive pressure against entrenched authoritarian governments and thus to undermine their popular legitimacy. The authors offered 12 case studies, of which 4 are especially relevant to the modern era: the Russian revolution of 1905, Gandhi's protest against British rule of India in the 1920s and 1930s, Solidarity's protest against Poland's communist government in the 1970s and 1980s, and opposition to South Africa's apartheid in the 1980s and 1990s.

The first case was the outbreak of popular protest against tsarist rule of Russia in 1905. Disruptions such as marches and strikes led by intellectuals, activists, and urban workers were aimed not at toppling tsarist rule, as Ackerman and DuVall wrote, but at urging democratic and economic reforms. Initially, the government responded with violence, but it eventually offered limited reforms, such as a stronger role for the Duma (parliament) and other elements of constitutional monarchy, plus economic changes aimed at faster industrialization, greater economic growth, and a more equitable distribution of wealth. However, after violent street battles instigated by Bolsheviks, the tsar took a stronger hold again and remained for the next decade or so in command of a monarchical and authoritarian government. Economic growth stalled, and the public at large was not significantly better off. This lack of progress along with three years of brutal losses in World War I set the stage for the revolution that overthrew the tsar in 1917. In this violent insurrection, democratic leaders were overtaken by the Bolsheviks led by Lenin, Trotsky, and others. A bloody civil war resulted in a totalitarian communist government whose oppression far exceeded that of the tsar. The lesson drawn by Ackerman and DuVall is that when civic movements succumb to violent tactics, even if they are successful at seizing power, they risk reinforcing or worsening the ills of dictatorship.

Ackerman and DuVall argue that although violent revolution did succeed in toppling governments in Russia and China during the 20th century, it often fails, because entrenched governments typically can muster more military power than can revolutionaries. For this reason, they argued, nonviolent revolutions often stand a better chance of succeeding because they avoid confronting governments in their areas of strength and instead undermine them in areas where they are potentially vulnerable. Such movements, even though nonviolent, may nevertheless be coercive, by employing such tactics as mass protests, strikes, economic boycotts, public information campaigns, and legal maneuvers, all aimed at damaging the capacity of governments to operate effectively and undercutting their legitimacy in the eyes of the public. The types of strategies employed by the opposition and the government greatly affect the outcome. Typically, wrote Ackerman and DuVall, such struggles unfold over a period of years and even decades. Governments can sometimes defuse opposition through a combination of counterpressures and reforms, but sometimes they may lose leverage in the face of growing power by the civilian-based movements.

The modern model of nonviolent action, wrote Ackerman and DuVall, is Mohandas K. Gandhi's challenge to British colonial rule of India in the 1920s and 1930s. Opposition to British rule began to emerge shortly after World War I, when the Indian Party Congress, known for its moderation, endorsed the goal of Indian home rule through constitutional reform. Gandhi, a lawyer, emerged as an unconventional leader of a growing nationalist movement that spread across the country. While Gandhi's ultimate goal was self-rule and independence for India, Ackerman and DuVall said, he realized that the process would be gradual and time-consuming. Accordingly, he sought first to change India's civil society through such measures as lessening of the caste system, increasing the cooperation of Hindus and Muslims, and improving care for the poor. As Indian society became mobilized under his guidance, he sought to pressure British rulers into granting a series of concessions aimed at enlarging Indian control over local government and laws. Although riots and other forms of violence periodically erupted outside his control, Gandhi's principles for confronting the British were strictly nonviolent. Among his tactics were resignations of Indian civil servants, refusal to pay taxes, civil disobedience against laws deemed unjust, mass protests, occupation of government buildings, blockage of traffic, and picketing. The goal was to weaken Britain's capacity to govern India, to heighten the cost of preserving India as part of the British Empire, and to undermine the legitimacy of British rule among the Indian people. At key junctures, Ackerman and DuVall wrote, Gandhi proved willing to negotiate with British rulers and to strike bargains with them, agreeing to decreases in civil disobedience in exchange for British reforms. British concessions were often followed by a period of renewed crackdown, but gradually British control weakened. World War II was decisive; it left a badly damaged Britain focused on its own recovery and unable to preserve its empire. In 1947, in a culmination of Gandhi's strategy, India and Pakistan were granted independence.

The third case is that of the Solidarity movement in Poland, which erupted in 1980–1981. It originated in 1970, when Polish shipyard workers went on strike against increases in food prices imposed by the communist government under Prime Minister Wladyslaw Gomulka. The crisis was settled only after police shot some workers at a shipyard gate in Gdansk, killing 4 and wounding 15. Order was restored when the government backed down on the price increases, and the situation was mostly stable for the next several years as Poland's economy went through a period of growth. In 1976, however, food prices again were raised, shipyard workers again went on strike, and again, after violence in the streets, the crisis was settled after police restored order and the price increases were rolled back. But organizers had begun developing permanent committees to build support for future confrontations with the government. Among their tactics was the printing and circulation of journal articles, books, and pamphlets criticizing the government, and creation of a "Flying University" of lecturers to lead discussions of political issues with small groups across the country.

When economic conditions turned bad again in early 1980, Ackerman and DuVall wrote, the government resorted to price increases as well as wage freezes. The arrest of a popular workers' leader, Anna Walentynowicz, triggered outrage; the core organization that would become Solidarity was born. Led by Lech Walesa, the organization started with workers at the Gdansk dockyards who were enraged by the failure of the trade unions that were created and staffed by the government to represent them fairly. Their group's main demand was for free trade unions, led by workers, that could negotiate with the government for terms favorable to workers. Solidarity was not seeking to overthrow communist rule in Poland. Aware that earlier violent protests had triggered repressive crackdowns, Walesa and others emphasized nonviolent discipline, but their strategy was nonetheless confrontational, aimed at pressuring the government into concessions. In August 1980, shipyard workers at Gdansk and other places went on strike, occupying dockyard buildings and public gathering places. The government came under pressure from its Soviet overlords to end the strike, but the workers' leaders refused to make concessions on the demand for free trade unions. The government capitulated to the workers. Within this new space in Polish society, Solidarity grew rapidly and soon had 10 million members. By early 1981, tensions were again rising: protests were spreading across the country, and membership in the Polish Communist Party was falling. The Soviet government perceived Solidarity to be a threat to socialist rule, and it began a series of menacing military exercises that were a transparent reminder that what had happened to Hungary in 1956 and to Czechoslovakia in 1968 could happen to Poland, too. Poland's Prime Minister Wojciech Jaruzelski, fearful of losing economic support from Western nations, made further concessions during 1981, but they were not enough to quell the growing protests by a population that had begun to question not only economic policies and political rights, but the very legitimacy of communist rule as well. By December 1981, Jaruzelski's government struck back, imposing martial law on Poland and imprisoning Walesa and his fellow Solidarity leaders.

For the moment, Ackerman and DuVall wrote, the Communist Party seemed to have regained its capacity to govern while avoiding a Soviet invasion. But the confrontation with Solidarity had changed Polish society and exposed vulnerabilities in the dictatorship. Solidarity went underground, where its leaders continued to agitate, and other opposition groups formed. Pope John Paul II, a Pole, encouraged a revival of Catholicism in Poland, which further undermined communist rule. Poland's economy continued to deteriorate, thus provoking further dissatisfaction with communist rule. In early 1988, a new set of government-decreed price increases provoked a new wave of strikes. The government started negotiations with the workers, but it was rapidly losing legitimacy and power. In April 1989, the government was compelled to permit free trade unions, expanded freedom of press, an independent judiciary, and parliamentary elections. In June 1989, Solidarity overwhelmed the Communist Party in national elections, and communist rule of

Poland was finished. It would soon be finished across all of Eastern Europe, and then in the Soviet Union as well.

Ackerman and DuVall gave much of the credit for this stunning outcome to Walesa and Solidarity. Although they noted that it sometimes made mistakes by overplaying its hand, they credited Solidarity with using skillful strategies to expand workers' rights and political freedoms, and thus ultimately with the destruction of communist rule. Moreover, Ackerman and DuVall concluded, by emphasizing nonviolent conduct, Walesa and Solidarity helped create a Polish civil society that proved capable of constructing democracy in its place.

Ackerman and DuVall's examination of the battle to end apartheid in South Africa focused on the role of nonviolent action in a setting that saw considerable violence between 1977 and 1994. South Africa had been organized on a principle of strict racial segregation, dividing European whites (just 20 percent of the population), from Indians or "colored," a small minority, and black Africans, the large disenfranchised majority, many of whom lived in economic squalor. Under the inspiration of Nelson Mandela, imprisoned from 1964 to 1990, and cleric Desmond Tutu, protest against apartheid was led by two political groups: the African National Congress and the United Democratic Front. Initially, black agitation was met by severe repression from the regime, but over a period of years, such actions as mass protests, boycotts, strikes, civil disobedience, and local community-building gained growing public support and gradually wore down the regime. International opposition such as trade sanctions increased the pressure, especially during years when the South African economy was not performing well. An advantage possessed by black Africans was that they performed many key jobs in the mining and manufacturing industries and elsewhere, and they also were the purchasers of many of the products sold by white businesses. Slowly they gained such rights as unions and better living conditions, but during "state emergencies," many blacks were still arbitrarily imprisoned and denied legal rights such as trial by jury. Finally, a new South African president and the regime's white business supporters concluded that apartheid was no longer sustainable. A political deal was reached in which black Africans would gain majority rule but the rights of the white minority would be respected. In national elections in 1994, the African National Congress won 60 percent of the vote, and Nelson Mandela was elected president by the parliament.

Ackerman and DuVall presented other case studies to buttress their claims for the effectiveness of nonviolent resistance, including Danish and Dutch resistance to the Nazis in World War II; resistance campaigns in El Salvador, Argentina, and Chile; the restoration of Philippine democracy; the

American civil rights movement; and the Palestinian Intifada. In these cases, the authors argued, nonviolent action could succeed because it built public support, weakened the legitimacy of the regime, and relied on skillful strategies aimed at undermining economic and military support for the dominant regime. In many cases, they wrote, modern communications and information systems aided movements that otherwise might have been isolated and fragmented by the regime. Ackerman and DuVall also made the argument that nonviolent conduct fosters civic discipline and experience in democratic organizing among the mass public, whereas violent insurrection may set the stage for new authoritarianism after the regime has been overthrown. They concluded that victory can be achieved through nonviolent mass action by unified civic movements, and that their case studies disprove the notion that violence is always necessary to defeat an oppressor or win rights.

The question that their book suggests is: What are the prospects for nonviolent action in the early 21st century in countries and regions where oppressive regimes still hold power? Ackerman and DuVall pointed out that the way in which Polish resistance to the Soviet Union spread across almost all of Eastern Europe in the late 1980s to end communist rule suggested that civilian-led revolutions may sometimes spread elsewhere to topple other authoritarian governments. Similarly, hopes grew elsewhere in 2004–2005, when democratic protest groups had success in Ukraine, Georgia, Lebanon, and Kyrgyzstan (although some of these successes have since turned sour). Authoritarian governments are now seeking to suppress nonviolent movements by limiting the activities of Western NGOs who support democracy-building and by shrinking the space in which indigenous civil society groups can operate. It is unclear how well they will succeed. Such questions will be crucial in the Middle East and Central Asia, where many repressive regimes rule and the need for democratization is apparent, but the danger is significant that rebellions could produce equally bad regimes. The spread of modern communications and information systems in these and other regions may, however, help tilt the odds more in favor of nonviolent protests. The book by Ackerman and DuVall shows that nonviolent resistance can succeed when it is carried out strategically, although it may have a hard time against authoritarian regimes that employ repression sparingly, defuse protests with minimal concessions, and generate enough economic growth to retain public legitimacy.

Kent E. Calder: Defense and Security Affairs in Asia

Whereas Europe's growing stability and unity have removed a longstanding danger, and the greater Middle East's chaotic affairs are clearly a major source of threats, Asia's future direction is uncertain. The Asian region has been empowered both by the overall globalization process and by increasingly strong regional economic ties. The new economic strength of the region has made its stability even more vital to American interests. If Asia can be rendered peaceful and stable, this will contribute greatly to global progress, but if it slides into turmoil as a result of geopolitical tensions, the result could present the United States and its allies with the Herculean task of handling security tensions in both the Middle East and Asia concurrently.

Asia's future is problematic not only because its security system is highly fragmented—the region lacks a collective security structure—but also because new technologies are having a profound impact there. Modern information networks have bonded countries into increasingly tight communications. Growing economies allow many countries to pursue more ambitious agendas than in the past. Asian military forces are also becoming stronger and more technologically sophisticated, magnifying the capacities of many Asian countries and enhancing their ability to project their powers across the region and beyond. These changes further complicate efforts to predict where Asia is headed.

Although public attention has focused recently on North Korea's pursuit of nuclear weapons and delivery systems, Asia's future will be shaped by a broader set of security issues. Much will depend upon how Asia's major powers, especially China and Japan, interact not only in economic affairs but in security and defense affairs as well. Over the course of one or two decades, this interaction has great potential to alter the Asian security system. Whether the effects will be good or ill is hard to determine, but they will be critical for the Asian region and U.S. security interests, and for global peace and prosperity.

Kent E. Calder's 1996 book, *Pacific Defense: Arms, Energy, and America's Future in Asia,* was one of the first comprehensive efforts to bring this complex subject into focus.[11] Many of his propositions continue to have resonance a decade later. Calder steered away from the temptation to brand North Korea and China as future enemies and the sole cause of troubles. He also avoided the polar-opposite temptation of portraying Asia's booming economic progress and integration as a guarantee that future regional security and defense affairs would be stable and peaceful. Calder viewed the entire Asian security system as a powerful variable in the strategic calculus. He drew particular attention to emerging Asian defense affairs, including the empowering impact of new military technologies.

The tone of Calder's book differed significantly from the optimistic analyses put forth by such neo-Kantians as Thomas Friedman. His basic thesis was that the emerging Asian security system might have the potential to descend into unstable balance-of-power rivalries of the sort that wrecked Europe during the late 19th and early 20th centuries. Calder did not question the influence of Asia's booming economies on the strategic priorities of regional powers. He acknowledged that practically all Asian countries, including China and Japan, are pursuing regional trade and foreign investments to power their economic growth. Asia's regional economic system, operating increasingly independently of the globalizing world economy, is bringing Asian countries closer to each other. But he dismissed optimism that this economic trend might be a harbinger of stability and peace in security affairs, much less a source of multilateral political integration. He pointed out that a century ago, Europe experienced comparable economic integration but descended into geopolitical rivalry and war for political reasons that transcended economics. Asia, Calder said, is vulnerable to the same dynamic, especially along the "arc of crisis" in Northeast Asia.

Calder portrayed the competitiveness of Asian economics as a potential source of geopolitical rivalry. Almost all modernizing Asian economies will need access to assured energy supplies, especially oil and natural gas, for continued economic growth. This requirement, he said, makes Asian countries potential rivals over access to cheap Persian Gulf oil and over control of the lengthy sealanes from the Persian Gulf to East Asia, including the vital Straits of Malacca and other critical waters in Southeast Asia. In addition, interstate competition could arise over large oil deposits in the East China Sea and the South China Sea. Moreover, Asia's principal countries, especially China and Japan, have long histories of viewing each other in terms of fear, rivalry, and domination. Calder warned that these two emerging powers might be on a collision course over control of Asia's future. Others in the region, including Russia, India, North and South Korea, Taiwan, Australia, Indonesia, and Vietnam, view security in national terms, not in terms of multilateral cooperation. All of them are growing in strategic power as their economies expand. As a result, he concluded, a complex Asian security system composed of multiple major powers, including India, could lead to multipolar geopolitical maneuvering, instability, and war.

Calder dismissed Asia's existing multilateral economic and security institutions such as ASEAN, the APEC forum, and the Asian Regional Forum, calling them far too weak to contain nationalist rivalries and unstable security affairs. Asian military affairs and technological trends will be key variables in the strategic calculus. Asia was not motivated to disarm, as Europe was, by the end of the Cold War. The growing wealth of virtually all countries is instead enabling them to elevate their defense spending in ways that may eventually have profound strategic consequences. A source of potential instability arises as Asian countries use new information technologies to reshape their militaries. They will try to take advantage of these technologies to achieve the ability to project power outside their borders and thus to influence regional security trends. As of 1996, when Calder wrote, this trend was already well under way, and it seems likely to accelerate as more countries become rich enough to purchase new technologies and weapons.

Calder identified nuclear proliferation as an especially menacing trend. While acknowledging the dangers of North Korea's pursuit of nuclear weapons, he argued that it is destined to collapse and give rise to a unified Korea under the Republic of Korea. This successor state might itself choose to be a nuclear power because it is surrounded by China, Russia, and Japan. A greater danger, he warned, is that China, already a nuclear power with small forces, may expand its nuclear arsenal and strengthen its conventional forces to enhance its strategic and military leverage across Asia. Fear of China's emergence as a coercive nuclear power, Calder wrote, seems likely to push technologically sophisticated Japan across the threshold into deploying its own nuclear weapons and delivery systems in an effort to protect itself and its regional interests. To Calder, the prospect of China and Japan engaged in nuclear competition, with nuclear-armed Russia, India, and Korea in the background, spelled trouble.

Calder also pointed to destabilizing trends in conventional military forces and technologies: China, Japan, Korea, and other countries are poised to gain access to the space systems, technical intelligence assets, and communications networks that make the U.S. military capable of modern strike operations. Calder foresaw future rivalries in naval, air, and missile forces, although perhaps not in ground forces. Disagreeing with those who believe that China would continue to be a mainland power as it had historically been, he pointed out that it was already trying to build a blue-water navy with submarines, surface combatants, amphibious craft, lethal missiles, and perhaps eventually small aircraft carriers. While China intends this blue-water navy for protection of its long coast, it might also give China the ability to coerce Taiwan, control oil in Asian waters, or intimidate foreign navies, including that of the United States.

This trend, wrote Calder, would inevitably threaten Japan's ability to control the sea lines of communication and trade routes that link Northeast Asia to Southeast Asia and the Persian Gulf. Thus, Japan would have a powerful motive to build a blue-water navy of its own, with submarines, surface combatants, and even carrier battlegroups capable of projecting power across East Asian waters. This, in turn, could push other Asian countries to bolster their own naval forces for self-defense. Calder saw a trend toward an Asian naval arms race already under way in 1996, and he expected it to accelerate in future years as Asian countries become wealthier.

Calder portrayed similar trends in Asian air and missile forces. Many Asian countries are quietly buying significant numbers of modern combat aircraft for air defense and strike missions. The acquisition of sophisticated command, control, communications, computers, intelligence, surveillance, and reconnaissance (C^4ISR) systems, smart munitions, and long-range missiles would make these modernizing air forces even stronger and more lethal, capable of offensive strike missions against countries far beyond their borders. China and Japan were triggering this Asian arms race in air weaponry, but Calder argued that modernization and competition were spreading to other countries as well. In summarizing these strategic developments, Calder sketched an Asian security system bristling with growing naval and air forces that would give many countries offensive power and long-range strike capabilities, making them able to inflict great damage on potential military and civilian targets. Such future military forces and capabilities, he said, in a setting of fluid geopolitical maneuvering would create a highly dangerous Asian security system prone to the kinds of rivalries, confrontations, and crises that historically afflicted Europe.

For many years, Calder said, the principal hope for Asian stability has been the United States, which has the role of protecting Japan and other countries, deterring North Korea, and dissuading China while peacefully integrating it into the Asian security system. However, said Calder, the United States cannot go on performing this demanding role forever. One reason is that the American economic and military advantage is diminishing as Asian countries grow stronger. Another reason is that the United States is likely to grow reluctant to continue to bear major security responsibilities in Asia as the American public starts to see Asia as a source of unfair burdensharing and unfair trade practices. A decline of American power, said Calder, would remove a key foundation of stability. This development would liberate China, an increasingly nationalist and rising power led by an autocratic government, and allow it to begin throwing its weight around. Japan would be motivated to abandon its current emphasis on economics and increasingly assert its power in regional security affairs in order to counterbalance China and protect its own interests. These developments could motivate other countries, fearing for their own safety, to begin thinking and acting in similar terms.

In the final chapter of his book, Calder offered several policy principles intended to help the United States cope with Asia's troubled future in an era when multilateral security institutions will not provide reliable solutions. He urged the United States to treat both economics and security affairs in Asia as equally important, rather than to assume that economic progress would solve security problems. He called for the United States to remain active in Asian security affairs and to maintain a strong military presence there. He urged attention to Asia's energy needs and U.S. encouragement of multilateral co-operation among Asian countries. The task of shoring up U.S.-Japanese security ties in spite of growing strains, said Calder, is imperative so that they can perform new security missions together and preserve their cooperation. He also urged U.S. attention to the Korean Peninsula and even-handed treatment of China. He urged that the U.S. Government, business community, and academic community should all become more knowledgeable about Asia's underlying dynamics and future trends. None of these steps would ensure a peaceful future in a big, dynamic region that the United States may be able only to influence, not to control. But, he said, they may help tilt the odds toward stability, while helping the United States protect its interests even if the future proves stormy.

When it was published in 1996, Calder's book was inconsistent with the policy premises of observers who tended to see Asia's future mainly in terms of economic cooperation. The Clinton administration's security policies in Asia mainly focused on reaffirming U.S. commitments to Japan and South Korea, pressuring North Korea not to acquire nuclear weapons, and sending aircraft carriers to warn China not to attack Taiwan. When the Bush administration took power in 2001, its views were closer to Calder's, but it initially focused on China as a potential adversary, not seeing the entire Asian security system as a source of trouble. Since September 11, 2001, U.S. attention to Asia has declined as it has become preoccupied with the war on terror in the greater Middle East. Relations with China have improved, and U.S. attention to Asia has been devoted mainly to North Korea's nuclear ambitions. But in future years, a growing focus on Asia seems inevitable for many of the reasons cited by Calder: its growing economic power, scarce energy supplies, political animosities, multipolar rivalries, and modernizing military technologies.

Today, experts are likely to offer diverse opinions of Calder's book. Optimists about Asia's future, such as Thomas Friedman, might say that Calder was too engrossed in Asia's security problems and paid insufficient attention to economic and political forces that are integrating Asia and pushing it toward peaceful progress. Pessimists are likely to say that Calder was on target then, and remains so today, although negative trends may be unfolding slower than he expected. Both would have to agree that, while Calder's specific arguments were contentious, he successfully identified key issues that remain alive today. Some of the military trends that he forecast are slowly emerging, such as North Korea's stubborn quest for nuclear weapons and China's accelerating military modernization. Others, such as Japan becoming a nuclear power with an imperial navy, have yet to appear. Only some of Calder's political forecasts have come to life. A hopeful evaluation is that, provided the United States continues to carry out assertive policies in Asia of the sort recommended by Calder and others, the region's most dangerous potential dynamics can be restrained. Yet there can be little question that if Calder's worries prove accurate, the threats facing the United States and its allies will multiply.

Jessica Stern: Religious Terrorists

Jessica Stern's 1999 book, *The Ultimate Terrorists*, focused on the threat that terrorists might use weapons of mass destruction against their targets.[12] In her widely acclaimed book of 2002, *Terror in the Name of God: Why Religious Militants Kill*, she set out to explain the underlying reasons why religious militants resort to violent terrorism in the name of their religious values.[13] She argued that modern-day terrorism is being empowered by religious intoxication and hatred and is being magnified by modern technologies, including information networks that allow terrorist organizations to coordinate their actions and project their power to great distances.

Acknowledging that religious terrorism is inherently evil, Stern urged that its root causes and different manifestations must be understood if it is to be countered and eliminated. Stern defined *terrorism* as an act or threat of violence against noncombatants to create fear and dread to achieve revenge, coercion, intimidation, or other specific political goals. Her argument was that terrorist acts normally are not random or purposeless but are carried out with a specific agenda. While she focused on Middle East terrorism, she also examined other religious terrorists, including right-wing extremists in the United States, al Qaeda terrorists in South Asia, and Islamic fundamentalists in Indonesia. Her book began by examining the motives of individual terrorists and the operations of terrorist organizations. Her methodology relied on abstract reasoning, original analysis and, of particular value, interviews with many terrorists from Islamic fundamentalist groups and others. Her book shed a great deal of light upon a critical and growing threat.

Stern ascribed religious terrorism to a variety of psychological and political motives rather than a single rationale. Many terrorists, she said, are motivated by rejection of the modern world, deep spiritual crises, or combinations of angst, alienation, and humiliation. Many view themselves as victimized by an evil enemy, often the United States or Israel, which threatens their core values, lifestyles, and ambitions. These perceptions, she wrote, may be anchored in reality or may be fantasy or rationalization, including a desire to blame others for their own faults and failures. Some individual terrorists may be motivated by sheer greed for political power, land, or money, and act as sociopath predators rather than as idealists. Regardless of their motives, she said, terrorists view their own religious faith in absolutist terms and regard people who practice other faiths as infidels or sinners. They thus view the world in black-and-white terms, which leads them to act with unambiguous purposes and to undertake "purifying" actions. Because they fear their religious faiths or political goals are in jeopardy, they believe that emergency conditions prevail, and that this makes the killing of innocent victims morally permissible. What unites religious terrorists of all faiths, Stern said, is self-righteous certitude coupled with inflamed anger toward adversaries that results in a lack of empathy for their victims. This produces the ability to kill without remorse or hesitation, even in people who lead otherwise moral lives.

Stern pointed out that such terrorism, driven by spiritual intoxication that perversely results in addiction to violence, is nothing new. In the 1st century, the Zealots-Sicarii group used terrorism to try to incite the Jews against the Greeks and Romans. During 1090–1275, the Assassins seriously threatened the Turkish Empire in Persia and Syria by using terrorism to seek to spread a purified version of Islam. In the late 19th century, Europe was plagued by sensational assassinations: nearly every year during the 1890s, a head of state was killed, including the president of France, the empress of Austria, and the king of Italy. In 1901, U.S. President William McKinley was assassinated. The 1914 assassination of Archduke Ferdinand of Austria at Sarajevo triggered World War I. This legacy, said Stern, shows the persistence of terrorism, its complex emotions, and its recurring use to provoke fear and dread to coerce government and peoples to meet terrorists' demands.

Stern launched her analysis of contemporary religious terrorism by pointing out that it is often anchored in grievances. She examines the issue of why some people respond to these grievances by joining terrorist groups, and why they remain as members, given that life as a terrorist is usually risky and costly. She concludes that terrorists receive offsetting benefits that are partly spiritual, partly emotional, and partly material. For example, some Islamic fundamentalists become terrorists because of the promise of heavenly rewards; others fear punishment in the afterlife if they do not participate in jihad; yet others seek financial rewards for themselves and their families. Some seek adventure, and some want comradeship and approval. Initially, she said, most terrorists are motivated by ideology and altruism. Over time, however, cynicism often takes hold; terrorism becomes a career as much as a passion, and such incentives as thrills or profit, as well as coercion from their peers and social groups, keep terrorists involved.

Stern focused on the specific motives of several different types of terrorists. Looking at right-wing terrorists in the United States who use violence against abortion clinics, she judged that while they may be inspired by genuine hostility to abortion, it is a deep-seated alienation from contemporary American life and culture that makes them willing to join violent cults. The principal motive of Palestinian terrorists in the West Bank and Gaza who join such organizations as Hamas, she said, is anger at being humiliated by their own poverty and by perceived Israeli oppression, U.S.-inspired globalization, secular materialist values, corrupt Western culture, and capitalist commercialism. Such sentiments are shared by other groups, such as Hezbollah and al Qaeda. Some of these terrorists, she said, become suicide bombers because their leaders promise heavenly salvation for themselves and financial rewards for their families. Most, however, do not choose the path of suicide, instead seeking to inflict violence while keeping themselves alive in hope of better days. Islamic terrorists in Indonesia, Stern found, arose amid shifting demographic patterns resulting in clashes between Islamic and Christian or other social groups. Right-wing Israeli terrorists, Stern says, are motivated by history in their attempts to resurrect Jewish temples while destroying Muslim holy sites. Pakistani jihadists are mainly motivated by the Pakistani-Indian struggle over Kashmir.

Stern also examined how religious terrorist groups are organized and operate. She identified a wide spectrum of models, ranging from virtual networks to highly stratified and structured organizations whose leaders act through multiple committees in command of a large, widely dispersed membership. Almost all terrorist organizations, she said, are shaped by the need to be both resilient and capable. Resilience calls for a loose structure, while capability calls for tight organizations. The task of juggling these two imperatives accounts for the variation in approaches.

Key to all terrorist organizations, wrote Stern, is the relationship between inspirational leaders and their followers. In the United States, right-wing terrorist groups are typically "virtual organizations" in which inspirational leaders set the basic ideological tone and agenda, while responsibility for specific actions is decentralized to subgroups, diverse "franchises," and lone-wolf "freelancers." In the Middle East and South Asia, she said, terrorist organizations also rely upon inspirational leaders but tend to be more structured, although they, too, rely on franchises, affiliates, and lone wolves. The pattern of al Qaeda and similar bodies is an elaborate structure, with leaders, commanders, subordinate cadres, committees, training camps, and detailed operational plans. Management committees are responsible for raising funds from diverse sources, recruiting and training terrorists, and coordinating complex operations of the sort carried out against the United States on September 11, 2001. She noted that these terrorist organizations often diversify into organized criminal activities—such as drug trafficking, money laundering, and support for corrupt governments—in order to raise money for their main activity, terrorism. While these terrorist organizations are partly influenced by religious ideology, she said, their cynicism also becomes apparent when they are examined up close. Their leaders may live in luxury; they often recruit poor and ignorant low-level members who are then brainwashed or coerced to carry out the organization's dirty work; and they may shift missions, abandoning one terrorist cause for another to preserve their organizational reasons for being.

Stern portrayed al Qaeda as an extreme form of terrorist organization, with its sophisticated structure, globally deployed assets, and complex, carefully planned operations, manifested in the United States, Europe, the Middle East, Africa, and Asia. She showed how terrorist organizations of this sort rely on modern communications systems, including the Internet, cell and satellite phones, computers, and encryption devices and systems. Thus, al Qaeda and other terrorist groups have information technologies previously available only to wealthy, powerful governments and nation-states. The combination of religious fanaticism and modern technology, she warned, creates a grave danger to world peace that threatens to grow exponentially if such terrorist groups acquire weapons of mass destruction.

Stern recommended some policies to combat religious terrorism, especially that of Islamic fundamentalists. She offered no ready cure for the alienation, humiliation, rage, and spiritual emptiness that seems to infect cultures that are failing to cope with modernity. Instead, she called for efforts to penetrate terrorist groups, to apply law enforcement to them, and to employ military action against them when necessary. But she cautioned against exclusive reliance on military solutions or other forms of suppression. She called for a public diplomacy that challenges the claim of radical Islamic fundamentalism to moral superiority and that portrays Western modernization and culture in a more favorable light. A U.S. foreign policy of "smart geopolitics" should avoid actions that especially inflame Islamic terrorism, such as unquestioning support of Israel, economic sanctions that unduly punish Arab peoples, support for corrupt Arab governments, and a high-profile U.S. military presence in the Persian Gulf and Middle East.

Stern's book is among the best to emerge on this topic since September 11, 2001, because it tried to explain this phenomenon, not just describe it. It gives insight into the sources, motives, and conduct of religious terrorism. It points out that because terrorism is conducted in pursuit of a conscious political agenda—for example, to drive the United States out of the Middle East—it is not, as it is often portrayed, indiscriminate in its use of violence, nor oblivious to negative consequences if its enemies respond forcefully. Her observation that while terrorist leaders often are willing to send their lowest-level cadres to martyrdom and death, they normally want to stay alive themselves and to line their own pocketbooks, may suggest an approach to combat terrorism.

Robert A. Pape: Suicide Bombers

Pape's 2005 book, *Dying to Win: The Strategic Logic of Suicide Terrorism*, provides an important complement to Stern's book and a valuable discussion of the extreme case of an empowered individual, the suicide terrorist.[14] Pape catalogued all 315 identified acts of suicide terrorism from 1980 through 2003. From this data, which he describes as "the first complete universe of suicide terrorist attacks worldwide," Pape drew several important and unexpected conclusions about the nature of suicide terrorism and the appropriate U.S. policy response.[15] Pape sought to explain three fundamental things about suicide terrorism: the strategic logic, the social logic, and the individual logic. He used the data he amassed to highlight characteristics of suicide terrorism and to question conventional wisdom on the subject. He concluded that suicide terrorism is not driven primarily by religious fanaticism in general, nor by Islamic fundamentalism in particular, as Stern implies. Rather, "modern suicide terrorism is best understood as an extreme strategy for national liberation against democracies with troops that pose an imminent threat to control the territory the terrorists feel view as their homeland."[16] This finding contradicts the argument for a U.S. counterterror strategy that focuses on Islamic fundamentalism or that relies on a substantial American military presence in the Middle East.

Acts of suicide terrorism, Pape wrote, overwhelmingly occur as part of a distinct campaign, clustered in time and aimed at specific, stated objectives. Therefore, he says, it is more important to explain the logic of the campaign—the strategic logic—than the logic or motivation of the individual. The database Pape assembled demonstrates that the major objective of every group mounting such a campaign over the last two decades has been to coerce a foreign state that the terrorists see as occupying their homeland to remove its military forces. That is, the goal is nationalist rather than religious. Moreover, the target states have been democracies, which terrorists see as having a low tolerance for the costs their attacks impose and as being constrained from responding brutally to them. An important point is that such attacks seem to work: history shows many cases in which concessions were made in response to suicide campaigns, after which attacks diminished. This suggests that such campaigns will continue in the future (and indeed, the phenomenon has increased since 1980), and that they are not, as some assume, illogical or irrational.

Pape devoted particular attention to an aspect of his findings that some would find counterintuitive: it is not religion, he said, but nationalism stimulated by occupation, that drives terrorism. While he examined the activities and motivations of numerous groups, he looked most closely at al Qaeda, a group whose international nature and clear ties to radical Salafist Islam would seem to contradict this conclusion. Pape argued, however, that al Qaeda's target selection and avowed aims show that its primary goal is to end Western military occupation of Muslim nations, particularly on the Arabian Peninsula. As evidence, he cited al Qaeda's proclamations, from Osama bin Laden and others, that have consistently described evicting the United States and others from Muslim nations as al Qaeda's primary goal. He points out also that al Qaeda has targeted only those Western nations with troops in the Middle East and has offered truces to those that agree to withdraw their troops. It has avoided targeting Israel, which a religiously driven strategy might have suggested as a prime target. Its attacks began only after the 1990–1991 Gulf War, when America's military presence in the Gulf became dominant. Al Qaeda's suicide bombers are overwhelmingly from countries that Western nations could be said to occupy.

Pape did, however, also demonstrate that religion plays a very important role in suicide terrorism. Looking at the social logic of such acts, he explained that the existence of a religious difference between the terrorist group (whether Islamic or otherwise) and the occupying force seems always to be found where there are acts of suicide terrorism. The data show that certain factors are associated with nearly every suicide terrorism campaign: a territory is occupied by a foreign power; the foreign power is of a different religion; and the foreign power is a democracy. Religious difference is important because, Pape argued, a suicide terrorism campaign depends on having a deep and often broad reservoir of popular support. While the occupation of a homeland is itself a provocation for violent action, if the occupying force has a different religion than the citizens of the territory it occupies, terrorist groups can more easily draw a distinct line between "us" and "them." It can stir fears of a risk to the nation's core identity, which is linked more closely to religion, Pape wrote, than to language or any other factor. This dynamic makes it possible to generate the popular support needed to sustain a campaign of suicide terrorism, and in particular, to create a culture of martyrdom. Support for such attacks is all the more likely, according to Pape's data, if they are seen as the last resort against an occupier who has already been resisted by other means.

Pape then delved into what motivates an individual to commit an act of suicide terrorism. The conventional wisdom sees suicide terrorists as mostly poor, uneducated, socially isolated religious fanatics; Pape's findings, however, indicated otherwise. His study of the demographics of suicide bombers shows that they are often secular, relatively well educated, and integrated into society. Many are venerated after their deaths. Pape wrote that their acts are best explained by altruism: the desire to do good for the community. Their posthumous status as martyrs provides clear confirmation to other potential suicide bombers that their final act would be valued by their community.

These findings on the strategic, social, and individual logic of suicide terrorism have potential implications for U.S. policy. Pape proposed a new U.S. strategy that takes into account that America's enemy is not Islamic fundamentalism, and that America is targeted by suicide terrorists not for what it is—its values and culture—but for what it does, specifically, its maintenance of a large military presence in the Middle East. "American military policy in the Persian Gulf was the pivotal factor leading to the 9/11 attacks," Pape wrote; his data led him to conclude that the U.S. presence on the Arabian Peninsula made that and other al Qaeda attacks much more likely.[17] America, he wrote, must find a way to defeat the current generation of terrorists while stopping the development of a new one. It must do so, however, while continuing to look out for its energy interests in the Persian Gulf. Thus, Pape recommended that the United States return to an "off-shore balancing" posture by withdrawing its military forces from the Gulf while maintaining local alliances and the capability to return quickly. This strategy would take into account the fact that offensive military operations are often an ineffective tool for fighting terrorism and that U.S. withdrawal would undercut the main motivation for the current campaign of suicide terrorism. It would also reflect Pape's conclusion that, the salutary effects of democracy notwithstanding, future terrorist recruits will not be dissuaded by heavy-handed Western attempts at remaking Muslim societies.

Throughout the book, Pape tempered his analysis and policy prescriptions with some cautionary notes on the value of his study. While he stood firmly by his analysis of the causes of past suicide terrorism, Pape acknowledged its predictive limits. The nature of suicide terrorism could change, especially as its power to coerce is more widely appreciated, and the threat could arise even in the absence of a struggle to end an occupation by a democratic foreign power with a different religion.

Pape's book leaves some aspects of suicide terrorism and related U.S. policy unaddressed or inadequately examined. It is largely silent on the security tradeoffs America would make if it withdrew from Iraq before that country had a stable government. With a data set that ends in 2003, it does not address the implications of more recent Sunni-Shi'a suicide bombings in Iraq. Describing the U.S. presence in the Persian Gulf from 1992 to 2001 as an "occupation" is a stretch, especially since it looked a lot like his recommended "non-occupying" strategy for the future, involving close alliances and a rapid return capability. Nevertheless, *Dying to Win* is a valuable contribution to the body of literature addressing the question of how to deal with the increasing threat posed by devastatingly empowered groups of suicide terrorists.

Stephen Flynn: Empowerment Makes America Vulnerable

Flynn's 2004 book, *America the Vulnerable*, highlights the domestic security weaknesses that the terrorists described by Stern and Pape will seek to exploit.[18] Flynn is a homeland security veteran; a former Coast Guard officer, he was a contributor to the Hart-Rudman Commission on National Security and the author of its well-regarded 2002 report.[19] Flynn's message is that both the Government and the citizens of the United States have failed to take adequate steps, even after September 11, 2001, against the threat of a catastrophic terrorist attack on U.S. soil. *America the Vulnerable* paints a grim picture of the challenge facing the Nation but counsels against simply dismissing it as insurmountable. The purpose of Flynn's book was to propose a new framework for the post-9/11 world and suggest solutions to specific vulnerabilities.

Flynn detailed domestic weaknesses, charging that the spasm of post-9/11 homeland security activity apparently did little to improve U.S. defenses. Federal Government money and attention remained focused on a forward defense: stopping terrorism overseas before it can reach the homeland. Meanwhile, local government, which bears much of the homeland security burden, is fiscally overwhelmed, and private industry, left to its own devices, takes a minimalist approach.

Three trends, says Flynn, contribute to the threat. The first of these is anti-Americanism. Taking a different view than Pape, Flynn argued that regardless of its policies, as long as America is a superpower, it will remain a magnet for discontent, and terrorist groups will not lack for recruits willing to strike the United States. This threat is exacerbated by the second trend, also noted by Stern and others: technology may offer nonstate actors lethal capabilities, from plentiful small arms to loose fissile material. To the motivation and the means, Flynn adds a third feature of the era, the opportunity offered by openness: in a modern economy that depends on sophisticated networks to move people, money, energy, goods, and information, security has taken a backseat to efficiency. The open U.S. economy is easy to strike, but it is also vital to U.S. power, as both terrorists and potential rivals such as China recognize.

Flynn identified a spectrum of three prevailing but inadequate schools of thought on how to cope with the terrorist threat to the homeland. Advocates of security at any cost maintain that no price is too great to prevent another attack. At the other end of the spectrum are those who hold that the terrorists essentially win if America takes preventive actions that impose additional costs or limits on personal freedom. Flynn identified as a third school those who hold the "escapist view that sidesteps homeland security altogether by advocating a go-to-the-source approach." This, he wrote, is the prevailing view held by the Bush administration and many others in Washington. It is an attractive view in that it plays to America's military strength and offers the prospect of limiting domestic sacrifices but, said Flynn, it ignores the fact that future terrorists, just like the 9/11 terrorists, could conduct their attacks from within the United States.

Having dismissed all three approaches as insufficient, Flynn pointed out that the Nation's homeland security challenges are manifold. They include its lengthy borders, across which flow massive volumes of goods and people; an underfunded security and response apparatus; and no real strategy. But if the Nation truly comes to grips with the problem, he wrote, pragmatic solutions are possible: solutions that aim to limit, not eliminate, the risk of attack, concentrate on the highest priority areas, and complement rather than conflict with market forces. Terrorists need successes, Flynn wrote, and therefore they can be deterred by security measures that decrease their chances of success.

Flynn sketched an arresting illustration of America's vulnerability: a scenario of a coordinated dirty bomb attack that could easily circumvent existing defenses and, by paralyzing the container shipping industry, threaten the entire U.S. economy. He then addressed the scope of the Nation's insecurity, cataloging resource-related problems of underfunding and understaffing, and the strategic deficiencies that led to them. The chief strategic shortcoming is that the United States continues to treat national security and homeland security as two distinct issues. Flynn charged that the United States has not even really debated whether security money should continue to go overwhelmingly to outward-focused activities as it does, leaving state and local governments and private entities starved for resources even as they must bear most of the domestic security burden.

Flynn found the reasons for America's inaction in a political and fiscal landscape in which homeland security had no natural constituency. A strong domestic Federal role runs counter to conservative convictions, while the left is resistant to the prospect of reductions in civil liberties and discretionary spending for social programs. The national security establishment prefers to keep its focus outside of America's borders. State and local governments are left to take up the slack, but they do not have the resources to do what needs to be done. The private sector is immobilized by the "tragedy of the commons," the lack of individual incentives to act for the common good; thus, no company is willing to shoulder security costs voluntarily because to do so would put it at a competitive disadvantage. Flynn held that the general public, for its part, is blindly hopeful that it is being protected.

To rouse the Nation, Flynn mapped out basic principles of action. As complete defense against an attack is impossible, America must aim to reduce key vulnerabilities while acknowledging that security efforts will reach a point of diminishing returns. He called for a layered approach that would focus on deterring attackers by increasing the odds of failure. By the same token, America must also prepare to manage the consequences of a successful attack. He noted that it is vital that the measures the country takes be politically and economically sustainable. Security planners must ask where security can reinforce the market's desire for efficiency and other valued public policy goals.

Flynn devoted two chapters to plans for specific threats. Reflecting the scenario sketched out earlier, Flynn proposed a container security regime in some detail. He touched briefly on other high priority areas, including the food supply and the chemical industry, and high priority threats such as the availability of radioactive material and chemical and biological weapons. He also addressed issues of response preparedness including the lack of trained, coordinated first responders and the difficulty of returning complex systems to service after an attack. Flynn emphasized, in these passages and elsewhere, that the economic consequences of a terrorist attack might be multiplied by the drastic measures needed to contain the initial damage.

Other themes ran through Flynn's treatment of these high-risk areas. The consequences of America's failure to prevent an attack, or at least prepare for its consequences, could be catastrophic, but feasible measures could lower the risk and mitigate the consequences. These measures could complement market needs; an example is detailed manifests and GPS receivers attached to shipping containers, measures that also have logistics benefits. Many are also applicable to nonterrorist events, such as improvements in the capacity to identify and react to food supply contamination. They could be introduced both with incentives (such as fast-track container importing for compliant companies) and disincentives (such as stiff regulatory penalties), but all such measures must be introduced and enforced by the Government; they cannot rely on private sector initiatives. By reducing a terrorist's odds of success, such measures create deterrence that could keep a terrorist act from taking place. As Flynn emphasized, deterrence is the goal, and it is attainable.

Flynn proposed a new kind of homeland security apparatus by which the Federal Government could mobilize both civil society and the private sector. He outlined a homeland security structure modeled on the Federal Reserve System, which he called the Federal Security Reserve System. This system would be self-funded and would tap the expertise available outside Washington, lowering the burden on the Federal Government and avoiding sometimes unworkable one-size-fits-all or top-down solutions.

Flynn concluded by insisting that the United States must not be daunted by the enormity of the task. He stated his belief that the American people are willing to hear the truth about their vulnerability, and that the Government therefore should be transparent about U.S. security shortcomings. The citizenry and the Government together must make sacrifices to shore up the Nation's defenses. A strategy based on risk management and emergency preparedness can be executed in a way that is not unreasonably costly and that can have other benefits. America must not, Flynn warned, remain in denial about its homeland security.

America the Vulnerable is compelling on the point made in its title: America *is* vulnerable, and the book is a provocative call to action. Along with his enumeration of the Nation's weaknesses, Flynn also proposed principles to shape a new homeland security regime, and he recommended action to make the Nation more secure. The book has shortcomings: Flynn was perhaps too dismissive of the role of national security efforts focused outside U.S. borders, and he does not critically examine the presumption that terrorists can be deterred. But, as Flynn's preface noted, serious scholarship on domestic security is limited, and his book contributes to a much-needed debate.

Judith Miller, Stephen Engelberg, and William Broad: Biological Warfare and Bioterrorism

Threats posed by chemical and biological warfare have been a growing concern in recent years. Both types of threats can magnify the power of states, and can also empower terrorist groups and even individuals. Especially in the hands of terrorists, these are worrisome threats because of the great damage that they can inflict on innocent people. Biological threats seem especially fearsome: infectious diseases such as smallpox, turned loose on a population the size of America's, could kill millions. Other forms of germ warfare could include anthrax, botulism, Ebola and Marburg viruses, salmonella, cholera, and even bioengineered germs. Modern public health efforts prevented most massive accidental outbreaks of the sort that devastated entire populations in past centuries. Today's risk is that rogue governments or terrorist groups might manufacture and employ deadly germs to attack victims in the United States and elsewhere.

Concern peaked in late September 2001—shortly after the terrorist attacks on the World Trade Center and the Pentagon—when anthrax powder was discovered in Florida, New Jersey, New York City, and Washington, DC. Although anthrax is not communicable from person to person, inhalation of only a few spores can be enough to kill. Five people died, but quick use of antibiotics and disinfectants prevented other deaths. Despite intense investigation, the culprits, foreign or domestic, were not found. With public concern about bioterrorist attacks widespread, the 2001 book *Germs: Biological Weapons and America's Secret War*, became an instant best seller.[20]

Steering away from sensationalism, this journalistic book by *New York Times* reporters Judith Miller, Stephen Engelberg, and William Broad strove to present a balanced and accurate account anchored in the history of biological warfare during the Cold War and afterward. During the 1950s and 1960s, the U.S. military funded a research program on the potential offensive and defensive use of bacteriological warfare, but in 1969, President Nixon halted work on all offensive measures. He declared that henceforth the United States would conduct biological research only on defensive measures, including vaccines and antibiotics. In 1972, the Biological and Toxin Weapons Convention was opened for signature, and it took effect in 1975. In time, over 100 governments had signed it.

Although the Soviet Union signed the treaty, the authors present evidence that it secretly carried out a massive biological warfare program for many years afterward. Accusations about this secret effort first began appearing in the late 1970s, but initially the evidence was mixed, and the U.S. Intelligence Community was uncertain what conclusion to draw. As the Cold War ended and more evidence emerged, however, it became clear that the Soviet Union had carried out a major effort to craft offensive biological weapons. It conducted research not only on old-fashioned germs such as anthrax, but also on bioengineered pathogens. A single installation at Stepnogorsk, for example, was thought to be capable of producing enough anthrax spores to kill the entire U.S. population. Starting in the early 1970s, the Soviet germ warfare effort grew to 60,000 people at more than 100 installations. In the early 1990s, Russian President Boris Yeltsin promised to terminate this effort and clean up the environmental damage it caused, but the authors expressed doubts about whether this promise was ever fully carried out.

In the 1990s, public attention shifted away from Russia and toward Iraq's efforts to preserve its biological warfare capability. During the 1980s, the authors reported, Saddam Hussein's regime had launched major research efforts on biological warfare as well as chemical warfare and nuclear weapons. In the months leading up to the U.S.-led invasion of Kuwait in early 1991, senior U.S. military officials were worried that Iraq might try to use anthrax and other biological weapons to attack U.S. and allied forces; programs to vaccinate U.S. soldiers and give them antibiotics were launched. During the war, Iraqi use of biological agents was not encountered, but afterward, UN inspectors found that U.S. airstrikes had not destroyed the facilities used by Iraq to conduct biological research and to manufacture weaponized agents and delivery systems. The early to mid-1990s saw persistent efforts by UN inspectors to identify and destroy Iraqi biological warfare facilities as well as chemical and nuclear programs. A great deal of success was achieved, but when Iraq expelled the UN inspectors in 1997, skeptics doubted that Iraq's germ warfare program had been entirely shut down. As Miller and her colleagues were writing in 2002, the question had not been resolved, and would not be until after the U.S.-led invasion of Iraq in 2003.

Public concern about terrorists gaining access to bacteriological and chemical agents rose in spring 1995, when an obscure religious cult called Aum Shinrikyo released deadly sarin nerve gas in a Japanese subway, killing 12 and injuring some 500 more. Subsequent investigations showed that this cult, whose charismatic leader claimed that their religion authorized mass killing, had secretly built laboratories to try to produce weaponized versions of anthrax, botulinum, and Q fever. Initially, the incident was viewed as Japan's problem and limited to the actions of a single religious cult. But when the U.S. Federal building in Oklahoma City was destroyed in April 1995 by bomber Timothy McVeigh, awareness began spreading that terrorists— from abroad or homegrown—might also try to employ chemical or biological agents against the U.S. population. Indeed, as Miller and her colleagues noted, such an incident had already occurred: in the mid-1980s, a religious cult known as the Rajneeshees had unleashed a salmonella attack in a town in Oregon.

The authors describe how the U.S. Government awoke to the biological warfare threat and began to develop defensive measures. Initial efforts began when the military preparation to eject Iraq from Kuwait exposed the inadequacy of stocks of vaccines and antibiotics and the difficulties of administering protective measures. Initially, governmental attention was mostly focused on protecting the U.S. military from chemical and biological attack during overseas operations. But dispersed and moving military forces are not as vulnerable to such attack as stationary and congested civilian populations in big urban areas are. Awareness of this risk led the Clinton administration to focus on practical measures to strengthen homeland security against both types of attacks. But in the years preceding September 11, 2001, this effort was mostly limited to Government officials and scientists; it suffered from a lack of both funding and public awareness. The terrorist attacks of September 11 and the subsequent release of anthrax on the East Coast galvanized the Bush administration to increase funds for vaccines and antibiotics for the prevention and treatment of smallpox and other diseases. The authors ended their book with a call for greater attention to the threat of germ warfare. They warned that, as of 2002, the United States was at best partly prepared and expressed skepticism that sufficient attention would be paid to this important enterprise.

The book can be criticized for not adequately exploring the difficulties of using chemical and biological agents against large militaries and civilian populations. For example, chemical agents such as mustard gas are best dispersed by air, but they are quickly dissipated by the wind. Biological agents—bacteria and viruses—are not easily weaponized, and many die when exposed to sunlight or other natural elements. Some biological agents, like anthrax, are not communicable from one person to another. Even communicable diseases such as smallpox can be contained by medical procedures and are subject to control by vaccines and antibiotics. Nonetheless, the authors clearly were correct in judging that, next to nuclear weapons, biological weapons present terrorists with the best way to kill large numbers of people quickly and cheaply and to escape detection. Almost all experts agree that the threat of chemical and biological attacks on the United States is real, and that large, sustained government preparedness programs, as part of an overall strategy for homeland security, are needed.[21] The authors deserve credit for being at the forefront of efforts to call attention to this threat.

Graham Allison: Nuclear Terrorism

Graham Allison's 2004 book, *Nuclear Terrorism: The Ultimate Preventable Catastrophe*, addressed a fearsome prospect: that al Qaeda or other terrorist groups might gain access to nuclear weapons and detonate them in American cities or elsewhere.[22] Allison portrayed the threat of terrorists with nuclear weapons or radiological dirty bombs as the most dangerous threat of the current era. His main argument was that American cities are highly vulnerable to nuclear devastation by terrorists, but that such destruction could be prevented by denying terrorists access to these weapons. He offered a multifaceted program of vigorous initiatives to accomplish this task, ranging from homeland security measures and military strikes against terrorists, to control of "loose nukes" in Russia and other places, to preventing proliferation among countries not already possessing nuclear weapons. He urged that the United States should join with Russia and other partner countries to fund this program and carry it out urgently and vigorously.

Allison argued that unless the right steps are taken, the nuclear destruction of one or more cities in America or its allies is all but inevitable. Allison asserted that al Qaeda and other terrorist groups want to do so, are potentially capable of doing so, and would need only a supply of small nuclear weapons, which could be carried surreptitiously in a suitcase, car, or container. Such a supply of nuclear weapons, Allison said, is readily available. One source is Russia, which possesses thousands of tactical nuclear weapons that are not well secured and that might be stolen by terrorists or sold abroad by corrupt Russian officials. Another source is Pakistan, a politically unstable state that has recently developed nuclear weapons, and a sizable portion of whose Islamic citizens are sympathetic to al Qaeda. Pakistani scientist Abdul Qadeer Khan developed his country's nuclear bomb, but also, as Allison recounts, made a fortune by selling nuclear parts and services abroad before he was caught. Both North Korea and Iran are striving to develop nuclear arsenals. North Korea, Allison said, could sell nuclear weapons and materials to rogue governments and clients in exchange for the hard currency it badly needs. Islamic fundamentalist Iran might give nuclear weapons to terrorists because its government would welcome the results, not least because it could not be held directly responsible.

Allison also warned that nuclear weapons might be manufactured by terrorist groups. Creating the necessary highly enriched uranium and weapons-grade plutonium requires access to special nuclear reactors and other manufacturing technologies. However, Allison wrote, terrorists could purchase these materials from a number of countries that have the appropriate reactors and a willingness to sell the materials. A relatively small amount of material— perhaps 30 pounds of uranium, or an even smaller quantity of plutonium— could produce a nuclear bomb of several kilotons, enough to flatten and irradiate a major portion of a big American city. Once in possession of these materials, Allison wrote, terrorists could readily assemble one or more nuclear weapons, based on engineering techniques already published in the open literature.

Allison urged stronger U.S. homeland security measures, including enhanced inspections of containers aboard ships coming into U.S. ports. He also advocated continued military strikes against terrorist camps in Afghanistan and elsewhere, and international law enforcement efforts against terrorists. Arguing that such measures cannot be enough, however, he urged a three-part international strategy aimed at denying nuclear materials and weapons to terrorists. He described the three goals as:

- no loose nukes
- no new nascent nukes
- no new nuclear weapons states.

To further movement toward the first goal, Allison proposed greatly enhanced funding of the Nunn-Lugar program (also known as the Cooperative Threat Reduction program) aimed at rendering Russia's nuclear arsenal and materials more secure through better storage and installation of mechanisms to prevent unauthorized detonation of weapons. Allison, portraying the Bush administration and the U.S. bureaucracy as insufficiently supportive of this effort, urged the personal backing of President Bush and President Putin. Allison also urged that the United States, Russia, and China should work with the International Atomic Energy Agency (IAEA) to establish a global standard according to which the stockpiles and nuclear reactors of all countries would be rendered secure.

To carry out Allison's second component requires that the major powers and the IAEA prevent the creation of any new national capabilities to enrich uranium or reprocess plutonium. Under Article 4 of the Nuclear Non-Proliferation Treaty, nonnuclear states can legally develop facilities for enriching uranium to create fuel for nuclear reactors and for reprocessing spent reactor fuel to extract plutonium. Allison's plan would rewrite Article 4 to prohibit this. It would instead provide that countries with peaceful nuclear reactors would receive all the fuel they need at one-half production cost, and they would also agree to remove all spent fuels. But it would deny existing nonnuclear countries the option to create any nuclear materials that could be used for nuclear weapons. Allison proposed not only powerful economic incentives for compliance, but also powerful punishments for noncompliance, including strong economic sanctions and potential military force. Allison would apply this plan, for example, to Iran in hope of supporting its legitimate nuclear needs for peaceful energy while denying it the capacity to produce nuclear weapons. His "grand bargain" for Iran would include incentives intended to motivate its Islamic regime: the West would pay for its nuclear supplies and removal of used material, would offer economic trade and investment as well as a U.S. agreement not to use military force to change its regime, and would express willingness to discuss Iran's legitimate security concerns.

The third component is closely related to the second and focuses in particular on North Korea. In order to bring about the freeze and dismantlement of North Korea's nuclear program, Allison proposed another grand bargain full of concessions and carrots: shipment of food and fuel from South Korea and Japan, an oil pipeline from Russia through North Korea, other forms of economic assistance, and bilateral negotiations with the United States aimed at reassuring North Korea that it would not be threatened militarily by the United States. But if North Korea failed to comply with this deal, Allison recommended a U.S. military attack on it aimed at destroying its nuclear facilities. Allison would apply the same logic of military attack to Iran or any other state that sought to become a new member of the nuclear club.

Allison's book performs a worthy service by calling public attention to a dangerous threat. Likewise, his ambitious strategy and its three components have virtues. No serious observer would quarrel with the idea of controlling loose nukes, shutting down the production of weapons-grade nuclear materials, or trying to stem further nuclear proliferation to new countries. All of these measures are already being pursued by the United States, many of its allies, and the United Nations. The real issue is whether pursuit of them in the vigorous and costly ways envisioned by Allison is politically possible, and whether this effort to stem the flow of nuclear materials into terrorist hands could succeed. Allison is hopeful on both fronts, but other observers might question this.

Allison's book offers a coherent strategy, which has obvious attractions because it employs two different types of potentially powerful instruments. The first instrument, concessions, relies upon diplomatic bargaining; the second instrument, coercion, relies upon economic sanctions and on military power as a last resort. The core issue is whether such a strategy can feasibly be executed and whether it could achieve its goals. Allison has a valid point in that, if the U.S. strategy is to work, its instruments must be strong enough to succeed.

While Allison's strategy might not overcome the stubbornness of nuclear proliferators, the U.S. willingness to carry out his prescription of big carrots and big sticks might be another constraint. For several reasons, the United States may be reluctant to make wholesale concessions to countries that violate international norms and menace American allies. For equally valid reasons, the United States may be willing to employ economic sanctions but unwilling to employ military force if the risks and costs of military action are seen as too high. Allies and partners of the United States may feel even more constrained from making concessions or employing military force. These uncertainties, too, reduce the effectiveness of deterrence.

Many of Allison's practical recommendations make sense. Undeniably, the prospect of nuclear weapons falling into the hands of terrorists willing to use them is a serious and growing threat. Allison appears to be correct in charging that the United States, its allies and partners, and the international community are not doing enough to lessen this risk, and that a more vigorous effort could yield tangible results: perhaps it could not eliminate the risk, but it might be able to reduce it significantly. In this sense, Allison's book is an important contribution to the literature on nuclear proliferation, a key political and technological danger of today's world.

Moisés Naím: Illicit Trafficking and International Organized Crime

Although public attention in recent years has focused mostly on the threats posed by global terrorism carried out for political ends, a comparably menacing dynamic has quietly been gaining momentum: the growth of illicit trade and trafficking carried out by empowered criminal networks, many of them transnational in structure and operations. Moisés Naím's 2005 book, *Illicit: How Smugglers, Traffickers, and Copycats are Hijacking the Global Economy*, calls attention to this threat and proposes methods to bring it under greater lawful control.[23] A former senior government official in Venezuela, Naím is now editor of the journal *Foreign Policy* and has devoted considerable study to international organized crime. His book warned that illicit global trade in illegal commodities and services, empowered by technology, has risen dramatically in recent years, to a point where governments and law enforcement systems can no longer control it; this has led to the criminalization of politics in several countries. His book urged a stronger, more focused effort by many governments, and greater international collaboration, to prevent further damage not just to law enforcement but to the international system itself. Illicit trade and international organized crime, he said, are undermining legitimate government and civil society in many countries and thus threatening the stability of international politics.

Naím argues that illicit trafficking in human beings, weapons, drugs, commercial manufactured products, biological organs, intellectual property rights, art, and money has soared in the past decade. Illicit trade is no longer carried out just in secrecy; in many places, it has come out into the open and is often carried out alongside legal trade or concealed and legitimized by it. Some criminal networks, said Naím, conduct licit businesses to help conceal activities and profits in their much larger illicit businesses. International criminal bodies employ complex, fluid transnational networks to acquire illicit products, transmit them to distant markets, distribute and sell them at high profits, and conceal the profitable financial transactions through elaborate money-laundering techniques.

The reasons for this fast growth and increasing brazenness, he said, are several. A main reason is simple supply-and-demand dynamics. There are large demands for illicit goods, large supplies of them, and huge profits to be made. Globalization has made illicit trafficking far easier because it has opened national economies, knocked down trade barriers, integrated global markets, and facilitated currency exchange and international financing. In response, international criminal groups, said Naím, have mutated to achieve higher levels of proficiency and profit, while insulating themselves from criminal prosecution. They have evolved from structured hierarchies into flexible transnational networks that employ the Internet and modern communications and can quickly adapt to emerging markets while avoiding law enforcement. Another contributing reason, argued Naím, is that governments simply lack the wherewithal to deal with them. Even in modern democratic governments, including the United States and Europe, law enforcement systems are subject to rigid and hierarchical bureaucracies, and they cannot fully protect porous borders, react swiftly to changing criminal patterns, or collaborate effectively on the world stage. Many governments in underdeveloped areas where much illicit trade originates have been penetrated and suborned by criminal groups and have themselves become not just failed states but criminal states. As a result, he said, illicit trade, organized crime, and smugglers are ahead in the global battle with governments and law enforcement.

Naím devoted much of his book to examining illicit trade in several areas, starting with weapons. Illicit trade in small arms and ammunition has, he found, soared since the end of the Cold War left superfluous arsenals for sale on the world market. This trade, Naím said, is mainly carried out through middlemen who buy small arms cheaply in such places as Eastern Europe, airlift them to such violent areas as sub-Saharan Africa and the Middle East, and sell them at high profits. The result, he said, has been the global proliferation of large quantities of rifles, machine guns, grenades, mortars, missile and rocket launchers, and man-portable air defense systems capable of downing aircraft. Much of this business is being carried out by private criminal groups, Naím said, but even some governments surreptitiously support it as a source of revenue. For example, he wrote, Transdneister, a de facto independent region of Moldova, has become a criminal government that officially supports arms smuggling for profit. Criminals have even gotten into the business of selling components for building nuclear weapons. Abdul Qadeer Khan led Pakistan's efforts to build nuclear bombs, and then was caught selling specialized parts for building centrifuges and other equipment to Libya. Naím argued that Khan was far from alone in such activity, little of which is detected.

In a lengthy chapter Naím showed how illicit drug trafficking and smuggling are steadily growing due to growth in both demand and supply. Demand for opium, cocaine, heroin, and other drugs, he said, comes from the United States, Europe, and other regions where drug use is growing. Supply comes from places such as Afghanistan (opium poppies for heroin), Colombia (cocaine), Mexico (marijuana), and other countries. Complex drug shipment and distribution networks run through Central America, Southeast Asia, Turkey and the Balkans, Nigeria, and elsewhere. Naím explains how the Internet and modern financial networks, plus the availability of shipping and other modes of transportation, have greatly enhanced the ability of drug smugglers to pursue great profits at low risk. The high-profile drug rings of the past, such as that of Pablo Escobár and the Medellín cartel, may have been broken up by law enforcement, but they have been replaced by more flexible networks that operate without much detection. In Colombia, both left-wing and right-wing revolutionaries and terrorist groups have used drug smuggling to raise money. There and in Bolivia, poor farmers are so dependent upon cocaine production for their livelihood that they block law enforcement, and many governments have been penetrated by drug traffickers. This pattern is repeated in many other countries, where governments may oppose drug smuggling in public but nevertheless rely upon it for revenue.

Another area of illicit trade identified by Naím is that of stealing intellectual property rights and making counterfeit items, such as fake apparel and accessory brands like Rolex watches, Gucci handbags, or Pierre Cardin shirts, sold at cheap prices worldwide. Counterfeiting has expanded into such dangerous areas as the manufacture and sale of fake drugs that may fail to work or even endanger the people taking them. Music, videos, and software are being counterfeited, with much of this business originating in China, South Korea, and elsewhere in Asia. Automobile and industrial parts are now also being counterfeited. This multibillion-dollar business is steadily growing because there is a high demand for brand-name goods, and because criminal groups can sell them profitably without much fear of being caught, arrested, and prosecuted.

A particularly grim area of illicit trade is the smuggling of human beings. Criminal groups sell passage aboard ships to the United States to large numbers of Chinese, or abet illegal immigration from Mexico to the United

States. The United States is far from the only focus of this illegal activity. Large numbers of South Asians are smuggled into European countries. Many of these migrants pay for passage, often in dangerous conditions, in hopes of finding jobs that will provide them a better life. Worse is human trafficking, in which a migrant is coerced and even sold; human trafficking involving the sale and prostitution of young girls and boys in Europe, the United States, and elsewhere is growing. Naím estimated the size of the trade in human beings at $7 billion–$10 billion per year.

Yet another area of growing illicit trade is the selling of human organs including kidneys, corneas, livers, pancreases, hearts, lungs, and even genitals. The demand far exceeds the legal supply, so illicit networks for acquiring, transmitting, selling, and implanting human organs have sprung up in several countries, including India, China, Brazil, Romania, the Philippines, Israel, and South Africa. There is also considerable illicit trade in endangered species and in wildlife, food and plants, and stolen artwork. In these areas, as in others, porous borders and weak law enforcement, plus global information networks, fluid global finances, and sophisticated money laundering techniques, have enabled criminal groups to operate profitably outside the law.

Naím acknowledged that law enforcement bodies occasionally achieve successes that make newspaper headlines, such as the capture of huge amounts of cocaine and heroin. Low-level retail sellers are often caught, sometimes wholesale distributors are caught, and occasionally even big-time criminals such as Pablo Escobár are brought to justice. But the effect, said Naím, is mostly minor disruption of otherwise booming businesses. Captured criminals are quickly replaced by others, and criminal networks adapt, finding new ways to circumvent law enforcement or new businesses to make profits. Law-abiding governments, societies, and countries, warned Naím, are losing the war with illicit trade and international organized crime to the point where the stability of the international system is threatened. Naím expressed special worry about the growing cooperation between illicit trade networks and terrorists, and about the growing corruption of entire governments in underdeveloped areas, which could produce a cascade of failed states and criminal societies.

Naím offered some explanations of how the globalizing world economy makes it easier for criminals to pursue their trade, just as it enables legitimate businesses. But he also blamed incompetent law enforcement in the United States, Europe, and elsewhere. Wealthy countries, he said, may possess the financial and human resources to perform better, but they fail to allocate sufficient resources to the task. An example is weak border controls and port inspections in the United States. Governmental law enforcement bureaucracies are often too hierarchically structured, constrained by rigid procedures, and unable to cooperate, Naím said, while governments lack the capacity to perform the multilateral cooperation needed to control illicit trade. In addition, Naím said, governmental strategies for law enforcement are often ineffective; for example, they focus on controlling supply-side sources rather than demand-side consumption.

Naím ended his book with a call for stronger law enforcement in the United States and elsewhere. The terrorist strikes of September 11, 2001, produced a new public atmosphere of awareness that could, he said, be mobilized to help deal with illicit trade. He called for development of new technologies that could help detect the flow of illicit goods, and creation of more flexible government agencies that could bring together multidepartmental teams of experts to address criminal networks. Strategies are needed to control demand as well as supply. Naím also called for a focus on achievable, prioritized goals; for example, he argued that decriminalizing marijuana use could leave governments free to focus on more serious drugs such as cocaine and heroin. He called for major increases in multilateral cooperation on behalf of law enforcement.

As one of the first books on this neglected topic, Naím's 2005 volume started to close a huge hole in the literature on new global dangers. He covered a wide spectrum of illicit activities and showed how they form an overall mosaic of crime. Although his book is better at diagnosing this growing problem than at suggesting concrete remedies, it is an eye-opening introduction to a subject whose importance is on a par with global terrorism.

Taking Stock of New Technologies, Opportunities, and Threats

The books examined in this chapter help illustrate the ways in which new opportunities and threats are being influenced by emerging technologies that had begun to make their mark in the 1990s and have since acquired even greater impact. Together, they illustrate the age of empowerment reflected in the rising relative power of nonstate actors, as van Creveld's book outlined. The first cluster of books showed how stability, peace, democratization, and economic progress are affected by the military predominance by the United States and its allies over potential adversaries, the use of space, the ongoing advance of economic globalization through new business patterns, and prospects for nonviolent protest against authoritarian governments. The second cluster of books illuminates the extent of new threats, and how a combination of old and new technologies is empowering the state and nonstate actors that create these threats, magnifying their capabilities and enabling them to project their influence to distant areas.

In the early 1990s, many people writing about new threats were commonly portrayed as engaging in unsubstantiated speculation or worst-case fear-mongering. Today, most of their forecasts seem tame when compared to the threats that have appeared. Potential threats now cover a wide spectrum of once-unimagined dangers, ranging from genocidal slaughter in impoverished regions, to terrorists exploding nuclear bombs in U.S. cities, to a competition between the United States and China for control of Asia's destiny. The books surveyed here help record and document these threats. However, many threats have caught the United States Government by surprise, and this gives rise to the troubling question of what new and different threats may now be gathering that could catch the United States by surprise again.

Even if no new threats appear, the current ones must be addressed by U.S. policy and strategy. As the threat-oriented books of this chapter make clear, each must be addressed on its merits, with uniquely tailored policies that may be little help with other threats. The effect of multiple simultaneous threats is to create major new requirements and burdens for the United States. Moreover, threats cannot be addressed solely by suppressing them through policies aimed at attacking their symptoms and outward manifestations: their underlying causes must also be addressed, which further magnifies the expense and difficulty of dealing with them. Whether today's threats can be successfully managed through either soft power or hard power or the use of both is explored in the next chapter. What is clear from this chapter is that as analysts and policymakers study the elephant, they should not be blind to the effects of empowerment through technology.

Chapter Five

U.S. National Security Goals and Constraints

Ever since the Cold War ended, the United States has been struggling to shape a new foreign policy and a new national security strategy. Initially, perhaps, the task seemed simple because the major threat to U.S. interests had receded and peace seemed to be ascendant. By the mid-1990s, however, the world appeared increasingly dangerous and the future uncertain. National security could not be taken for granted, and it was clear that the United States would face stiff challenges in pursuing its goals abroad. The sense of threat has grown far greater since September 11, 2001, when terrorists struck the U.S. homeland and the Bush administration embarked upon a global war on terror.

Thus, the United States must now deal with a world that is partly neo-Kantian—the wealthy democratic community—and partly neo-Hobbesian—in regions facing instability, chaos, and conflict. To deal with this bifurcated world, what goals should U.S. national security strategy pursue abroad in the early 21st century? What priorities should it establish? What are the policy options at its disposal? What actions should it take in its diplomacy, economics, and military power?

To provide a conceptual framework for seeing this part of the elephant, this chapter organizes a number of influential books on U.S. grand strategy into four different schools of strategic thought: traditional conservatives, progressive multilateralists, assertive interventionists, and the offshore balancers. These four schools do not array themselves logically along a linear spectrum as they might have during the Cold War, when grand strategy was measured by attitudes toward the Soviet Union. Today's approaches to grand strategy are best described in a matrix, which highlights their policy motivations and their attitudes toward the instruments of national power (see tables 5–1 and 5–2).

As table 5–1 shows, their similarities and differences are more complex

Table 5–1. Motivations and Preferred Instruments of Power		
Motivation		**Instrument**
Create Democracies	*Balance Power*	
Assertive Interventionists	Traditional Conservatives	Military Power
Progressive Multilateralists	Offshore Balancers	Soft Power

than a single-dimension linear spectrum could show. Those whom we call *traditional conservatives* see the U.S. role in contemporary world affairs in terms of classical power-balancing, military relationships, and achieving equilibrium in dealing with other great powers, such as China and Russia. *Progressive multilateralists* are those who believe that the United States should focus on acting multilaterally as leader of the democratic community, including NATO, and that it should employ consensus-building diplomacy in order to seek global progress when dealing with terrorism and other threats in the Middle East and endangered areas. *Assertive interventionists* are those who argue that the United States should assert its military and economic power, unilaterally if necessary, to deal with endangered areas and new threats. Later in this chapter we explore the limits and constraints on American national security policy. Out of that discussion emerges a fourth, rather new, general national security approach called *offshore balancing*. It differs from the other three in being more neo-isolationist, with an emphasis on withdrawing deployed American troops from much of the world. There are neo-isolationists in both the liberal and conservative communities.

This table shows how a progressive multilateralist (or political liberal) could, by changing some assumptions about policy instruments and the need to use force, become an assertive interventionist (or political neoconservatives): both share similar foreign policy motivations, that is, seeking the spread of democracy. It also illuminates some of the bitter debates within the Republican Party between the traditional conservatives and the neoconservatives because, even though both support significant use of hard power, their fundamental foreign policy motivations are different.

The three books we discuss that come from the category of traditional conservatives are:

- Henry Kissinger, *Diplomacy* (1994) and *Does America Need a Foreign Policy? Toward a Diplomacy for the 21ˢᵗ Century* (2001)
- Richard N. Haass, *The Opportunity: America's Moment to Alter History's Course* (2005).

The books by progressive multilateralists include:

- Zbigniew Brzezinski, *The Grand Chessboard: American Primacy and Its Geostrategic Imperatives* (1997) and *The Choice: Global Domination or Global Leadership* (2004)
- Joseph S. Nye, Jr., *Soft Power: The Means to Success in World Politics* (2004).

We discuss three books that are in the category of assertive interventionists:

- Walter Russell Mead, *Power, Terror, Peace, and War: America's Grand Strategy in a World at Risk* (2004)
- Niall Ferguson, *Colossus: The Price of America's Empire* (2004)
- Robert J. Lieber, *The American Era: Power and Strategy for the 21ˢᵗ Century* (2005).

We describe six books that focus on the limits of American power, including the offshore balancers, a few pages below.

Each of these books sought to evaluate the U.S. national security strategy particular to its time. When the Clinton administration took power in early 1993, it inherited a world apparently characterized by neo-Kantian dynamics in the wake of U.S. victories in the Cold War and the Persian Gulf War. The global scene was mostly peaceful; relations among the big powers were tranquil; democratization and economic integration were accelerating; and security problems, such as those in the Balkans, seemed to exist at the margins of an otherwise stable world order. The Clinton national security strategy therefore focused mainly on fostering further enlargement of the global democratic community.[1] By the time the Clinton administration entered its second term, in early 1997, the global scene was worsening in an upsurge of neo-Hobbesian dynamics, with ethnic warfare in the Balkans, failed states in Africa, an increase in terrorism, troubles in the Persian Gulf, security strains in Asia, and a slowdown of democratization and economic integration. In response, the Clinton administration shifted strategic gears to focus more on global engagement, deepened its involvements in the Balkans and

Table 5–2. Premises of National Security Strategy Philosophies				
	Traditional Conservatives	**Progressive Multilateralists**	**Assertive Interventionists**	**Offshore Balancers**
Kant versus Hobbes	Mostly Hobbes	Mostly Kant; some Hobbes	Mostly Hobbes; some Kant	Mostly Hobbes; some Kant
Nature of Major Threat	Unstable big-power relations	Chaotic southern arc, terrorism	Chaotic southern arc, terrorism	American overstretch
Role of Alliances	Important	Very important	Less important	Very important
Instruments of Power	Hard military power and diplomacy	Soft power and diplomacy	Hard military and economic power	Soft power and diplomacy
Mechanisms of Success	Power-balancing and major-power equilibrium	Persuasion and coalition-building	Suppression of threats and promotion of democratization	Balancing and using regional powers
U.S. Leadership Style	Architect of big-power concert	Consensual leader of multilateral alliances	Path-setting leader of ad hoc coalitions	Less engagement
Attention to Limits of U.S. Power	Moderate emphasis	Major emphasis	Little emphasis	Strongest emphasis
Also called	Realists	Liberals, idealists	Neoconservatives	Neo-isolationists

other troubled regions, and articulated a new strategic concept of *shape, respond, prepare* ("Shape the international security environment in ways favorable to U.S. interests. . . . Respond to the full spectrum of crises. . . . Prepare now for an uncertain future").[2] The three books we discuss by Kissinger and Brzezinski assess how the Clinton administration carried out this transition to a more security-minded strategy for the world of the middle to late 1990s.

By the time the administration of President George W. Bush entered office in early 2001, the world appeared even more neo-Hobbesian. The terrorist strikes of September 11, 2001, marked a major strategic departure as growing threats directly menaced the interests and safety of the United States and its democratic partners. The highest profile feature of the September 2002 National Security Strategy, which was aimed at handling this dangerous environment, was the "strategy of preemption" as one option for handling terrorism and the proliferation of WMD.[3] However, the document was broader in scope: it also articulated visions for promoting democracy, reforming alliances, encouraging global economic growth, defusing regional tensions, and improving big-power relations. Even with these elements, however, the Bush strategy was unquestionably marked by an elevated sense of global danger and by a greater U.S. willingness to use military power, unilaterally if necessary.

Brzezinski's second book and those written by Walter Russell Mead, Joseph Nye, Niall Ferguson, Robert Lieber, and Richard Haass were prepared in the context of the 2002 National Security Strategy.

The books described above address basic goals and priorities for U.S. national security strategy, but they do not pay much attention to the constraints facing the United States as it operates on the world stage. Accordingly, this chapter also examines six books that do so. From at least one of those books (by Stephen Walt) flows a new strategy of offshore balancing that responds to the weaknesses of the assertive interventionists. The books are:

- Paul M. Kennedy, *The Rise and Fall of Great Powers: Economic and Military Conflict from 1500 to 2000* (1987)
- Ivo Daalder and James Lindsay, *America Unbound: The Bush Revolution in Foreign Policy* (2003, rev. ed. 2005)
- Samuel P. Huntington, *Who Are We? The Challenges to America's National Identity* (2004)
- Robert Kagan, *Of Paradise and Power: America and Europe in the New World Order* (2004)
- Stephen M. Walt, *Taming American Power: The Global Response to U.S. Primacy* (2005)
- Fareed Zakaria, *The Future of Freedom: Illiberal Democracy at Home and Abroad* (2004).

A new National Security Strategy issued by the Bush administration in March 2006 updated the 2002 strategy; we offer our own review of the more neo-Kantian 2006 strategy near the end of this chapter:

- *National Security Strategy of the United States of America* (March 2006).

Henry Kissinger: In Search of a New Balance of Power and Global Equilibrium

Henry Kissinger's writings on U.S. foreign policy for the post–Cold War era are contained in two books. *Diplomacy* was published in 1994, and *Does*

America Need a Foreign Policy? Toward a Diplomacy for the 21ˢᵗ Century, was published in 2001, shortly before the terrorist attacks of that year.[4] Since the 1950s
and his seminal book *A World Restored: Castlereagh, Metternich, and the Restoration of
Peace, 1812–1822*, Kissinger has been a geopolitical realist who emphasizes
clear thinking and wise diplomacy as key to advancing U.S. interests and
preserving peace.[5] His two books for the contemporary era similarly urge the
United States to think globally and to strike a sensible balance between its
idealist principles and the geopolitical realities of world affairs.

Kissinger is a strategic thinker who views contemporary geopolitics
through the lessons of history. Accordingly, he devoted most of *Diplomacy*'s
912 pages to recounting how great powers managed their relations from the
time of France's Cardinal Richelieu, when foreign policy by *raison d'état* was
born during the early 1600s. Throughout the subsequent centuries, Kissinger
wrote, national leaders, especially in Europe, have struggled with the problem of asserting their state interests while establishing peaceful relations with
other powerful countries that were pursuing their own interests. During the
first two centuries of this period, Europe witnessed a succession of violent
conflicts, culminating in the Napoleonic wars. Then, after Napoleon's defeat
at Waterloo in 1815, stable relationships were attained when Austria's
Metternich, Britain's Castlereagh, Prussia's von Hardenberg, and France's
Talleyrand established the Concert of Europe at the Congress of Vienna and
in subsequent negotiations. The Concert, wrote Kissinger, employing such
tools and doctrines as maintenance of equilibrium, acknowledgment of one
another's legitimacy, and balance of power, kept Europe mostly peaceful for
40 years and prevented general war for a full century. However, this broke
down in the 20ᵗʰ century with a succession of catastrophes: World War I,
when Europe's stable balance of power suddenly collapsed; World War II,
when Nazi Germany tried to conquer all of Europe; and the Cold War, when
the Soviet Union tried to impose communist ideology on Europe. This historical legacy, wrote Kissinger, with its mixture of success and tragedy, provides
reason for both hope and concern as the world enters the 21ˢᵗ century.

Kissinger offered a similarly mixed appraisal of the role the United States
played during the tumultuous 20ᵗʰ century. By tradition an isolationist country, the United States entered the 1900s with a newfound but ambivalent
willingness to begin asserting its power on the world stage. Unlike Britain
and other great powers with considerable experience in global politics, wrote
Kissinger, the United States had no unified strategic doctrine to guide its
conduct. Instead, it was torn between two competing concepts, the conservative realpolitik of Theodore Roosevelt and the liberal idealism of Woodrow
Wilson. As a result, said Kissinger, the country was prone to vacillate among

lingering isolationism, temporary surges of military power to crush menacing enemies, and moral campaigns seeking to propagate democracy and humanitarian values worldwide. Thus, Kissinger wrote, the United States briefly played a big-power role under Roosevelt's leadership, shifted to liberal internationalism under Wilson in World War I, reverted to isolationism during the 1920s and 1930s, and launched global campaigns to defeat Nazism in World War II and then to contain communism in the Cold War. The effect by the end of the 20th century, Kissinger wrote, was to make the United States the world's strongest power, but one not necessarily well endowed with the habits of strategic thinking needed to carry out its superpower leadership role in the post–Cold War era.

In anticipating what would follow the collapse of the Soviet Union in the early 1990s, Kissinger dismissed optimistic hopes that the world would achieve growing peace, democracy, and progress from forces of global unity and integration. Instead, he predicted a murky, uncertain, and turmoil-filled future capable of producing either progress or tragedy, depending upon the diplomatic skills of the major powers. The world would be marked by a contradiction between two powerful trends, as globalization drew the world closer together in complex webs of growing ties, while fragmentation shattered attempts at achieving unity and cohesion. Although economic and military power might temporarily be concentrated in the United States, Kissinger wrote, it would become distributed more equally among the big powers, including the European region, Russia, China, India, and Japan. Many medium powers, small powers, and transnational groups would acquire the strength to act increasingly independently in a stage wired together by modern communications systems. The result, predicted Kissinger, would be great pluralism, change, and uncertainty that would make it hard for all countries to steer their foreign policies in sensible directions, and might make them unable to preserve peace if their interests and identities collided.

Kissinger portrayed a future more like Europe in the 18th and 19th centuries, fluid and multipolar, rather than like the 20th century, with its bipolar confrontations and universalist ideologies. The principal challenge would be for the major powers to establish a new balance-of-power system on a global scale, anchored not only in mechanical power balancing, but also in such principles as equilibrium, legitimacy, shared values, and moderate conduct. Kissinger warned that this would be a demanding challenge because none of today's major powers have recent experience in this enterprise: managing a global balance of power is a lost art from two centuries ago. Indeed, said Kissinger, it is an art entirely foreign to the United States, which has never even participated in a multipolar balance-of-power system, much less managed one.

Moreover, Kissinger said, managing such a complex system is especially difficult for a pluralist democracy because it cannot carry out nuanced policies.

For these reasons, Kissinger predicted a lengthy period of difficulty for U.S. foreign policy as it tried to carry out its global responsibilities. He rejected any return to isolationism as impractical. While urging strong U.S. activism and leadership abroad, he also rejected any new moral campaign of Wilsonian idealism aimed at propagating democracy and other American values to the far corners of the Earth. Instead, he urged a concerted effort by U.S. statesmen to balance realism and idealism in their diplomacy, and to find a workable synthesis of strategic realpolitik and moral principles aimed at managing the realities of world politics while advancing the cause of democracy and peace effectively. Such a foreign policy, Kissinger said, should not be misguided by a mistaken belief that U.S. power is so supreme that its designs can be imposed on the world, or that its liberal values can be transplanted to cultures that are anchored in entirely different values. Instead, Kissinger urged pragmatic thinking about vital U.S. national interests. The United States must strive to ensure that neither Europe nor Asia fall under the control of a hostile power capable of menacing U.S. interests, and it must search for partners to help it manage global security affairs.

Kissinger wrote that the best hope for achieving peaceful progress in a world of pluralism and danger is to craft a new equilibrium among the world's great powers, giving all of them a stake in creating stability and moderation to enable cooperative conduct to flourish. Kissinger was thus arguing for a return of the Concert of Europe's moral and strategic principles to guide U.S. foreign policy and global security affairs: not to re-create a global version of Europe in the early 19th century, but to craft a stable structure of peace that could handle the new dangers and opportunities of the early 21st century. The challenge, said Kissinger, would be for shapers of U.S. foreign policy to think in terms that had never before been mastered, and indeed, had often been disdained. In suggesting this strategic orientation for U.S. foreign policy, Kissinger wrote not as a neoconservative, willing to exert U.S. military power in order to propagate democratic principles abroad, but from the perspective of a traditional conservative intent on blending old-style diplomacy and restrained use of military power to craft a stable equilibrium and avoid calamitous wars.

Whereas his 1994 book *Diplomacy* was historical and philosophical, Kissinger's 2001 book, *Does America Need a Foreign Policy?* addressed the practical realities of contemporary world politics and the legacy of the Clinton administration's foreign policy for the 1990s. As in *Diplomacy*, this book portrayed a complex world of great turmoil owing to globalization, modern communications systems, shifting agendas of nation-states, new regional dynamics, post-Westphalian norms, and the rise of nonstate actors, including terrorists and multilateral institutions. While acknowledging American global preeminence, Kissinger continued to predict that the United States would face major challenges abroad that would test its resources and wisdom to their limits. He called for a U.S. foreign policy that would blend interests and values, realism and idealism. He warned of the need to craft a strategic concept and a long-range strategy thoughtfully, not just relying upon ad hoc responses driven by domestic politics. U.S. foreign policy, he said, must address five main challenges:

- coordinating the world of democracies, including Europe, Russia, and the Western Hemisphere
- guiding Asia toward equilibrium
- managing the Middle East and Africa, regions in transition
- shaping the politics of economic globalization
- crafting new norms and rules for intervention.

Kissinger wrote that although Europe was now peaceful and integrating, the Atlantic alliance was adrift in a crisis of identity and purpose. U.S.-European relations were drifting apart because the old Cold War threat posed by the Soviet Union had disappeared. In addition, he said, the inward-looking European Union was developing an identity apart from the Atlantic alliance. The United States and Europe increasingly disagreed on how to handle the Middle East and other regions; transatlantic economic frictions were intensifying. Fearing U.S.-European rivalry in world politics, Kissinger called for the United States to continue supporting European integration, and also to seek Europe's cooperation to develop common strategic policies toward areas outside Europe, especially the Middle East. He also called for U.S. policies aimed at preserving NATO's cohesion as it enlarged and at upgrading its military capability to perform new missions. He proposed a new structure for Atlantic relations with an Atlantic Steering Group to manage the evolution of NATO and the European Union, and a Transatlantic Free Trade Area to promote economic integration.

Kissinger portrayed U.S. relations with Russia as partly an extension of U.S. relations with Europe, and as partly unique because of Russia's size and geopolitical role in world affairs. While acknowledging Russia's steps to establish democracy, Kissinger warned that full democratization would take years, and could fall short by producing a government with lingering elements of authoritarianism. The main challenge would be, said Kissinger, not to influence Russia's domestic affairs, but to influence its foreign policy constructively. Kissinger rejected the idea of admitting Russia into NATO and the EU any time soon, but he urged that U.S. foreign policy should show respect for Russia's legitimate security interests and promote Russia's economic integration into the world economy. Kissinger warned, however, that the United States would need to maintain a balance of power, by being partly forthcoming and partly dissuading, to discourage any reappearance of Russian imperial conduct.

Kissinger noted Latin America's progress toward democracy and its economic growth but pointed to major challenges in this region. Some countries, Venezuela among them, face the risk that democracy could give way to a renewal of authoritarianism; others, such as Colombia, are beset by internal violence and crime. Dealing with such threats on a case-by-case basis, said Kissinger, would be important for U.S. policy. Kissinger's main recommendation was to create a Free Trade Area of the Americas in order to help promote capitalist markets and economic progress, while heading off rivalry between NAFTA and the Brazilian-led MERCOSUR (Southern Cone Common Market).

Kissinger proposed a U.S. foreign policy toward Asia that would seek to maintain an equilibrium despite profound changes in Asian economics and security affairs. Unlike Europe, Kissinger noted, Asia has no multilateral political and security institutions to help integrate its countries, many of which distrust each other profoundly. The United States can realistically aspire neither to democratize all of Asia, Kissinger said, nor to create strong bodies similar to NATO and the EU. But it can aspire to a regional balance that would allow political and economic progress to unfold gradually. Kissinger proposed a multipart U.S. strategy in Asia that would maintain U.S. military strength and multilateral alliances, prevent domination by any hegemonic power, and build greater regional integration.

In particular, Kissinger urged careful attention to preserving close relations with Japan, the bedrock of U.S. security strategy in Asia. He predicted that a sea change in U.S.-Japanese relations would be brought about by Japan's worries over China and Asia, and by its nervousness at relying wholly on the United States for its security. What must be avoided, said Kissinger, is both a remilitarized Japan playing a freewheeling role in Asian security affairs, and a cowed Japan dominated by China. Kissinger proposed a U.S. policy aimed at encouraging Japan to strengthen its military forces gradually while remaining in close partnership with the United States and contributing constructively to a stable Asian security order.

On the Korean Peninsula, Kissinger endorsed continued security collaboration with the Republic of Korea, coupled with multilateral diplomacy aimed at containing North Korea and halting its pursuit of nuclear weapons.

Kissinger's main focus on potential dangers, however, was China's emerging role in Asian security affairs and its relationship with Japan. The United States should treat China neither as a strategic partner nor as an implacable adversary. A growing economic and military power, China has an authoritarian government that might embrace nationalism and hegemonic ambitions and might seek to subordinate its neighbors and drive the United States out of Asia. However, wrote Kissinger, this bleak future is not inevitable. He urged a balanced U.S. policy of both firmness and moderation toward China, aimed at dissuading it from menacing conduct while welcoming it into the world economy and global security system if it chooses to act responsibly.

In South Asia, Kissinger proposed a U.S. policy aimed at building improved relations with India, which is becoming a major power, while stabilizing the Indo-Pakistan rivalry.

Kissinger portrayed the Middle East as a troubled region in transition, facing multiple difficulties, including Arab-Israeli tensions, turbulent geopolitics in the Persian Gulf, Islamic fundamentalism, menacing conduct by Iraq and Iran, and authoritarian governments. Kissinger blamed the failure of the Oslo peace process on Palestinian leader Yasir Arafat's refusal of a generous offer by Israeli Prime Minister Ehud Barak in 2000. Rather than continued pursuit of an overall settlement, Kissinger urged a step-by-step negotiation aimed at gradually ameliorating tensions by creating a Palestinian state while protecting Israel's security. He portrayed Iraq and Iran as continuing threats to peace in the Persian Gulf as well as to U.S. interests. Writing before the invasion of Iraq, he viewed efforts to negotiate with Saddam Hussein as a failure and concluded that regime change was the only viable choice. Regarding Iran, he expressed doubt that unilateral concessions would motivate it to abandon its pursuit of nuclear weapons and support of terrorism. Kissinger therefore urged a joint U.S.-European diplomacy of firmness, with concessions if Iran reciprocated.

Africa, too, was identified by Kissinger as a troubled region in transition. He expressed doubt that U.S. calls for regional democratization could solve the continent's problems. He called for a multilateral approach, led by the United Nations, to lessen genocidal violence, reduce poverty, and promote effective governance.

In both issues of economic globalization and of Western intervention in local crises such as the one in the Balkans, Kissinger pointed to the need for wise U.S. diplomacy and political leadership. Like Friedman and Gilpin, Kissinger expressed the belief that globalization offers the prospect of bringing economic growth to poor regions that can capitalize on its opportunities, but that it could leave unprepared countries in the backwaters of an increasingly competitive world economy. While the Western model of democracy and capitalist markets may provide a path to rapid economic progress, he warned that it often cannot be adopted by poor countries because of the social and political disruption that accompany it. He urged U.S. leadership in such institutions as the G–8, the World Bank, and the IMF in safeguarding the world economy against shocks and recessions, and in helping poor countries develop competitive economies.

On the subject of Western intervention in the Balkans and other violent regions, Kissinger observed that the old Westphalian standard of respecting national sovereignty is giving way to the principle of preventing dictators from committing genocide against their own people, as in Bosnia and Kosovo. But Kissinger also urged U.S. caution in this arena, pointing out that while Western intervention in Bosnia and Kosovo may have temporarily suppressed violence, it has not yet brought political stability to the Balkans.

In these two books, Kissinger attacked what he described as a strain of naïve Wilsonian idealism in U.S. foreign policy. Kissinger was critical of some Clinton administration policies, although in its later years, the Clinton administration was moving in some of the general directions Kissinger recommended. In contrast, the subsequent Bush administration rejected many of Kissinger's traditional conservative suggestions in favor of assertive interventionist concepts. Kissinger's emphasis on establishing equilibrium with other major powers, and on acting prudently in the face of intractable regional problems that do not lend themselves to easy solutions, is cautionary advice to those who regard assertion of American power and preeminence as ready solutions to the world's problems.

Despite his knowledge and experience, Kissinger, like many others, failed to anticipate the degree to which global terrorism would erupt as a central challenge only a few months after his second book was published. The question, however, is whether the sense of history, geopolitical realism, and regional priorities he outlined are appropriate guides for U.S. foreign policy. Kissinger undeniably provided valuable insights in calling for an equilibrium among major powers through a skillful blending of idealism and realism.

Richard Haass: Traditional Conservatism After Iraq

In his 2005 book, *The Opportunity: America's Moment to Alter History's Course*, Richard Haass articulated a U.S. strategic agenda of updated traditional conservatism.[6] In an earlier book, *The Reluctant Sheriff*, Haass had argued for a U.S. global leadership role to bring stability to post–Cold War security affairs.[7] In his 2005 book, he assessed the new U.S. role in the aftermath of the

Iraq invasion. Acknowledging the argument of those who favor use of U.S. primacy and power to quell the threats of terrorism and WMD proliferation in the Middle East, Haass argued that the United States had gone too far in this direction, and in doing so risked poisoning its cooperative relationships with other major powers. Haass faulted the Clinton administration for devoting too little attention to global security affairs, but was also critical of the Bush administration's handling of the war on terrorism. He called the Bush Doctrine "less a coherent policy than a mix of counterterrorism, democracy promotion, preemption, and unilateralism."[8] The purpose of his book was to outline a new U.S. foreign policy doctrine of integrating the major powers into cooperative relationships capable of meeting the challenges of a globalizing world.

Like Kissinger, Haass envisioned the creation of a new Concert of Europe in which the United States, Europe, Russia, China, Japan, and India would work constructively together, not only to quell terrorism and WMD proliferation, but also to forge peace and economic progress across the world. To achieve such a high degree of major power integration and cooperation, Haass said, the United States must take the lead, but it could not rely on unilateral assertion of American military power or a unilateral strategic agenda, which would polarize the major powers and provoke opposition. Instead, he argued, the United States must employ persuasive diplomacy and consensus-building to enlist the major powers to work collaboratively. The United States must listen carefully to the major powers, respect their legitimate interests, embrace their goals when appropriate, and, if need be, modify some of its foreign policy options in response. Such negotiations and bargained relationships would, he argued, help the United States form a truly powerful coalition that could achieve its legitimate aims in the Middle East and elsewhere.

The early 21st century is unusual, Haass wrote, because for the first time in centuries, the major powers are not directly at geopolitical odds with each other on the world stage, nor are they pursuing conflicting ideologies; rather, they share many similar interests and aims. This creates an unprecedented opportunity for a solid consensus among the major powers; common policies, rules, and regulations could aim at halting genocide, quelling terrorism and WMD proliferation, minimizing wars, and promoting global economic growth through open trade. But this opportunity is fleeting, he warned; if it is lost, the world could descend into a new dark age of anarchy and violence, a new Cold War between the United States and China, or both.

Because of its unique status and strength, Haass said, the United States may be capable of forging this new concert of major powers. But its preoccupation with its own primacy and tendency to assert its military power unilaterally may cause the United States to miss this opportunity. To its own peril and that of world peace, the United States is mostly driving the major powers away rather than bringing them closer. Moreover, the United States is not being effective at carrying out its own foreign policy in the Middle East; it is finding out that, although its military power can be used to win wars, it cannot readily be used to win the peace afterward. Iraq is an example, he said, of an unwarranted war, although he agreed that, having started it, the United States must bring it to a successful conclusion.

Haass argued that if the United States shows flexibility in its own positions, the major powers can be persuaded to accept the broad framework of values and goals that animate U.S. policy in the Middle East and elsewhere. Much of his book is devoted to spelling out how these cooperative relationships could be manifested in a number of important policy areas, including terrorism, WMD proliferation, and global trade policy.

Haass proposed creation of a global coalition dedicated to quelling terrorism, with an immediate goal of reducing terrorism to its pre–September 11, 2001, levels. He argued that the reason radical Islamic fundamentalists hate the United States is not its cultural values, but rather specific U.S. policies in the Middle East and elsewhere. Accordingly, he proposed U.S. policy shifts aimed at lessening this hatred, including reducing U.S. support for authoritarian Arab regimes, reducing the U.S. military profile in the Persian Gulf, and increasing support for a Palestinian state on the West Bank and for political reforms and economic modernization, if not rapid full-scale democratization, across the Middle East.

In order to slow or halt WMD proliferation, Haass proposed stronger enforcement of the Nuclear Non-Proliferation Treaty to make it harder for countries to acquire enriched uranium and plutonium that could be used to make nuclear weapons. He also proposed accelerated U.S. and Russian nuclear reductions, stronger efforts to control Russian nuclear stockpiles, a reconsideration of current U.S. plans to develop a new generation of nuclear weapons, and a U.S. declaratory policy of no first use of any unconventional weapon of mass destruction. Haass said that the tough cases of North Korea and Iran could best be handled through multilateral diplomacy employing economic sanctions and inducements to persuade the two countries to abandon their nuclear efforts. While he did not rule out use of military force as a last resort, he pointed out that as a practical matter, military strikes against either were not likely to be successful. He also expressed doubts that policies aimed at changing the regimes of these countries would work.

Haass proposed that a global coalition of major powers should seek to expand economic integration so as to broaden the benefits of globalization.

A main mechanism of accelerated globalization would be pursuit of open trade coupled with efforts to lower tariffs and other protectionist or trade-distorting measures. Poor countries could, he said, best achieve economic progress if they were allowed to sell their agricultural products in Western markets, and if they encouraged foreign direct investment. He also called for efforts to develop alternative sources of energy, coupled with policies aimed at reducing energy consumption in the United States and elsewhere.

Haass ended his book by arguing that creation of a global coalition of major powers is a realistic goal. China and Russia are mostly focused on their own economic development, he said, while India has shed its reflexive anti-Americanism; all would now prefer cooperation with the United States. Japan is gradually coming out of its shell and is increasingly willing to play a constructive global role under U.S. leadership. Europe is a more complex case; Haass argued that the main U.S. goal should be to ensure that Europe emerges as a partner of the United States rather than becoming increasingly inward-looking, or else becoming a rival. Thus, he called for U.S. policies aimed at fostering partnership with Europe, coupled with diplomatic efforts to bring in Russia, China, Japan, and India in order to achieve the goal of a global coalition.

A strategy of diplomatic persuasion, wrote Haass, could build consensus among the major powers, and globalization offers opportunities to help achieve this goal. He seems correct in arguing that the United States cannot handle this demanding job on its own, that it needs help from strong and committed allies, and that a wise, patient U.S. diplomacy could broaden the scope of collaboration there and elsewhere. Haass may or may not be correct about the feasibility of creating a strong global coalition of major powers, but it is undoubtedly true that even modest progress toward greater consensus would enhance the odds that the United States and its allies can succeed at suppressing new threats and fostering global peace and economic progress. A principal task facing U.S. foreign policy, Haass would agree, is to perform better at the twofold task of asserting American power and strengthening global partnerships, rather than pursuing one at the expense of the other.

Zbigniew Brzezinski: Geopolitical Chess in Eurasia and Dealing with Islamic Fundamentalism

Brzezinski's books fall into the category of progressive multilateralism because of his insistence that the United States should work closely with its European allies to enlarge the democratic community that could help handle geopolitical troubles. In *The Grand Chessboard*, published in 1997, Brzezinski analyzed the new era in geopolitical terms and updated the analysis presented in his 1993 book (which we discussed in chapter three).[9] He set out to craft a comprehensive and integrated U.S. geostrategy for managing the vast Eurasian region that stretches from Europe to Asia, with *geostrategy* defined as the conscious management of geopolitical interests. Brzezinski started from the premise that the United States is now the world's only global superpower, with an unusual degree of supremacy everywhere. The United States presides over a hegemonic but liberal "global system," leading a large alliance network and an economic order anchored in market capitalism. Brzezinski deems this system "liberal" because it enjoys the consensual support of its members; this consent is what sets it apart from earlier empires, which were hierarchical and coercive. While this global system serves U.S. interests, it also serves the interests of its many other members, bringing them security and economic prosperity. However, he noted, it does not cover major parts of the globe; most of Eurasia, for example, lacks unifying institutions and values.

Brzezinski predicted that U.S. global supremacy is transient: other countries will gain relative power in the coming years. However, he wrote, if the United States acts skillfully, with a conscious geostrategy in mind, it may be able to guide a dynamic, dangerous future toward peace and stability. Brzezinski argued for Eurasia as the main focus of U.S. geostrategy. The United States must act, he said, to avert both anarchy and the emergence of a hostile coalition against its interests.

Brzezinski characterized the current U.S. hegemony in Eurasia as shallow, being derived from influence rather than control. Eurasia's five prime "geostrategic players" are France, Germany, Russia, China, and India; also important are Britain, Japan, and Indonesia. He identified five "geopolitical pivots"—Ukraine, Azerbaijan, South Korea, Turkey, and Iran—whose conduct could substantially influence the future. Shaping this complex interaction will not be easy, because many of these countries do not share common interests or strategic concepts with the United States or with each other. Eurasia has the physical potential to dominate future world politics, he pointed out, but it currently is simmering in geopolitical instability.

Brzezinski's proposed U.S. strategy for this "Eurasian chessboard" began with Europe, a potential democratic bridgehead to Russia, Central Asia, South Asia, and Asia. Brzezinski noted that Europe is endeavoring to unify under the EU and bring democracy, markets, and community to the whole continent. Beneath this façade of progress, however, Europe suffers from major problems; Brzezinski identified these as continued dependence upon the United States, a pervasive decline in economic and cultural vitality, an inward perspective that is escapist and isolationist, and a lingering potential to fall back into nationalism and fragmentation. Europe's key leaders, noted Brzezinski, are France and Germany, which are now cooperating, unlike in the past. Their motivations differ: France seeks to regain its historic position as leader of Europe, while Germany hopes for redemption from its 20th-century history by building a unified Europe. Even so, Brzezinski portrayed this French-German reconciliation as a gain for Europe.

Brzezinski expressed concern, however, that if France, Germany, and other continental powers do not act wisely, Europe might drift away from the United States and fall into political conflict with Russia. The United States, too, must act wisely in handling Europe, especially its quest for unification. Brzezinski urged a geostrategy anchored in continued U.S. leadership, preservation of the Atlantic alliance, a co-equal role for Europe as a genuine partner, and greater German and French influence in NATO. The United States should encourage eastward expansion of NATO and the EU, to include Ukraine as well as other countries in Eastern Europe and the Balkans. Such a U.S. geostrategy, said Brzezinski, could create a more genuine transatlantic partnership; a united Europe could serve as a powerful democratic bridgehead to all of Eurasia, while acting as a close partner of the United States.

The collapse of the Russian Empire, wrote Brzezinski, created a geopolitical power void in the critical center of Eurasia. The new Russia, he wrote, is struggling to create democracy but faces serious political and economic troubles and a struggle to regain primacy in the unstable regions around its borders (its "near abroad"). Brzezinski expressed hope that a democratic Russia could become a source of progress in Eurasia, but he also acknowledged concern that Russia might backslide into internal authoritarianism, neoimperial reassertion in Central Asia, and opposition to European enlargement. He urged a U.S. geostrategy toward Russia that would balance firmness and cooperation, aimed at producing a truly democratic Russia that would seek integration with Europe and the United States. The United States should strive to ensure the independence and democratic evolution of Ukraine and other countries around Russia's borders.

What Brzezinski called the "Eurasian Balkans" stretches from the Caucasus—Georgia, Armenia, and Azerbaijan—to Central Asia, including Kazakhstan, Uzbekistan, Turkmenistan, Tajikistan, Kyrgyzstan, and Afghanistan. The "Eurasian Balkans" constitute a region marked by unstable governments, Islamic fundamentalism, poverty, and instability. The area also contains considerable potential riches in oil and natural gas. In the Eurasian Balkans, therefore, a power vacuum tempts outside intervention by Russia, the United States, Europe, Iran, India, and China; the potential for chaotic turbulence and great power competition is high. Reasoning that the United States cannot neglect this important zone, Brzezinski urged a strategy aimed at preserving its geopolitical pluralism, ensuring Western access to its vital resources, and aiding its gradual, steady transition to competent governance and economic progress.

Brzezinski called Eurasia as a whole a region of "metastability," characterized by rigidity and little flexibility. He predicted that if there were a powerful jarring blow, major shifts could produce a destructive chain reaction. Brzezinski especially worried about the interaction among the United States, China, and Japan. China might employ its growing economic and military power to exert influence over Asia to advance its interests, dominate Japan, and lessen U.S. influence. Much will depend, he said, upon whether China's ambition is a modest zone of influence around its seacoasts or a neoimperial dominance of much of Asia, including Southeast Asia.

The greatest danger, he warned, would be an intense multipolar rivalry involving an assertive China, a rearmed and frightened Japan, and a weakened United States struggling to protect its interests. In articulating this fear, Brzezinski's analysis was similar to that of Kissinger: to safeguard against this danger, the best strategy would aim at accommodating China's legitimate designs for an enhanced sphere of influence, while dissuading it from imperial ambitions. Rather than see Japan rearm, he said, the United States should continue protecting it, while encouraging it to lead other nations in multilateral economic and political cooperation. Such a strategy, he said, would require continued U.S. protection of South Korea, Taiwan, and other friends, accompanied by diplomacy aimed at defusing tensions with potential adversaries and promoting gradual reconciliation with them. Brzezinski thus argued against a U.S. strategy of treating China as an adversary by seeking to contain and deter it. Instead, he endorsed a long-term U.S. strategy of accommodating China's rise to power by seeking to include it in a large web of cooperative diplomacy and mutual adjustment, while protecting U.S. and allied interests.

Much of Brzezinski's strategic thinking has been confirmed by the passage of time. Although *The Grand Chessboard* did not address the Middle East, its focus on Eurasia has been validated. As Brzezinski said, although the Middle East is important, control of Eurasia is most critical to whether the world evolves toward anarchy or new great power rivalries, or instead achieves greater stability, peace, and community.

Brzezinski's book received some criticism for relying too heavily upon geopolitical concepts, and for being too preoccupied with giving U.S. foreign policy a geostrategic focus. However, management of the U.S. relationship with Eurasia is, first and foremost, an exercise in geopolitics. As Brzezinski argued, broad visions of democratic integration, economic globalization, communications networks, and community building can be pursued only if the United States can first master underlying Eurasian geopolitics to help lay a foundation of stability. Likewise, Brzezinski's policy recommendations may be criticized by some as being too ready to accommodate China, as well as France and Germany, too eager to carve up Russia's fading empire, or too neglectful of the critical roles played by Britain and Japan as powerful and indispensable allies of the United States. Like Kissinger's books, Brzezinski's 1997 volume has been criticized in retrospect for failing to foresee the dangers of transnational threats, especially terrorism. But his geopolitical perspective on Eurasia and his insistence on a comprehensive U.S. strategy of multilateralism provide considerable food for thought.

In his 2004 work *The Choice: Global Domination or Global Leadership*, Brzezinski focused more specifically on the Middle East, Islamic fundamentalism, terrorism, and the imperatives of multilateralism.[10] He again portrayed American hegemonic preeminence as fleeting and said that the principal challenge is for the United States to use its power wisely. He expressed concern about whether a democracy with fractious domestic politics can consistently carry out a conscious geopolitical strategy. Brzezinski again called upon the United States to develop a global strategy that would strive to integrate Russia into the democratic community and to keep East Asia stable. Rather than focus on all of Eurasia as he did in *The Grand Chessboard*, Brzezinski mainly addressed U.S. strategy in the Middle East and throughout the "Global Balkans," the critical subregion between Europe and the Far East. He urged that the United States should not focus its policy solely on suppressing terrorist threats, should not think only in military terms, and should not act unilaterally. In these respects, he was critical of the Bush administration and the neoconservative principles of some of its members.

The 2003 invasion of Iraq showed manifestations of a growing trend toward unilateralism, said Brzezinski. He refrained from passing judgment on the invasion, but he was critical of how the Bush administration handled the global politics of the pre-invasion period. He expressed concern that if the United States develops a reputation for acting unilaterally in using military power against threats, counter to the weight of international consensus, it will become isolated and lose its political power to lead other countries. He advanced cautionary principles for the handling of future crises: in deciding whether and when to launch U.S. military attacks against threats arising from this geographic zone, Brzezinski urged that a distinction be made between *preemptive* attacks—ones launched in the face of a truly imminent threat, in the short period before a well-armed adversary strikes the United States or its allies—and *preventive* attacks—ones launched before a threat is imminent, and designed to prevent an adversary from assembling the physical assets to attack at a later date.

Many preemptive attacks, said Brzezinski, are necessarily unilateral and conducted with great urgency. Preventive attacks, however, allow time for mobilization of international political pressure aimed at forestalling the undesirable from occurring; they should take place only after other remedies have been exhausted and deterrence is no longer viable. The invasion of Iraq, he said, was often portrayed as preemptive, but it was actually preventive, and debate over its necessity would have been appropriate. Regardless of how the invasion of Iraq is appraised by history, Brzezinski argued that the United States should not be quick on the trigger in dealing with future threats, should try to avoid resort to military force if possible, and should act multilaterally when feasible.

Beyond this, said Brzezinski, the United States must think broadly in political and strategic terms rather than focusing mechanically and narrowly on crushing threats. The whole Middle East and Global Balkans, wrote Brzezinski, are beset by dysfunctional politics and societies and are reacting angrily to the threat posed by economic globalization to their traditional values, which they blame on American imperialism. The United States thus faces a task of monumental scope and complexity that, if mishandled, could inflict grave damage on the world as a whole. Terrorism and WMD proliferation must be addressed decisively, he said, and the Israeli-Palestinian conflict must be settled. But he identified as the basic challenge the pacification and modernization of this region and, in the long run, the promotion of cooperative organization there. Critical to the region's progress will be efforts to bring greater economic prosperity, responsible governance, and social reforms. Today's threats, he said, are manifestations of deeper problems that must be remedied if this vital region is to be moved beyond turmoil and violence to a better future.

To meet this strategic challenge, Brzezinski said, the United States and Europe must work together; the United States must approach Europe with a broader perspective and not treat it as subordinate or selectively recruit shifting subcoalitions of allies to participate in the crisis du jour. He argued that the United States must view Europe as a true partner, ceding to it appropriate influence over policy and strategy, and that the Europeans must reciprocate. Above all, Brzezinski cautioned against letting the Atlantic alliance fall apart or, worse, letting the United States and Europe become global rivals. Such a development, he said, would gravely damage both and would cripple their capacity to deal with the Middle East, leaving it, as well as the Global

Balkans, to descend further into violent turmoil. Brzezinski did not express hope that Europe could emerge as an equal partner of the United States any time soon, owing to its current military weakness and political fragmentation. But he judged that, with military and political reforms, it could become a "complementary partner," contributing in vital ways to supplement American power.

The core theme of Brzezinski's book was that the United States should endeavor to lead rather than dominate allied partners and the global security system. While he worried about the future if the United States fails to lead properly, he hoped that wise U.S. leadership could manage the risks of widespread turmoil, by creating a global community of shared interests, shared convictions, and cooperative conduct. Such a global community, he wrote, must be anchored in close U.S.-European cooperation that expands outward to include other countries. He called for a U.S. leadership strategy with five specific features:

- a rational and balanced policy of self-protection that addresses serious threats to American society without provoking an excessive sense of insecurity in others
- a patient, protracted effort to pacify those volatile regions of the globe characterized by the emotional hostility that fuels violence
- a sustained effort to engage the friendly parts of the world in a joint framework to eliminate or contain the sources of greatest danger
- recognition that globalization is not only an opportunity for enhanced trade and profit, but also a phenomenon with a moral and cultural dimension
- an effort to foster a democratic political culture that acknowledges the complex responsibilities inherent in global interdependence.

Two of Brzezinski's basic prescriptions—that the United States and Europe should work closely together, and that they should think about the Middle East in strategic, long-range terms aimed at resolving basic problems—are hard to refute. Indeed, many other observers share them. The challenge for U.S. policy lies in implementing this wise guidance when intense crises erupt and the two would-be partners differ over how to respond. As Brzezinski pointed out, a close and frank dialogue between the United States and Europe is needed if the Atlantic alliance is to be preserved and to remain relevant.

Brzezinski raised valid points about the distinction between preemptive and preventive attacks on adversaries, yet even making this distinction does not resolve all of the issues around such attacks. In both cases, thoughtful judgment is necessary. The debate over invading Iraq involved assessment of a series of strategy choices such as whether continued containment was still viable, whether forceful regime change was necessary, and whether nationbuilding there could be successful. Future crises are likely to produce similarly contentious debates, even if there is clarity about preemption versus prevention. Similarly, Brzezinski's call for U.S. cooperation with Europe makes sense, but it is equally true that the Europeans must be willing to accept new roles and burdens in managing difficult security affairs. They cannot leave this responsibility to the United States, and then criticize it when its judgment is not subject to a European veto.

While arguments will persist regarding military intervention, many observers will agree with Brzezinski that the United States must seek to lead rather than to dominate, and that it should be guided by strategic principles more nuanced than simply attempting to crush threats when they appear. In this sense, Brzezinski resembles Kissinger, even though their geopolitical analyses differ in some details. In order for the United States to play a strong leadership role, partners must play complementary and supportive roles. As Brzezinski acknowledged, Europe's stance toward cooperation with the United States is uncertain, as are its unity, willpower, and physical capacity to assert power beyond its borders. Mobilizing Europe may not be easy, even if some European governments want to cooperate with the United States, and even if the United States adopts the forthcoming attitude endorsed by Brzezinski. Yet even partial steps in the direction he advises could provide important payoffs.

Curing the Middle East and the Eurasian Balkans of their deep-seated problems will be difficult challenges. As Brzezinski pointed out, a holistic cure is needed for this vast region to foster stable security affairs and modern governments, economies, and societies. The bottom line is that Brzezinski's strategic vision has undeniable force, but the feasibility of implementing it can be questioned. The United States is likely to face suboptimal circumstances in dealing with its allies as well as the globe's tumultuous zones.

Joseph S. Nye, Jr.: Making Better Use of Soft Power

Nye falls into the category of progressive multilateralist, in part because of his emphasis on using *soft power*—a country's capacity to persuade other countries to accept its agenda by convincing them of its merits—to enlarge the circle of countries willing to cooperate with the United States. Nye has written many books on world affairs and U.S. foreign policy. His 1990 book, *Bound to Lead: The Changing Nature of American Power,* questioned the idea, then popular, that the United States was doomed to decline as a result of imperial overstretch (as suggested by Paul Kennedy in his 1987 book, which we address below).[11] By contrast, Nye's 2002 book, *The Paradox of American Power: Why the World's Only Superpower Can't Go It Alone*, cautioned against the belief that American and Western values are destined to spread over the world. In it, he argued that the United States needs cooperative allies in order to pursue a demanding global agenda of managing security affairs.[12] In his 2004 work, *Soft Power: The Means to Success in World Politics*, Nye addressed issues of hard and soft power, arguing that current U.S. foreign policy needs a greater infusion of the latter.[13] Nye argued that the right mix of hard (military and economic) and soft (persuasive) power yields the kind of "smart power" that won the Cold War. Nye had originated the term *soft power* more than a decade earlier, and in his 2004 book, he developed the concept in detail.

Nye wrote that to carry out foreign policy, *power* entails more than the possession of physical assets, but also the ability to get things done and to influence the behavior of others to favor or accept the outcomes that it wants. Thus, Nye said, power is relative: it must be judged in relation to the situations being encountered and the national goals being pursued. The correct measure of power is not the level of resources possessed and expended, but whether success is achieved. If a country is immensely strong in military and economic might, but cannot attain the political outcomes that it seeks abroad, it is not truly powerful.

Hard power, said Nye, refers to a country's capacity to use inducements (carrots), threats (sticks), and physical coercion to achieve its goals. Hard power is anchored in military and economic resources and is measured in terms of a country's ability to command others to support its agendas. By contrast, he wrote, soft power uses persuasion and attractiveness to shape the preferences of countries being influenced. The soft power of a country rests on three resources, wrote Nye: its culture, political values, and foreign policies. A country has soft power if its culture is admired, its political values are shared by other countries, and its foreign policies are seen as legitimate and deserving of support. When a country possesses all three qualities, it is likely to have influence; if it lacks them, it will lack influence. Nye pointed out that soft power is a variable, not a constant; it can be created through wise actions, and it can be lost rapidly through activities that alienate other countries, their governments, and their people.

U.S. foreign policy in today's world, said Nye, requires both hard and soft power. Although its military and economic preeminence gives the United States more hard power than any other country, it is not nearly so dominant in soft power. It does exert substantial global influence through such media as entertainment, language, human rights, education, scientific research, and commerce. But he pointed out that other regions and cultures have soft power of their own. Europe's soft power arises from its reputation for high culture in arts and other arenas, its pursuit of liberal values and welfare societies, and its peace-seeking multilateralism. He noted that soft power gives some countries—for example, Norway—much more international influence than their hard power alone might suggest. Japan, too, possesses soft power in such areas as its extensive trade ties and scientific research. By contrast, China and other Asian countries possess little soft power. Meanwhile, Islamic fundamentalism is acquiring a persuasive soft power among cultures willing to embrace its religious values.

Nye expressed concern that the United States has been losing soft power in recent years. One reason, he said, is that as it plays a leadership role in the turbulent security affairs of many regions, it is acquiring a reputation for coercive behavior that appears menacing, even to neutral observers and allies. Another reason is that economic globalization is causing social and political disruptions in many areas of the world, resulting in angry backlash, and the United States is often blamed: some countries and regions have come to view globalization as an instrument of an American imperialism that deliberately exploits and oppresses them. A third reason, wrote Nye, is that the Bush administration has often behaved in what appears to be an arrogant, high-handed, unilateralist, and imperial style that relishes wielding hard power, ignores soft power, and tramples upon the wishes and interests of many countries and multilateral institutions. Nye pointed to the invasion of Iraq as the most obvious example. Other examples include the Kyoto climate accord and the International Criminal Court, where U.S. actions were contrary to prevailing world opinion.

Nye strongly urged the Bush administration to employ hard power less abrasively and to do a better job of developing and employing soft power. The Bush administration should, he said, downplay its reliance upon military might, economic leverage, and other instruments of coercion, while increasing its efforts at persuasion. While Nye acknowledged that the United States sometimes must act unilaterally, and that it cannot allow its decisions to be made at the United Nations or in foreign capitals, he argued that it should pay greater attention to the preferences of Europeans, other countries, and multilateral bodies, or at least consult more closely with them before taking controversial steps. The United States needs to do a better job of restoring its reputation, credibility, and popularity abroad; Nye especially urged a major U.S. effort to strengthen public diplomacy, including daily media communications, strategic communications about core themes, and cultural contacts with key foreigners through scholarships, seminars, and similar venues.

The United States was not skilled at public diplomacy early in the Cold War, as Nye points out, but it got considerably better over time. Such efforts as the Voice of America and the U.S. Information Agency (USIA) played crucial roles by explaining U.S. foreign policy and by highlighting the attractions of democracy over communism. Since the Cold War ended, however, these efforts at U.S. public diplomacy have noticeably slackened. The USIA has been dismantled; funding for other public diplomacy efforts has dried up and they no longer enjoy the attention of senior U.S. leaders; and few fresh initiatives aimed at addressing new challenges have been launched. U.S. foreign aid to poor countries is notoriously ungenerous. Nye charged that the United States has done a particularly poor job of public diplomacy in the Middle East and the Islamic world, where the U.S. image has declined and anti-Americanism has soared. Arguing that U.S. foreign policy has suffered because of this deficiency, he urged greater attention to public diplomacy and more funding for it.

Nye may underestimate the extent to which the United States employs soft power today. Even so, his book identifies a challenge confronting U.S. foreign policy and an area of trouble in its recent diplomacy. As other observers have noted, the United States is a lightning rod for criticism simply because of its size, wealth, and role in world affairs. It uses military power—in peace and war—mainly to protect allies, but distant countries whose security is not directly at stake often criticize such actions. Modern communications systems, moreover, transmit the bad features of American culture as well as the good. The United States is often blamed for drawbacks that are really due to economic globalization. Some of these problems would exist regardless of which political party governs in Washington, but in the eyes of many observers, the Bush administration has compounded them by inadequate use of soft power. Whether it will perform the functions of public diplomacy better in the future is to be seen; in the interim, Nye's book stands out as a well argued assessment of this important subject.

Walter Russell Mead: A New U.S. Grand Strategy of Millennial Capitalism and a Revival of Wilsonianism

We classify Mead's 2004 book, *Power, Terror, Peace, and War: America's Grand Strategy in a World at Risk,* as assertive interventionist, although he is highly critical of many neoconservative policies that are also in that category. Because of its synthetic thinking and bold arguments, the book is widely regarded as one of the more insightful and provocative writings on U.S. foreign policy to emerge since September 11, 2001, the launching of the war on terror, and the invasion of Iraq in 2003.[14] It is controversial, especially on the far ends of the political spectrum, but it has appeal for many readers of centrist instincts who are trying to sort out the strengths and weaknesses of the Bush administration's strategy and its alternatives.

Walter Russell Mead set out to appraise U.S. grand strategy in light of recent events, to explain why this strategy is changing in its fundamentals, and to offer insights on how it can be improved. Mead concluded that the Bush administration is, in many ways, pursuing a proper strategic agenda, but that its policy execution and public diplomacy could and should be better. Along the way, Mead offered a new conceptual formulation of the problems and prospects facing U.S. foreign policy in the early 21st century. Mead is one of the few writers to synthesize economics with security affairs and political ideology, creating a framework that can be used by supporters and critics alike to debate the intertwining issues at stake.

Mead began by arguing that ever since the onset of the Cold War, the United States has been pursuing an ambitious "American Project" aimed at reshaping global affairs. The core idea, said Mead, has been to protect U.S. security while building a peaceful world linked by common values and common prosperity. He identifies three interlocking U.S. instruments: military power and security alliances, or "hard power"; capitalist economics anchored in global trade, or "sticky power"; and the spread of democratic values to new regions, which he calls "sweet power." These three forms of power, said Mead, together create a fourth type, "hegemonic power," which creates a structural framework of global politics and economics within which other nations must act. By using these four instruments during the Cold War, wrote Mead, the United States experienced great success in carrying out its ambitious and revolutionary American Project while wearing down its principal opponent, the communist Soviet Union. It succeeded because the American Project benefited not only the United States, but also many allies and partners, which acquiesced or actively supported it.

Mead then argued that during 1989–2001, the United States lost its strategic bearings because it assumed that the American Project had become so successful that it could now be left on autopilot to sweep over the world on its own without top-down guidance and careful nurturing. Both the traditional conservatives who dominated the George H.W. Bush administration and the progressive multilateralists of the Clinton administration, he contends, took continued success for granted. The result, he wrote, was to leave the United States largely blind to a new set of strategic problems.

During that period, Mead said, while the U.S. security strategy pursued NATO enlargement, its other alliance commitments remained remarkably constant in their focus on containing such regional menaces as North Korea,

Iraq, and Iran. What changed, Mead said, was the approach to capitalism, both at home and abroad. From the 1930s onward, he wrote, the United States had pursued "Fordism," a combination of an industrial-era, production-line economy and a growing welfare state managed by the Federal Government. Aimed at dampening the disastrous effects of rampant Victorian capitalism during the Gilded Age, Fordism, as Mead described it, called for the state to regulate domestic economies to prevent economic depressions, and to provide social safety nets to protect disadvantaged classes. It also allowed for regulation of global trade in order to shield national economies from damaging external competition. Outside the United States, wrote Mead, Fordism was popular in many regions—wealthy and poor—because it offered a path to prosperity and social stability and a rationale for national governments to strengthen their roles in economic and strategic management.

By the 1980s, Mead argued, Fordism had outlived its appeal and was seen as a barrier to economic growth because it entrusted too much regulatory power to governments; this was said to strangle market competition, a principal engine of growth. In response, Ronald Reagan and Margaret Thatcher shifted to "Millennial Economics," a new form of capitalism that scaled back government regulation, liberated competitive markets, reduced social safety nets, and created international institutions to foster unfettered trade. Millennial economics, launched in the 1980s in the United States and Britain, began manifesting itself globally in the 1990s, said Mead, and became a main engine of globalization. It was only then that its full effects—both good and bad—became apparent to the world community.

Millennial economics proved popular in parts of Asia, where Japan, South Korea, Taiwan, and others took advantage of it to anchor their economies on exports and earn immense profits. But millennial economics came as a great shock to many other regions. In Europe, said Mead, it threatened not only welfare-state policies, which enjoyed widespread popular support, but also political power structures, especially rule by liberal democratic and socialist parties. In Russia, Latin America, and Africa, it endangered longstanding government management of national economies. It administered the greatest jolts, wrote Mead, in the Middle East, where the combination of assertive capitalist economics, fledgling democracies, accelerating communications, and the growing presence of U.S. military forces threatened not just governmental power structures and economic practices, but traditional social structures and values as well. The result was an angry religious backlash manifested in the form of Islamic fundamentalism and terrorism directed at the United States.

Mead urged the U.S. Government to be more aware of how its actions abroad provoked stress and turmoil in world affairs. The accelerating pursuit of millennial capitalism and "Revival Wilsonianism," the name he gave to the headstrong pursuit of democratization, is a major cause of the rising opposition to U.S. hegemony in Europe, the Middle East, Asia, and elsewhere. However, Mead did not call for the United States to abandon these two strategic concepts or their accompanying grand strategy. He pointed out that the new U.S. grand strategy enjoys strong consensual support among several powerful domestic constituencies: the Hamiltonian business community, traditional Jacksonians who believe in markets at home and strength abroad, neoconservative intellectuals, and evangelical Christians. All of these groups, said Mead, cluster within the Republican Party. A second reason to continue with this new American Project and grand strategy, anchored in vigorous capitalist markets and democratic enlargement, is that it has a great deal to offer to the entire world, said Mead: it offers organizing principles for a potential new global security structure and world economy anchored in stability, democracy, and prosperity.

Based on his appraisal, Mead approved of the strategic directions being pursued by the George W. Bush administration from 2001 onward. In important ways, said Mead, President Bush is moving with the tides of history, but equally important, there are no viable strategic alternatives. U.S. withdrawal into isolationism and a dismantling of the American-led system, he said, would trigger a worldwide descent into anarchy, chaos, and violence. Although an effort to cling to Fordist economics and politics might temporarily lessen the stress on many governments and societies, over the long term it would lead to permanent economic stagnation. Thus, the Bush administration is on the right strategic track, he argued, but it has not done an especially good job of implementing this new grand strategy, nor of explaining it at home or abroad.

Surveying U.S. policy in the Middle East, Mead viewed the war on terror and the invasion of Iraq as necessary strategic choices. The United States, he said, was correct to treat terrorism as an act of war, not a legal problem, and it had no choice but to invade Afghanistan in order to deal with the Taliban and al Qaeda. Continued containment of Saddam Hussein of Iraq was not a viable choice because, he said, this strategy had irretrievably failed. The choice facing the United States, as Mead saw it, was to let Saddam Hussein recapture his regional power and engage in increasingly menacing conduct, or else to pursue regime change through military intervention. In Mead's view, the Bush administration made the right choice to invade, but it did a poor job of publicly explaining the strategic rationale because it focused on weapons of mass destruction rather than on the many other threats posed by Iraq's dictator, and on the positive opportunities for opening the door to regional democratization.

Elsewhere in the world, Mead wrote, the Bush strategy has much to recommend it, although this does not imply that the United States should have a hard-right foreign policy or that only the Republican Party can lead effectively. The Bush administration was correct, in Mead's view, to shift U.S. foreign policy from its previous Eurocentrism, where its strategic goals had been mostly attained by the late 1990s, to a focus on the Middle East, South Asia, and East Asia, where the new issues, challenges, threats, and partners are. In Asia, Mead wrote, the Bush administration has been pursuing a sensible strategy, aimed at preserving a stable security structure among China, Japan, and other big powers while using economics to foster greater political integration. Mead views the Bush administration as correct in favoring informal coalitions and partnerships rather than relying upon formal multilateral institutions such as the United Nations and the World Trade Organization, both of which get too mired in seeking consensus to make major strategic innovations. Moreover, he said, the United States must be prepared to act unilaterally when its citizens, homeland, and vital interests are threatened.

Yet the Bush administration failures are readily apparent, said Mead, and need to be corrected before greater damage is done. Mead sharply criticized the administration for failing to prepare for the occupation of Iraq. He faulted it for poor public diplomacy in failing to explain its reasons for the invasion of Iraq and for other aspects of its assertive foreign policy. Poor public diplomacy further inflamed an already damaging confrontation with the Europeans, he said, brought about by the confrontational tactics of France's Jacques Chirac and Germany's Gerhard Schroeder. He also faulted the Bush administration for neglecting Latin America and for taking other controversial actions without explaining its reasons, thus alienating leaders in many countries, even some that are normally friendly to the United States. This abrasive, unforthcoming style of diplomacy, wrote Mead, was the fault of some neoconservatives in the Bush administration who were deaf to the opinions of others. Overall, in his view, the Bush administration has often acted soundly for the right strategic reasons, but has done so with an overbearing style that is counterproductive.

What directions should U.S. foreign policy and strategy take in the future? At the end of his book, Mead rejected a return to the "ahistorical 1990s" as infeasible and undesirable. Indeed, he said, even the Clinton administration was moving toward a more assertive foreign policy during its last years. Thus, he cautioned against any temptation to blame America's current troubles solely on the Bush administration, which might suggest that they could easily be corrected if a different foreign policy team were in place. Foreign policy in today's world, said Mead, is a difficult enterprise, and it inevitably is accompanied by mistakes, especially as a new U.S. strategy is being launched and its details worked out.

Mead endorsed a strategy of "forward containment" aimed at suppressing terrorists on their home ground, along with efforts to build healthy societies in the Muslim world that could counter their appeal. He urged strong U.S. efforts to win the war of ideas: most of today's terrorists, he said, are "Arabian Fascists" whose dark ideas must by countered by democratic ideals and encouragement of moderate Islamic values. He also called for U.S. policies aimed at settling the Palestinian-Israeli dispute, which inflames Arab public opinion against the United States and produces more terrorists.

In addition, Mead called for the United States to mend fences with its European allies and to encourage them to work closely with the United States in handling dangerous regions outside Europe. He called for better U.S. public diplomacy to explain the strategic rationale and justification for the Bush strategy. He recommended U.S. policies aimed at reforming multinational institutions, including the United Nations and various regional bodies, rather than wholly abandoning them in a misplaced emphasis on American unilateralism. Finally, he called for greater foreign aid to underdeveloped countries, to help these countries benefit from the globalizing economy and take advantage of millennial economics.

Perhaps Mead's greatest conceptual contribution comes from his identification of changing economic conditions as a fundamental dynamic that is altering world politics and how governments behave at home and abroad. Mead doubtless is correct in pointing to the importance of this powerful dynamic. Yet critics might suggest that sometimes he makes too much of it, while neglecting the extent to which new security affairs have a powerful impact of their own. For example, the political conflict between India and Pakistan is not fueled by economic issues, while if China and Japan fall into rivalry, the reason will be traditional great power rivalry, not differences in their view on millennial economics.

Nonetheless, Mead's book does a good job of critiquing the Bush administration's national security strategy by acknowledging both its strengths and its liabilities. His defense of the Bush strategy as sound at its fundamentals, if flawed in its execution, is thought-provoking; it reflects centrist, bipartisan, integrative thinking, qualities that are needed in the current era of divisive argument. As Mead suggests, a visionary national security strategy that is not effectively implemented and that does not recognize its own limits, thereby failing to attain its goals, cannot be judged a success without improvements.

Another key issue raised by Mead is whether new-era global economics and security affairs require a new U.S. national security strategy that is significantly different from that of the 1990s, and whether the Bush strategy is, in fact, correct about many fundamentals. While these issues seem likely to be debated in the years ahead, Mead has staked out an important position.

Niall Ferguson: Can the American "Empire" Be Sustained?

The idea that the United States is an imperial power presiding over a global empire has been a staple of the European political left for some time. In recent years, this idea has gained traction on both sides of the political spectrum in the United States, and a number of scholars have used it to provide a conceptual framework for their writings on U.S. foreign policy and world politics. The 2004 book by Niall Ferguson falls into the latter category and thus belongs to the assertive interventionist school. *Colossus: The Price of America's Empire* portrayed the United States as presiding over an empire in the broad sense of the term: a large geographical area outside its borders over which it has considerable influence.[15] The American version, he wrote, is not an empire in the extreme historic sense of an ancient imperial hegemon that exercises dictatorial and exploitative control over oppressed vassals and tributaries. But judged in terms of its influential presence and functional activities in so many regions, he said, the American influence does have many of the trappings of empire.

Ferguson did not portray this "empire" as malevolent. He characterized it, rather, as a "liberal empire" that not only serves U.S. interests but also performs valuable public services: encouraging democracy and human liberties, promoting economic progress through capitalist markets, and safeguarding peaceful stability in endangered regions. The world would be far worse off if the United States were to abandon its empire or somehow lose it, said Ferguson, because the consequence would be an "apolar" world: not one of multipolar rivalry among great powers, but an amorphous, unstructured world of anarchy and violence. The core problem, said Ferguson, is that the United States is not very effective at empire management and does not relish the task. Ferguson expressed concern that the American government and people will tire of the burdens of empire, withdraw from global leadership, and leave the world to chaos. His main policy recommendation was that the United States should consciously commit itself to sustaining its empire over the long haul, and that the Europeans should be encouraged to help it, rather than seeking to shape a competitive empire of their own. Thus, Ferguson essentially calls upon the United States to be a Hobbesian global Leviathan for the 21st century.

Ferguson reviewed the history of empires. Centuries ago, the Roman Empire presided over the Mediterranean zone. During the 19th century, the British Empire ruled much of the world but, on the eve of World War I, it was challenged by the German, Austro-Hungarian, Russian, and Ottoman Empires for control of Europe and distant colonies. World War I and World War II washed away these empires and, as Ferguson tells it, two new empires rose to replace them: the Soviet Empire and the American Empire. He portrayed the Cold War as a global contest for supremacy between these two empires and the ideologies that they represented. When the dust settled, the Soviet Empire had dissolved, leaving the United States as a global superpower leading a large liberal empire, confronting anarchical chaos in many turbulent regions.

Americans deny having an empire, said Ferguson, or ever trying to create one, yet their current empire is a product of a long and often deliberate series of actions. The Americans settled the North American continent during the 19th century through overt, step-by-step imperial expansion. Then, he wrote, they took control of the Atlantic and Pacific oceans along their borders, and expanded steadily outward to seize Hawaii and the Philippines, dominate Cuba, Puerto Rico, and other Caribbean countries, and invade several Central American countries in the pursuit of "dollar diplomacy." During the early 1900s, President Theodore Roosevelt was an exponent of imperialism. During World War I, however, the United States was led by Woodrow Wilson, whose anti-imperial values called for dismantling of the German, Austrian, and Ottoman Empires. During World War II, Ferguson wrote, President Franklin Roosevelt similarly embraced liberal values, calling not only for the destruction of Nazism, fascism, and Japanese militarism, but also for decolonization and the dismantling of the many colonies held by European powers, including Britain and France. The result, said Ferguson, was a power vacuum in Europe and elsewhere that mandated U.S. intervention. This set the stage for the emergence of a de facto U.S. Empire, paradoxically erected on an anti-imperial ideology opposed to empires and colonies.

Today's American Empire, said Ferguson, bears some resemblance to the ancient Roman Empire, which endured for centuries. The American Empire, however, is animated by a liberal moral and strategic philosophy that, to Ferguson, better resembles that of the British Empire of 1850 to 1930. Britain's Victorians, Ferguson argued, were partly motivated by a self-serving quest for natural resources and raw materials, investment and trading opportunities, profits, and competition with other colonial powers. But they also had loftier goals: they sought to create integrated commodity and financial markets, to foster oceangoing commerce, and to create a 19th-century version of globalization. They aspired to develop effective government, educated workforces, and modern societies in the countries that they occupied, and to build new institutions, infrastructure, and capitalist economies. They also favored developing democracy in places where it appeared to be feasible to do so. Although they typically occupied colonies for decades, said Ferguson, they eventually departed from nearly all of them, and in many cases the countries they left behind were better off because of the British presence. The British Victorians, said Ferguson, acquired their empire—which at its height ruled nearly 25 percent of the world's land surface—by happenstance as much as by design, but they took to the task of imperial management eagerly. Thousands of talented, well-educated English gladly left their homeland to spend their careers in India or other far-off places, serving their empire while ruling colonies and seeking to elevate them toward democracy and capitalist prosperity.

America's Empire, said Ferguson, is different from the British Empire in many respects. For example, it commands less land, but it possesses far more military and economic power. Yet it is driven by similar core principles and values, although few Americans realize the degree to which they resemble modern-day Victorians. The United States, said Ferguson, experienced considerable success at empire-building during the Cold War's initial years; it occupied Germany and Japan and presided over their security, democratization, and economic progress, which helped rebuild Western Europe and East Asia. This success was achieved, however, partly because the Americans were dealing with modern societies capable of democracy and capitalism. The United States was not, as Ferguson notes, especially successful in other places, achieving only a standoff in the Korean War, and defeat (albeit with few lasting consequences) in Vietnam. Nor did U.S. forays elsewhere, such as in Latin America and the Caribbean, have particularly good results. Thus, he concluded that American imperialism during the Cold War had a checkered record.

Charging the Clinton administration with an unwillingness to accept the tough security challenges of the new era, Ferguson supported the decision of the Bush administration to throw the United States into the Middle East and Central Asia to rescue these regions from terrorism, dictators, WMD proliferation, aggression, Islamic fundamentalism, poverty, and other evils. Quite apart from whether Saddam Hussein possessed WMD, Ferguson said, the Bush administration had ample reasons for invading Iraq; indeed, he argued, the invasion should have been mounted years earlier. Ferguson approved of Bush's lofty goals of bringing democracy, freedom, and capitalist prosperity to the Middle East. He also argued that the United States must be the leader; neither the United Nations, nor Europe, nor NATO are up to the task. But he also pointed out that the United States has taken on a monumental job in a region that does not welcome its imperial presence, does not share its values, and may not be capable of taking the steps needed to achieve success in the foreseeable future. Ferguson pointed to the difficulties encountered by the British and French—both of whom had considerable prior experience as colonial occupiers—when they tried to pacify and democratize the Middle East during the early 20th century. They managed to create modern states in many countries. But soon after they left, or were driven out, most of these countries slid into dictatorships, with stagnant economies and premodern societies.

Ferguson did not question the moral intentions and strategic judgments of the U.S. Government in abandoning its traditional distance to wade ashore in the Middle East. The United States is not, he contended, seeking oil or looking to serve the Israeli government; nor is it, as sometimes charged, blind to the legitimate aspirations of Arabs. The problem, he said, is that unlike the Victorian British, the United States is not a patient colonizer, occupier, and empire-builder. The British understood that such efforts take years or decades, and they were willing to spend the necessary time, blood, and treasure. By contrast, he said, the Americans deny their own imperial intentions and obligations and are typically unwilling to commit the necessary money, talent, or manpower. They also suffer from an attention deficit, he wrote: preoccupied elsewhere, they only intermittently focus on the gritty, frustrating tasks of empire, which often do not show immediate payoffs. Ferguson's more fundamental charge is that the Americans do not have an overseas mind-set, much less an imperial mind-set; they are, he said, preoccupied with the opportunities and pleasures of life on their own continent. They have a record of stubborn persistence in regions where their vital interests are at stake, such as Europe and Northeast Asia, but elsewhere, he wrote, they are willing to assert themselves only when victory can be achieved promptly and almost painlessly. Evidence of this attitude, he said, is the U.S. Government's desire to democratize Iraq quickly so as to depart from the country as soon as possible. Such a stance, he said, is incompatible with the difficult realities of the Middle East.

Ferguson expressed fear for the future: if the United States abandons its imperial missions in troubled regions such as the Middle East, the consequence could be a rapid descent into anarchy, chaos, and violence that would damage the Western democracies and global peace. Even if the consequence is not a new dark age, he said, many underdeveloped countries do not have the wherewithal to overcome bad governance and impoverished economies unless they get help from a sponsoring imperial power. Ferguson saw no viable alternatives to U.S. constancy and leadership; he viewed the United Nations and other multinational bodies as too prone to bickering and indecisiveness to act boldly and strongly. Nor is the European Union a candidate for leadership; its federalist aims are inward-looking rather than attuned to any renewal of European imperial leadership. Ferguson also dismissed, as both foolish and contrary to Europe's own interests, the idea of the EU acting as a global counterweight and rival to the United States; Europe's better choice is to act as its partner. Even if Europe continues to lack the military power for major combat operations outside its continent, he said, it does have the military capability to undertake occupation, peacekeeping, and nationbuilding tasks, and to contribute in other ways, including economic aid and diplomacy.

Ferguson concluded with a call for the United States to keep its strategic bearings. If presiding over a global empire may not have been America's original intent, he said, this is now its duty, to itself and to the rest of the world: "Unlike most European critics of the United States, I believe the world needs an effective liberal empire and the United States is the best candidate for the job."[16]

Questions can be asked about Ferguson's use of the term *empire* to describe U.S. foreign policy in the contemporary world. Recent presidents and other senior government officials have insisted that empire is not their intention and that the term is an inappropriate one for their motives or their actions. Indeed, this traditional definition of *empire* does not accurately characterize current U.S. foreign policy: dictionaries and textbooks commonly apply the term to situations in which a hegemonic power holds absolute sovereign control over subordinate countries and peoples, and governs with its own interests primarily in mind, to the point of exploiting occupied territories.

Ferguson tried to solve the problem by qualifying the term, but *liberal empire* does not seem an apt characterization for the U.S. involvement in most regions. Ferguson's comparison with the British Empire seems a stretch: the United States neither governs big countries such as India and Egypt nor controls much of Africa. America's greatest involvements—political, military, and economic—are in Europe and Northeast Asia, and there could be no serious claim that the United States maintains an "empire" in Europe, liberal or otherwise, nor in Northeast Asia. There, as in Europe, the U.S. military presence has its origins in security treaties reached to protect Japan and South Korea from external threats and to remove their incentive to pursue nuclear arms. The United States is sometimes accused of having acted as an imperialist in Latin America; today, however, it is more often accused of neglecting this region by failing to contribute enough to its democratization and economic progress. Only in the greater Middle East does the "empire" metaphor seem remotely plausible, largely because the U.S. invasions of Afghanistan and Iraq seem like actions that the British Victorians would have taken in similar circumstances.

Robert Lieber: How Should American Power Be Asserted?

After the terrorist attacks of September 11, 2001, important departures in U.S. national security strategy were launched. The United States invaded Afghanistan and Iraq and, after toppling the Taliban and Saddam Hussein governments, chose to remain in both countries to try to achieve stability and security and to develop democracy. Elsewhere, the U.S. Government has been active in pursuing the war against terror, opposing WMD proliferation, seeking to help democratize the Middle East, and mobilizing international coalitions to help pursue these goals. These far-flung and ambitious efforts have been conducted under the rubric of the Bush administration's National Security Strategy. Published in late 2002, it unveiled a new U.S. assertiveness on the world stage in the aftermath of September 11.

Robert Lieber, in his 2005 book, *The American Era: Power and Strategy for the 21ˢᵗ Century*, examines questions pertinent to this strategy. For example, to what degree have these global efforts been appropriate? To what degree have they succeeded or failed? How can the performance of U.S. national security strategy be improved? Lieber's book provided a reasoned defense of the Bush administration's strategy in the global war on terror.[17] It articulated many of the premises embraced by neoconservatives in the Bush administration, and it sought to rebut criticism of the Bush strategy. Lieber did criticize the Bush team and the U.S. Government bureaucracies for ineffectiveness in implementing interventions abroad, including in Iraq, but he endorsed the strategic principles that have animated them.

Lieber approved of an assertive U.S. strategy anchored in power, primacy, and a willingness to act decisively including, sometimes, the use of military force and of preemptive attack. Such a bold, power-wielding strategy, he said, is needed for three reasons. First, the deadly combination of global terrorism and WMD proliferation poses a threat of a wholly new magnitude. This threat, motivated by the nihilistic evil of radical Islamist terrorism, has the potential to inflict catastrophic destruction on the United States and its democratic allies. Classical deterrence mechanisms are ineffective; WMD-armed terrorists who cannot be identified and retaliated against cannot be deterred, as the Soviet Union was in the Cold War.

Second, the United Nations and other international institutions are mostly inadequate to handle the most urgent and deadly problems of today. Their incapacity has been revealed not only in Iraq, but in Rwanda, Sudan, and other crisis spots. As a result, says Lieber, the United States—acting with other countries where possible, but alone if necessary—must wield power effectively and constructively to counter and contain terrorism, WMD proliferation, and other threats.

Third, wrote Lieber, in an international system with no central authority, the United States is the preponderant power, and other countries will look to it for leadership. If the United States does not take action on the most dangerous perils, no other country is likely to do so. Effective multilateralism can be achieved only if the United States leads and if other countries lend their weight to the cause.

These premises lead Lieber to conclude that preemptive strategies are needed in order to deal with terrorism and WMD, and that preemption is supported by international law and the just war tradition. U.S. primacy is necessary, he argued, because a large disparity of power is more likely to deter challenges by malevolent actors than to provoke them. Lieber argued that while the United States should make use of allies and multilateral institutions when they are capable of being helpful, its freedom of action should not be limited to cases where there is prior approval by allies or by the UN Security Council. Thus, he endorsed American unilateralism when the situation demands, but he also called for a judicious blend of multilateralism, peacetime engagement, and diplomacy in order to mobilize allies, lessen dangers, and reduce the need to use military force.

In Lieber's eyes, today's dangerous world demands a strategy of U.S. primacy and assertiveness, and this is a better choice than any other alternative. Lieber acknowledged that power and primacy do not necessarily add up to influence and effectiveness, and that the use of military force does not necessarily mean that American political goals will be attained. Effective implementation is vital, as he noted, and requires diplomatic as well as military skill. Provided such a strategy is carried out wisely, said Lieber, it is better than the two competitors: liberal internationalism (what we have called progressive multilateralism) and realism (closer to the views held by those we have called traditional conservatives). A strategy of realism, said Lieber, would mean that the United States would refrain from assertiveness abroad, fearing overcommitment and believing that upsetting the status quo would trigger unpredictable and possibly unmanageable consequences. The problem with realism, Lieber wrote, is its reluctance to address gathering dangers and unwillingness to press for necessary changes. The problem with liberal internationalism, he wrote, is that it leaves the United States hostage to the views of other countries and multilateral institutions that may be unwilling or unable to act, even in the face of great danger.

Although Lieber argued that the risk of imperial overextension is often exaggerated, he acknowledged that there are limits on American power and influence. American military advantages over potential adversaries are increasing, he said, yet the United States already has difficulty carrying out occupation of foreign countries and nationbuilding, missions that can become quagmires that erode domestic public support for interventions abroad. The United States, he wrote, must guard against excessive involvements, and it also must avoid spending so much on defense and national security that it damages its economic health. For these reasons, the United States cannot try to make the entire world secure and prosperous; it should focus on those places where nuclear proliferation and radical Islamic terrorists pose particular threats. Such a focused strategy can work because, he wrote, the United States possesses enough power to carry it out.

Lieber rejected the argument that an American strategy of primacy and assertiveness would alienate Europe and turn it into an adversary of the United States. He noted the opposition in France, Germany, and other countries against the invasion of Iraq, but he also pointed out that the British, Italian, Polish, and several other governments supported the invasion. Acknowledging that some European countries resent American predominance and disagree with the Bush administration's foreign policy, he argued that disputes within the Atlantic alliance are nothing new and have been surmounted before. Today, the alliance is strained by structural factors, including the lack of a Cold War threat and the EU's internal focus on its unification; however, he noted, the dynamics of transatlantic solidarity are also at work. The United States and Europe share basic interests and values, and they have a common cause in combating terrorism and WMD proliferation. Moreover, they need each other in this endeavor; neither can attain its goals without help from the other. Europe lacks military capabilities for power projection comparable to those of the United States, he wrote, but it can contribute in some areas such as peacekeeping and nationbuilding. He concluded that although it is uncertain whether the United States and Europe can achieve greater cooperation in diplomacy and military intervention in the Middle East, a complete rupture of the Atlantic alliance is unlikely.

Lieber was critical of interpretations that blame rampant anti-Americanism on the Bush administration's assertive policy toward terrorism and WMD proliferation. He argued that foreign attitudes are often ambivalent and noted that, although globalization is spreading American culture around the world in ways that sometimes trigger jealousy and resentment, the United States is still admired in many places because of its democracy, openness, and protection of its allies. He attributes recent public opinion polls that reveal anti-Americanism to the views of media elites rather than to enduring or widespread attitudes. Most countries in Asia, including Japan, place a high value on their alliance relationships with the United States, he said, and they identify these relationships as a source of regional stability and progress. In the Middle East, the source of the angry backlash against the United States, Western values, and globalization is found in deep-seated problems of identity in Islamic and Arab societies brought about by social, economic, and political stagnation.

Countering critics of the U.S. invasion of Iraq, Lieber said that the Bush administration was justified in its decision to use military force to overthrow Saddam Hussein. He argued that after September 11, in the climate of mounting fear over terrorism and WMD proliferation, the United States could not afford to leave Saddam Hussein in power, whether or not he possessed chemical and biological weapons at that particular time. Lieber argued that the containment and sanctions regime previously imposed on Saddam Hussein was rapidly eroding and could not be restored, that Saddam Hussein was moving toward a renewed capacity to play a destabilizing role, and that he was supporting terrorism in the Persian Gulf and Middle East. The only option open to the United States, Lieber argued, was to seek regime change, and this could only be accomplished by military invasion. Lieber acknowledged that, after the invasion, the United States did not perform effectively at occupying Iraq, stabilizing it, reenergizing its economy, or installing a new government. However, he judged these to be problems of implementation rather than problems of strategic intent or design. The United States, he said, is on the correct track in asserting its power and leadership in the Middle East and attempting to bring it peace and democracy. The threats posed by global terrorism, WMD proliferation, and radical Islamic fundamentalism, he concluded, leave it no other option, and all allies of the United States would be better off if they cooperated with the United States in dealing with these common dangers.

Limits and Constraints on U.S. Foreign Policy: Toward Offshore Balancing?

Because the U.S. global agenda is so demanding, limits and constraints upon its power and effectiveness must be considered in setting goals and priorities. The books surveyed in this section identify several of these limits and constraints and assess their implications. Our discussion here is intended to touch on five constraints: imperial overstretch, limitations in the executive branch, changes in national character and will, the reluctance of America's allies, and the difficulties of democratization.

Paul M. Kennedy: Imperial Overstretch

One constraint arises from limits on U.S. money, manpower, and other resources. In the late 1980s, Paul Kennedy articulated a theory of "imperial overstretch": his 1987 book, *The Rise and Fall of Great Powers: Economic and Military Conflict from 1500 to 2000*, combined military strategy and economic history to explain the balance of power over five centuries.[18] Kennedy concentrated on the history of Europe and its empires up through the Cold War. His main thesis was that states need wealth to attain military power, and they need military power to acquire and protect wealth. If a state devotes too much of its resources to military purposes instead of to the creation of wealth, this is likely over the long term to lead to a weakening of national power. Kennedy argued that a state at its military height is usually already in a period of relative economic decline. He made the case that many previous great powers, especially those presiding over big empires, spent themselves into bankruptcy trying to pay for external activities that they could not afford.

The first section of Kennedy's book deals with the pre-industrial world, charting the rise of Europe as the seat of power in world affairs. Comparing the decline of the Ming, Ottoman, Japanese, and Russian Empires and the rise of Western Europe, Kennedy argued that a nation in a state of competition is more likely to undergo dynamic changes in order to gain power relative to its competitors. The Ming and Ottoman Empires, in self-imposed isolation, failed to achieve major technological or social change. In contrast, a decentralized Europe gave rise to competitive interaction. The "gunpowder revolution" brought about technological changes for the military as well as such social changes as the end of the feudal system, brought about by the ability of cannon to destroy feudal castles.[19] At the same time, colonial expansion helped fuel European commercial growth.

This period saw the rise and fall of the Habsburg Empire, which fought wars all over Europe to increase and protect its territory. The costs of making war rose as the "fortress revolution" led to larger armies and the "revolution of sail and shot" led to the expansion of navies with heavily armed galleys. Spain, unable to afford the cost of waging war on several fronts, lost possessions in France, Austria, and the Netherlands. Although France mishandled its economy and experienced domestic turmoil, it became such a continental threat under Napoleon that the rest of Europe banded together to form a coalition to defeat it. In contrast, trade gave England a robust economy, enabling it to afford a powerful navy; moreover, it was quick to take advantage of the Industrial Revolution.

Kennedy then describes the period of relative peace and economic growth after the Concert of Europe in 1815. Britain led the world in manufacturing and commerce, yet maintained a smaller army than other powers, devoting its military resources to its navy and colonial empire. Prussia was preoccupied with unification; the Habsburg Empire in Austria was weak; France made no real gains, although it played a key role in maintaining the balance of power in Europe. Russia fell behind Europe economically and technologically, as the Crimean War revealed. Meanwhile, the United States was growing into an economic giant, but its resources were diverted by its Civil War.

Kennedy refers to the period from 1885 to 1914 as the "multi-power" world. Italy, unified, was seen as the weakest of the great powers. Germany under Bismarck grew in industrial, commercial, and military terms. Austria-Hungary suffered from a poor economy and lack of national cohesion. France saw growth in industry but was declining relative to Germany in terms of trade. Britain's grip on industry and commerce began to erode, while its navy increased. Russia's industry grew, as did its military, but it still lagged in industrial output compared to Europe and the United States. The United States enjoyed the largest per capita income in the world by 1914; it traded extensively on the foreign market and had begun to assert itself diplomatically.

This period was also marked by the alliance diplomacy that triggered World War I. Germany, with the advantages of a strong, organized, well-trained military, and a large population and industrial base, had emerged as the next threat to take over the European continent. American dollars and industry arrived to prop up the war efforts of Britain and France, as Germany's manpower and economy began to weaken. Even after losing World War I, Germany remained the strongest economic power on the European continent. It began to remilitarize during the interwar period, as did Italy and Japan, in another bid to assert power. Britain and France, although weakened, remained central to the diplomatic power struggle. The industrial bases of the United States and Russia grew quietly during their self-imposed isolation, setting the stage for World War II, its outcome, and the subsequent bipolar Cold War world.

Writing near the end of the Cold War, Kennedy suggested that the imperial overstretch thesis might then apply to the Soviet Union and the United States, both of which he viewed as overburdened. His examination of the Soviet economy and industry led him to predict the eventual decline of the Soviet Empire. Kennedy's thesis proved prescient with respect to the Soviet

Union, which shortly thereafter collapsed, partly because of a bankrupt economy that could no longer sustain its huge military.

For the United States, too, Kennedy predicted a decline, because it also "runs the risk of what might roughly be called 'imperial overstretch'; that is to say, that the sum total of the United States' global interests and obligations is nowadays far larger than the country's power to defend them all simultaneously."[20] He pointed to the Middle East as the most likely location for war, and he predicted that American unpopularity in that region would prove a challenge for U.S. policy planning. However, throughout the 1990s, his predictions about the United States did not come true. Instead, the U.S. economy continued growing, while world affairs posed only modest demands on its resources. Its defense budget shrank to only $250 billion in the mid-1990s, about 3 percent of its gross domestic product, a considerable decline compared to 6 to 7 percent during the Cold War.

Today, however, some analysts are reconsidering the applicability of Kennedy's thesis to the United States. In October 2005, Kennedy was quoted as pointing to "an increasing mismatch between U.S. commitments and ground forces carrying out those commitments."[21] Because the world has become more dangerous, resource requirements of U.S. national security have increased. The U.S. defense budget has increased to nearly $500 billion, taking into account the cost of the wars in Iraq and Afghanistan. U.S. active-duty military manpower, numbering 1.4 million, is now stretched thin, necessitating the repeated call-up of many Reservists to sustain operations in Iraq.[22] Numerous analysts are beginning to question whether future requirements and commitments can be met. Such factors as tax cuts, the growth of spending on Social Security and healthcare, costs for disaster relief, and mounting current-account deficits combine to pose potentially serious economic constraints. While the United States may be able to sustain current defense expenditures, it might be hard-pressed to increase them in real terms. If so, this would hamper expansion of commitments abroad and, perhaps especially problematic, could prevent any increase of stabilization and reconstruction missions. Kennedy's recommendation is that the United States should avoid overextension by concentrating its overseas involvement on areas significant to its strategic power.

Ivo Daalder and James Lindsay: Executive Branch Constraints

A second potential constraint on U.S. foreign policy arises from the nature of U.S. decisionmaking and decision implementation. In books discussed earlier, Kissinger and Brzezinski wrote of the difficulties faced by a pluralist democracy, with powers that are deliberately divided between the executive branch and Congress, in trying to make and implement foreign policy. The vagaries of domestic politics, along with constant media attention, often impose pressures that can erode a coherent national security strategy. Public opinion also has an impact. During the Cold War, the American people largely supported an assertive and burdensome foreign policy; the decline in support for the Vietnam War was the exception. It is uncertain whether they will continue to support a similarly demanding strategy in the early 21st century, in Iraq or in other places where prolonged military involvements and expensive foreign aid policies are needed. Public opinion has already shown decreasing support for the Iraq war; public support for what the Pentagon calls the Long War against terrorism is uncertain.

A key variable in the national security calculus is the performance and effectiveness of the executive branch. A 2003 book by Ivo Daalder and James M. Lindsay, revised in 2005, provides a template for thinking about Executive decisionmaking and implementation.[23] In *America Unbound: The Bush Revolution in Foreign Policy*, Daalder and Lindsay set out to explain the reasons for the bold choices of the Bush administration in launching the war on terror, invading Afghanistan and Iraq, and pursuing other controversial departures that, in many ways, flouted international opinion. The authors pointed to debates within the Bush administration between neoconservatives (whom we call assertive interventionists) and traditional conservatives. Rejecting the thesis that the "Bush revolution" is a product of advisers and other political appointees, the authors attributed both credit and blame to President George W. Bush himself. During 2001–2003, they wrote, President Bush emerged as a strong President, imposing a new strategic vision on his administration and on the world. Bush's main intent, they said, was to unshackle the United States from past constraints and to assert American power on the world stage on behalf of U.S. interests and new strategic principles.

Daalder and Lindsay considered Bush's policies a "revolution" in American foreign policy: not in its goals, but in how those goals should be achieved. It was a revolution that relied on unilateral exercise of American power and diminished emphasis on "reactive" strategies of deterrence and containment and on traditional uses of treaties and alliances. It stressed regime change and the value of preemptive action. These changes, Daalder and Lindsay concluded, have marked politics at home and abroad.[24] But the implementation of these policies, they wrote, presented considerable difficulties.

Daalder and Lindsay criticized Bush's strategic doctrine, arguing that while it might bring short-term gains, in the long run it is destined to backfire and bring major reversals. This judgment may be shared by some and dismissed by others, but their assignment of responsibility to President Bush rather than his advisers seems credible. Moreover, because the Bush national security team was filled with many experienced and talented people from the NSC staff, the Department of Defense, and the Department of State, and precisely because so many of these appointees supported Bush's goals, a clear, well-conceived execution of the new foreign policy should have been the result. Instead, write Daalder and Lindsay, the result was poor execution and implementation of many aspects of the Bush strategy, including management of the international debates before Iraq was invaded and planning for the postcombat occupation. In this, their criticism resembles that of Walter Russell Mead, whose book (discussed earlier) similarly faulted the Bush administration for unsuccessful implementation of a policy of which he generally approved.

Historians are likely to debate why the Bush administration experienced such troubles. But longtime analysts of U.S. foreign policymaking are unlikely to be surprised that these troubles arose even when the White House was occupied by a strong, determined leader with a clear vision. Prior to the Bush administration, many scholarly studies had documented the problems that can arise even when White House guidance is clear. One problem stems from interagency bureaucratic politics: the tendency for agencies such as the NSC staff, the State Department, and the Defense Department to quarrel over how policies are to be defined and pursued. A second problem is intellectual and analytical: the sheer difficulty of determining options, evaluating them, and then developing associated plans, programs, and budgets. A third problem is implementation: ensuring that field agencies, including diplomats and military forces, fully carry out policies approved by the President and his team. It has become clear that many civilian agencies have little capacity to deploy their personnel quickly to troubled areas of the world.

If the Bush administration encountered problems in all three areas, it will not have been the first to do so. Indeed, such troubles have plagued most administrations going back to the Cold War and before. The same applies to intelligence analysis, whose troubles were documented by the special commission that assessed events leading up to the terrorist strikes of September 11, 2001.[25] Since then, major efforts have been launched to reform the Intelligence Community by creating a new Director of National Intelligence, by reworking the Central Intelligence Agency, and by strengthening how the Intelligence Community operates. While these efforts may address some of the problems, future challenges facing the executive branch in shaping U.S. national security strategy are likely to reflect many of the same issues.

Samuel Huntington: National Character and Will

American society is changing in ways that will have consequences for foreign policy. That presents a possible third set of constraints. In his controversial book of 2004, *Who Are We? The Challenges to America's National Identity,* Samuel P. Huntington observed that through the centuries, Americans have defined the substance of their identity in terms of "race, ethnicity, ideology, and culture." The first two of these have now largely been eliminated, with Americans identifying themselves as being multiracial and multiethnic. Huntington called what is left the "American Creed," which is based on a distinct Anglo-Protestant culture. But Huntington argued that America's once-dominant Anglo-Protestant culture is now being eroded by a new wave of immigration from Latin America and Asia, by the acceptance of doctrines of multiculturalism and diversity, and by the growing acceptance of Spanish as a second language. He fears that, as a result, the United States faces a high risk of growing fragmentation.[26]

Huntington expressed worry that the erosion of this American Creed and thus of U.S. national identity could weaken the social and political consensus in the United States, which in turn could keep the U.S. Government from acting with vigor and consistency in domestic and foreign policy. Huntington's controversial solution was a reassertion of Anglo-Protestant culture and Christian religious values. Whether Huntington's proposal is correct can be debated; we disagree with many of his recommendations. But clearly, U.S. society today is less dominated than it was by ethnic groups from Northern Europe, and America's focus of power has become less anchored in the Northeast. As U.S. society becomes more multiethnic and its center of gravity shifts westward, this trend could produce a change in attitudes on foreign policy. Huntington is concerned that this could reduce support for America's current international role.

A larger issue raised by Huntington is whether the American people, who have historically preferred isolationism, will continue to support costly foreign policy involvements in faraway places such as the Middle East and Asia. If the American people see such involvements as only peripherally related to vital national interests, they might tire of them and withdraw support. A shift to a "fortress America" mentality could arise if its people believe that the United States is too big and powerful to be menaced by any coalition of overseas powers: it has wealth and technology, and its population now numbers nearly 300 million, more than double the 140 million during World War II. Such strength prevents invasion of its shores and might yield indifference to events abroad. Against this trend are globalization and the information age, the fact that fully one-fourth of the U.S. economy depends upon overseas commerce, and perhaps most visibly, the threats posed by terrorism and weapons of mass destruction. The American people seem to have no taste for empire, yet they appear willing to support an ambitious foreign policy—provided it does not damage their wealth, brings them safety, does not produce high wartime casualties, and is succeeding.

Robert Kagan, Stephen Walt: The Cooperation of Reluctant Allies

A fourth constraint on national security policy is whether other nations are willing to cooperate with the United States as it carries out national security efforts along the southern arc of instability (the Middle East, South-Central Asia, and East Asia). In his 2003 book, *Of Paradise and Power: America and Europe in the New World Order*, Robert Kagan argued that it is time to stop pretending that the United States and Europe share a common view of the world.[27] The United States and Europe are drifting apart in their core strategic cultures, he wrote: whereas the United States remains willing to carry weighty strategic burdens, most Europeans (more from Western Europe than from Eastern Europe) have embraced an inward-looking culture of liberal pacifism. Europe is turning away from the use of power in international affairs, he argued, and is instead focusing on a self-contained world of laws, rules, negotiations, and cooperation. In short, Kagan says, Europeans have embraced the world according to Kant, believing that they have realized Kant's state of "perpetual peace." The United States, meanwhile, remains mired in the anarchic world of Hobbes where international rules and laws are unreliable and military power is often needed. Kagan wrote that "on major strategic and international questions today, Americans are from Mars and Europeans are from Venus: They agree on little and understand one another less."[28]

These differences, Kagan wrote, do not spring naturally from differing national characteristics. A peaceful strategic culture for Europeans is relatively new, he argued, as is the present American reliance on the use of force. Over the last century, European and American cultures have traded places. According to Kagan, the change is the result both of a reversal in the relative military power of the two groups and of the different historical experience each has had during the past century. He fears that because the new division is the result of both power and ideology, it may be impossible to reverse. As a result, Kagan concluded, Europeans cannot be counted upon to assist the United States in foreign policy efforts that involve the use of military power and require a willingness to face danger.

Critics argue that Kagan carries a partly valid idea too far. They question the idea that Europe, only recently a hotbed of nationalism and world war, has become pacifist. After all, Britain remains a staunch ally of the United States; NATO fought a war with Serbia over Kosovo, and today 90 percent of the NATO troops in Kosovo are European; the European Union commands operations in Bosnia; many European countries have contributed to military tasks in Iraq, and NATO commands International Security Assistance Force (ISAF) operations in Afghanistan. In addition, the European members of NATO field militaries that total 2.4 million troops and spend more than 200 billion dollars each year on defense. Kagan is right, however, that most European countries would rather rely upon diplomacy and soft power than on military power to address foreign troubles and threats. It is also true that Europeans cannot rapidly project sizable military forces outside of Europe, trailing the United States in power projection capability by a factor of four.[29] For these reasons, their willingness to support U.S. foreign policy in the Middle East and elsewhere is limited and conditional. Moreover, Europe does not speak with one voice on such matters.

In 2005, Stephen Walt made an alternative case related to this fourth constraint that arises from U.S. relationships abroad.[30] In *Taming American Power,* Walt argued from a realist perspective that the European resistance to America's recent policies is not necessarily the result of a culture of pacifism, but is instead part of a global response to America's unprecedented primacy. He argued that this is an effort, by friend and foe alike, to tame America's power, and that it is a response not to U.S. policies that are aimed at maintaining the status quo but rather at those intended to "increase [U.S.] influence, to enhance its position vis-à-vis potential rivals, and to deal with specific security threats."[31] Walt asserted that there is a large gap between the way America perceives its own global role and the ways that role is perceived abroad, and that Americans do not understand this.

Walt then explored various strategies that other countries might use to deal with a dominant America. Those who seek to oppose U.S. primacy could choose a strategy of *balancing,* either by aligning with others or by mobilizing their own military and other resources, perhaps even acquiring weapons of mass destruction. They could choose a strategy of *balking,* by ignoring U.S. requests for help. They might pursue a strategy of *binding,* using institutions or norms to limit U.S. action. They could seek concessions through *blackmail,* or they could attempt *delegitimation* of U.S. policies, portraying them as selfish or bankrupt.

States that have misgivings but still choose to cooperate with the United States might follow other strategies. They could *bandwagon,* or accommodate U.S. power to avoid being pressured or attacked. They could engage in *regional balancing,* Walt's term for seeking U.S. protection against, for example, a resurgent Russia or China or against terrorist threats. States could try *bonding,* supporting some U.S. policies in the hope that they might influence those or other policies as, Walt said, Great Britain does. States might try *penetrating* the American body politic by lobbying to affect policies from the inside. Penetration is most effective, noted Walt, where open societies have considerable cultural proximity.

Walt argued that the United States cannot realistically continue to strengthen its power relative to others; instead, its best strategy is to seek to preserve its current position for as long as possible. To accomplish this task, Walt wrote, the United States cannot squander its power, nor should it create incentives for others to strengthen their relative power. It should avoid policies that tend to force America's adversaries to band together. It should use military force only with forbearance and should abandon its doctrine of preemption. The best path for the United States, Walt argued, is to follow a policy of "offshore balancing." This policy, which is gaining support in the academic community, is based on the assumption that the United States does not need to control foreign territory, but just needs to prevent it from being controlled by hostile forces. Rather than deploy troops that become targets, Walt suggested, the United States should work through local actors to help uphold a regional balance of power. Under an offshore balancing policy, the United States would reduce its overseas military presence significantly in Europe and the greater Middle East, keep troops in Asia, and maintain a distance from various regional powers. Under this policy, the United States would intervene only if overt aggression occurred and vital U.S. interests were directly concerned.

A recent historical example of offshore balancing—one that illustrates both the strengths and weaknesses of the strategy—is the U.S. support for Iraq to balance the strength of revolutionary Iran during the 1980s. It worked for a while at low cost to the United States, but in the process, America supported Saddam Hussein, who then undertook wars against Iran, Kuwait, and his own people. While Walt claimed that the offshore balancing strategy is not an isolationist strategy, it would include a major withdrawal of U.S. forces from the Middle East and Europe with a greater reliance on naval and air forces; Walt's critics could well call it neoisolationism.

Fareed Zakaria: Limits of Democratization

A fifth constraint turns on whether countries in the Middle East and surrounding regions can advance toward democracy and economic progress as envisioned by contemporary U.S. foreign policy. In his 2003 book, *The Future of Freedom: Illiberal Democracy at Home and Abroad,* Fareed Zakaria argued that even when democracy takes hold, it is not necessarily liberal.[32] Zakaria acknowledged that Islam can produce democracy, pointing out that the two biggest Islamic countries, Indonesia and Turkey, are democracies, if fairly recent ones. But he argued that the Arab Middle East, with its fundamentalist Islamic values, is another matter: Zakaria defined a *democracy* as a country in which public elections are held to determine governmental leaders but, he said, this does not necessarily mean that a "liberal democracy" exists. Elections do not guarantee liberal constitutional values if the society is illiberal. In such a society, he said, the result can be "illiberal democracy," where elections produce governments that oppress minorities, deny civil rights, attack neighbors, or lead to populist dictatorships. Venezuela is a Latin American example of elections producing a populist dictator, said Zakaria, and the Arab Middle East is a prime candidate. The election of Mahmoud Ahmadinejad to the presidency of Iran and the Hamas election victory in Palestine, both occurring after Zakaria's book came out, exemplify the problem.

Zakaria's concern over mass elections producing illiberal governments is not new. Indeed, James Madison and the other Founding Fathers designed the U.S. Constitution on the principles of federalism, separation of powers, and checks and balances partly because they feared mob rule. During the 1930s, Hitler was voted into power in Germany because his Nazi ideology appealed to many voters; similarly, Mussolini's fascism also enjoyed popular support among Italian voters. Zakaria's book, nevertheless, is pertinent to conditions prevailing today. His trenchant thesis identified a potential flaw in the quest to spread democracy, raising the question of whether true liberal democracy can be developed in the Middle East and neighboring regions any time soon.

Current trends suggest that public support for democratization is growing, but authoritarian regimes still cling to power in many countries, and their commitments to true reform are uncertain. The scholarly literature is replete with analyses arguing that democracy is unlikely to take hold or succeed in countries that lack a solid middle class, a civic culture, modern social values, a cohesive society, and respect for private property.[33] Many countries in the Middle East and elsewhere lack such prerequisites. Similar constraints apply to hopes for rapid economic progress in these countries, many of which do not have the consistent governance, trained workforces, infrastructure, resources, or other assets needed for rapid growth. It is no accident that these countries have been left behind in the globalization sweepstakes. Democracy and economic progress may often be mutually dependent: the former cannot succeed unless the latter is achieved, and vice versa. The daunting task facing these countries is to pursue both democratization and economic progress simultaneously, so that one reinforces the other. To the extent that this agenda cannot be achieved, it spells trouble for these countries, and is thus also a constraint upon U.S. policies for promoting democratization.

Appraising the Limits of American Power

Although these five constraints do not prevent the United States from acting like a superpower and pursuing an ambitious strategy abroad, they limit its capacity to achieve its most ambitious goals. They are variables in the strategic calculus: they may rise or subside in importance. A principal challenge facing the United States is to act within the framework of the limits they impose and to pursue policies that take them into account. This challenge enhances the importance of employing sophisticated thought and analysis in crafting U.S. national security strategies that respond not only to strategic goals and ambitions, but also to the limitations affecting American power.

The 2006 U.S. National Security Strategy: A More Kantian Approach to a Hobbesian World

In March 2006, the Bush administration released its *National Security Strategy of the United States of America*.[34] This document superseded the earlier strategy released in early 2002, shortly after the terrorist attacks of September 11, 2001. In this section, we describe it in terms of the philosophies and approaches discussed above.

The new strategy has both neo-Hobbesian and neo-Kantian elements. It describes a very dangerous world, with the major challenge coming from terrorism fueled by an aggressive religious ideology. Indeed, the President's cover letter for the strategy document begins with the Hobbesian statement that "America is at war." Yet the strategy also declares that the United States has an unprecedented opportunity to lay a foundation for peace by promoting human freedom and democratic ideals; this focus on democratic solutions is classic Kant.

Consistent with earlier Bush administration stances, it endorsed the basic strategy we call assertive interventionism. But shifting somewhat from the earlier 2002 strategy, it championed aspects of progressive multilateralism by calling for greater efforts to work closely with allies and partners and by emphasizing elements of soft power. It also contained elements of traditional conservatism by calling for careful management of big-power relations, with Russia, China, India, and others. It did not, however, pay much attention to the limits of power discussed above. Critics may identify this as its principal shortcoming: its tendency to be too ambitious, and its reluctance to discuss the impact of constraints and limits on U.S. foreign policy.

The new strategy declared that two inseparable priorities–fighting and winning the war on terror, and promoting freedom and democracy as the alternative to tyranny–will continue to guide U.S. foreign policy. The strategy connects these two issues by treating democracy as the antidote to terrorism. *Democracy* is a key word in the strategy; it is mentioned over 120 times. In this respect, the strategy's focus is similar to that of the Clinton administration's 1994 strategy of enlarging the family of democratic states. However, the means it proposes to achieve this end differ. The other key word in the latest strategy is *terrorism*, with forms of that word also appearing over 120 times. These two terms unite the Hobbesian description with the Kantian prescription in the first of two key concepts of the strategy. Elements of this formula existed in the 2002 Bush strategy, but it was overwhelmed by the public focus on preemption and use of force.

The second key concept in the 2006 National Security Strategy, which does not appear until almost halfway through this 49-page document, is the more Hobbesian endorsement of the preemptive use of force by the United States. The concept of preemption is not new to American foreign policy or international law, but it was only in the 2002 strategy that preemption was raised to the level of declared national doctrine. That document and subsequent debates tended to blur the difference between preventive use of force and preemptive use of force. Prevention implies a fairly early use of force, well in advance of a potential attack; thus, the Israeli attack on Iraq's Osirak nuclear reactor in 1981 was an example of a preventive use of force, because it countered a long-term but not immediate threat. By contrast, preemption implies the use of force in response to an impending attack, such as the Israeli strike during the 1967 war, when an Arab attack seemed imminent. From the point of view of international law, it is easier to justify the preemptive use of force (although with hindsight, no one in the West today seriously criticizes the preventive Osirak raid). The American attack on Iraq in 2003 was in this sense preventive rather than preemptive, because an Iraqi attack on the United States was not imminent.

On the subject of preemption, the 2006 U.S. strategy stated, "The place of preemption in our national security strategy remains the same." It probably would have been difficult for the Bush administration to abandon the strategy, given its high profile in the 2002 strategy; however, some care was taken in the 2006 document to place preemption more clearly in context. The document noted that preemption need not involve military force; that the strong preference of the United States is to address concerns through international diplomacy; and that any U.S. preemption would take place only in the context of the possibility of a devastating WMD attack. It warned that the preemption policy should not serve as an excuse for others to take aggressive action. The strategy concluded that "we do not rule out the use of force before attacks occur, even if uncertainty remains as to the time and place of the enemy's attack." Nonetheless, the shift from a Hobbesian tone in 2002 to a more Kantian tone in 2006 is evident.

In assessing progress made by the United States since 2002, the new strategy noted that the United States had remained on the offensive against terrorist networks, leaving the enemy weakened but not yet defeated; brought down the Taliban regime in Afghanistan, and aided a new democratic government there; focused attention on the proliferation of dangerous weapons; toppled the Saddam Hussein regime in Iraq, and worked with the Iraqi people to secure a united, stable, and democratic Iraq that could be a new ally in the war on terror in the Middle East; promoted the spread of democracy in the broader Middle East; expanded efforts to encourage economic development in poor regions, and focused these efforts on reform and results; and cultivated stable and cooperative relations with all the major powers in the world.

In continuing on this path, the new strategy asserted, the U.S. approach would be "idealistic about our national goals, and realistic about the means to achieve them." Addressing means, the new strategy said that the United States must expand its national strength and maintain a military without peer while maintaining economic prosperity and a healthy democracy. It also said that U.S. strategy should rest on strong alliances, friendships, and international institutions. The document declared that the U.S. aim is to promote freedom and justice abroad while leading a growing community of democracies in effective multinational efforts. It said that "a world of democratic well-governed states that can meet the needs of their citizens and conduct themselves responsibly in the international system . . . is the best way to provide enduring security for the American people."

Within this overarching framework, the new strategy outlined U.S. policy in addressing nine specific tasks. First, addressing aspirations for human dignity, the strategy document lauded recent democratic progress in Afghanistan, Iraq, Lebanon, Ukraine, and elsewhere, but noted that some tyrannies still exist and that many democratic governments are fragile, are only partially committed to freedom, or are regressing. It called for ending tyranny, promoting effective democracies, and advancing freedom through actions that are "principled in goals and pragmatic in means."

Under the task of defeating global terrorism, the new strategy portrayed the war on terror as a battle of arms and of ideas, but not of religions. It called for assertive actions against terrorist networks and their supporters, and actions that would be effective in denying terrorists access to WMD. It acknowledged that eradicating terrorism requires nurturing democracy and human freedom. It outlined a threefold strategy for Iraq, composed of political efforts to build democracy, security efforts to build competent Iraqi security and military forces, and economic efforts to restore and strengthen the Iraqi economy. It outlined a similar strategy for Afghanistan.

Under the third task, working with others to defuse regional conflicts, the strategy noted recent successes in Sudan and Liberia, in Israeli-Palestinian and India-Pakistan relations, and in Ireland. It noted challenges in Darfur, Colombia, Venezuela, Cuba, Uganda, Ethiopia-Eritrea, and Nepal. It outlined a U.S. strategy focus with three elements: conflict prevention and resolution, conflict intervention, and postconflict stabilization and reconstruction.

As part of preventing WMD proliferation, the new strategy declared that to forestall or prevent WMD attacks by adversaries, the United States might act preemptively in exercising its inherent right of self-defense. The document noted recent nonproliferation efforts such as the Proliferation Security Initiative launched in May 2003 to control trafficking in WMD and related materials and systems, efforts to strengthening the International Atomic Energy Agency, and success at persuading Libya to dismantle its nuclear program. It also noted ongoing problems in Iran and North Korea and with terrorist networks. Current U.S. goals include closing loopholes in the Nuclear Non-Proliferation Treaty that allow production of fissile materials under cover of a civilian nuclear power program, and keeping fissile material out of the hands of rogue states and terrorists. The strategy proposes use of diplomatic action and deterrence to help achieve these goals. It defended the attack on Iraq, which had once possessed and used WMD and which threatened to acquire them again, as part of this strategy.

Under the heading of the task of igniting economic growth, the new strategy pointed to several new global, regional, and bilateral economic initiatives such as WTO negotiations, the Central America Free Trade Agreement, and free trade agreements with countries in Latin America, Asia, and the Middle East. The new strategy proposed opening markets and integrating developing countries, opening and diversifying energy markets, and reforming the international financial systems to ensure stability and growth.

Discussing the task of expanding the circle of development and democracy, the strategy noted successes and frustrations, including trying to turn the tide against acquired immunodeficiency syndrome and unleashing the power of the private sector. For the future, it highlighted transformational diplomacy and the goal of making foreign assistance more effective.

Under the task of developing cooperative action with other main centers of power, the strategy noted successes in U.S. cooperation with foreign governments, especially in Europe and Asia. It articulated principles that would influence U.S. relations with main centers of global power, including the importance of regional and global institutions, a state's treatment of its own citizens, the U.S. need to hedge against another state's potential aggressive behavior, and the possible need for the United States to sometimes act alone.

With regard to the task of transforming America's national security institutions, the strategy pointed to creation of the Department of Homeland Security, reorganization of the Intelligence Community, and the Defense Department's new focus, which encompasses traditional, irregular, catastrophic, and disruptive challenges. *Traditional* military challenges include conventional war; *irregular* challenges are the kind faced in Iraq today; *catastrophic* challenges imply weapons of mass destruction in the hands of terrorists or rogue states; and *disruptive* challenges would include significant technical advances by potential military rivals such as China. For future goals, this section proposed improving interagency capabilities and creating a civilian reserve corps for postdisaster relief and postconflict reconstruction.

The final task addresses the opportunities and challenges of globalization, including pandemics, illicit trade, and environmental destruction. To meet these transnational challenges would require, said the strategy, unity of effort by all Federal agencies, and in some cases cooperation with other countries in coalitions of the willing capable of quick response.

The 2006 National Security Strategy thus reflected a continuation of the assertive strategic principles that have been pursued by the Bush administration since the 2002 strategy. It articulated a comprehensive view, specifying goals, values, and action agendas, and offering appraisals of successes. It repeated its endorsement of the possibility of U.S. preemption and of unilateral action. However, its overall tone was more multilateral and pragmatic than the 2002 document. The issue critics are likely to home in on is whether the new strategy is too ambitious in its goals and aspirations and insufficiently realistic about the constraints and limits that will face U.S. national security strategy.

From Grand Strategy to Policy Prescriptions

Four broad policy prescriptions emerge from our review of the schools of strategic thought and of the 2006 National Security Strategy just described. The first policy prescription flows from the assertive interventionists who build on elements of democratic peace theory and introduce the notion of forceful change. This might be called the *democratic regime change* policy, which the current Bush administration has championed in Iraq, in Afghanistan, and in its National Security Strategies. It presents democracy as an antidote to terrorism and seeks to set up model democracies to demonstrate to others in the greater Middle East and elsewhere that this form of government can provide both stability and freedom. Democratic regime change is also part of what the Pentagon has called the Long War against terrorism. This experiment is under way, with mixed results as of mid-2006.

The second policy prescription might be called the *great power concert* approach. Flowing from the views of the traditional conservatives, it calls for a broad coalition of major powers dedicated to fighting terrorism. That coalition would also include nondemocratic states such as China and Russia, since they are major powers. This policy would play down the current focus on spreading democracy as an antidote for terrorism and would turn to historical patterns of major power solutions to deal with current problems. Some elements of this policy prescription are evident in the Bush administration's approach to Iran in the summer of 2006.

The third policy prescription, flowing from the progressive multilateralists, might be called *global democratic partnerships.* This approach recognizes that the nature of today's challenges requires a broad multilateral approach and, like the traditional conservatives, this approach favors formation of a new international coalition. However, under this approach, such a coalition would include only democratic partners, not just major powers but all true liberal democracies. It would not focus primarily on creating new democracies in the greater Middle East. The global democratic partnership approach would aim to repair the flaws in the current system of international institutions so as to improve means of defeating the terrorist threat. Consistent with this approach, NATO is considering developing global partnerships with Japan, Australia, South Korea, and others.

The fourth policy prescription, with a focus on the limits of American power, would call for a significant American disengagement from its current overseas posture and commitments. This policy, called *offshore balancing*, has been championed by Stephen Walt, Robert Pape, and others. It is a radical change from America's current overseas posture, but in the Middle East it would not differ much from pre-1980 U.S. deployments. It is an echo of President Richard Nixon's Guam Doctrine. It would rely on regional allies to balance potential threats. This approach has been rejected as too isolationist by most progressive multilateralists, traditional conservatives, and assertive interventionists. However, it may begin to meet with more favor in American public opinion as U.S. casualties mount in the greater Middle East.

Some of these four policy prescriptions overlap and could be combined; others are mutually exclusive. Several are reflected in elements of current U.S.

policy, while others present stark contrasts to it. The first policy prescription, democratic regime change, suggests continued high levels of U.S. military deployment and intervention to promote and protect democracies and to deal with a long war. The fourth prescription, offshore balancing, is a reaction to this current policy direction and suggests a neoisolationist reversal of neoconservative policies. These two policies are mutually exclusive. The second and third prescriptions, great power concert and global democratic partnerships, present two different ways to multilateralize current U.S. policies that are viewed by traditional conservatives as well as by progressive multilateralists as excessively unilateralist and as excessively demanding of American resources.

Given the growing public unease with America's current military involvement in the greater Middle East, support for the first policy prescription, democratization via forced regime changes, is declining rapidly. Given the reluctance of today's national security elite to move toward isolationism, the offshore balancing concept is also unlikely to emerge as a dominant policy alternative. The second and third prescriptions provide alternative ways to reduce some of America's burden without abandoning a policy of a robust American engagement overseas. American national security strategy in the future is likely to move in the direction of these two middle alternatives. Indeed, the 2006 *Quadrennial Defense Review* calls for a new focus on building partner capacity. The key will be whether the new alliances and coalitions will be based more on common democratic values or on the need to organize the major powers for common purpose. What is essential is that policymakers see, as clearly as possible, as much of the elephant as possible; the books we review contribute to this goal.

Chapter Six

U.S. Defense Strategies

As the United States has sought to reshape its foreign policy and national security strategy, it has also been struggling to shape a new defense strategy and military posture. This chapter addresses this aspect of the elephant, beginning with three books that survey the need for new operations and for new capabilities that have arisen in the recent wars in Kosovo, Afghanistan, and Iraq. The chapter then discusses several books that examine alternative approaches to defense transformation, that is, the process of providing U.S. military forces with new technologies, operational concepts, and organizational structures to give them the capabilities they need for a wide spectrum of operations. Next, it describes a book that discusses the affordability of future transformation. Finally, this chapter outlines the elements of the Defense Department's 2006 *Quadrennial Defense Review*.

The defense issues discussed here have a clear connection with the world views described in the first chapters of this book. In a neo-Kantian world, defense spending can be trimmed. A neo-Hobbesian world with a focus on possible great power conflict would require increased defense spending with an emphasis on high-technology warfare. However, a neo-Hobbesian world dominated by conflict with small groups of terrorists or rogue states that are empowered by globalization requires a third defense model, with a greater emphasis on ground forces, special operations, and cultural intelligence. Elements of all 3 of these defense policy models have been in effect at different times during the past 20 years. The neo-Kantian model led to dramatic reductions in defense spending from 1986 to 1996. A neo-Hobbesian model with a focus on high-tech warfare drove the defense budget increases and military transformation between 1997 and 2003. A neo-Hobbesian model focused on defeating empowered terrorist groups and on stabilization operations has shaped defense budgets and planning since 2002.

This chapter's main theme is that U.S. defense planning will continue to face major challenges as it prepares for a complex future. Owing to its supremacy in technology and warfighting capabilities, today's U.S. military is the world's best fighting force and is capable of prevailing in traditional combat operations. Yet today's wars are a mix of traditional and untraditional combat, including messy conflicts that require stabilization and reconstruction (S&R) operations after the main battles have been fought. Transformation in the coming years will require the U.S. military not only to acquire new weapons and information networks to preserve its strategic dominance and warfighting supremacy, but also to strengthen its capacity for S&R missions, irregular operations, small wars, and other expeditionary missions in the Middle East and other distant areas. Because affording both types of capabilities will not be easy, priorities will have to be established. The books reviewed here provide guidance toward setting these priorities.

The books that address the experience of three recent wars tend to be neo-Hobbesian in their assessment of both the international environment and the means necessary to deal with the new challenges. Those books are:

- Wesley K. Clark, *Waging Modern War: Bosnia, Kosovo, and the Future of Combat* (2001)
- Tommy Franks, *American Soldier* (2004)
- John Keegan, *The Iraq War* (2004).

The books that describe various approaches to transforming for tomorrow's military missions are:

- Hans Binnendijk, ed., *Transforming America's Military* (2002)
- Hans Binnendijk and Stuart Johnson, eds., *Transforming for Stabilization and Reconstruction Operations* (2004)
- Douglas A. Macgregor, *Transformation Under Fire: Revolutionizing How America Fights* (2003)
- Max Boot, *The Savage Wars of Peace: Small Wars and the Rise of American Power* (2002)
- James Dobbins et al., *America's Role in Nation-Building* (2003) and *The UN Role in Nation-Building* (2005)
- Thomas P.M. Barnett, *The Pentagon's New Map: War and Peace in the Twenty-first Century* (2004).

The book that discusses budgetary pressures is:

- Michael E. O'Hanlon, *Defense Strategy for the Post-Saddam Era* (2005).

And finally, we address the official concept statement for the future U.S. defense posture:

- U.S. Department of Defense, *Quadrennial Defense Review* (2006).

This chapter begins with the three books that draw lessons from recent wars.

Wesley K. Clark: Waging War in Kosovo

In today's setting, it is easy to forget that U.S. defense strategy during the 1990s was focused mainly on being prepared for two major theater wars (MTWs). The two hypothetical contingencies came to preoccupy the work of force planners and budgeters in the Pentagon. Both were scaled-down versions of the *Desert Storm* campaign of 1991, and both reflected a carryover of threat-based thinking and reliance upon contingency-based planning inherited from the Cold War. Both hypothetical MTWs involved, for planning purposes, a three-phase operation: an initial U.S. and allied effort to halt invasion of allied territory; rapid deployment of large U.S. forces overseas as reinforcements; and a big counterattack to eject the enemy and occupy its territory. One hypothetical MTW was a North Korean invasion of South Korea. The other MTW involved a repeat Iraqi invasion of Kuwait plus Saudi Arabia, this time with a smaller Iraqi force moving fast to try to seize oilfields quickly before U.S. forces could arrive. Because, for planning purposes, these two invasions were presumed to erupt nearly simultaneously, the Department of Defense would need sufficient forces and capabilities to deal with both of them concurrently. The two-MTW approach provided DOD with a strategic focus as well as a rationale for preserving an active military of about 1.4 million troops with combat forces about 70 percent the size of the Cold War posture. As the U.S. military shrank from its Cold War levels, DOD's budget was also declining; it reached a post–Cold War low of about $250 billion in the mid-1990s. By the late 1990s, the budget had started to rise toward $300 billion to increase readiness and to begin to fund transformation and modernization with new weapons systems.[1] DOD remained focused on the two MTWs, fitting all of its planned forces and budgets within that framework.

A clear sign that the two-MTW plan was eroding and that a new era of wars was emerging came in 1999 when war broke out in Kosovo. This war erupted in Europe, rather than Asia or the Persian Gulf as the two-MTW plan had presumed. It was not a war in which an enemy attacked a U.S. ally, but instead a war in which the United States and its NATO allies chose to attack a brutal Balkan dictator because he was committing ethnic cleansing against his own people. It was not a war in which a balanced posture of U.S.

ground, naval, and air forces rushed to the scene, as in *Desert Storm*; this time, airpower was the main instrument, and it benefited from the recent steps toward transformation and modernization of new information networks and smart munitions. The conduct of the war was not dictated by a military calculus in which battlefield victory was the sole aim. Instead, it was powerfully influenced by politics and the diplomacy of coercion. It was a messy conflict in which a large, unruly multilateral alliance attempted to wage limited war for limited purposes in a highly complex and unstable region. It was a sobering introduction to the realities of modern warfare in the early 21st century.

General Clark wrote his book, *Waging Modern War: Bosnia, Kosovo, and the Future of Combat*, shortly after he guided NATO forces to victory in Kosovo.[2] Although he was the first general in memory to win a war without suffering a single battlefield fatality among his troops, he was rotated out of his job in May 2000, months ahead of the normal schedule. His controversial departure reflected the complex political and military currents around U.S. and NATO forces as they tried to coerce Serbian dictator Milosevic into leaving Kosovo in spring 1999. This difficult war involved an unusually contentious process; it was waged by airpower alone and was conducted mostly by U.S. military forces, although it was NATO that was calling the shots.

The Kosovo war's origins, as Clark described them, were the same as those that had earlier produced the war in Bosnia: ethnic and religious strife prompted Western intervention in the name of peacekeeping. In late 1995, the Bosnia conflict had been settled by the Dayton Accord. Territory was divided between the Bosnian Muslims and Serb Orthodox Christians, and 30,000 NATO peacekeepers were deployed to enforce the treaty. By 1998, ethnic tensions were erupting in Kosovo, pitting the majority Kosovar Albanians (who are Muslims), against the dominant minority Serbs, whose harsh rule was backed by Milosevic in Belgrade. Local violence by Kosovar Albanian rebels triggered brutal crackdowns by the Serbs. When the Serbs appeared to be preparing to commit ethnic cleansing, the United States and European governments became alarmed. Believing that outside intervention was needed, wrote Clark, they decided to use NATO, rather than the United Nations, because NATO had been more successful than the UN in Bosnia. Moreover, Russia, a friend of Serbia, seemed likely to block UN intervention. Initially, the United States and its allies tried to use diplomacy by seeking to broker a deal at Rambouillet, France, early in 1999. However, the effort broke down when Milosevic sent thousands of Serb troops into Kosovo to terrorize, displace, and kill Kosovar Albanians. As violence spread and Serbs began to force Albanians into boxcars, the NATO allies decided, as Clark wrote, to use military force to stop this "ethnic cleansing."

Although there was a widespread agreement on the need to intervene militarily, said Clark, forging an operational strategy and precise plan for intervention was not easy. Initially, the United States wanted the Europeans to provide most of the forces. With 10,000 American troops already deployed in Bosnia, the Pentagon believed that few additional U.S. forces could be spared from the two-MTW strategy focused on the Persian Gulf and Korea. The Europeans, however, lacked the capacity for projecting power swiftly into a combat setting outside NATO's borders, even as near as the Balkans. Thus, it was left to the U.S. military, which was capable of expeditionary missions, to meet the bulk of the requirements. On both sides of the Atlantic, political leaders wanted to avoid the high casualties that might come from close combat with the Serbian military. As a result, wrote Clark, they turned to coercive airpower. Their hope was that U.S. and European aircraft could employ their smart bombs and cruise missiles to force Milosevic into complying and thus could halt the ethnic cleansing in Kosovo.

Under the title Operation *Allied Force*, NATO bombing began on March 23, 1999. Initially, the bombing focused on suppression of Serbia's air defenses and its command and control system, but soon it was broadened to other targets in Serbia and Kosovo. Clark wrote that NATO hoped Milosevic would buckle after only a few days of bombing, as he had in Bosnia. Milosevic, however, accelerated his ethnic cleansing of Kosovo, apparently hoping that he could achieve success there before NATO's bombing did much damage. This stubbornness, wrote Clark, compelled NATO to lengthen its bombing campaign and to add more aircraft and munitions. The number of aircraft quickly grew from 300 to 900 and then more; Clark had to request U.S. reinforcements in the form of Air Force fighter wings and Navy carriers. The Pentagon authorized the reinforcements, but grumbled about the diversion from the two-MTW plan. The intensification of the air war, in turn, gave rise to a transatlantic debate about air strategy. Reluctant to bomb Belgrade and other civilian targets in Serbia, France and other European countries wanted to focus the bombing on Serb troops in Kosovo, where the ethnic cleansing was occurring. But U.S. air generals, doubtful of their ability to find and destroy targets among dispersed Serb troops in Kosovo, wanted to conduct strategic bombing of Belgrade and other Serbian targets in hope of maximizing the pressure on Milosevic. The result, said Clark, was a compromise air strategy that split attacks between both target sets but did not maximize damage on either.

Execution of this air strategy was complicated by the requirement that Clark seek approval of his targets from both Washington, DC, and NATO headquarters in Brussels. The Pentagon and the White House, wrote Clark, scrutinized every single target and vetoed some strikes. In Brussels, the European allies tended to focus on classes of targets, rather than individual targets, but this did not stop the French and other countries from vetoing some strikes. At NATO military headquarters, Clark and his frantic staff had to develop target plans each day, staff them through Washington and Brussels, deal with the media, discuss the war with their political masters, and monitor events on the battlefield.

Fortunately, Serbia's air defenses were able to shoot down only one NATO aircraft, whose U.S. pilot was quickly rescued. Nevertheless, the air war had political downsides. U.S. and European pilots were accused of bombing innocent civilians and causing other collateral damage. A NATO strike mistakenly destroyed the Chinese embassy in Belgrade, provoking intense protest from Beijing and other countries. Meanwhile, wrote Clark, the tactical bombing in Kosovo did not adequately suppress the Serbian military, which was clever at dispersing and hiding its tanks and other vehicles. As Serbian ethnic cleansing of Kosovo began to produce hordes of refugees, the media began claiming that NATO's air war was failing.

As the weeks went by, Clark concluded that ground intervention might be needed. At a minimum, he wrote, the threat of a NATO ground attack might be enough to scare Milosevic into complying. But creating a credible threat, he recognized, meant that NATO ground forces had to move close to the Balkans. Clark's initial step was to request that U.S. Apache attack helicopters be sent to Albania, where they could mount attacks into western Kosovo to aid the Albanian rebels in their combat with Serbian troops. But the Pentagon initially objected, and even after it relented, the Apaches moved slowly, took time to establish a logistic infrastructure, experienced trouble flying in the mountains, and never did go into combat.

Frustrated at these delays, Clark set out to develop a plan for a full-scale ground intervention. The European allies were willing to intervene with a small ground force that would seek to defeat the Serbs through guile and maneuver, he wrote. Because U.S. forces would dominate the operation, however, American ground commanders thought in more traditional, less risky terms. They judged that defeating the well-armed Serbian army would require a large NATO invasion force of many divisions and up to 200,000 troops. As Clark wrote, he ruled out an attack into Serbia from the north, via Hungary or Romania. Instead, he favored an attack directly into Kosovo from the south, moving from Albania and Macedonia. Assembling such an intervention force could not be done quickly; the Pentagon again resisted, complaining of diversions away from its two-MTW plan. The European allies were more willing to participate, but they lacked the logistics and ships to move large forces quickly. Thus, NATO would not be able to mount a ground invasion until late summer or fall, when it could assemble the necessary forces and logistic support. The issue was debated at a stormy NATO summit in Washington in late May, after which NATO slowly began moving toward consensus on the need to prepare for a ground attack. However, it sought to delay a final decision to invade.

Fortunately, Milosevic buckled. On June 8, he agreed to a Russian-brokered deal in which Serbian troops would withdraw from Kosovo, and a NATO ground force of 60,000 troops, plus a small Russian contingent, would enter the province on a peacekeeping mission. The particular reasons for Milosevic's capitulation, wrote Clark, were unclear. The mounting damage to Serbia's command centers, government buildings, bridges, and economic infrastructure apparently contributed, along with the increasing readiness of NATO to use ground forces. A final reason may have been that Russia, previously a diplomatic supporter of Serbia, withdrew its support in early June. The war was over after 11 weeks of airstrikes, fractious alliance politics, and coercive diplomacy. When Serbian troops departed Kosovo, there were large numbers of Kosovar Albanians dead. Thousands of returning refugees found their homes destroyed. Meanwhile, Serbia's economic infrastructure was a wreck; for example, the destruction of bridges over the Danube River blocked a vital commercial line for all of the Balkans and the rest of Europe. In Kosovo, NATO forces faced the daunting task of putting a destroyed province back together amidst continuing ethnic tensions and uncertainty about Kosovo's future relationships with Serbia.

Writing two years later, Clark sought to discern lessons from the Kosovo conflict. This, NATO's first attempt to wage war, might not have felt like a victory, he said, but coercive diplomacy worked in the sense that the alliance achieved all of its goals: withdrawal of Serb forces, return home of refugees, a ceasefire, successful use of a NATO peacekeeping force, and the opportunity for a political settlement. This war was won, said Clark, because NATO's members, realizing that they could not afford to lose it, had to show persistence and teamwork. The victory also was due, Clark wrote, to NATO's multilateral mechanisms, which worked, although they were a headache to navigate. They preserved the alliance's cohesion while enabling military commanders to pursue effective combat operations. Because NATO is likely to be involved in future limited wars, wrote Clark, care should be taken to preserve its cohesion and to update these mechanisms.

Clark noted that when the Kosovo crisis was brewing in 1998, the Western allies had been loath to intervene and had allowed the crisis to intensify. When the Western allies did intervene, he said, they initially relied mainly upon diplomacy and made the mistake of keeping the military option off the table for too long. This reduced their credibility with Milosevic, he said, and diminished their ability to negotiate an early end to the crisis. In the next crisis, he urged, the Western allies should be ready to intervene early and to use military power as a credible threat, rather than seek to separate diplomacy from war. In order to be prepared to launch combat operations at the required moment, Clark wrote, NATO's military commanders should be allowed to prepare war plans well in advance of crises, much as U.S. commanders do. During the early stages of the Kosovo war, the war plan that had been hastily contrived was, said Clark, so driven by diplomacy—it was basically a small air bombardment for political effect—that it violated virtually all principles of effective conduct of war, including decisive operations. As the conflict unfolded, however, NATO commanders adapted their operation, bringing it into better alignment with these principles and ultimately succeeding. Clark urged that better war plans must in the future be prepared in advance and must focus on how to operate decisively for political-military effects.

The NATO military command suffered from lack of intelligence collection capabilities, wrote Clark, and from lack of staff assets for analysis of intelligence, operations, and logistics. This, he said, left NATO dependent upon U.S. military staffs, which fortunately were available in Europe. Clark's book urged NATO improvements in these areas. He was not overtly critical of European forces, but he pointed out that it was the United States that flew 60 percent of the air combat missions and over 70 percent of the air sorties. Other writers have pointed to European shortfalls in such areas as smart munitions, all-weather and day-night capabilities, refueling, and modern C[4]ISR networks.[3] Clark was aware of such shortfalls: at the Washington Summit held during the Kosovo War, he had vocally supported adoption of NATO's Defense Capability Initiative, a multiyear plan aimed at improving European forces in these areas.

Clark also called for improvements in how the United States plans to conduct limited wars, arguing that the two-MTW framework is too narrow and restrictive, and must be broadened to provide greater flexibility. Clark was also critical of the decisionmaking process in Washington. As Supreme Allied Commander, Europe, he said, he was required to wade through too many administrative layers in the Pentagon to reach the Secretary of Defense and the President. (Similar complaints would be voiced several years later when General Tommy Franks, U.S. Central Command [USCENTCOM] commander of the invasion of Iraq, wrote his war memoirs, discussed below.) Although airpower provides a powerful instrument that can help win wars, Clark wrote, it requires effective tactical intelligence, reconnaissance, poststrike assessments, and on-the-spot observers capable of guiding aircraft to their precise destinations. Moreover, he said, airpower usually cannot win wars on its own, and ground forces will be needed. He urged that the U.S. Army be made more mobile so that it would be able to respond to urgent needs for ground power in distant areas.

Clark's conclusion was that limited wars of this sort are likely to be a main feature of modern warfare. He urged that instead of avoiding them until they become critical, the United States and its allies should tackle them head-on with appropriate political strategies, military plans, and decision procedures. When NATO is involved, he wrote, the United States should avoid the temptation of acting unilaterally, because preserving alliance cohesion is as important as gaining tactical military advantages. Many observers came to the conclusion, after Kosovo, that the United States should never again "fight wars by committee" and thus should avoid using NATO. Clark, however, judged that NATO's multilateral machinery worked adequately even though it required a lot of diplomatic effort: his complaints were more about dealing with Washington, DC, than with NATO. While the desire to avoid casualties is understandable, Clark said, the United States and its allies must be prepared to take risks and accept costs, for this is the best way both to avoid wars and to win them. Limited wars like the one in Kosovo, however undesirable in the eyes of diplomats and soldiers alike, may be a wave of the future, he wrote; if they are handled correctly, they can be waged effectively and won.

Tommy Franks: Revolutionary Concepts for Waging War in Afghanistan and Iraq

Following September 11, 2001, the two biggest U.S. military campaigns in the war on terror were the invasions of Afghanistan, initiated in October 2001, and of Iraq, begun in March 2003. In his 2004 book, *American Soldier,* former USCENTCOM Commander General Tommy Franks described how the plans for both invasions were shaped and carried out.[4] Crafted under the leadership of Secretary of Defense Donald Rumsfeld, both plans discarded old approaches to warfare, wrote Franks; they reflected revolutionary approaches to warfare by blending "transformational" thinking with professional military guidance. Both plans strove to incorporate not only new information systems and smart munitions, but also new doctrines aimed at making U.S. force operations truly joint and focused more effectively on their battlefield goals. Both plans embodied new approaches to shaping a multi-Service force posture that would blend air and ground operations in actions intended to overcome the enemy quickly and decisively. Both plans, said Franks, quickly succeeded in winning the major phase of combat operations, toppling the Taliban government in Afghanistan and the Saddam Hussein regime in Iraq. In the wake of these stunning victories, however, came lengthy occupations. These two long-tyrannized countries, lacking any tradition of democratic governance, required S&R operations that were still under way when Franks retired in summer 2003 and that have far outlasted his tenure.

Planning for the invasion of Afghanistan began immediately after September 11, 2001. As Franks explains, existing USCENTCOM plans for Afghanistan operations, inherited from the Clinton administration, envisioned a limited use of force for limited goals, such as cruise missile strikes against al Qaeda training camps. Dismissing such plans as inadequate in the new context, the Bush administration wanted a new plan for a major force intervention aimed at toppling the Taliban government and crushing al Qaeda. A major ground invasion similar to *Desert Storm* was deemed both impossible and unnecessary. Franks and USCENTCOM decided to plan for use of those U.S. and allied forces that realistically could be rapidly made available, but to employ them in revolutionary ways, taking advantage of new information systems and smart munitions. Their new plan brought together four components: U.S. airpower, Special Operations Forces (SOF), Afghan forces from the so-called Northern Alliance, and a later buildup of conventional U.S. ground forces of no more than 10,000–12,000 troops. The plan had four phases, beginning with speedy force deployments to Afghanistan, moving to initial combat operations, then major combat operations that would produce military victory, culminating in a postwar occupation aimed at preventing re-emergence of the Taliban or al Qaeda.

Crafted with great urgency and unusual speed, the new plan took shape within less than a month. Meanwhile, U.S. air and naval forces were moving toward Central Asia and nearby waters. Initial combat operations, largely in the form of U.S. airstrikes, began on October 7, 2001. Operations during the first 10 days encountered some problems in identifying fleeting targets quickly and hitting them. Coordinating U.S. airstrikes with Northern Alliance operations—which employed 20,000 friendly troops against at least twice as many Taliban and al Qaeda—also proved difficult. All of this changed, however, when U.S. Special Operations Forces troops were fully deployed. Small SOF teams joined with Northern Alliance formations moving against enemy troops. This enabled the SOF teams to use laser target designators and GPS to provide precise targeting data to U.S. fighters and bombers flying overhead, which carried smart munitions capable of pinpoint strikes. The result was a series of airstrikes that blew apart enemy formations, which could then be overrun by Northern Alliance forces. A cascade of battlefield victories, with few American casualties, followed. By late December, the Taliban government had been driven from power and Kabul was occupied.

As of early 2002, wrote Franks, most of Afghanistan had been liberated, but remnants of al Qaeda and the Taliban were still operating in eastern provinces near Pakistan. A combined U.S.-Afghan operation at Tora Bora in December 2001 failed to capture the senior al Qaeda leaders there (possibly including Osama bin Laden) because there were too few ground troops to close off escape routes. The numbers of U.S. ground forces then increased in February 2002 as elements of the 101st Air Assault Division and the 10th Mountain Division began to arrive. The United States still had only about a single brigade of infantry present. While these troops had some attack helicopters and mortars, they lacked armor and artillery. In combination with Northern Alliance troops, these U.S. forces attacked a Taliban–al Qaeda stronghold in the Shahikot Valley, a narrow valley between two steep mountain ranges, in Operation *Anaconda.*

Franks wrote that, at the time, he told his subordinates that the plan for Operation *Anaconda* was basically sound, but seemed insufficiently joint: the various components and their operations did not seem well coordinated with one another. This proved prescient. Anticipating only light enemy resistance, the plan called for friendly Afghan forces to enter the valley from the west and south. At the same time, four U.S. infantry companies were flown by helicopter to the eastern mountain slopes, where they were to block escape routes. Other troops were to form concentric rings around the valley at greater distances to block escape routes. Operation *Anaconda* thus was a classic hammer-and-anvil plan that was intended to trap enemy forces in the valley, where they could be overpowered and disarmed by the allied Afghan troops.

This plan fell to unanticipated frictions of war. Friendly Afghan troops halted short of the valley when they drew enemy fire. After they were accidentally attacked by a U.S. aircraft, they retreated toward their home bases. Arriving U.S. infantry were thus alone on the eastern slopes to face an enemy that proved to be larger, better armed, and more aggressive than expected. The result, wrote Franks, was sharp combat and a difficult fight. U.S. infantry forces had only a few mortars and several attack helicopters, which were badly damaged in the fighting. U.S. combat aircraft, which originally had been told that they would not play a major role, were quickly called in. Although they were armed with smart munitions, they faced difficult conditions: a narrow valley, enemy troops scattered among mountains in many concealed places, and the need to strike targets without hitting nearby U.S. troops. Initial problems in establishing smooth command and control procedures between the ground and air components added to the difficulty.

For three days, combat was intense; then, enemy resistance began to slacken in the face of U.S. air and ground firepower. More experienced Afghan troops arrived to join the fight. By day seven, the fight was mostly over; it was declared officially ended about a week later. Operation *Anaconda*, wrote Franks, was a decisive victory. Hundreds of enemy troops were killed, and losses to U.S. and allied troops were light. Enemy forces thereafter sought to avoid major combat with U.S. forces. However, *Anaconda* exposed fault lines and controversies in joint operations that would need to be corrected before the next war, which erupted when Iraq was invaded a year later.

Successes in Afghanistan helped clear the way for a growing focus on Iraq. From the time he took over as USCENTCOM commander in 2000, wrote Franks, he had viewed Saddam Hussein as a serious threat, and leaders of many friendly Arab governments shared his views. In 1998, the U.S. Congress had officially endorsed a policy of regime change aimed at removing Saddam Hussein from power. Achieving this goal had then been impossible, but September 11, 2001, wrote Franks, created new necessities and new possibilities.

Franks wrote that Secretary of Defense Rumsfeld first asked him in late November 2001 about USCENTCOM's operation plan (OPLAN) for the Persian Gulf, entitled OPLAN 1003. President Bush insisted that the war on terror should include not only strikes on terrorist groups, but also action against rogue countries that sponsored or encouraged terrorism or otherwise posed grave dangers to Western interests. Iraq, Bush would later declare, was part of an "axis of evil." Rumsfeld wanted an early sense of USCENTCOM's options and capabilities for going to war, so he would be prepared if a decision for war were made, or if Saddam Hussein committed a casus belli that made war unavoidable. As Franks knew, it normally took months to write a new OPLAN, and additional time would be needed to put forces in place and work out relationships with allies.

Rumsfeld and Franks decided that OPLAN 1003, last updated in 1998, was badly out of date. Although the force levels required by the plan had been trimmed from 500,000 troops to 400,000, they were still too large; moreover, it did not incorporate transformation concepts or newly emerging lessons from Afghanistan. In the following months, wrote Franks, he worked with Rumsfeld and USCENTCOM on a new Commander's Concept that tailored joint force operations to the specific missions that would have to be performed in a war with Iraq. He also worked to whittle down the size of the force, to emphasize joint operations, to blend use of airpower and SOF with ground maneuvers, and to achieve speedy deployment and wartime execution. He crafted a spectrum of options that offered choices depending upon how much cooperation was offered by allies and friendly countries. Similar to the plan for Afghanistan, his concept, which aimed at regime change in Iraq and elimination of WMD, had four phases: preparation; shaping the battlefield; decisive operations; and post-hostility operations.

Franks wrote that his concept was sufficiently developed by March 2002 to lay the foundation for OPLAN 1003V. USCENTCOM's work on the new plan got under way on March 22; a spectrum of options was under consideration, and many complex issues had to be addressed, including plans for the movement of forces and supplies to the Persian Gulf. Moreover, the task of invading Iraq promised to be harder than merely ejecting the Iraqi army from Kuwait, as the U.S. military had done in 1991. By August, enough issues had been settled to allow the OPLAN to take shape. It provided for about 135 days to prepare and shape the battlefield in Phases I and II, followed by about 90 days of decisive operations in Phase III. Phases I through III, Franks wrote, would require a maximum of 250,000 troops in Iraq. The duration of Phase IV, he wrote, would be unknown in advance, but the plan provided for troop levels to be substantially reduced as it unfolded successfully.

In the following weeks, Franks wrote, he briefed the new OPLAN to the interagency community, and worked with Rumsfeld and Pentagon staffs to refine it. No final decision to go to war had yet been made. Iraq was being debated at the UN, and there were still prospects for a diplomatic resolution. Franks wrote that this period provided the opportunity to fine-tune the sequencing of force deployments, to tailor tactical battle plans, and to conduct simulations and war games to test battle plans. Along the way, the OPLAN mutated into a new version called Hybrid 1003V. It envisioned that an invasion could begin before all forces had arrived in the Persian Gulf, that air and ground operations could begin simultaneously, and that U.S. ground forces would move quickly toward Baghdad along multiple axes. Although it called for U.S. and allied forces to face much larger Iraqi forces, speed and momentum would compensate. On November 8, the United Nations passed Security Council Resolution 1441, which called for Iraq to report in detail on all of its weapons of mass destruction and to provide unimpeded access to international weapons inspectors. During this period, Franks wrote, USCENTCOM continued its work on the OPLAN, and the U.S. Government intensified its discussions with Britain and other participating countries and with friendly Arab countries. Turkey's stance was especially important, because the plan provided for the 4th Mechanized Division to move across Turkey to invade Iraq from the north, as other forces advanced from Kuwait in the south. The Turkish government, however, decided against the idea. USCENTCOM therefore revised its plan: the 173[d] Airborne Brigade would be airlifted into northern Iraq, while the 4th Mechanized Division would be rerouted through Kuwait.

By the time Operation *Iraqi Freedom* began on March 19, 2003, the allied coalition had assembled a force of 290,000 military personnel from all U.S. Services and Components as well as forces from Britain, Australia, and many other countries.[5] The invasion itself was remarkably successful, although some tactical adaptations had to be made as it unfolded. For example, on the roads to Basra and Baghdad, Franks wrote, U.S. and British forces discovered Iraqi stocks of brand-new equipment for operating in a chemical warfare environment, including masks, protective suits, nerve gas sensor alarms, atropine, and field decontamination trucks loaded with detergent solutions and high-pressure spray tanks. Since the Iraqi army knew that U.S. and British forces did not have chemical weapons, Franks reasoned, it was preparing to protect itself while using its own chemical weapons against U.S. and British forces. Franks wrote that USCENTCOM had expected to be attacked with chemical weapons, and that before the invasion, friendly Arab leaders had warned him about such attacks. No such attacks, however, took place, and after the war, no offensive chemical and biological weapons were found—leaving an unresolved mystery, as Franks wrote.

U.S. and allied forces moved quickly to Baghdad despite severe sandstorms on the way. On April 9, Saddam Hussein's statue in Baghdad was toppled. A week later, major combat operations were deemed over, far sooner than the OPLAN had originally estimated. U.S. and British casualties were remarkably light, and damage to oilfields and bridges was far less than had been feared. Writing afterward, Franks expressed satisfaction with this quick and successful campaign, which he described as unlike any other in modern warfare. While he had some complaints about some frustrating debates with Pentagon bureaucracies, he praised Secretary Rumsfeld, President Bush, USCENTCOM, and the U.S. and allied servicemembers.

Franks left USCENTCOM and retired from active duty in early July 2003, before the insurgency in Iraq began to reach high levels of violence. His 2004 book responded to those who accused him, the U.S. Government, and USCENTCOM of neglecting preparations for the occupation, stabilization, and reconstruction duties of Phase IV. Franks argued that major attention had been given to Phase IV, and that Office of Reconstruction and Humanitarian Assistance Director Jay Garner had done a good job of identifying the missions, requirements, and priorities likely to arise. As a result, he wrote, USCENTCOM and Presidential envoy J. Paul Bremer, head of the Coalition Provisional Authority, went into Phase IV well aware of the challenges ahead. They knew, for example, that ex-Ba'athist leaders, terrorists, felons let out of prison by Saddam Hussein, and even Saddam himself would be roaming the country.

Franks' optimistic assumptions with regard to the postconflict period in Iraq, reflected both operationally and in his book, were challenged by Michael R. Gordon and Bernard E. Trainor in their 2006 book, *Cobra II: The Inside Story of the Invasion and Occupation of Iraq*.[6] Gordon and Trainor described the postwar reconstruction team led by Jay Garner as having had little time to plan, having few real resources to complete the mission, being badly understaffed, and having prepared for the wrong missions, such as disaster relief. Efforts by State Department officials to point out these problems resulted in their removal from the Garner team. When the Garner team was deployed to the region, it remained in a hotel in Kuwait while the war was fought. Meanwhile, Gordon and Trainor point out, postwar planning in Washington continued based on faulty assumptions about de-Ba'athification, the nature of the Iraqi police, and the speed at which Iraqi military forces could be reconstituted. According to Gordon and Trainor, one person who accurately assessed the situation was Lieutenant General John Abizaid, then Franks' deputy, who concluded: "We are an antibody in their [Iraqi] society. It would be crazy to keep the U.S. Government in charge for too long."[7]

These books make it clear that General Franks' great successes were the use of transformed U.S. military capabilities to fight high-tech wars in both Afghanistan and Iraq with minimal American casualties, and that his mistake was in misunderstanding the nature of the postconflict problems that lurked in the wake of his military victories.

John Keegan: The Iraq War in Strategic Perspective

Where General Franks provided an operational perspective on the Iraq war, British scholar John Keegan provided the strategic perspective of an eminent historian and author of 17 previous books on military affairs. Keegan's 2004 book, *The Iraq War*, set out to explain three mysteries of what he called a "mysterious war"—its political origins, its military character, and the postconflict occupation.[8] He analyzed not only America's conduct, but Britain's as well, an important subject often neglected by American writers. He also assessed the behavior of France and Germany in the UN debate over whether to invade Iraq. Whether Keegan fully succeeded in explaining and evaluating the Iraq war will be up to future historians to decide, but his book offered many cogent insights and interpretations that are likely to be benchmarks for some time.

After briefly describing Iraq's history and Saddam Hussein's rule, Keegan reviewed the complex political interactions that led U.S. and British forces to invade Iraq in March 2003. Keegan cited the terrorist attacks of September

11, 2001, as a decisive turning point because they produced a new, assertive strategic mentality in the United States. Previously, said Keegan, the United States had viewed the world as mostly safe and stable, subject only to problems at the margins such as the Balkans. After September 11, however, many Americans adopted the view that the world was dangerous, volatile, and full of threatening enemies. The newly arrived Bush administration, said Keegan, was not reluctant to assert U.S. military power unilaterally. In this, the neoconservatives who led the Bush administration were, Keegan judged, reflecting views that had become more widely held by Americans and that were also consistent with an established U.S. record of reacting angrily and powerfully to attacks on its homeland or its interests abroad.

Problems arose, however, because the United States was focusing on the Middle East, a region that it did not well understand and from which it had previously kept its distance. The Americans, wrote Keegan, had a poor grasp of Middle East politics and of militant Islamic fundamentalism, which is not well understood by British and French experts on the Middle East either. The angry upsurge of militant Islam is a product of centuries of decline, wrote Keegan, and a reaction to the spread of Western culture and economics. Out of the decolonization of recent decades had come new countries that did not embrace the West and were dominated by autocratic governments, which embraced nationalism and power politics, and by resurgent Islamic fundamentalism, which took over Iran, influenced other societies, gave rise to the Taliban regime in Afghanistan, and provided a safe haven for al Qaeda. Keegan pointed out that nationalist regimes, such as Saddam Hussein's Iraq, are more secular than religious, but they are nevertheless willing to use military force and terrorism to advance their national causes, often at expense of Western interests. Islamic militants justify anti-Western terrorism as attacks on infidels and are willing to accept help from secular despots. After September 11, wrote Keegan, all of this was a volatile mix: the United States was rolling up its sleeves for a military showdown, and Islamic militants were eager for a violent encounter. Meanwhile, Saddam Hussein failed to grasp the threat facing him.

The Bush administration, said Keegan, failed to distinguish between the religious violence of militant Islam and the power politics of Saddam Hussein. The administration viewed Saddam Hussein as a leader of an axis of evil that was facilitating terrorism and endangering the Middle East in other ways. This U.S. view, wrote Keegan, was shaped by Saddam Hussein's malevolent conduct of many years; he was truly a serious threat to the region as well as to common Western interests. Quite apart from whether he actually possessed WMD and was helping al Qaeda, Keegan pointed out, Saddam

Hussein was a tyrant who had committed genocide against his own people, used chemical weapons, invaded two of his neighbors, ignored multiple UN Security Council resolutions, resisted no-fly zones enforced by the United States and Britain, sponsored terrorism against Israel and other victims, tried to assassinate a former U.S. President, and kept a large army that had recently been used to threaten both Kuwait and Israel.

The United States, wrote Keegan, was no longer willing to tolerate Saddam Hussein's menacing presence and volatile behavior. As a result, it decided to force regime change in Iraq as soon as it became confident of winning quickly in Afghanistan. It was this earlier U.S. decision for regime change, not the subsequent UN debate over WMD, said Keegan, that was a key step toward war. Another key step was the decision of Prime Minister Tony Blair, based on moral and strategic grounds, to support the Bush administration's commitment to regime change, including the use of military force if necessary. Keegan offered no judgment on whether the invasion was the best or only choice, leaving this contentious topic to be debated by others. However, he made it clear that the U.S. and British governments believed that they were standing on sound legal and strategic ground when they decided to invade.

France's Jacques Chirac and Germany's Gerhard Schroeder, Keegan said, were genuinely doubtful that invading Iraq was a wise step. They also were partly motivated by anti-Americanism and by their desire to shape the European Union into a power bloc capable of rivaling the United States on the world stage. In addition, he said, France's profitable economic relations with Iraq made it more willing to let Saddam Hussein stay in power. More fundamentally, wrote Keegan, the EU had developed an "Olympian" view—what we would call a neo-Kantian view—of world politics, believing that reason and diplomacy could replace the use of military force in resolving political confrontations. This Olympian view may have been appropriate for governing the EU's internal affairs, wrote Keegan, but it was inadequate for global realities. Many Eastern European countries recently admitted to NATO and the EU agreed with the United States and Britain, noted Keegan; however, enough Western European countries agreed with France and Germany to embolden them at the UN, where they sought to block authorization to use force against Iraq.

At the UN, the United States and Britain gained passage of Security Council Resolution 1441 in November 2002. The resolution firmly warned Saddam Hussein of impending trouble if he failed to both relinquish the WMD he was believed to have and comply with other Security Council resolutions. The UN then dispatched WMD inspectors to Iraq under Hans Blix;

they encountered a combination of cooperation and resistance. Blix reported that while his inspectors did not find WMD systems, they could not verify that Iraq had dismantled those known to exist when UN inspectors were expelled in 1998. The Bush administration, which by now was impatient with the delay-inducing UN debates, was ready to treat Resolution 1441 as authority to invade Iraq, but Britain's Blair wanted a second resolution that more explicitly authorized use of force. Seeking such a resolution, the United States and Britain encountered opposition from several Security Council members, including Germany. Chirac ended the matter when he announced that France, a permanent member, would veto it. The United States and Britain saw the way clear for invasion of Iraq, but without the second Security Council resolution, controversy remained.

Turning to the military challenge, Keegan wrote that U.S. and British forces would be trying to conquer a country whose geography had long resisted invasion. Outnumbered in military forces by a 2-to-1 ratio or more, they would face an Iraqi army that fielded 22 divisions, including 6 Republican Guard divisions that were thought to be capable of serious combat operations. Iraq would be defending terrain, with two large rivers, that it had had years to prepare. However, its lack of air defenses and other components of modern warfare, coupled with poor training and readiness, were key liabilities. For the invasion, wrote Keegan, the United States deployed a joint force of three Army/Marine divisions plus three independent brigades and Special Operations Forces, six fighter wings plus bombers, six carrier battlegroups, and many naval combatants. Another Army division, the 4th Mechanized, was on the way. To this formidable U.S. force, the British added an armored division composed of an armored brigade, an air assault brigade, and a commando brigade, plus fighter aircraft, an aircraft carrier, and numerous ships. The Australians provided a small force of SOF, fighter aircraft, and ships; Poland contributed 200 SOF troops. This U.S.-led coalition force, wrote Keegan, may have been outnumbered by the Iraqis, but it packed a big offensive punch, and was vastly superior in information networks, weapons, munitions, doctrine, training, joint operations, air superiority, air-to-ground strike power, and other aspects. As a result, the major combat phase of the war yielded a rapid victory for the coalition, rather than the hard-fought contest some had predicted.

Keegan praised U.S. forces for their well-conceived, speedy drive to Baghdad, which was briefly slowed only by a sandstorm and the need to bring supplies to combat troops from a long distance. He provided a clear step-by-step portrayal of how Army and Marine forces advanced up the Euphrates and Tigris rivers, capturing key terrain features, passing through danger zones, crossing bridges, and accomplishing other objectives. The rapidity and distance of their advance, he said, was unprecedented in history. The powerful U.S. attack showed good planning coupled with mastery of modern warfare, including the blending of ground forces, airpower, and Special Operations Forces; the Iraqi army would have been quickly defeated, said Keegan, even if it had decided to mount serious opposition, but in the event, it melted away in the face of U.S. air bombardment and the arriving U.S. ground forces. Some Republican Guard units and other forces tried to fight, but they were quickly defeated. Soldiers of many regular Iraqi army divisions simply discarded their uniforms and walked home, abandoning prepared fortifications and failing to destroy key bridges. Keegan speculated that this flight was mainly caused by fear of combat, but it also may have been aided by earlier U.S. contacts with Iraqi generals, who were persuaded not to mount a hopeless defense. Most Iraqi citizens were unwilling to put much effort into saving Saddam Hussein's regime. They might not welcome Western invaders, but they did not regret Saddam Hussein's departure.

The U.S. ground force speedily arrived at Baghdad, easily overpowered resistance by disorganized Ba'athist fanatics, and swept over the city. There was no sign of the Stalingrad-like resistance that some had predicted. With so little major combat, and nearly all of it one-sided, American forces suffered few losses.

British forces, Keegan wrote, were charged with invading southern Iraq, populated by Shi'a who generally had good relations with Britain. They aimed to occupy Iraq's second biggest city, Basra. British tactics were somewhat different than U.S. tactics: instead of charging directly into the city, the British surrounded it and applied pressure, then entered it a few days later when Iraqi forces were on the verge of collapse. Like Baghdad, Basra was captured with few losses to coalition troops. Keegan credited British forces with fighting well and playing the role of "esteemed junior partner" in the invasion.

The problems with the invasion, as Keegan wrote, came after major combat operations had ended and Baghdad had fallen. The Saddam Hussein government neither surrendered nor was captured. Instead, it melted away into Iraq's cities and countryside, where it soon began mounting opposition through terrorist attacks. It was joined by terrorists from other countries and was aided by common criminals. In contrast to the relative tranquility that settled over the Kurdish zone in the north and the Shi'ite zone in the south, said Keegan, the Sunni triangle around Baghdad, with about 20 percent of Iraq's population, descended into violence and turmoil, even as U.S. occupiers were trying to establish a new Iraqi government with a democratic constitution. Saddam Hussein was eventually captured and his sons killed, but even this decapitation of the former Ba'athist regime did not abate the growing violence.

In Keegan's view, some of this chaos and violence was inevitable, but unlike General Franks, he sharply criticized the U.S. occupation strategy and many of its initial decisions, saying that the U.S. warfighting and diplomatic postwar scripts did not mesh well. The British were successful in the south, he said, because they adopted a pragmatic approach. Aspiring to reestablish law and order quickly, they worked with anybody willing to cooperate, even former Ba'athists. As a result, electricity was soon restored, and schools and hospitals were quickly put back into running order. Crime was controlled, streets were safe, and terrorism was quelled.

In contrast, wrote Keegan, the Americans sought an immediate transition from tyranny to functioning democracy. They dismantled the Iraqi army and police force and made no effort to reestablish the administrative apparatus of the former government. The resulting failure to restore essential services, outbreak of chaos and crime, and lack of public safety or restoration of a functioning economy caused growing disillusionment among Sunnis in and around Baghdad. Only as violence began growing in following months, wrote Keegan, did the Americans begin to turn to essential tasks of stabilization and reconstruction. They sought to build a new Iraqi army and police force, and promoted nationwide cooperation to create a true democracy. Such steps held out some promise of eventual success, but in the interim, the stage had been set for a great deal of violence and terrorism directed not only at Americans, but also at Iraqis willing to cooperate with them. A brilliant military victory descended into a prolonged occupation struggle.

Although Keegan's writing was analytical and even-handed in tone, many of his arguments about the "mysteries" of the Iraq war are controversial. His portrayal of Saddam Hussein as a dictator whose overall menacing behavior validated the invasion is rejected by those who view the presence of WMD as the sole legitimate justification for the war. His portrayals of the Bush administration as already intent on regime change in Iraq shortly after September 11 and of Tony Blair as a brave if moralistic prime minister who resisted public opinion and betrayal by parts of his own Labor Party are also controversial, as is his unsympathetic treatment of France and Germany.

Also contentious is his attribution of the swift victory mainly to the failure of Iraqi forces to offer a credible defense, although he did acknowledge the skilled performance of U.S. and British forces. Keegan does not speculate about what would have happened if Iraqi forces had given serious battle; presumably the contest would have been a bloodier affair, but the coalition would still have won. Nor does he discuss the idea that the Saddam Hussein regime consciously adopted a strategy of offering terrorist resistance during the postwar occupation, rather than dying on the battlefield or surrendering. Keegan does not express his views on these key issues.

However, his critical treatment of the early U.S. occupation strategy is amply clear. It would doubtless anger those who crafted or supported this strategy, but to many outside observers, it may have the ring of truth. So, too, do many of his other arguments. The great strength of his book is that it examines the Iraq war in strategic terms and provides a comprehensive sense of the whole. At a minimum, it provides a powerful frame of reference for future historians of this conflict.

Hans Binnendijk and the NDU Team: U.S. Military Transformation

In writing the book *Transforming America's Military*, one of the authors of this volume assembled a team of experts who analyzed U.S. defense planning in the early stages of the Bush administration.[9] Written in 2002, as the war on terror was getting under way but before the invasion of Iraq, it took as a point of departure the Pentagon's *Quadrennial Defense Review (QDR)*, issued in late 2001.[10] *QDR 2001* was pathbreaking in many ways. It swept away the much criticized two-MTW formula, and in its place offered a "1-4-2-1" formula: U.S. forces should be sized to provide for homeland defense, to conduct peacetime military engagement in four regions, to be able to respond to two nearly concurrent MTWs, and to carry out a counterattack and occupation of enemy territory in one MTW. This formula generated flexibility by stripping away counterattack forces for one MTW, although it preserved them for the other. The effect was to liberate some forces for missions other than the two major theater wars.

With this switch in formulas, *QDR 2001* discarded "threat-based" planning in favor of "capability-based" planning. DOD would no longer design its forces solely on the basis of a few specific hypothetical contingencies. Capability-based planning called instead for U.S. forces to be designed to handle diverse crises and wars across a wide spectrum of missions and operations that would range from small to large and would require different types of military responses. Forces would be flexible, modular, and adaptable, capable of being packaged and repackaged in different ways. After surveying a wide range of options, *QDR 2001* had concluded that the current force posture provided an adequate array of forces for such operations, so it imposed no changes in force size or mix. It called for an increased emphasis on joint operations in which all components would work closely together and for changes to the U.S. overseas presence to improve power-projection capabilities.

QDR 2001 identified transformation as the main engine for shaping future forces and capabilities. It endorsed such new technologies as information networks, smart munitions, missiles for long-range strikes, and space systems. However, it did not articulate a full strategy to guide transformation, nor did it say much about exactly how future U.S. force operations were to be conducted. It centered on the concept of joint expeditionary warfare for full-spectrum operations. This meant that future U.S. operations were to be truly *joint,* that is, with components highly integrated together rather than operated separately but side by side; future operations would also be *expeditionary,* or conducted at long distances for specific reasons and of relatively brief duration. Operations would be conducted across a wide spectrum of missions and settings, ranging from small crises and interventions against terrorists and WMD sites to MTWs with medium-sized powers and to bigger wars against larger opponents. To support this central concept, the Chairman of the Joint Chiefs of Staff issued his *Joint Vision,* which offered a host of subsidiary concepts, including networked operations, precision strike, dominant maneuver, focused logistics, and full-dimension protection.[11] More concepts were later added by the Joint Staff and the services, such as the Navy's network-centric warfare concept, the Army's rapid decisive operations, and the Air Force's effects-based operations. Subsidiary concepts included dispersed formations, simultaneous operations, high-tempo maneuvers, and synergistic leverage. For all their focus on new-era operational warfare, these concepts, like *QDR 2001,* said little about how exactly transformation was to be implemented.

The 2002 book *Transforming America's Military* sought to help fill this conceptual gap. It portrayed transformation as a response to strategic changes abroad as well as to new technologies and doctrines. At the time, some transformation advocates were calling for a bold leap by which an entire generation of legacy weapons—those already developed and ready for procurement—would be discarded in favor of pursuit of exotic futurist weapons then only found on the drawing boards. A lengthy period of 10 or 20 years might be required before these weapons might be produced, but "leap-ahead" advocates argued that the world was then entering a "strategic pause": a period of calm in which big wars would not be fought. As a result, they asserted, leap-ahead was a low-risk, high-payoff strategy. Essentially, leap-ahead advocates were focused on a high-technology rivalry with China in the distant future, but they discounted imminent conflicts such as messy limited wars in the Balkans, the Middle East, Central Asia, and elsewhere. The leap-ahead theory failed to anticipate the war on terror, which would require use of existing forces and technologies, not exotic technologies unavailable for a decade or two.

Transforming America's Military rejected leap-ahead as too risky, but it also rejected the opposite approach, a "steady-as-you-go" crawl into the future. Instead, it proposed that transformation should be guided by a "purposeful and measured" strategy that paid appropriate attention to the near term, to the midterm, and to the long term. It advocated attention to the near term using transformation concepts to help fight the war on terror. It also highlighted the need to focus innovative ideas on the midterm (6 to 12 years in the future) as a bridge between the near term and long term. It defined transformation in broader terms than just the acquisition of new weapons and new technologies. Transformation, it said, should be a holistic effort aimed at reconfiguring U.S. forces for information-era operations through a combination of new weapons and technologies, operational concepts, doctrines, and organizational structures. The biggest gains could be made by combining changes in all of these areas and by coordinating them in such a manner that U.S. forces could gradually absorb them without being disrupted by them.

Employing this philosophy, the authors of the book's various chapters addressed specific forces, missions, and challenges. Chapters on air forces and naval forces concluded that the U.S. Air Force and the U.S. Navy were well situated, with new weapons, technologies, and information systems suitable for taking advantage of transformation, but that they faced challenges in affording all of their programs. The same applied to space systems, a favorite of transformation advocates in the Pentagon. Homeland security was assessed as an area for vigorous transformation and enhanced spending, particularly because the terrorist attacks of September 11, 2001, had revealed so many deficiencies. Cyberspace security needed substantial efforts but was capable of swift progress. Authors of chapters on the Army, joint transformation, and multilateral transformation reached more cautious conclusions: the Army was expected to face trouble if it continued its pursuit of a futurist, high-tech Objective Force of lightweight armored vehicles and sophisticated information networks, while neglecting to invest in upgrading the legacy forces that would continue to provide the backbone of Army capabilities for years to come. Joint transformation was assessed as troubled, not only because integrating multiple cross-Service programs was difficult, but also because the Services were not yet fully committed to operating jointly. Multilateral transformation was also seen as troubled, because the European allies did not fully understand transformation and lacked the money for major investments.

The Air Force and the Navy were generally seen as doing a good job of developing new information systems and smart munitions that would enhance their capacity to conduct standoff strikes, a priority highlighted by *QDR 2001*. Moreover, although their current weapons systems were aging, the new weapons systems about to become available offered many improved capabilities, even if some critics portrayed them as insufficiently transformational. The authors concluded that the problem facing both Services was affording these new weapons, but they noted that the Bush administration was increasing the defense budget, which could within a few years begin to fund a sustained procurement effort. The Army's main problem was that it had acquired a reputation for stodgy thinking in the past few years, in contrast to the Marine Corps, which had become known for its innovative attitude. The two new weapons in the Army's research, development, testing, and evaluation pipeline, the Crusader artillery tube and the Comanche helicopter, were both denigrated by critics as legacy systems (and indeed, both were later cancelled). The Army's transformation strategy, the authors wrote, was in fact truly leap-ahead: it proposed creation of ultrasophisticated information systems for networking all of its forces from top to bottom. It also proposed lightweight weapons—called Future Combat Systems (FCS)—that were to replace such heavy stalwarts as the Abrams tank and the Bradley infantry fighting vehicle. As replacements, the Army plan sought to develop a whole new generation of vehicles that would be sufficiently lightweight to fit aboard C–130 transport planes. As a bridge to the Objective Force, the Army conceived of an "Interim Force" based on the 18-ton wheeled *Stryker* vehicle, which would serve as a test model for FCS concepts. This ambitious plan to create a future Objective Force faced three problems, according to critics: the new weapons would take many years to create; they might not possess the necessary firepower, mobility, and survivability even if created; and in the interim, most Army combat forces would benefit from few new weapons programs.

The pursuit of joint transformation was also assessed as problematic. The Services were perceived as mostly inward-looking rather than joint in their orientation and as viewing transformation mostly in Service-centric terms. The Navy and Marines were assessed as best at joint thinking; they belong to the same military department and regularly integrate their forces to create a joint capacity for naval and amphibious warfare. The Air Force was portrayed as being at the cutting edge of modern technology and lethal strike capabilities, but the authors expressed concern that it was focusing too much on strategic bombardment to the neglect of providing close air support for the Army. The Army was said to be not innovating enough to create the rapidly deployable, modular forces needed to work closely with the Marines, Navy, and Air Force in fast-moving expeditionary missions. The authors identified joint operations as a key aspect of transformation, and expressed hope that the U.S. Joint Forces Command could foster improvements.

The authors found even more to be concerned about with multilateral transformation. The NATO allies in Europe were, they wrote, facing two major problems. They lack the physical capacity for swift projection of large forces, especially ground forces, outside their borders for expeditionary missions. They also lack the information networks, smart munitions, and modern doctrines needed to operate alongside U.S. forces. As U.S. forces increasingly pursue transformation, the Europeans will be left further behind. The resulting transatlantic gap in capabilities might not be bridgeable in demanding situations. Despite low European budgets for investments, the authors concluded that the task facing NATO is not hopeless. Some European countries, they noted, are starting to buy information systems that, although not as sophisticated as U.S. systems, may be adequate to connect with American networks. These countries, they wrote, are also buying stocks of smart munitions and are interested in new force structures and doctrines. The creation of a few European forces capable of swift power projection and networked operations, they said, might be a more feasible and affordable proposition than critics realize. The authors thus created a sense of hope that the widening transatlantic gap in modern forces and transformation capabilities could be closed with planning and innovative thinking at NATO headquarters.

Viewed in retrospect, *Transforming America's Military* seems to have put a finger on issues that also were on the minds of senior DOD officials. In 2002–2003, the services presented "transformation roadmaps" that articulated their visions of the agenda ahead.[12] The Air Force reaffirmed its need for expensive new F–22 and F–35 Joint Strike Fighters as well as space systems, but also made clear its commitment to expeditionary warfare. In future years, it proposed to acquire a growing number of robot-piloted unmanned combat aerial vehicle fighters. The Navy presented an ambitious plan to grow from 295 ships to 370 ships by 2022, with much of the increase coming from acquisition of 56 littoral combat ships, which are decidedly transformational in nature. The Navy added transformation technologies to its designs for new carriers, surface combatants, and submarines. It also set out to reorganize its combatants into fresh formations, such as carrier strike groups. Like the Air Force, its main problem would be affordability, not strategic design.

The Army, too, began responding. After losing Crusader and Comanche, the Army discarded its earlier formula of Legacy Force, Interim Force, and Objective Force. In its place came a new two-part formula, Current Forces and Future Forces. The Army's revised plan called for increased investments in Current Forces so that near-term and midterm missions could be carried out effectively. The Army continued to pursue FCS vehicles but specified that this program would be managed with regard for battlefield capabilities

as well as information networks and light weight. The Army also began crafting a plan to reorganize its combat forces, emphasizing brigades as the centerpiece of a modular, diverse posture. As the Army's transformation plans
came into better focus, the growing concern was no longer strategic wisdom,
but affordability. Army spending requirements were growing, but the Army
investment budget was still less than half that of either the Air Force or the
Navy. Moreover, ground operations in Afghanistan and Iraq were diverting
ever-larger sums away from investments.

    In order to help ease this problem for all services, DOD sought and
obtained special budgetary supplements to pay for Iraq and Afghanistan, so
as to leave the normal peacetime defense budget untouched. Even so, a variety of factors have slowed the growth of the defense-wide procurement budget. Formerly slated to rise from $70 billion in 2002 to $120 billion by 2012,
it had only reached $75 billion by 2004.[13] Even so, progress on transforma-
tion was accelerating. It was not limited to the services acting individually;
interest in joint transformation was growing, prompted not only by transformation theories, but also by battlefield realities. The invasion of Iraq in 2003
was expressly designed to be conducted by a relatively small force that would
employ modern doctrine to defeat a much larger enemy. The services had
no choice but to operate jointly, and under the guidance of General Franks
and USCENTCOM, they did so to an unprecedented degree.

    Growing hope was also coming from the direction of NATO. At the
Prague Summit of 2002, NATO took several important steps. It adopted the
Prague Capabilities Commitment aimed at channeling European defense
investments into high-priority areas. It reformed its command structure by
creating a new Allied Transformation Command located alongside the U.S.
Joint Forces Command in Norfolk, Virginia. This new command was charged
with the mission of helping transform European and NATO forces so that
they would be interoperable with U.S. forces. NATO also decided to field a
new Response Force, a small, high-tech strike force that could deploy outside
Europe quickly and could work closely with sophisticated U.S. forces. It was
to include about 21,000 personnel: a ground brigade, a fighter wing, and a
surface action flotilla, with appropriate support assets. It was designed to be
ready to move within 7 days and to have 30 days of sustainment. Under its
rotational concept, one NRF would be on duty for six months, while a second NRF would be training to assume future duty, and a third NRF would
be standing down and recovering from previous duty. These three rotating
multinational forces would give all NATO allies the opportunity to participate. The hope was that, as they rotated through the NRF, European forces
would learn transformation concepts and then bring this thinking back to

their parent services. Public attention to the NRF faded when the debate over Iraq erupted shortly thereafter. But a year later, the NRF had made rapid progress, with full operational capability expected in 2006. Its rapid progress provided hope that NATO and the Europeans would not be left behind by transformation or sidelined by transatlantic squabbling over political and diplomatic issues.

Within the United States, transformation was off to a good start by 2002. Whereas its advocates initially had conceived it as a long-term leap to exotic technologies and weapons in a distant future in which China might be a main enemy, transformation now focused on the near term and midterm, striving to prepare U.S. forces for expeditionary operations anywhere from the Middle East to Central Asia and the East Asian littoral. Even so, transformation unfolded slowly, changing the American military in stages, and initially affecting only a small part of it. The war on terror, generating unanticipated demands of its own, had to be waged with the forces at hand, and thus it required transformation steps that could be achieved in a hurry.

In 2002, *Transforming America's Military* had offered a cautionary observation: "If the American military appears able to win victories at low cost, war might become a preferred instrument of diplomacy rather than an instrument of last resort."[14] The United States subsequently reached rather quickly for the military instrument in Iraq. The experiences of Iraq and Afghanistan suggest that while winning wars in a military sense is one thing, winning the peace can be something else, and that different U.S. military capabilities may be needed for each.

In 2004, a second book addressing how to win the peace followed up on *Transforming America's Military*. Edited by Hans Binnendijk and Stuart Johnson, *Transforming for Stabilization and Reconstruction Operations* called for the U.S. military to strengthen its forces and capabilities for S&R missions.[15] It noted that although America's transformed network-centric military and its effects-based operations targeting concept could quickly collapse a regime, elements of the regime and its military might then go underground from where they could make the postconflict period more difficult. As a result, new U.S. capabilities are needed to deal with a "stabilization and reconstruction gap." The book noted that S&R operations would typically require specialized capabilities in such areas as light infantry for urban operations, military police, civil administration, construction engineers, medical services, intelligence, psychological operations, and logistic support. Often these assets are not present in adequate numbers in traditional combat forces, leaving a critical capabilities gap, as in Iraq.

The 2004 book noted that even after the situation in Iraq is resolved,

S&R operations could be required in other places, even in countries larger than Iraq. History shows that such an operation can be successful, as in Germany and Japan after World War II, but it takes time and resources. Accordingly, the book proposed organizing a flexible, modular force of two division equivalents, with one Active and one Reserve Component totaling about 30,000 troops, as well as joint and interagency capabilities for future S&R duties. This is quite a different form of transformation than had been envisioned earlier. S&R units of this sort, it argued, appropriately trained and equipped, could deploy to a contingency early, so that they would be immediately available when major combat operations began the transition to S&R missions. S&R units might be created by reorganizing existing Army forces, but if this were not possible, an expansion of Army manpower could be needed.

Transforming for Stabilization and Reconstruction Operations noted that new U.S. military capabilities are not enough for success; new strategic concepts are also required. Unity of effort, a consistent and compelling strategic message, full-spectrum planning, better cultural intelligence, early demonstrable successes, and early use of indigenous capabilities are all needed for enduring success in an operation of the type likely to be undertaken during the Long War. The book listed several new technologies that could help with these operations, such as tagging devices, handheld translating devices, non-lethal weapons, and ordnance detection devices. It noted the importance of improving the capacity of the Pentagon's partners, both in other U.S. departments and agencies, and among America's allies. In the 2 ½ years since publication of this book, the Pentagon has adopted many of its recommendations.

Douglas A. Macgregor: Transforming the Army Under Fire

Colonel Macgregor wrote *Transformation Under Fire: Revolutionizing How America Fights* on the eve of his retirement from a long Army career in which he was a successful leader of armored cavalry operations in *Desert Storm* and afterward a persistent advocate of Army reform.[16] His earlier book, *Breaking the Phalanx*, argued that the organizational structure of the Army needed to be changed. It raised eyebrows in the Army in the late 1990s but had an important effect on the thinking of many junior officers.[17] *Transformation Under Fire*, written in 2003 shortly after the invasion of Iraq, also raised eyebrows, perhaps even higher. Macgregor's book on preparing the Army for high-intensity warfare was controversial, but it was scholarly in its approach to warfare and offered specific proposals for Army innovation.

Looking at the Army's experiences since *Desert Storm* in 1991, Macgregor expressed concern about its ability to handle the expeditionary wars expected during the coming decades. In *Desert Storm*, Macgregor said, the Army had been slow to deploy to the Persian Gulf and ponderous in its attack against Iraqi forces that followed. Eight years later, Macgregor pointed out, the Army was entirely left out of the Kosovo war, partly because it was unable to assemble quickly enough to deploy usable force packages to the Balkans. Its only contribution was a small force of Apache attack helicopters that deployed rather slowly to Albania and then did not take part in combat because they could not operate properly in the mountainous terrain. Similarly, Macgregor said, in the 2001 invasion of Afghanistan, the Air Force, Navy, and Marines rapidly converged on the scene with usable force packages, but the Army did not, apart from its SOF, because it was configured to deploy only as extremely large divisions and corps. The Army deployed a division headquarters and a few brigades, but it did so only two months after the major battles that toppled the Taliban regime. The Army entered the fray in March 2003 with Operation *Anaconda*, but it did not perform well because its forces lacked the appropriate assets for battle against a dispersed enemy hiding in mountains.

Macgregor wrote that the Army did better in Operation *Iraqi Freedom*, during which it joined with the Marine Corps to seize Baghdad in only three weeks, but even there, he found cause for worry. Once again, he said, the Army was slow even with just half as large a deployment as for *Desert Storm* (three divisions and two independent brigades). While the Army quickly overpowered enemy opposition, said Macgregor, this was no real test, because the Iraqi army was far overmatched, and its large massed formations on flat desert terrain made perfect targets for U.S. air and ground fires. Future enemies, noted Macgregor, are unlikely to be so accommodating: they are likely to be armed with better weapons and have had better training and are likely to disperse on more rugged terrain such as forests, mountains, and cities. Macgregor therefore called for rapid transformation of the Army in order to fight the war on terror. The purpose of "transformation under fire," he said, is to use structural reform so as to win real-life battles, not to prepare for a distant future with notional exotic technologies. He charged that the Army's existing transformation plan was neither well conceived nor adequately revolutionary. He described it as largely a marginal change to a philosophy inherited from World War II that is reliant upon rigid hierarchies and large, tightly meshed formations that deploy gradually and then crush the enemy through attrition by firepower and logistic sustainment. This traditional philosophy, said Macgregor, leaves the Army resistant to the major changes in structure, doctrine, and joint operations that are needed for the war on terror and other future wars.

Macgregor charged that DOD's overall approach to joint transformation of all services is also misguided. It relies upon information networks and smart munitions to use standoff fires to defeat the enemy from the air by classical attrition mechanics. Essentially, he argued, this is an attempt to use airpower to compensate for the Army's lack of capacity for winning ground battles rapidly through swift maneuver and strike. The problem with this technology-centered and air-dominant approach to joint warfare, said Macgregor, is that airpower cannot work effectively if enemy ground forces are not compelled to mass together in readily identifiable and vulnerable formations. Such massing could be expected on future battlefields, Macgregor wrote, only if the enemy must concentrate its forces to block a U.S. ground advance. Macgregor did not dispute the growing importance of airpower and standoff strikes in modern battle, but he argued that they cannot be used effectively unless U.S. forces fight jointly and unless Army forces can play their critical roles by maneuvering rapidly and striking lethally. Dispersed formations, flatter command hierarchies, decentralized initiative, and joint assets must, he said, be concentrated at lower echelons.

Surveying the specific features of the Army's transformation plan, Macgregor found fault with the interim Stryker combat brigades. The Army's six Stryker brigades are being equipped with thin-skinned, infantry-carrying vehicles of an earlier Marine Corps design. Although these Stryker vehicles, wrote Macgregor, may be rapidly deployable aboard C–130 aircraft, they lack the firepower and survivability to perform on the modern battlefield. They would enable the six brigades, mainly equipped as mechanized light infantry, to conduct peacekeeping and light combat, but not to prevail in intense close combat with a well-armed enemy. He also criticized the Army's accelerating effort to field Future Combat Force vehicles in the next decade or so. The futurist FCS vehicles are also designed to be lightweight and to fit aboard a C–130. Macgregor acknowledged strengths of the Army's plan, including its emphasis on creating sophisticated information networks, robotics, missiles, and other standoff attack assets. But he expressed concern that the FCS vehicles are likely to lack the firepower, survivability, and tactical mobility to prevail in close intense combat. Thus, the future Army might be able to defend ground positions, but it would not be capable of conducting powerful offensive maneuvers. Airpower would be required to outmaneuver and destroy the enemy, leaving ground combat forces to clean up the battlefield afterward.

Macgregor offered an alternative transformation design aimed at building a better joint command structure for expeditionary operations and at assuring the future Army of a significant role in joint operations. Turning first to multi-Service joint operations, he called for a change in the U.S. military's command structure in battle zones. The existing structure is insufficiently joint because it still relies mostly on Service-centric command staffs that engage in stovepiped thinking and are not attuned to the tasks of creating truly integrated joint operations. In order to help solve this problem, Macgregor proposed creation of Standing Joint Force Headquarters (SJFH) in each regional (now called geographic) combatant command. Such a deployable joint headquarters would be organized functionally into four sub-elements, all of them joint: maneuver, strike, sustainment, and information, intelligence, surveillance, and reconnaissance (IISR). Each SJFH, he said, should be commanded by a three-star general with a highly expert staff and should be able to assert direct, on-the-spot command over operations like the invasions of Afghanistan and Iraq. It should focus on carrying out effects-based operations, a concept that would designate military targets whose destruction would have a significant political impact; it should seek to fracture the enemy's cohesion through an integrated ground-air combination of fire and maneuver, rather than through the traditional calculus of Service-centric firepower and attrition.

Macgregor proposed even more sweeping changes for the Army. His plan would transform the Army in the near term, not by rushing new weapons and technologies to the field, but instead by reorganizing the Army into new combat force structures to improve maneuver and strike capabilities. His proposal aimed to design a new Army that could easily be embedded in joint multi-Service operations with the Air Force, Navy, and Marines. His specific goal was to create the ability to field reorganized Army forces that could deploy abroad more swiftly, disperse on the battlefield, and employ fire and maneuver. Macgregor sought to decentralize the Army by concentrating fire and maneuver assets at lower levels. This would be achieved with a focus on the brigade as the echelon at which to bring together a full spectrum of combined assets: armor, infantry, artillery, air assault, SOF, and logistic support. As Macgregor pointed out, many combined assets are now brought together at the level of the division or corps, but brigades are not currently equipped like old-style regiments, which had all necessary assets permanently assigned to them. Assigning critical assets to the division and corps might have enhanced the capability of their senior commanders to allocate these assets flexibly among their constituent units, but it also yielded rigid, top-heavy hierarchies, leaving brigades and their subordinate battalions with little capacity to operate independently on a dispersed battlefield.

Seeking a way to flatten command hierarchies, Macgregor considered the idea of doing away with the division echelon entirely, speculating that division and corps headquarters might be blended into his proposed SJFH.

However, Macgregor's main focus was on making the brigade more effective by giving it a full set of assets for combined operations. He proposed that the brigade be replaced by a new organization called a combat maneuver group (CMG). It would include about 5,000 troops under a brigadier general, and would function as a junior-sized division. It would comprise a robust mix of IISR, armor, infantry, artillery, attack helicopters and stand-off attack systems, and logistic support. To provide offensive capabilities for close combat, Macgregor would equip a CMG with 114 tanks, 131 IFVs, 51 artillery tubes and heavy mortars, 9 multiple launch rocket systems, and 12 attack helicopters: considerably more weapons than are now fielded by a standard U.S. Army brigade. The result would be a heavily armed CMG shaped along the lean, offense-oriented lines of armored cavalry.

Macgregor also proposed creation of additional formations of similar size: light reconnaissance strike groups, airborne/air assault groups, and aviation combat groups. His proposed Army would be composed of about 25 CMGs plus enough of the other formations to yield roughly 33 total combat groups: similar to the number of combat brigades presently in the Army. In order to populate higher echelons with enough assets to direct and support the operations of these combat units, Macgregor proposed, as additional units, a joint C^4I group, an early deploying support group, and a theater air and missile group. These combat and support groups, he said, would all be modular and self-contained so they could be combined and recombined to form diverse force packages tailored to the situations at hand. Their readiness would take a rotational form, similar to the way the Navy maintains its carriers in rotational status: at any time, one-third of the groups would be ready for quick deployment, another third would be standing down from recent duty but recallable on short notice, and the remaining third would be training for future high-readiness status.

Such a staggered readiness profile, Macgregor said, should provide enough combat strength to handle almost any fast-breaking emergency, plus the assets to generate increased strength within a few weeks. These independent units could be quickly brought together in varying numbers, providing scalability for operations from large to small. The Army's deployment rates could, he argued, be accelerated by trimming unnecessary logistic support assets inherited from the old firepower-heavy, indefinite sustainment philosophy of the Cold War. Macgregor pointed out that currently Army deployment plans are based on big corps formations of three divisions each. Under his new structure, said Macgregor, the Army could plan for a smaller, corps-sized formations of five or six combat groups each. Forces with a high tooth-to-tail ratio would thus be capable of firing and maneuvering quickly on a dispersed, fast-moving battlefield and not be burdened with the large command hierarchies and large logistic tails that might slow deployment and make operations on the battlefield ponderous and inflexible.

Macgregor's book can be evaluated by looking at how the Army subsequently changed its approach to transformation. His work was not the only influence: the Army was responding to many sources of advice and to its recent experience in the Iraq war and subsequent occupation. The Army was credited for its battlefield success in Iraq, but it was also criticized for deploying too slowly and not performing well in the stabilization and reconstruction missions of occupation. Whether because of Macgregor's book or otherwise, the Army adopted his core recommendation to focus on combat brigades and made them more independent and modular. The Army transferred to its brigades some of the assets previously held by the division commander, including artillery, attack helicopters, C⁴ISR, and logistic support. The Army, however, did not endeavor to create the muscular brigades of 5,000 troops envisioned by Macgregor. Instead, it decided to field more brigades by reducing the size of each brigade: it removed one maneuver battalion, leaving each brigade with just two battalions. The freed battalions were to be formed into additional brigades of two battalions apiece, and the Army thus would grow from 33 to 42 active-duty brigade combat teams, augmented by 28 National Guard brigade combat teams.

Observers of this plan noted that the Army was thus making a conscious tradeoff: it will have more brigades, which can be deployed to more geographic places and perform more missions. It will be better able to carry out long-term rotational occupations of Iraq and elsewhere, while still having enough extra maneuver units to handle additional contingencies and requirements. The downside is that each brigade will have fewer maneuver battalions than before. The removal of a battalion from each brigade is supposed to be offset in part by gains elsewhere, such as more artillery, reconnaissance, and attack helicopters. Nonetheless, critics worry, these assets may not be able to compensate fully for the lost battalion in situations where numbers of infantry and armor are critical. This plan for tradeoff of more but smaller and weaker brigades has admirers as well as detractors.

Another issue noted by critics is whether the transfer of assets from the division to the brigade would be a net plus. The advantages of enhanced modularity and dispersal are obvious, yet this plan leaves the division commander with fewer assets to allocate among the brigades in response to their changing situations. Some express concern that this plan might overload the brigade commander with too many new functions: the commander will be required to direct not only combat operations, but also such rear-area support functions as maintenance and supply. Certainly, the brigade command staff will need to be large and diverse enough to perform both its old and its new functions.

Critics of the current Army plan also question the impact of Future Combat Systems. If lightweight FCS weapons, when they become available, prove to be less potent than current tanks and IFVs, the new smaller brigades may be too weak to perform their combat missions. The Army is seeking to maximize the firepower of the FCS. But critics argue that when the design standard is lightweight, combat power will probably be sacrificed. A fair appraisal is that the Army will need to study the combination of smaller brigades and lighter weapons closely.

A third question has to do with occupation missions and whether the current combat brigade team structure will give the Army enough units to perform stabilization and reconstruction missions, which tend to be of long duration. Critics charge that the Army's current configuration lacks sufficient S&R capabilities, citing as evidence the need to mobilize and deploy large numbers of Reservists trained for these missions. The practice may have worked thus far, but continuing to rely on Reservists for these missions has obvious downsides; they cannot be kept in active status forever. The Army is now trying to create more active-duty units for noncombat S&R duties. However, it has resisted calls for organizing large formations, such as brigades and divisions, expressly tailored for S&R.

Macgregor wrote about the need to prepare for joint operations, but he called in particular for preserving an Army that can win difficult ground wars mostly on its own in situations where effective combat air support is not available. This is a core reason why Macgregor insisted on muscular Army brigades with many tanks and firepower, and plenty of offensive punch. The Army's current transformation plans, by contrast, seem to depend upon the reliability of networked capabilities and airpower to support ground forces. In this sense, it is riskier than Macgregor's plan.

Max Boot: Waging Savage Wars in Distant Places

When the war on terror erupted in late 2001, President Bush acknowledged that it was likely to be a long war, with many small operations conducted in many distant places. How should the United States react to the growing prospect of lengthy and messy military involvements in distant parts of the underdeveloped world, including small to medium wars followed by troubled occupations? This is quite a different prospect from U.S. military planning and operations during World II and the Cold War. Those conflicts required large forces, in war and peace, for deterrence and defense of vital interests in Europe and Asia. But in the early 21st century, U.S. interests in the greater Middle East and nearby regions are less clear, wars are less easy to win in decisive and final ways, and occupied countries are less easily guided to democracy or capitalism.

Max Boot, although not the only writer envisioning messy wars ahead, has focused in particular on their implications for the U.S. military. In his 2002 book, *The Savage Wars of Peace: Small Wars and the Rise of American Power*, Boot tried to provide a reassuring answer by reminding Americans of their long history with distant conflicts.[18] Throughout the 19th century, Boot wrote, the United States was frequently involved in small, messy wars and related intervention operations in the Western Hemisphere and also in Asia and North Africa. Indeed, the Navy and Marines have long regarded such wars and operations as core to their missions, and have developed an organized doctrine for handling them. Such involvements began with the Barbary pirates during Thomas Jefferson's Presidency. Thereafter, as Boot wrote, came numerous uses of small military forces to open economic doors in the Far East and to take over territory in the Pacific, including the Hawaiian Islands. In the 1840s, after border disputes, the United States invaded Mexico, defeated its army, and occupied its capital. After the U.S. Civil War, small clashes occurred in Asia and elsewhere, even as the U.S. Army engaged in guerrilla warfare with Indians on the Great Plains.

With the transition from the 19th century to the 20th century, Boot wrote, the United States started to become a global and imperial power, which brought about a surge of small wars and prolonged occupations. Quick victory in the Spanish-American War of 1898 resulted in the U.S. occupation of the Philippine Islands after the Spanish departed. Although many Philippine citizens welcomed the United States until they could achieve independence, a violent insurrection broke out in some places. During the 3-year war that followed, the U.S. military deployed a sizable force, ranging from 30,000 to 70,000 troops. The guerrilla war was fierce: over 4,000 American troops were killed, along with large numbers of Filipinos. The insurrection was finally quelled, Boot wrote, not just because U.S. troops fought hard and well, but because they also performed stabilization and reconstruction tasks, such as securing villages, building roads, and establishing schools and hospitals.

A similar pattern, Boot said, prevailed in a host of smaller U.S. military interventions in the Caribbean and Central America, including Cuba, Haiti, the Dominican Republic, Mexico, Nicaragua, and Panama. Some of these interventions were motivated by economic gain, yet in other places where American business interests were greatest, the U.S. military was not used: never in Costa Rica and Guatemala, for example, and only once in Honduras.

America's motives, wrote Boot, were mainly strategic: they included building the Panama Canal, forestalling European interventions that would give hostile powers a foothold in the Western Hemisphere, and quelling local violence that threatened the lives of Americans and Europeans living there.

The United States preferred to rely upon diplomacy and economics, so-called Dollar Diplomacy, and to turn to military power mainly as a last resort. When it intervened militarily, it normally did so with small forces, and then left as soon as order was restored. When it stayed longer, Boot said, its military forces tried to help establish competent local governments and to improve economic infrastructure. Boot pointed to Haiti and the Dominican Republic as examples of prolonged U.S. stays that helped the occupied countries, and where trouble increased after U.S. troops left. When prolonged combat against guerrillas was necessary, Boot said, the U.S. Marines shunned big-unit maneuvers. Instead, they learned to divide into small groups, deploy into numerous villages, and work with local citizens to establish secure zones. This small-unit strategy of dispersal and local engagement, Boot said, was highly successful, and it became the model for a Marine Corps manual on small wars and distant occupations.

Any national willingness to wage small, messy wars in distant places diminished after the U.S. experience in the Vietnam War. There, wrote Boot, the task had been especially hard because the South Vietnamese were unable to build their own government. Equally important, the U.S. military ignored the lessons of its own history, relying mainly on massive firepower and search-and-destroy missions to suppress a guerrilla foe that could usually slip away into the jungle. The U.S. military should have made greater use of operations aimed at protecting local villages and pacifying nearby areas, said Boot; such a pacification program was launched but never became large enough. Moreover, the U.S. military tried to create a South Vietnamese army like itself, patterned for big-unit operations, not local security. When the time came for the South Vietnamese to fight big battles with the North Vietnamese army in 1972, they were fairly successful because they enjoyed U.S. air support. But in 1975, with U.S. airpower and logistic support gone, the South Vietnamese army collapsed when the North Vietnamese launched a major invasion aimed at conquering the entire country.

The Vietnam War might have turned out better, Boot concluded, had the U.S. military fought more wisely. But rather than recognize its own failings, he said, the U.S. military simply recoiled from the idea of further wars of this type, and so did the rest of the country. The United States, having disengaged from Southeast Asia, focused its military on the burgeoning Cold War competition with the Soviet Union in Europe. The U.S. military thus turned back to the big-battle mentality of World War II. Along with it, Boot wrote, came the Powell Doctrine, which rejected interventionist wars except in cases where vital U.S. interests were clearly engaged, the American people solidly supported intervention, the operation promised to be neat and clean, decisive victory was assured, and an exit strategy was spelled out.

Perhaps the Powell Doctrine made sense 20 years ago, wrote Boot, but it no longer makes sense as a guide to fighting today's war on terror. For a long time to come, small, messy wars and prolonged occupations will be necessary. There will be repeated need for military interventions where vital U.S. interests are not clearly threatened and where declarations of war and wholehearted public support are lacking. The U.S. military will be asked to intervene in the internal affairs of occupied countries; it will need to perform occupation duties that involve nationbuilding; and sometimes it will need to adjust to the presence of allied soldiers, or even to operate under foreign command. The United States, said Boot, can handle this challenge by remembering its history, for it has faced such challenges before.

In the past, wrote Boot, American military interventions have been most successful when the goal has been to protect U.S. strategic and economic interests, or to punish foreign governments for transgressions. Results have been more checkered when the goal has been to permanently pacify a troubled country and to foster democracy there. Success was achieved in Germany and Japan after World War II because the necessary conditions were present, but Boot warned that such favorable conditions are not likely to attend many future interventions. In this regard, his caution proved prescient on Iraq. Boot wrote that a tough struggle lies ahead, but that the United States should not shrink from the task, pointing out that although there are costs to intervention, there are also costs—perhaps much greater—to not intervening. Boot recommended that the U.S. military should be configured to perform the full scope of missions in the small and savage wars ahead, and in the occupation duties and nationbuilding missions that accompany them. Boot concluded that the United States unavoidably has the mission of carrying out a Pax Americana in the 21st century like the Pax Britannica of the 19th century.

Critics have accused Boot of being soft on imperialism, yet Boot was writing mainly with an eye on the future, not the past. He was right that in many ways, the wars of the early 21st century are more like the small wars of a century ago than like World War II and the Cold War. Yet there are differences as well. Global information networks and advanced technologies make modern wars unlike the imperial adventures of Theodore Roosevelt. Then, terrorists and insurrectionists were unable to communicate by email and cell phones, or to gain access to weapons of mass destruction, or to fly airplanes into

New York skyscrapers. Nor were occupied countries then animated by an ideology like Islamic terrorism. While Boot is correct that we can learn from past small wars, analysts must also recognize the differences.

James Dobbins and the RAND Team: Building Nations

While Max Boot's book focused on fighting small wars, James Dobbins and the RAND Corporation produced a two-volume series on a closely associated element, namely nationbuilding or rebuilding. These two books examined the level of success, lessons learned (or not learned), and nature of U.S. and UN approaches to nationbuilding over the last 60 years. In addition to evidence from the historical record, the authors augmented their research with a quantitative approach. They examined the level of inputs in each case, measured in military and police presence, duration of mission, timing of elections, and economic assistance. They measured outcomes in terms of military casualties, returning refugees, growth in per capita GDP, and quantitative measures of peace and democracy.

The first of the two volumes, *America's Role in Nation-Building: From Germany to Iraq,* systematically compared eight cases: U.S. involvement in nationbuilding in Germany (1945–1953), Japan (1945–1952), Somalia (1992–1994), Haiti (1994–1996), Bosnia (from 1995 through the date of the study), Kosovo (from 1999), Afghanistan (from 2001), and early results in Iraq (from 2003).[19] Dobbins' team sought to discover why the United States was successful in rebuilding and transforming Germany and Japan after World War II—cases that show the best of what nationbuilding can achieve—but was less successful elsewhere. The simple answer is that Germany and Japan were already highly developed and economically advanced nations that were ready to be transformed into peaceful and democratic societies, and each society was largely homogenous in makeup, without potentially destabilizing ethnic and sectarian divisions. However, the authors contend that the most critical factor was the level of effort—time, manpower, and money—put into the rebuilding. America and its allies were committed to transforming these nations, and they expended great resources and time in order to do so.

Although this commonsense answer may seem overly simplistic, the RAND display comparing its quantitative measures visually across case studies shows a more complex picture of the details of each case. The authors explain that the citizens of both Germany and Japan were war-weary at the conclusion of hostilities; victory was decisive and the losing side did not dispute that it had been defeated militarily. Comparing this with experiences in Somalia, Afghanistan, and Iraq, Dobbins' team found that when conflicts ended less definitively and less destructively, postconflict security challenges loomed larger. Swift and fairly bloodless victories may leave the defeated combatants able to challenge the victor's presence. However, far from advocating scorched-earth policies in terms of warfighting, the authors argue that the potential for insurgent violence in these circumstances must be met with robust policing and security.

Security proved illusory in Somalia, the first post–Cold War effort by the United States to lead a multinational nationbuilding effort. The initial mission of the Unified Task Force was narrowly focused on security for humanitarian and relief operations. However, the objectives quickly expanded. The changing mission objectives and a chaotic command and control environment undermined coordination and unity of effort. The major lessons of the Somalia effort, wrote the authors of the RAND study, were that nationbuilding objectives should be scaled to available forces, resources, and staying power; that unity of effort is as important in peace operations as in war; and that regional or external dimensions of instability must be taken into account when undertaking nationbuilding.

After its experience in Somalia, the United States defined its objectives more narrowly in its next intervention in Haiti and sought to accomplish them as quickly as possible. Although the operation went smoothly and major reconstruction goals were met, the rapid withdrawal of U.S. personnel then undermined the formation of democratic institutions. Using the RAND study's methodology of comparing input versus output, the authors convincingly argued that resources and duration directly affected the degree of success. Dobbins and his coauthors find in this case the lesson that reconstruction efforts and funding must be coupled with a commitment of enough time to foster self-sustaining stability.

The United States learned from its experience in Bosnia that while free elections may be an important milestone in building a democratic nation, holding them prematurely could strengthen the hand of rejectionist elements and return to office precisely those leaders whose ambitions had been a primary cause of destabilization. Continued lack of coordination among civilian and government entities implementing reconstruction efforts played a major role in undermining transformation, as did disruptions by organized crime.

The authors contend that the best managed post–Cold War nationbuilding endeavor was the one that took place in Kosovo. It included broad participation among international organizations and coalition countries that allowed for extensive burdensharing. There was also unity of command on the civilian side with the UN at the helm. Moreover, large-scale assistance spurred Kosovo's economic well-being; second only to postwar Germany, Kosovo had the most rapid economic recovery of the cases studied.

The authors pointed out, however, a number of lessons to be learned from the experience in Kosovo. Chief among them was the fact that mobilization of international civilians to participate in peace operations was slow and that resulting delays proved costly.

The followup to quick U.S. defeat of the Taliban in Afghanistan marked the next major U.S. nationbuilding effort. In contrast to previous endeavors, peacekeeping forces on the ground had a much smaller footprint. For example, there were 18.6 peacekeepers per 1,000 people in Bosnia, and 20 per 1,000 in Kosovo, but only about 0.18 ISAF soldiers per 1,000 Afghanis. The RAND study emphasized that here, too, a low input of military and civilian resources correlated with a low output of security, democratic transformation, and economic development. The authors criticized U.S. strategy for not taking into account the lessons learned from previous peace operations, although they noted that the short period between September 11 and the invasion of Afghanistan left little time to plan for its aftermath.

The second volume of the RAND study, entitled *The UN's Role in Nation-Building: From the Congo to Iraq*, focused on nationbuilding by the United Nations rather than the United States.[20] Using the same methodology, it examined UN peacekeeping operations in the former Belgian Congo (1960–1964), Namibia (1989–1990), Cambodia (1991–1993), El Salvador (1991–1996), Mozambique (1992–1994), Eastern Slavonia (1995–1998), East Timor (1999 through the date of the study), and Sierra Leone (1998 onward). Because the UN and U.S. roles in global order are interdependent, this volume also took into consideration the cases discussed in the first volume. As a whole, many of the same lessons of the U.S. study are confirmed in the UN book: unity of command and shared vision are essential; the cooperation of neighboring states can buttress efforts; quick mobilization of civilian elements of reconstruction is key; premature withdrawal almost always undermines incipient democratic and civil society institutions.

Again comparing quantified inputs and outputs, the second book contended that, in the cases studied, the UN has had a higher rate of success than the United States in its nationbuilding efforts, beginning with its first major action in the former Belgian Congo. The authors attributed this to the fact that UN goals in each of the examined cases were far more limited. In the case of Congo, for example, large-scale civil conflict was averted, although the nation later came under the rule of a corrupt dictatorship; democracy-building had not been part of the Security Council resolution that authorized UN action. While the UN success rate is justified by the authors' data, it might give the misleading notion that, all things being equal, the UN does nationbuilding "better" than the United States. However, all things are far from equal, and the authors point out that U.S. missions have generally taken place in much more demanding circumstances, have required larger forces, and have attempted to achieve much more ambitious objectives. The authors point out that even the largest UN peacekeeping operation (Congo with 20,000 troops) was not as big as the smallest U.S.-led mission (Haiti with 23,000 troops).

The authors argue, however, that the United States has comparatively shallow institutional knowledge in nationbuilding, compared to the UN, where peacekeeping best practices are better preserved and cultivated. Dobbins and his coauthors argued that the UN has learned more from its mistakes, compared to the United States, and that therefore the UN sets smaller and less ambitious goals that are agreed upon through negotiation and consensus. In contrast, U.S. statements on nationbuilding objectives often "tend toward the grandiloquent" as part of an effort to build congressional and public support for costly endeavors. Accordingly, the authors argued, past U.S. Presidents have generally tried to avoid nationbuilding missions. New global threats have changed this, placing stability and reconstruction operations at the forefront of U.S. national security strategy.

The limited scale of UN nationbuilding objectives resulted not only from past UN experiences, but also from resource limitations. An additional obstacle is that many governments are not ready to commit troops to international peacekeeping missions. In part because of these resource limitations, the RAND study concluded that the UN does a better job in brokering reconciliation in coalescing states than it does in holding together collapsing ones.

Both books also address efforts in Iraq. Although produced between 2003 and 2005, the volumes accurately predicted how early-stage U.S. failures in postconflict Iraq would lead to long-term challenges. It is hard to argue with the authors' contention that the United States failed to implement the lessons of nationbuilding that it could have drawn from its own experience, not to mention that of the UN. Coupled with the slow pace of training and deploying an adequate indigenous military and civilian policing presence, these shortcomings in the reconstruction process meant that insecurity would inevitably plague rebuilding efforts. Without security, the three other pillars of reconstruction—justice and reconciliation, social and economic well-being, and governance and participation—cannot stand. Exacerbating this dynamic, Iraq combines the worst features of the cases examined earlier: lack of a previous democratic tradition, potential for ethnic and sectarian strife, decrepit economic and industrial infrastructure, and lack of support from neighboring countries.

The quantification of current Iraqi nationbuilding and the comparison with past stability and reconstruction operations are very striking. While not offering any magic numbers for success in planning for troop and police strength and funding over time, the visual comparisons presented in the books' graphs provide useful benchmarks for the manpower costs of previous cases. For example, for the United States to reach the per capita levels of troop concentration in Iraq that would be equivalent to those in Kosovo, it would need about 526,000 troops on the ground, or roughly 400,000 more than the mid-2006 presence. Dobbins and his coauthors also note that, while force size affects success of peace operations, it is but one factor in the input-output equation. They point out, for example, that it would be important for these forces to be culturally sensitive, and that force protection should not take priority over acquiring adequate local knowledge.

Regardless of how the United States and the UN approach the endeavor of nationbuilding, neither can avoid the responsibility. Operations in Iraq and elsewhere will continue to tax U.S. and international organizations seeking to foster global peace and stability. Dobbins and his coauthors do an admirable job of documenting, assessing, and analyzing past operations, and identifying lessons. The fact that the lead author, James Dobbins, played key roles in managing many U.S.-led nationbuilding operations of the post–Cold War years lends a special credibility to the two volumes. Future planners for peace operations would do well to examine this analysis closely and take its lessons to heart.

Thomas P.M. Barnett: The Pentagon's New Map

What strategic principles should guide U.S. national security policy and defense strategy in the future? How should the U.S. military posture be shaped for the missions ahead? Thomas Barnett's 2004 book, *The Pentagon's New Map: War and Peace in the Twenty-first Century*, attempted to provide answers to these key questions.[21] Partly because of its eye-catching title and provocative writing, the book was a best seller, a status seldom achieved by others on this topic. It offered an insightful synthesis of many ideas about world affairs and policy directions.

Barnett advanced five key ordering principles for future U.S. policy and strategic planning, since Afghanistan and Iraq have been invaded and occupied. First, like many of the other writers discussed above, he argued that globalization, a key dynamic of the modern era, is separating the world increasingly into what he calls the "Core"—the wealthy democracies, with Russia, China, and India striving to join—and the "Gap," that is, the Middle East and southern arc, sub-Saharan Africa, and the Caribbean. Second, he argued that the United States can play an effective global leadership role by helping bring the benefits of economic globalization to the Gap counties. It should try to connect the Gap countries to the globalizing world economy so that they, too, can become wealthy, democratic, and peaceful. Third, Barnett argued, the United States can promote this connectivity by helping establish security "rule-sets" in the countries of the Gap; security rule-sets would, he said, allow the Gap to develop economic and political connections to the Core and to the globalizing world economy. Collective security would foster peace in the Gap, and peace would foster connectivity and integration, which would in turn bring economic prosperity, democracy, and community. Fourth, Barnett recommends that the United States should play the military roles of "Leviathan" and of "System Administrator" to help manage the Gap's security affairs. In its Hobbesian role of Leviathan or warfighter, the United States should be willing and able to punish or coerce rogue states, terrorists, and other transnational actors that do not abide by U.S.-dictated rule-sets that prohibit malevolent conduct and mass violence. In its role of System Administrator, the United States should act as necessary to preserve the peace, even to the extent of occupying invaded countries in order to guide their transition to postwar democracy and capitalism. Finally, Barnett recommends that the future U.S. military should be divided into two components: a smaller, high-tech posture that can function as a Leviathan, and a larger, lower-tech force that can function as System Administrator in peacetime and postwar occupations. Over time, he said, the former would be able to shrink in size, while the latter should grow.

To what degree do Barnett's five ideas provide a sensible approach to future U.S. national security policy and defense strategy? Barnett's first idea is, we believe, correct: few serious observers of world affairs question the idea that globalization is a defining trend, or that its dynamics are contributing to a bifurcation of global society between the haves and have-nots. In the early to mid-1990s, the Clinton administration's national security strategy explicitly acknowledged that globalization is a central dynamic of our time and declared that it must be guided wisely to promote progress and avoid instability.[22] Increasingly during that decade, many writers and public officials in the United States and abroad expressed concern about whether the underdeveloped world could compete in the globalizing economy or if it would be left behind. The Bush administration echoed this concern when it entered office in early 2001.

Barnett's second idea—that the United States should try to help bring the benefits of globalization to the poorer "Gap" countries—also makes sense. The Clinton administration shaped much of its national security strategy around the goal of using economic globalization to help promote prosperity and democracy in the underdeveloped world. This is one reason why it sought more global and regional trade agreements, and why it tried to use such institutions as the World Bank and IMF to help achieve this goal. When it entered office in early 2001, the Bush administration was less inclined to view globalization as an automatic engine of global prosperity and peace. But it did seek accelerated trade negotiations and a doubling of U.S. economic aid to poor countries through Millennium Challenge Accounts (aid designed for better managed nations) and through debt forgiveness.

Barnett's third idea, employing U.S. power and leadership to help establish security rule-sets in the Gap countries, is also sound as a strategic principle; however, the devil lies in the details. As long ago as the mid-1950s, Henry Kissinger argued that establishing codes of conduct, rules of the road, regulations, and common accords was key to global and regional peace. Since the early 1990s, Kissinger, Brzezinski, and many others reviewed in this book have been arguing for the application of such security concepts to the new era. The U.S. Government has, to some extent, accepted such thinking: the Clinton administration, for example, promoted NATO enlargement into Eastern Europe with this calculus in mind, and the Bush administration promoted further NATO enlargement for the same reason. For similar reasons, both administrations chose to continue longstanding U.S. security commitments to Asian allies, several of them poor countries. Barnett acknowledged that the process of establishing security rules must be embedded in a larger diplomatic approach that is carefully tailored to each region, but he did not discuss specific details of how to implement these ideas.

Barnett labels himself an "economic determinist" but correctly notes that economic progress cannot take place in the absence of proper security conditions. As he acknowledged, security rules and regulations cannot merely be proclaimed, but must enjoy the consensual support of the major powers. If they are violated, someone must enforce them. Establishing security rules has been successful in Europe and parts of Asia, but considerably less progress has been made in the Middle East and surrounding regions. Experience in Europe and Asia shows that, before consensus can be built in support of particular rules, key countries must be assured of their security and safety and must be willing to cooperate. Multilateral agreement on rule-sets thus is a result of stable and collaborative security affairs, rather than a way to achieve them. This is a "chicken and egg" problem—which comes first?—in regions that lack both a stable security architecture and agreement on rules, such as the Middle East. Barnett's book articulated a sound strategic theory, but it did not offer practical guidance on how to create architectures and rules at the same time, apart from proposing that the United States should enforce rules proposed by itself.

Barnett's fourth idea was especially bold and provocative. He wrote that the United States should first act as a Leviathan, by setting and enforcing the security rules in troubled times, and then act as a System Administrator by watching over their observance in more peaceful times. He did not address some key questions: for example, by what authority the United States could presume to justify setting the security rules for others to obey; what these rules should be, apart from the obvious prohibition against mass violence; and which violators of these rules should the United States attack with military force, and when and how.

As part of his rule enforcement regime, Barnett suggested that after the United States succeeds in pacifying Iraq, it should impose regime change on North Korea, by force if necessary, and on Iran, too. This, he argued, is appropriate conduct for the Leviathan. Barnett argued that U.S. strategy should not be limited to launching attacks against menacing dictators, but he argued that such attacks are permissible when done according to principles of justice and on behalf of rule-sets that would promote economic globalization. After the United States performs its Leviathan missions, Barnett argued, it can settle down to the less provocative task of acting as System Administrator. In making these recommendations, Barnett was undaunted by the limits of American power. He did acknowledge, however, that the United States would need some political and military help from friends and allies.

Barnett's fifth idea—that of separating the U.S. military into two different components, one with a warfighting and one with a peacebuilding posture— is highly controversial. Barnett's core argument is that in order to perform the Leviathan function, the United States must have powerful, high-tech forces equipped to fight major wars, but once this function has been successfully performed, the United States can transition into a dual posture, with warfighting units in the minority, and the majority of units optimized for peacekeeping, occupations, and other System Administrator duties.

However, Barnett's proposal seems to ignore the likelihood that, even if at some future time medium-sized rogues are no longer on the scene, the United States must still keep up its military guard against a future threat from China or another rising power. Barnett discounted any such need, arguing that China would not be an enemy even if it did become a superpower, noting that it has already embraced globalization (and that Russia and India have done so, too). Whether the U.S. Government would be wise to adopt Barnett's reassurances as to future big-power conduct seems dubious. Since his book was written, Russia has begun veering away from the model of democratization. Barnett judged that China wants to join the democratic globalizing Core, but it continues to be ruled by a communist government, and its future leaders might have a different Core in mind, one that does not look to the United States as the rule-setter for economics or security. Barnett's notion that globalization will neutralize China and Russia as potential enemies may be a good strategy, but it is not necessarily a good prediction.

Many of Barnett's critics have focused on his proposed System Administrator force. They argue that it would be large, weak, and vulnerable; that it would divert resources from the warfighting force; and that a well-trained warfighting force could also perform this function as a secondary mission. Yet recent experience in Iraq and Afghanistan indicates that Barnett has a point: the forces designed primarily for high-intensity warfighting are not optimally trained and equipped for peacewinning missions. Enhanced specialty forces such as civil affairs, psychological operations, engineers, military police, medical units, and intelligence units would be needed to augment the Leviathan force so as to give it System Administrator capabilities.

To respond to his critics and develop his argument, Barnett published a followup book in 2005 called *Blueprint for Action*.[23] Focusing on the implementation of concepts developed in his 2004 book, this book expanded on the historical underpinnings of his Leviathan force, with reference to the transformational network-centric warfare concepts of Andrew Marshall and Arthur Cebrowski. He also expands on his System Administrator force concept by discussing irregular and so-called fourth generation (insurgency-based) warfare, as defined by William Lind and others.[24] Linking his two-force proposal to these two contending views of American military policy—stand-off warfare and boots on the ground—Barnett is saying in essence that the United States can have some of each capability. That, however, may be difficult to achieve if defense budgets do not continue to grow. Barnett's 2005 book does acknowledge that the U.S. military cannot be the sole System Administrator: it will need partners both among other U.S. agencies and among international allies. The main thesis of this book is that it will take a major and unified effort on the part of the Core to "shrink the Gap." Barnett persuasively argues that economic assistance and other nonmilitary measures are key to winning the peace by ending disconnectedness.

Michael O'Hanlon: Setting Future U.S. Defense Priorities

As many of the other authors discussed in this chapter have argued, DOD will face a host of future issues about its plans, programs, and budgets. Its forces will probably continue to occupy Iraq and Afghanistan while it begins an expensive, across-the-board effort to procure new weapons for modernization and transformation. Up to mid-2006, the wars in Iraq and Afghanistan have mainly been funded by special congressional supplements that, in theory, have protected DOD's normal peacetime budget from being diverted to war expenses. However, the lengthy occupations have begun to stretch Army and Marine manpower to their limits. In early 2004, the Pentagon announced that the Army would temporarily be increased by about 30,000 active troops. In fall 2004, the Pentagon announced that over the coming 6 years, about $30 billion more would go to the Army to enhance its capabilities, with the money coming out of Air Force and Navy procurement programs, including the F–22 fighter aircraft and new surface combatants. Since then, however, this decision has been under review, and aspects of it may be reversed.

Michael O'Hanlon's 2005 book, *Defense Strategy for the Post-Saddam Era*, endeavored to assess such issues and to offer practical guidance on DOD budget priorities.[25] His main recommendation was that the United States should enhance near-term readiness by further increasing the size of its ground forces, while trimming back on expensive procurement for all Services over a period of 10 years or longer. O'Hanlon recommended reduced procurement funding, not because new weapons are unneeded, but because, he says, they are unaffordable within the defense budgets likely to be available. O'Hanlon recommended priorities and acknowledged the pain involved in choosing among them.

The strength of O'Hanlon's book is that it identified the defense budget shortfall that looms as spending requirements mount for both near-term expeditionary missions and long-term, high-tech transformation. O'Hanlon postulated that although the defense budget is likely to continue growing modestly in real terms for the foreseeable future, DOD will not be able to spend its way out of its fiscal dilemmas. In this context, he addressed a number of issues, including whether and to what extent the size of U.S. ground forces occupying Iraq and Afghanistan should increase; how DOD should approach manpower issues such as conscription, the overseas base structure, and military reform of allies; where and to what degree various U.S. procurement plans should be trimmed in order to save money; and how the U.S. defense planning framework should be adjusted for future years, after the demands of the occupation in Iraq diminish.

Some of O'Hanlon's recommendations lack detailed analysis, but even so, his judgments have found favor in some quarters and deserve consideration on their individual merits. O'Hanlon began his appraisal by noting that DOD's fiscal year 2005 peacetime budget of about $425 billion (excluding wartime supplemental appropriations) can be expected to grow by about

$20 billion annually in the coming years. One-half of this increase reflects inflation, but the other half represents real increases. The effect will be to elevate the annual defense budget above $500 billion in 5 years. Bigger increases are unlikely, he wrote, because of Federal tax cuts, rising expenses for Social Security and healthcare, and the cost of Federal deficits. DOD will have to live within these fiscal limits, and thus it will have to set priorities, because not all of its proposed requirements will be affordable. Contributing to DOD's dilemmas, he said, are rising costs for manpower as well as for operations and maintenance; these demands squeeze funds available for investment, intensifying the need for setting priorities in procurement accounts.

As O'Hanlon pointed out, the prolonged occupations of Iraq and Afghanistan are beginning to strain the Army and Marines. Although DOD's active military manpower totals 1.4 million, the Army has only about 500,000 troops, and the Marines about 180,000. With 160,000 ground troops in Iraq and Afghanistan, in theory, nearly 40 percent of active-duty Army and Marines must be deployed abroad at any given time to maintain presence in these countries and in South Korea, Okinawa, and the Balkans. DOD has deployed thousands of Reservists to Iraq and Afghanistan to ease the strain, but even so, active units now face repeat rotational tours in Iraq and Afghanistan; meanwhile the Reserves, too, are becoming overtaxed. U.S. ground combat forces are being progressively worn down and stretched thin, wrote O'Hanlon, with negative effects on their endurance, readiness, and morale.

DOD has sought to generate more soldiers for active ground forces, as O'Hanlon wrote, by authorizing a temporary Army manpower increase of 30,000, by converting 10,000 military jobs to civilian contractor status, and by transferring about 50,000 active troops from less-stressed battalions such as artillery and air defense to such high-demand areas as military police and civil affairs. While these steps could help, O'Hanlon argued that a bigger active-duty increase is needed: he urged that DOD enlarge the active Army by another 40,000 troops, at least temporarily while the occupations of Iraq and Afghanistan remain so large. This combination of measures—internal reallocation and additional enlargement—would, he argued, generate enough new troops to meet requirements in Iraq and Afghanistan for a full year, giving currently deployed forces a needed break.

Others, too, have urged a larger Army and Marine Corps; some observers have called for as many as 100,000 more active-duty troops. In setting a figure of 40,000 for enlargement, O'Hanlon cautioned against creating large permanent forces for stabilization and reconstruction missions that do not involve combat. Creating some new forces for these missions—perhaps one active division and one Reserve division—might, he said, make sense.

Addressing the issues of conscription, the overseas base structure, and allies, O'Hanlon's book argued that any near-term return to the draft is unnecessary and would reintroduce many controversies experienced during the Vietnam War. Moreover, he pointed out, today's U.S. military has become so high-tech that it requires mainly professionals and volunteers. He also argued against any major effort to shift National Guard forces to the homeland defense mission or to ask them to be first responders to terrorist attacks against U.S. cities. While National Guard forces could be useful to maintain civil order, he said, disaster response is best handled by the civilian authorities—police, fire, and medical personnel—who are better trained and are more likely to be available immediately.

O'Hanlon broadly approved of the new peacetime U.S. overseas presence designed by DOD under Secretary Rumsfeld. Portraying DOD's plan as a long-overdue shift away from a Cold War legacy posture, he praised the efforts to reduce overseas manpower while shifting toward new bases and infrastructure in regions where the United States expects growing demands for operational involvement. He argued, however, against an excessive reduction of U.S. forces from Germany, because that would damage infrastructure that is useful for power projection outside Europe. He agreed that the Army presence of four heavy brigades in Germany could be reduced, but argued that DOD should leave behind two brigades—one heavy and one light—rather than the single Stryker brigade now being planned. He also warned against expectations that new bases in Eastern Europe would do much for DOD's ability to deploy forces outside the continent quickly, noting that they lack good rail, road, and air transport. O'Hanlon approved of the DOD plan to remove an Army brigade from South Korea and to consolidate command structures in Korea and Japan. But he argued for a sizable withdrawal of Marine combat forces from Okinawa, where he says they are no longer needed and could better be deployed to Guam, Australia, and other Asian Pacific locations.

O'Hanlon acknowledged the importance of inducing allies, especially the Europeans, to improve their forces for future expeditionary missions, including occupation duties, but he expressed skepticism that major gains would be likely any time soon. He did not propose concrete ideas for reconfiguring European forces beyond fielding the new NATO Response Force. His main point was that DOD should not expect European contributions to justify reducing the size and missions of U.S. military forces. O'Hanlon's concerns notwithstanding, however, improving allied capabilities need not mean the reduction of U.S. forces, because the scope of future missions and requirements is so large; it is surprising that a book so intent on restructuring U.S. forces and cutting U.S. procurement failed to examine how restructuring allied forces could contribute to this goal.

Addressing DOD's modernization and procurement effort, O'Hanlon wrote that although many current weapons are aging and will need to be replaced soon, there should be no "wholesale rush to replace most major weapons platforms with new systems that commonly cost twice as much as is necessary or affordable."[26] Describing DOD's plan as a wholesale rush seems a stretch, since it is scheduled to unfold over a period of nearly 20 years. Moreover, O'Hanlon presented little evidence to justify his claim that many new weapons cost twice as much as necessary. Stripped to its essentials, O'Hanlon's call for a sharp reduction in DOD's procurement stems from his argument that this ambitious and costly plan cannot be afforded. O'Hanlon instead urged a revised procurement plan focused on replacing or refurbishing aging equipment fast enough to keep it safe and reliable; purchasing only a modest number of costly next-generation weapons, such as F–22 fighters and new submarines, while otherwise making do with updated versions of existing weapons, such as the F–16; and relying upon modernized electronics, sensors, precision munitions, unmanned vehicles, and related computerization and miniaturization technologies to provide qualitative gains in force capabilities.

With these themes in mind, O'Hanlon proposed cutbacks to DOD procurement programs, including scaling back the planned deployment of homeland missile defenses to a force of 50 to 100 midcourse interceptors, while trimming theater missile defense programs. This step, he said, would save between $1 billion and $2 billion per year. Retiring 200 Minuteman intercontinental ballistic missiles and 2 more Trident submarines earlier than currently planned would save $1 billion per year. Reducing the Air Force's planned buy of F–22s from about 270 aircraft to 150 aircraft, while refurbishing F–15s to make up the difference, would yield savings of about $500 million per year for a total of $7 billion. Reducing the plan by the Air Force, the Navy, and the Marines plan to buy about 2,500 F–35 Joint Strike Fighters to only 1,500 aircraft, with refurbished F–16s and other fighters making up the difference, would save $2 billion annually for the next 10 years, and $50 billion overall, said O'Hanlon. He recommended trimming the Army's $92 billion plan for new Future Combat System vehicles by $2 billion per year for the next 10 years and beyond. Reducing the Navy's plan to buy 16 to 24 new DDX destroyers to just 8 ships and buying fewer *Virginia* class submarines would, according to O'Hanlon's calculations, result in annual savings of $1 billion to $2 billion.

These proposals for reducing procurement spending would save an estimated $7.5 billion–$9.5 billion per year over the next 10 years and beyond.

In its favor, proponents would point to the need to trim DOD's unaffordable procurement plan to manageable proportions and emphasize that the plan represents an extension of cutbacks already planned by DOD rather than a strategic departure. O'Hanlon's plan would spread the reductions uniformly among competing programs and would not completely cancel a single major new weapons system; rather, it would ask the Services to make do with fewer new weapons, extend the life spans of existing weapons, and emphasize other, cheaper ways to enhance force quality.

Some critics, including the military Services, are likely to argue that O'Hanlon's plan would damage the effort to procure new weapons that are vital for transformation and national security. They might question whether his plan would provide adequate missile defenses and nuclear forces to protect national security in an era of accelerating nuclear proliferation; whether cuts in the F–22 and F–35 program by nearly 50 percent would leave U.S. air forces able to perform their operational missions in an era when stealthy high-tech fighters will be needed; whether the Navy would be able to perform its missions with fewer new surface combatants and attack submarines; and whether the Army would get necessary new weapons fast enough to perform its duties.

Specific proposals for cutbacks by O'Hanlon or by others, including their priorities and tradeoffs, must be examined carefully. Perhaps better ways can be found to perform necessary trimming while leaving the defense plan properly balanced; cuts in spending on peacetime operations and maintenance or other accounts might, for example, reduce the need to slash valuable modernization programs.

O'Hanlon concluded his book by examining the question of sizing future U.S. combat forces. Believing that U.S. forces should remain at about their current size and mix, he proposed that the current 1-4-2-1 construct for force sizing should be changed to a 1-4-1-1-1 construct. It would provide forces for homeland defense, normal operations in four forward theaters, an occupation like that in Iraq or larger, a major war in Korea, and a naval battle with China over Taiwan. This would change the existing sizing construct by adding a naval war with China and dropping a war with a smaller rogue state. O'Hanlon points out that the U.S. military might have to perform future occupation missions in places as big as Pakistan, Indonesia, or Iran. Critics might point out that, as O'Hanlon's construct provides primarily for major war in Asia, it could leave other combatants, especially U.S. European Command and USCENTCOM, without adequate plans and forces to handle unanticipated contingencies in the Persian Gulf, the Middle East, or Europe. One key question is whether it is prudent to assume, as O'Hanlon appears to do, that after Iraq, the United States will no longer have to worry about major wars in regions that have seen four wars since 1990, while Asia remained at peace.

O'Hanlon's book makes an important contribution to the emerging literature on U.S. defense plans and priorities after Iraq. O'Hanlon provides specific recommendations, many of which are likely to be judged sensible, some of which need further analysis, and others of which are not so persuasive. His call for larger ground forces for as long as Iraq must be heavily occupied makes sense, as do his points about overseas presence. But while his cutbacks to procurement spending reflect a legitimate need for priorities, he acknowledges that they would cut into modernization plans that have a strong military rationale. O'Hanlon also underscores the need for adequate defense budgets for the twin goals of being prepared for expeditionary operations in the near term and pursuing high-tech transformation in the long term. O'Hanlon's book should help remind the national security community that the debate about America's future defense priorities will not stop even after U.S. involvements in Iraq and Afghanistan wind down.

Quadrennial Defense Review 2006

The Department of Defense's long-anticipated 2006 *Quadrennial Defense Review* was published in February 2006.[27] It reflected many of the ideas proffered by authors reviewed in this chapter. It sought to improve America's ability to dominate any high-tech war like those fought against Serbia, Afghanistan, and Iraq. At the same time, it sought to improve America's ability to fight the "small, savage wars" discussed by Max Boot. It also outlined steps to improve the U.S. ability to deal with postconflict stabilization and reconstruction operations, as discussed by Binnendijk and Johnson. Although it did not accept Barnett's dual-forces proposal, the overall capabilities of the force do show some signs of moving in this direction. However, the 2006 *QDR*, and the $440 billion defense budget request that accompanies it, does not address the budget constraints pointed out by O'Hanlon: no significant reductions in major battle platforms are recommended. As a result, defense budgets will rise by more than 5 percent in 2007. The budgetary dilemma will probably grow even sharper as America's budget deficits increase.

The 2006 *QDR* sought to be a document of both change and continuity. It began with a list detailing the changing nature of the international system—for example, from peacetime tempo to wartime urgency, from predictability to uncertainty, from single to multiple threats, and from crisis response to shaping the future. However, it did not launch a new beginning for U.S. defense policy; rather, it carried forth the strategic premises established by the Bush administration in *QDR 2001,* updating them to reflect U.S. experiences, including the wars in Afghanistan and Iraq and the paths taken by U.S. defense transformation. *QDR 2006* did, however, launch several new initiatives.

QDR 2006 especially focused on the challenge of fighting the Long War, meaning the diverse and lengthy military actions taking place in Iraq, Afghanistan, and other places where U.S. forces are fighting terrorists and other adversaries, many of which are not the regular military forces of nation-states. Since much of this Long War will be fought with other than traditional military means, the term *long struggle* might better describe the nature of this conflict.

In both Iraq and Afghanistan, *QDR 2006* pointed out, the major phase of combat operations ended successfully, but stability operations aimed at suppressing insurgents and terrorists have continued, along with efforts to build effective governments and military forces. In addition, U.S. military forces are being called upon to perform other missions on a global basis, such as helping governments in Africa and elsewhere build military establishments capable of maintaining order and quelling terrorism; conducting humanitarian relief efforts such as those in response to the tsunami of 2004 and the Pakistani earthquake of 2005; and helping the government of Colombia counter drug production, terrorism, and violence within its borders.

The Long War also means that DOD is more involved in homeland defense. It has created the U.S. Northern Command and has begun working with other Federal agencies to prepare for such contingencies as biological attacks or the use of other weapons of mass destruction. The Long War, said *QDR 2006,* has greatly increased the pressures on the U.S. military to perform more missions at higher operational tempos. It has also taught valuable lessons, such as the need for DOD to build better partnerships with other U.S. agencies and with foreign governments, to take early preventive measures to stop local problems from escalating, and to enhance the flexibility and freedom of action of U.S. forces. *QDR 2006* offered no blueprint of when and how to bring the Long War to an end, but it implied that U.S. military forces were steadily becoming better able to wage it effectively.

QDR 2006 presented a lengthy analysis of how the Department of Defense can best pursue the multiple components of the U.S. national defense strategy over the coming years. It acknowledged that although the United States possesses many advantages over opponents in traditional forms of warfare, it now faces a widened spectrum of potential challenges. These include not only traditional challenges, but also "irregular" challenges, such as terrorism, insurgency, and guerrilla warfare; "catastrophic" challenges, such as the use of weapons of mass destruction by rogue states on U.S. soil; and "disruptive" challenges, such as efforts to damage U.S. space systems or information networks. In order to prepare for such challenges, *QDR 2006* set four priority areas: defeating terrorist networks; defending the homeland; shaping the choices of countries at strategic crossroads; and preventing hostile states and nonstate actors from acquiring WMD.

Efforts to defeat terrorist networks will include U.S. combat operations, said *QDR 2006*, but will also encompass many other activities, including U.S. cooperation with foreign governments and militaries, and winning the battle of ideas and ideologies. This will require a cluster of capabilities, including enhanced human intelligence, persistent surveillance, Special Operations Forces, cultural awareness, prompt global strike capabilities to attack fleeting enemy targets, and the capacity to rapidly counter enemy propaganda.

Discussing the priority of defending the homeland, *QDR 2006* noted that whereas threats to the U.S. homeland in the past were posed by the nuclear missiles of hostile states such as the Soviet Union, threats today may be posed even by small groups of terrorists. They could attack using a variety of means, including hijacked aircraft or chemical, biological, or nuclear weapons. *QDR 2006* called for improving military capabilities for the direct defense of the United States, including air, missile, and maritime defenses. It also called for DOD attention to the threat of natural disasters such as Hurricane Katrina, and closer DOD cooperation with other Government agencies in dealing with such threats.

In addressing the goal of shaping the choices of countries at strategic crossroads, such as countries in the Middle East, Latin America, and other developing regions, *QDR 2006* called for strong U.S. efforts, supported by U.S. military programs, to help them to achieve democracy and capitalism. *QDR 2006* also called for U.S. efforts to build partnership relations with Russia and India, major powers now in geostrategic transition. It devoted special attention to China because of its size, fast economic growth, importance to the Asian security system, and potential capacity to compete with the United States militarily. *QDR 2006* noted that a goal of U.S. policy is to encourage China to play a constructive and peaceful role in the Asia-Pacific region, to become a partner in addressing common security challenges, and to pursue economic growth and political liberalization in its internal affairs. *QDR 2006* also noted, however, the extent to which China is increasing its defense budget, modernizing its military forces, and developing capabilities that could be used against Taiwan or elsewhere in Asia. Therefore, the United States must maintain strong forces in Asia, preserve and develop partnership relationships with key friends and allies, and improve U.S. military capabilities in communications, intelligence, missile defenses, long-range strike assets, and other important areas.

QDR 2006 emphasized the importance of preventing the proliferation or use of weapons of mass destruction. It singled out North Korea and Iran as countries in pursuit of nuclear systems, and said that in future years, other countries as well as terrorist groups might also seek them. *QDR 2006* recommended strong measures, such as the Proliferation Security Initiative, which is aimed at developing multilateral efforts for tracking and interdicting nuclear materials. *QDR 2006* also called for the United States to be able to respond to WMD proliferation in the event that preventive efforts fail; it declared that, although the United States would use peaceful and cooperative measures whenever possible, it must be capable of employing military force against WMD systems. This mission, said *QDR 2006*, requires the capacity to locate, characterize, and, if necessary, destroy dangerous WMD materials. Such options, said *QDR 2006*, require intelligence and surveillance systems, interdiction capabilities, Special Operations Forces, and other strike assets.

These four priorities mean a change to the force-sizing construct. *QDR 2006* appears to abandon the 1-4-2-1 formula discussed previously in favor of a threefold construct that includes:

- providing for homeland defense
- prevailing in the war on terror and conducting irregular (asymmetric) warfare, including steady-state and surge operations
- remaining capable of conducting and winning two nearly simultaneous conventional campaigns, or just one additional campaign if U.S. forces are already engaged in a large-scale, long-duration irregular campaign.

The main impact of this new formula is to call attention to the important roles the U.S. military now plays in operations against terror. This formulation clearly is intended to be global, rather than linked to specific regions, but the Middle East and adjoining regions will clearly be the main focal points of U.S. military actions in the coming years. A noteworthy feature of the new construct is that it retains the longstanding 2-MTW formula. *QDR 2006* concluded that the existing U.S. military posture will remain adequate for the years ahead, and that neither major force additions nor subtractions are desirable.

Although *QDR 2006* outlined no major changes in the size or basic composition of current U.S. military forces, it did call for improvements and reorientations in a number of *capability portfolios*, the assets from different

Services that together provide capabilities for a specific area of operations. The capability portfolios include:

- joint ground forces
- Special Operations Forces
- joint air forces
- joint maritime forces
- tailored deterrence assets and a new nuclear triad concept
- capabilities for combating WMD
- joint mobility assets
- intelligence, surveillance, and reconnaissance (ISR) and space capabilities
- network-centric assets
- joint command and control.

QDR 2006 derived specific plans and programs for all force components from this emphasis on building improved capability portfolios in specific areas. For ground forces, *QDR 2006* called for the Army to rebalance its posture by creating a total of 42 active combat brigades and 28 National Guard combat brigades, plus 75 active support brigades and 136 Guard/Reserve support brigades. It called for major increases in SOF assets, including a one-third increase in SOF battalions, additional psychological operations and civil affairs units, creation of a Marine Corps Special Operations Command, and more Navy SEAL units. For joint air assets, *QDR 2006* called for development by 2018 of a new land-based Earth-penetrating capability, modernization of existing bombers to support global strike operations, development of a carrier-based unmanned strike aircraft, doubling of unmanned aerial vehicle capability by acquiring more Predators and Global Hawks, extension of F–22 production, and a restructuring of Air Force wings to emphasize long-range strike capabilities. To improve joint maritime capabilities, *QDR 2006* called for a larger Navy fleet with 11 carrier strike groups, accelerated procurement of littoral combat ships, procurement of 8 maritime preposition force ships, an improved riverine capability, and return to a production rate of 2 attack submarines per year.

A variety of additional initiatives were declared in *QDR 2006*, such as:

- develop the capability to deliver precision-guided conventional warheads using Trident submarines
- expand the number of U.S. forces capable of participating in WMD elimination missions

- continue the acquisition of new wide-bodied cargo aircraft to increase U.S. strategic mobility
- develop new technologies to improve ISR capabilities
- acquire new communications systems to strengthen the global information grid
- activate additional Standing Joint Force Headquarters and develop better adaptive planning capabilities
- strengthen DOD capacity to make use of Reserve Component forces for homeland defense, natural disasters, and civil support missions
- improve joint training, transform the National Defense University into a National Security University, and broaden U.S. military language and cultural skills.

QDR 2006 also outlined steps to develop the Defense Department's ability to work with other departments and agencies of the U.S. Government and to cooperate closely with friends and allies abroad, acknowledging that globalization, complex information networks, and new missions make improvements in these areas imperative. In order to achieve greater interagency unity of effort, *QDR 2006* recommended creation of a National Security Planning Guidance process to direct the development of both military and nonmilitary plans and institutional capabilities. In field operations where multiple instruments are employed, it urged greater collaboration between military combatant commanders and civilian chiefs of mission.

QDR 2006 devoted special attention to U.S. capability for stabilization and reconstruction efforts in such countries as Iraq and Afghanistan. It noted that in 2005, the Department of Defense had issued guidance intended to place stability operations on par with combat operations. It asked that the State Department and other Governmental agencies strengthen their capabilities for stabilization and reconstruction missions and called for improved interagency coordination at all levels.

Finally, *QDR 2006* emphasized the need for the United States to work closely with international allies and partners in the coming years, especially NATO and European countries, many of which possess assets and capabilities that could assist U.S. military forces in future operations ranging from combat interventions to stabilization and reconstruction missions. *QDR 2006* praised NATO for such recent steps as creating the NATO Response Force and Allied Transformation Command, accepting leadership of the International Security Assistance Force in Afghanistan, and establishing the NATO Training Mission in Iraq. In addition to supporting further improvements to European combat forces, it called for creation of a NATO stabilization and reconstruction capability and a European constabulary force. It also called for strengthening the military assets of the African Union and for developing a more cooperative Defense Department relationship with the UN Department of Peacekeeping Operations. *QDR 2006* thus expressed the Department of Defense's willingness to work closely with capable friends and allies in the challenging future missions of the Long War.

Taking Stock of the Defense Strategy Literature

The authors discussed in this chapter addressed a wide spectrum of topics regarding future U.S. military forces and capabilities. Some common themes stand out. Since 1999, expeditionary wars have come to dominate the use of U.S. military forces abroad. Three such wars were launched between 1999 and 2003, and as of mid-2006, two have not been concluded. Their major combat operations are over, but their occupation phases are still being performed, and fighting is still going on. The future might produce additional expeditionary wars, or sizable operations that involve joint strikes against specific targets, such as WMD sites, terrorist camps, or rogue governments. Waging war, not just preparing for it as during the Cold War, could be a dominant practice of the U.S. military in the coming years.

Modern expeditionary wars are heavily influenced by nonmilitary factors. While battlefield operations have a military logic of their own, these wars are fought mainly to achieve political goals. Thus, U.S. military operations must be effects-based in a broad sense, aimed at achieving military ends that, in turn, produce political ends. Recent experience also shows that the U.S. military can expect to achieve its battlefield aims by crushing opponents quickly, but that achieving its political aims will not be so easy. Wars are not over until the vanquished agree that they are over and lay down their arms.

Equally difficult is the task of creating a stable political order within an occupied country and across a region. During the 1990s, the United States and its NATO allies used military power to coerce Serbia into accepting imposed settlements in Bosnia and Kosovo. Since then, NATO and EU forces have been deployed in both. Although enemy regimes have been toppled in Afghanistan and Iraq, stable democratic governments have yet to take their place. The entire greater Middle East and nearby regions remain hotbeds of instability without stable security structures. The complex politics of expeditionary wars are not easily mastered, and they do not always yield neat, clean, or permanent solutions. When they are fought, they must be guided not only by wise military planning, but also by wise political planning.

Recent experience validates a number of key Department of Defense decisions since 2000. The old geographic defense perimeters inherited from the Cold War are clearly no longer valid, and DOD has recognized that modern wars might be fought in many unexpected places. Future wars in the greater Middle East and along the vast southern arc of instability are possible; conflicts in Asia, perhaps on the Korean Peninsula or over Taiwan, cannot be ruled out. DOD also was wise to shift from threat-based planning to capability-based planning, seeking to create a flexible portfolio of U.S. military assets to deal with a wide spectrum of potential conflicts. The Defense Department has been slower, however, in developing stabilization and reconstruction capabilities. Knowing whether the current posture will provide a sufficient portfolio for tomorrow's missions requires careful analysis and continuing development of capability-based planning, a more useful tool than such force-sizing constructs as 1-4-2-1.

Defense transformation has thus far been a success in the sense of bringing information-age networks, technologies, and doctrines to U.S. military forces, greatly enhancing their combat power. The physical and operational gap between U.S. forces and opponent militaries will remain large and could even grow as transformation continues. Yet achieving and preserving technological dominance is not the only strategic imperative: an equal imperative is developing the ability to use U.S. military power to achieve U.S. political-military goals, even in the messy wars of the present and the future. This includes winning wars, and also winning the peace that follows; occupation duties, including stabilization and transformation, will have to be performed successfully. A second military transformation may now be required that focuses on very different skills. Striking a balance between preserving technological dominance for high-intensity warfare, while assembling the forces and capabilities needed to prevail in messy near-term conflicts, will present a difficult challenge in the coming years. Moreover, constraints on budgets and manpower mean that priorities will need to be set and difficult decisions reached with wisdom. The more clearly we can see the elephant, the wiser our decisions may be.

Chapter Seven

Seeing the Elephant

This chapter summarizes the main insights we derived from the more than 60 books covered in the previous chapters, in order to offer guidelines about how the United States should view the elephant of modern world affairs, and how it can employ its national security strategy and defense policy to guide the elephant in the future evolution. Here, we try to answer two questions: Does the material in this book add up to a coherent way of viewing the world of the early 21st century, and does it offer guidance about the global role of the United States?

The Elephant Now Can Be Seen Better

Seeing the elephant of world affairs is undeniably a difficult task, far more challenging than it was during the Cold War. Compared to the simple bipolarity and frozen terrain of the Cold War, today's world is significantly more complex and is, moreover, changing rapidly. Globalization, the changing roles of the nation-state and other actors, new political ideologies, shifting security conditions, the hotly competitive world economy, the empowerment of new technologies, transformed military forces, and other trends add to this complexity. The consequence is that our view of the world is obscured by a dense fog, and the signals coming through the fog are often confusing and even downright contradictory at times. As a result, building a theory of today's international system is truly difficult. Many factors are at work, and their interactions are highly complex and multidimensional. There are limits to human knowledge and understanding as we try to see the elephant of today and tomorrow. The elephant is not only in the fog but also is still changing shape. While some things about the current and future world are already known or can be known, there are many other things that are not known or knowable at all. Even the best experts are sometimes confused and often surprised by events. All of us are going to be living in uncertainty for a long time; recognition of this fact should lead to a measure of intellectual humility.

Yet we argue that there are reasons for believing that the elephant of world affairs can now be seen more clearly and accurately than it could only a short while ago. The elephant of the early 21st century has been slowly revealing itself over the past 10 or 15 years, and especially since 2001. It helps that scholars and writers have published books and other studies about the elephant; the books reviewed in this volume are a sample of the sizable literature that has appeared in the Western world. Although each of these books makes an important contribution, none of them by itself gives a view of the entire elephant. But when they are brought together, and their collective themes are assessed, they shed light on the elephant as a whole. Collectively, they create an intellectual history of national security affairs during the past decade and a half.

Fifteen years ago, we were perhaps mostly blind, but today, although we may not fully see and understand the elephant, we are no longer sightless. Additional thinking, research, and writing are necessary to develop the conceptual lenses that will enable us to see with the accuracy that will be required. Continuing analytical work is necessary because the elephant is developing and changing. The intellectual theories of today are doubtless better than those of a decade ago, but if they remain stagnant, they may be rendered anachronistic by the changes that lie ahead in world affairs. This is a time for a continuing, ceaseless quest for truth and prudent judgment.

Summarizing the World Views

The literature seeking to describe this emerging elephant has come in three overlapping waves. The first wave consisted of what we have called neo-Kantian literature, which dominated the first half of the 1990s with books like those by Fukuyama and Huntington and continued with more recent works like those by Keohane and Slaughter. The second wave, which we have called neo-Hobbesian literature, started soon after the first with books by Brzezinski, Mearsheimer, Kaplan, Pfaff, Power, and others. This second wave reflected changing world events, and it affected the attitudes of policymakers in Washington after the middle of the 1990s. The third wave of literature, with its focus on empowerment of nonstate and smaller actors, has amplified themes of both the neo-Kantian and neo-Hobbesian literature. After September 11, 2001, the realization and impact of this empowerment had a profound effect on American national security policy.

We will summarize the main themes of these three waves of literature, starting with the neo-Kantians:

- Francis Fukuyama (1992) and Samuel Huntington (1991) argued that liberal democracies are on the rise and that they form a solid basis for a core of nations that can act together to deal with troubled parts of the world.

- Charles Lipson (2003) explained why and how the democratic peace theory works.
- Thomas Friedman's analysis (2000) was similar to that of Fukuyama and Huntington, but he argued that it is economic globalization, more than democratization, that is strengthening the core and pulling it together.
- Daniel Yergin and Joseph Stanislaw (1998) argued that it was the retrenchment of big government in the 1970s, coupled with a restoration of open markets and free trade, that created the globalization championed by Friedman.
- Robert Gilpin (2000) pointed out that although globalization is likely to spread, it is fragile and depends on constant attention to the political system.
- Jeffrey Garten (1992) argued that it takes more than democracy and globalization to keep the core together; it takes sound management of alliances to overcome trends that might otherwise pull the major liberal democracies apart. Ronald Asmus (2002) describes the case of NATO enlargement in the 1990s that implemented the concepts articulated by Garten.
- Charles Kegley and Gregory Raymond (1994) put the ideas of Asmus and Garten in a larger context by arguing that multipolar great power relations, even including those among nonallies, can result in a stable international system if the powers share values and conduct wise diplomacy.
- Robert Keohane (2002) amplified the great power focus of Kegley and Raymond by arguing that pragmatic negotiations and sound multilateral institutions can help create the global governance needed to underpin globalization.
- Anne-Marie Slaughter (2004) developed Keohane's institutional arguments by stressing the importance of the growing international networks of government officials and their nongovernmental counterparts, and the role that such networks can play in stabilizing the international system.

The neo-Hobbesians of the second wave offered these views:

- Zbigniew Brzezinski (1993) forecast more anarchy and chaos than the neo-Kantians had done, arguing that in the "post-utopian" or post-ideological period, groups would fall back on their own experiences for identity and meaning, and this would result in a lack of common values.

- Samuel Huntington, in his neo-Hobbesian book (1996), took Brzezinski's analysis a step further to argue that the renewed search for identity will lead to greater adherence to traditional cultures, which could well lead to a clash of civilizations.

- John Mearsheimer (2001), focusing on the nation-state system rather than culture, forecast probable great power conflict based on his assessment that nations are inevitably motivated to be aggressive toward one another in an anarchical international system that is unconstrained by world government.

- Ross Terrill (2003) portrayed China as an unstable emerging empire that will face problems to its landward flank and, on its seaward flank, will challenge the United States as it seeks to expand its naval empire.

- Daniel Patrick Moynihan (1993) and William Pfaff (1993) both made use of elements found in Huntington's and Mearsheimer's logic to conclude that ethnic nationalism will be revived as a major force in international affairs and that this will result in interstate conflict.

- Robert Kaplan's neo-Hobbesian view (1993, 2003) was developed from the bottom up, based on his firsthand reporting on poverty and violence in failed states; these, he predicts, will produce postmodern anarchy.

- Samantha Power (2002) sought to explain the causes and consequences of the extreme neo-Hobbesian case of genocide caused by malevolent or failed states unconstrained by the intervention of the rest of the world.

- Bernard Lewis (1996, 2002, 2003) compared the failure of the Middle East to modernize with the modernization experience of the West, which, he argued, resulted in a colonial resentment in Islamic nations that now is focused on the United States.

- Kenneth Pollack's neo-Hobbesian view of developments in both Iraq (2002) and Iran (2004) led him to develop specific recommendations on how to deal with each.

The empowerment theorists of the third wave of literature extended both neo-Hobbesian and neo-Kantian concepts to nonstate actors newly empowered by changes in technology and culture:

- Martin van Creveld (1999) argued that the modern state is in decline, both because some of its functions, such as national defense, have become less important, and because technology now empowers other institutions and international organizations, giving them statelike attributes.
- Alvin and Heidi Toffler (1993) offer a somewhat contrary argument, that the mastery of information technology and knowledge by modern militaries will increase their power and thus that of the nations that employ them.
- Michael O'Hanlon (2004) applied the Tofflers' thesis to space technologies, concluding that current U.S. dominance in this domain will slowly erode as other nations develop both offensive and defensive capabilities in space.
- Kent Calder (1996) applied the Tofflers' argument to Asia, concluding that new technologies and growing economies are empowering those nations, thus creating new challenges, and that the region needs to be rendered stable so that U.S. attention can be turned to the greater Middle East.
- Thomas Friedman (2005) wrote about how Internet-driven economic globalization has empowered individuals, even in nations such as China and India, to create what he called a "flat world."
- Peter Ackerman and Jack DuVall (2000) described how effective strategies and new communications technologies can empower ordinary citizens to use nonviolent means to bring down dictators.
- Jessica Stern (2003) explained how religious intoxication magnified by modern technologies has empowered the resentful Islamists described by Lewis.
- Robert Pape (2005) argued that the motivation of most empowered suicide bombers is not religious but rather political, aimed at defeating foreign occupation.
- Stephen Flynn (2004) highlighted America's many new vulnerabilities that result from the empowerment of terrorist groups.
- Judith Miller, Stephen Engelberg, and William Broad (2001), focusing on one of those technologies, describe how biological agents such as smallpox or anthrax in the wrong hands could create existential threats to civilization.
- Graham Allison (2004) called nuclear technology in the hands of terrorists the most dangerous threat of the current era, but argued that it could be avoided by tough denial policies.
- Moisés Naím (2005) diagnosed the soaring growth of organized crime,

fueled by the demand for illicit goods and by technology, as a significant threat to legitimate governments and thus to global stability.

Having summarized key insights of the books discussed in chapters two, three, and four, we next suggest how these insights can be used together in a more successful effort to see the elephant as a whole.

Blending the Views

The neo-Kantian and neo-Hobbesian theories of the modern world can serve as analytical partners. With changes in politics, economics, and technology, today's world is being driven by powerful dynamics of both progress and peril, producing new opportunities but also new problems, threats, and dangers. The interplay of these dynamics is too complex to be reduced to simple sound bites, slogans, or bumper stickers. Today's world is a highly complex system of many interacting parts that cannot be reflected accurately in narrow, one-way, or deterministic theories of causality. Both neo-Kantian and neo-Hobbesian theories, augmented by empowerment theories, are required if the elephant is to be seen fully. From the perspective of the American policymaker, the mission is to solve the problems identified by the neo-Hobbesian and some of the empowerment authors so that the United States can take full advantage of the opportunities outlined by the neo-Kantian authors.

The sense of hopeful optimism in the neo-Kantian literature was a natural product of the times after Cold War threats had suddenly collapsed and before new dangers had shown themselves. Then the neo-Hobbesian literature began to appear as these dangers gained force. Not surprisingly, U.S. national security strategy and foreign policy reflected this important change in intellectual currents. The Clinton administration started out as mostly neo-Kantian, then shifted to a blend of Kant and Hobbes. The George W. Bush administration leaned heavily on neo-Hobbesian views such as unilateralism after September 11, 2001, but its subsequent calls for democratization in the Middle East showed that it had acquired a neo-Kantian vision of its own. Today's troubles with terrorism and instability in the Middle East lead some to conclude that neo-Hobbesian worries have triumphed and neo-Kantian hopes have faded. However, behind the scenes, neo-Kantian dynamics are still alive and well.

Within the global democratic community, neo-Kantian dynamics predominate for several reasons: democracy and capitalism are flourishing; many countries have or are achieving wealth; security and peace are mostly intact; and multilateralism is common practice. The democratic community, of course, is no monolith. Its "inner core"—the United States and Canada, most of Europe, the wealthy democratic countries of Asia, and some of Latin America—is predominantly neo-Kantian, even though its members face some problems, including terrorist threats and their own internal strains over politics, economics, and security affairs. The "outer core"—which includes most of Latin America, new and less prosperous Asian democracies, and a few democratic outposts elsewhere—faces more serious troubles, including shaky democracy, slow economic progress, and security concerns. Nonetheless, even for this outer core, the situation is better than it was 10 or 20 years ago.

However, a different and less hopeful situation prevails, to a greater or lesser degree, in the countries of the "transition regions." There is a combination of hopeful dynamics and worrisome trends in three major transitional states: Russia, China, and India. These 3 big powers comprise about 40 percent of the world's population, occupy a huge landmass, and are pivotal actors in global and regional geopolitics. Although Russia today is making efforts to adopt democracy, it may be losing ground. Meanwhile, it is regaining momentum toward economic progress as a result of high oil prices, and Russia's leaders have demonstrated their willingness to use oil and gas deliveries to gain political advantage. Meanwhile, it is searching for a new external identity in global politics and struggling with internal tensions in its southern regions. China is making fast economic strides, but it remains governed by its Communist Party, and it has not yet firmly decided upon its future role in Asian and global security affairs. India, a democracy, is making economic progress as market capitalism takes hold in many of its regions. Its future appears bright, but its troubled relationship with Pakistan remains a potential flashpoint for conflict in South Asia. For these reasons, all three countries can be characterized as halfway between the worlds of Kant and Hobbes.

The Middle East and nearly the entire southern arc of instability, plus major parts of sub-Saharan Africa, are mostly ensnared in neo-Hobbesian dynamics. A combination of major troubles—lack of democratization, poor governance, fractious societies, weak economic progress at best and deep poverty at worst, poisonous security affairs, and angry ideologies such as radical Islamic fundamentalism—produces a great deal of fragmentation, chaos, turbulence, and violence.

The empowerment described in chapter four has had a significant impact on both neo-Kantian and neo-Hobbesian dynamics. Empowerment, primarily through technology, gives new strength to the militaries of democratic states, as explained by the Tofflers, and also new opportunities to those oppressed by authoritarian rule, as explained by Ackerman and Duvall. But empowerment has had an even greater impact on the nature of the challenges to liberal democracies, as the books by Stern, Miller, Allison, and Naím highlight.

September 11, 2001, revealed the new challenges created by empowerment, with attacks that were nothing less than a neo-Hobbesian invasion of the inner core of the neo-Kantian sphere. Prior to September 11, the world described by Stern, Kaplan, and Power was seen by most in the developed world as awful, but not as particularly personally relevant: the liberal democracies perceived themselves as safe in their own sphere. When the Clinton administration intervened in the neo-Hobbesian world of the Balkans, some critics described this as "international social work" that was not vital to American interests. After the neo-Hobbesian world "invaded" the neo-Kantian world on September 11, 2001, however, the threat to the United States was clear, and many of those same critics considered intervention abroad to be necessary to further a vital American interest. The entire panoply of Cold War national security concepts and instruments had to be reconsidered. Concepts such as deterrence and arms control seemed anachronistic; new concepts such as preemption and unilateral action took their place. However, many of the policies developed since September 2001 have not been altogether successful.

Five Challenges

The perspectives that are presented in chapters two, three, and four of this book can be used to identify the major national security challenges now facing the United States. Their scope is broader than the challenges of the Cold War. Five such challenges present themselves.

The first challenge is whether the United States can still harness the neo-Kantian opportunities identified by Fukuyama, Huntington, Friedman, and others to capitalize on globalization, expand the number of liberal democracies, and shape the battle of ideas to its favor. Leaving globalization to develop untended will not meet this challenge; the United States must lead this process. The tools to do this are available, as Yergin, the Tofflers, and Ackerman explain. But there are limits, as Kennedy, Kagan, Zakaria, and others point out. To meet this challenge, the United States must maintain a strong defense posture, but it must also take steps to regain its lost status as a role model for the world.

The second challenge is whether the United States can contain, manage, or roll back the transnational neo-Hobbesian threats identified by Lewis, Kaplan, Stern, Power, Miller, Allison, Naím, and others. This is the dark side of globalization. Events in the troubled regions of the world can no longer be seen as isolated from American interests. As portrayed in chapter four, empowered small states or groups of individuals can now directly threaten the United States and its allies with weapons of mass destruction. Traditional concepts such as deterrence that carried the United States through the Cold

War are inadequate for addressing this challenge. A high degree of American engagement in these troubled areas is needed. The American will to engage may be in decline, but the events of September 11, 2001, show that failure to confront these new threats could lead to disaster.

The third challenge is whether great power rivalry can be alleviated, as Kegley and Raymond suggest, or whether instead the search for identity and sovereign interests will lead the great powers to clash, as Huntington and Mearsheimer predict. This concern especially applies to U.S. relations with large states such as Russia, China, and India that are growing economically but whose political directions are somewhat uncertain. If the major powers can cooperate, they can alleviate global dangers. If they fall into competitive rivalry, this could create a huge, potentially insurmountable problem. For the United States to defeat the transnational threats identified by the neo-Hobbesians, it will have to set a high strategic priority on good relations among the great powers.

The fourth challenge is whether the powerful members of the democratic community in North America, Europe, and Northeast Asia can protect their homeland security and also work together to address global problems that lie mostly outside their borders. The great lesson of the past five years is that the United States cannot deal successfully with the neo-Hobbesian world alone. The books by Garten and Asmus suggest that liberal democracies could cooperate more to address this challenge. Most of these threats cannot be settled by military force alone, but will require cooperation in economic aid, police work, shared intelligence, and coordinated public diplomacy. It will also take close cooperation with NATO, the European Union, and Asian and Middle Eastern allies. This challenge involves two problems relating to political will and the capacity of U.S. partners: first, decisionmaking among the liberal democracies will require greater consensus if the United States is to find its partners willing to cooperate, and second, sustained efforts will be required of allies to transform their capabilities.

The fifth challenge is whether the world economy can continue to grow steadily as Yergin suggests, or whether instead dwindling energy supplies and the political disruption discussed by Gilpin will undercut the benefits of globalization. Political stability is built upon the foundation of economic growth and vice versa; either could be upset by excessive competition for energy resources. Globalization must provide benefits for the world's poor, but along with the challenge of poverty in South Asia, Africa, and elsewhere comes associated challenges of poor governance, fast population growth, and social frustration. Failure to address these challenges successfully would greatly add to the dangers facing not just these regions but the entire world.

Together, these five challenges highlight most of the imperatives of global security affairs in the 21st century. If these challenges are handled effectively, the United States and the democratic community may be able to work with Russia, China, and India to bring steady progress to the Middle East and other troubled regions, and the threats of terrorism, WMD proliferation, genocide, and aggression could fade as impoverished regions make steady economic progress. But if these challenges are not handled well, the future could produce disasters: the democratic community could fall apart, the major powers could be at loggerheads, and the southern arc could remain a boiling cauldron, while global terrorism could grow, WMD proliferation accelerate, and poor regions sink into poverty and violence.

A central conclusion stemming from the intersection of neo-Kantian and neo-Hobbesian perspectives is that no single opportunity, problem, danger, or threat holds the key to the world's future. What matters is all of them together and how they interact in the coming years. The spread of democracy and liberty can help enhance peace if they result in governments that respect international norms, but in the Middle East and Latin America that has not always been the case recently. Efforts to promote globalization by integrating more countries into the global economy can help lessen frustrations, but this success will not itself solve underlying security troubles that stem from political and strategic issues. Democracy and economic integration can work together to encourage peace and multination cooperation, but both require a foundation of stable security affairs. The absence of stable security affairs in troubled regions can stall democratic reforms and economic progress, or even prevent them altogether, setting the stage for war.

In the security realm, defeating terrorism, quelling WMD proliferation, and containing rogue states in the Middle East and elsewhere will help lessen today's dangers. But such achievements will not, by themselves, ensure a peaceful future. These dangers are, to a significant degree, symptomatic of deeper problems brought about by how the world is evolving. If global progress toward peace and prosperity is to be achieved, all five challenges will need to be addressed: carefully crafted policies and strategies must help resolve or at least contain them. The United States and its partners have to muster the willpower and resources to address all five challenges. This agenda will be difficult and long-lasting, but defining it, and seeing it in all its elephantine scope, will help establish a framework for shaping U.S. national security strategy in the coming years and decades.

Future U.S. National Security Strategy

Chapter five discussed a number of books that talk about how U.S.

national security strategy should be configured to deal with these and other challenges. The chapter organized these books into several contending schools of thought, 3 of which have shaped U.S. national security policy during parts of the past 15 years.

The traditional conservatives emphasize a U.S. strategy that seeks equilibrium among the major powers. Their strength is their understanding of traditional geopolitics and their willingness to use force if necessary. Their weakness has been inadequate attention to new transnational threats.

The progressive multilateralists emphasize a U.S. strategy that seeks consensual cooperation with close allies such as Europe. Their strengths are their understanding of the value of soft power and of multilateral action. Their weakness may be a reluctance to use force.

The assertive interventionists emphasize a U.S. strategy that employs American muscle and leadership in the Middle East and other turbulent areas. Their strengths include a focus on the new threats and a willingness to use force. Their weaknesses are a disregard for allies and a lack of concern over the limits of military power.

Books discussing the limits of American policy reveal a fourth approach, offshore balancing. It differs from the three schools described above in that it would abandon American forward engagement and significantly draw down U.S. troops from overseas deployments.

No one of these four approaches alone can meet the complex challenges of the future; a combination of the best of these approaches is needed. Below we outline such an approach. This combined approach would have seven strategic features:

- It would recognize that the *primary threat* facing the United States for the next decade or so is weapons of mass destruction in the hands of rogue states or terrorists, as highlighted by Lewis, Stern, Miller and her colleagues, and Allison. This implies the possibility of what *QDR 2006* calls a Long War, analogous to the Cold War, which will be fought primarily by the use of police, good intelligence, diplomacy, ideas, and foreign assistance in addition to occasional use of military force.
- During this long struggle against terrorism, it is understood that, as Lieber and other interventionists recommend, *force* should be used in collaboration with others wherever possible, and unilaterally only if absolutely necessary. Soft power, championed by Nye, is also recognized as a powerful instrument.
- Nurturing healthy relationships among the *great powers* should be a

priority, as recommended by Kissinger and Haass, so that the United States can focus without distraction on the primary threat.

- This approach recognizes that there are *limits* to American power, as suggested by Kennedy, Walt, and others, and that if those limits are consistently exceeded, policies will begin to fail, as will the support of the American people.
- The limits of American power can be compensated for in part by harnessing the strengths of America's *alliances*, as suggested by Garten, Brzezinski, and Asmus.
- *International institutions and networks* must also be strengthened, as suggested by Keohane and Slaughter, with the purpose of addressing this primary threat.
- *Democracy and market economics* should be promoted globally, while recognizing, as Mead and Zakaria point out, that there are limits to how much can be accomplished, and that promoting them without due care could make things worse rather than better.

Using this combined approach, U.S. national security policy would move from assertive interventionism to a new mix of traditional conservatism and progressive multilateralism. It would seek to overcome the limits on alliances discussed by Kagan and Walt, both by convincing allies about the nature of the prime threat to their nations and by assisting them to develop an array of capabilities to deal with the threat. That process is already under way, but to succeed, the United States will need to show greater willingness to listen to the views of allies. The new approach would seek to create a new equilibrium among the great powers, which has been a central focus of the traditional conservatives. That would mean working to defuse problems with China and Russia over Taiwan, Chechnya, and other issues. The new approach would champion the spread of democracy but would also recognize the limits to this campaign and the need to conduct it with cultural sensitivity and more soft power. It would not adopt all of the ramifications of the offshore balancing thesis, but it could support a gradual withdrawal of U.S. troops from Iraq. Finally, the new strategy would be more sensitive diplomatically to the way in which American policies are presented both to the U.S. public and to the rest of the world. It would make more use of what the progressive multilateralists would call soft power and what many in the Pentagon call *strategic communications*. This new approach would give the United States its best chance at successfully meeting the five key challenges it faces internationally.

Future U.S. Defense Strategy

To meet the five challenges derived from the books reviewed in the first three chapters, and to fight what *QDR 2006* called a Long War, U.S. defense strategy needs continued revision. The military's missions have increased dramatically in scope in recent years. The military transformation codified in 2001 focused on high-intensity conflict, as described by Clark and Franks, a form of warfare that relies greatly on the replacement of massed forces with technology. The results were dramatic in Kosovo, Iraq, and Afghanistan, with a force designed to implement the Powell Doctrine of decisive force. But events in these three countries after each war was won indicated that winning the peace would be particularly difficult and would require new military and civilian skills during the stabilization and reconstruction phase of operations. A second military transformation is needed to fight the small, messy wars described by Boot, and to conduct S&R operations as described by Dobbins, Binnendijk and Johnson, and Barnett. That second transformation began in 2005.[1]

These two sets of missions, high-intensity conflict and S&R operations, were captured dramatically in Barnett's book, which described them as Leviathan force and System Administrator force. While the American military will need to perform two types of missions during the Long War, the United States cannot afford two separate forces. As O'Hanlon rightly points out, the rapid rise in defense budgets may soon have to give way to America's growing budget deficits. The 2006 *QDR* and the fiscal year 2007 defense budget proposal still sought to maintain a full spectrum of military capabilities, and as of mid-2006, most tough budget decisions had been postponed. But constrained defense budgets can be expected in the longer term, and even during the past five years, most of the funds spent on defense have gone to defense consumption items such as personnel costs, operations and maintenance, and to the wars in Afghanistan and Iraq. Defense investments in procurement and in research and development have not benefited nearly as dramatically.

The key question for defense policy in the decade ahead is how the United States can fight a Long War that requires a broad array of military capabilities and continue with efforts at military transformation while its defense dollars may be constant or decreasing. There are several possible approaches to this dilemma.

- The United States must get its grand strategy right. Facing a Long War against chaos in the greater Middle East while contending with a hostile Russia or China would create massive difficulties; therefore, reducing differences with the latter two nations would make defense planning easier.

- Accurate cultural intelligence is at a premium. The United States must place a much greater emphasis on human and cultural intelligence, rather than depending so much on technical means of collection.
- America's foreign policies must be shaped to rely on soft power first and on the use of military force only when absolutely necessary.
- More emphasis should be put on preventive action using a combination of tools such as coordinated public diplomacy, economic assistance, and military-to-military programs.
- America's military force must be agile, ready to perform an array of missions, and adaptable to adjust quickly to new needs. Some specialty forces are needed to augment warfighting forces in postconflict operations, but a separate constabulary force is not the answer. Services may need to stretch their capacities and develop more skills that are beyond their traditional domain; for example, naval forces could be helpful in stability operations.
- Relatively more defense dollars may need to be spent on ground forces, Special Operations Forces, and civil affairs. To compensate, purchases of new large battle platforms such as the F–22 and the DDX may need to be stretched out in time. Smaller networked battle platforms such as the Navy's littoral combat ship, the Army's future combat system, and the Air Force's unmanned aerial vehicles all have their place in the new inventory, although not to the exclusion of the larger battle platforms.
- If operations continue at current levels, the Reserve Component will need to continue its shift from a strategic reserve to an operational reserve. Such a shift would be difficult and costly, but it may be unavoidable.
- The Defense Department's civilian partners in other Federal departments and agencies must be trained and deployable for stability and reconstruction missions, so that their skills could allow an earlier end to military engagements; this could save billions of defense dollars.
- Finally, America's alliances need to be strengthened and transformed. Although significant progress has been made, particularly with NATO's creation of Allied Command Transformation and the NATO Response Force, more needs to be done, especially in the area of stability and reconstruction operations and NATO common funding for operations.

The current burden on America's military forces is already great, and it will probably expand during the next decade. There is considerable danger of overcommitment and of overstretching the force. America's national security strategy and diplomacy will need to take these limitations into account, but with wise strategy and policies, the United States can husband its defense dollars and provide security for the American people.

Final Thoughts

This book is an attempt to organize and assess a sampling of the best post–Cold War thinking on national security affairs. It has major gaps and omissions. We have not touched upon such areas as international environmental policy, energy policy, or new transnational threats such as pandemics. For academic readers, much more could be done to tie the books we have reviewed to contending theories of international affairs. Many more non-American authors could be reviewed. Nonetheless, we hope that this volume sheds light on the emerging international system and on America's role in it. We hope that, as a result, our readers can better see the elephant.

Notes

Preface

1. See James M. McPherson, *Battle Cry of Freedom: The Civil War Era* (New York: Oxford University Press, 1988). The phrase *seeing the elephant* was apparently brought to the Civil War from the California Gold Rush of 1849, where it had summed up both the great adventure and the danger of the enterprise: "Those planning to travel west announced they were 'going to see the elephant.' Those turning back claimed they had seen the 'elephant's tracks' or the 'elephant's tail,' and admitted that view was sufficient." From Jo Ann Levy, *They Saw the Elephant: Women in the California Gold Rush* (Norman: University of Oklahoma Press, 1992). The phrase seems to have originated with the folktale of a farmer on his way to market with a wagonload of produce who encountered a circus parade, led by an elephant. His terrified horses bolted, overturning the wagon but, said the farmer, "I don't give a hang, for I have seen the elephant." From "Trail of the '49ers," Central Nevada Emigrant Trail Association, available at <http://ourworld.compuserve.com/homepages/trailofthe49ers/elephant.htm>.

Chapter One

1. Norman Angell, *The Great Illusion: A Study of the Relation of Military Power in Nations to Their Economic and Social Advantage* (London: Heinemann, 1910).
2. Thomas Hobbes, *Leviathan* (Baltimore: Penguin Books, 1968 [original publication 1651]).
3. Ibid., part 1, chapter 13.
4. Ibid.
5. Immanuel Kant, *Critique of Practical Reason* (Cambridge, UK: Cambridge University Press, 1997 [original publication 1788]).

6. Immanuel Kant, *To Perpetual Peace: A Philosophical Sketch*, trans. Ted Humphrey (Indianapolis: Hackett, 2003 [original publication 1795]).

Chapter Two

1. Francis Fukuyama, *The End of History and the Last Man* (New York: Free Press, 1992).
2. Barrington Moore, Jr., *Social Origins of Dictatorship and Democracy: Lord and Peasant in the Making of the Modern World* (Boston: Beacon Press, 1966).
3. Francis Fukuyama, *Trust: The Social Virtues and the Creation of Democracy* (New York: Free Press, 1995).
4. Francis Fukuyama, *America at the Crossroads: Democracy, Power, and the Neoconservative Legacy* (New Haven, CT: Yale University Press, 2006).
5. Samuel P. Huntington, *The Third Wave: Democratization in the Late Twentieth Century* (Norman: University of Oklahoma Press, 1991).
6. Michael W. Doyle, "Kant, Liberal Legacies, and Foreign Affairs, Part I," *Philosophy and Public Affairs* 12, no. 3 (Summer 1983), 205–235; Michael W. Doyle, "Kant, Liberal Legacies, and Foreign Affairs, Part II," *Philosophy and Public Affairs* 12, no. 4 (Autumn 1983), 323–353; Michael W. Doyle, "Liberalism and World Politics," *American Political Science Review* 80, no. 4 (December 1986), 1151–1169; and Michael W. Doyle, "Liberalism and World Politics Revisited," in Charles W. Kegley, Jr., ed., *Controversies in International Relations Theory: Realism and the Neoliberal Challenge* (New York: St. Martin's Press, 1995).
7. Charles Lipson, *Reliable Partners: How Democracies Have Made a Separate Peace* (Princeton, NJ: Princeton University Press, 2003).
8. Ibid., 4.
9. Ibid., 151; see also Lars-Erik Cederman, "Back to Kant: Reinterpreting the Democratic Peace as a Macrohistorical Learning Process," *American Political Science Review* 95, no. 1 (March 2001), 15–31.
10. Thomas L. Friedman, *The Lexus and the Olive Tree* (New York: Farrar, Straus, and Giroux, 1999).
11. The White House, *A National Security Strategy for a New Century* (Washington, DC: The White House, 1997), available at <clinton2.nara.gov/WH/EOP/NSC/html/documents/nssr.pdf>.
12. For example, see Richard L. Kugler and Ellen L. Frost, *The Global Century: Globalization and National Security* (Washington, DC: National Defense University Press, 2001).
13. David Held, Anthony McGrew, David Goldblatt, and Jonathan Perraton, *Global Transformations: Politics, Economics, and Culture* (Stanford, CA: Stanford University Press, 1999).

14. Kugler and Frost.
15. Paul R. Krugman and Maurice Obstfeld, *International Economics: Theory and Practice*, 6th ed. (Reading, MA: Addison-Wesley, 2003).
16. Thomas L. Friedman, *The World Is Flat: A Brief History of the Twenty-first Century* (New York: Farrar, Straus, and Giroux, 2005).
17. Jeffrey E. Garten, *A Cold Peace: America, Japan, Germany, and the Struggle for Supremacy* (New York: Times Books, 1992).
18. Lester C. Thurow, *Head to Head: The Coming Economic Battle Among Japan, Europe, and America* (New York: Morrow, 1992).
19. Ronald D. Asmus, *Opening NATO's Door: How the Alliance Remade Itself for a New Era* (New York: Columbia University Press, 2002).
20. Charles W. Kegley, Jr., and Gregory A. Raymond, *A Multipolar Peace? Great-Power Politics in the Twenty-first Century* (New York: St. Martin's Press, 1994).
21. Daniel Yergin and Joseph Stanislaw, *The Commanding Heights: The Battle Between Government and the Marketplace That is Remaking the Modern World* (New York: Simon and Schuster, 1998).
22. Ibid., 13.
23. Robert Gilpin, *The Challenge of Global Capitalism: The World Economy in the 21st Century* (Princeton, NJ: Princeton University Press, 2000).
24. Robert O. Keohane, *Power and Governance in a Partially Globalized World* (London: Routledge, 2002).
25. Anne-Marie Slaughter, *A New World Order* (Princeton, NJ: Princeton University Press, 2004).
26. Ibid., 10.

Chapter Three

1. Zbigniew K. Brzezinski, *Out of Control: Global Turmoil on the Eve of the Twenty-first Century* (New York: Scribner, 1993).
2. Ibid., ix.
3. Ibid., 162.
4. Samuel P. Huntington, *The Clash of Civilizations and the Remaking of World Order* (New York: Simon and Schuster, 1996).
5. Samuel P. Huntington, "The Clash of Civilizations?" *Foreign Affairs* 72, no. 3 (Summer 1993), 22–28.
6. John J. Mearsheimer, *The Tragedy of Great Power Politics* (New York: Norton, 2001); John J. Mearsheimer, "Back to the Future: Instability in Europe After the Cold War," *International Security* 15, no. 1 (Summer 1990), 5–56.
7. Hans J. Morgenthau, *Politics Among Nations: The Struggle for Power and Peace*, 5th ed., rev. (New York: Knopf, 1978); Kenneth N. Waltz, *Man, the*

State, and War (New York: Columbia University Press, 1959); Kenneth N. Waltz, *Theory of International Politics* (Reading, MA: Addison-Wesley, 1979).

8. Mearsheimer, *The Tragedy of Great Power Politics*, 34.

9. Ross Terrill, *The New Chinese Empire: And What It Means for the United States* (New York: Basic Books, 2003).

10. Ernest H. Preeg, *The Emerging Chinese Advanced Technology Superstate* (Washington, DC: Hudson Institute, 2005).

11. Liah Greenfeld, *Nationalism: Five Roads to Modernity* (Cambridge, MA: Harvard University Press, 1992).

12. Daniel Patrick Moynihan, *Pandaemonium: Ethnicity in International Politics* (Oxford, UK: Oxford University Press, 1993).

13. William Pfaff, *The Wrath of Nations: Civilization and the Furies of Nationalism* (New York: Simon and Schuster, 1993).

14. Robert D. Kaplan, *Balkan Ghosts: A Journey Through History* (New York: St. Martin's Press, 1993).

15. Robert D. Kaplan, *The Coming Anarchy: Shattering the Dreams of the Post–Cold War* (New York: Random House, 2000).

16. George W. Bush, second term inaugural speech, January 20, 2005, available at <http://www.whitehouse.gov/inaugural/>.

17. Samantha Power, *A Problem from Hell: America and the Age of Genocide* (New York: Basic Books, 2002).

18. Resolution 260 (III), Convention on the Prevention and Punishment of the Crime of Genocide, adopted by the United Nations General Assembly, December 9, 1948.

19. Bernard Lewis, *The Middle East: A Brief History of the Last 2,000 Years* (New York: Scribner, 1996).

20. Bernard Lewis, *What Went Wrong? Western Impact and Middle Eastern Response* (Oxford, UK: Oxford University Press, 2001).

21. Bernard Lewis, *The Crisis of Islam: Holy War and Unholy Terror* (New York: Modern Library, 2003). Lewis later wrote that dictatorship should not be mistakenly viewed as the sole political model in the Middle East; indeed, democratic political and social order has put down roots in Iraq and begun elsewhere in the region, but its development will not be easy. Bernard Lewis, "Freedom and Justice in the Modern Middle East," *Foreign Affairs* 84, no. 3 (Summer 2005), 36–51.

22. Kenneth M. Pollack, *The Threatening Storm: The Case for Invading Iraq* (New York: Random House, 2002).

23. For more on Pollack's views on how *The Threatening Storm* influenced the 2003 Iraq War, see Pollack, "Spies, Lies, and Weapons: What

Went Wrong," *The Atlantic* 293, no. 1 (January/February 2004), 78–92; "Mourning After," *New Republic* 230, no. 24 (June 28, 2004), 21–23.

24.   Kenneth M. Pollack, *The Persian Puzzle: The Conflict Between Iran and America* (New York: Random House, 2004).

Chapter Four

1.   Martin L. van Creveld, *The Rise and Decline of the State* (Cambridge, UK: Cambridge University Press, 1999).

2.   For details, see chapter 7, tables 7–6, 7–4, and 7–3, *National Defense Budget Estimates for Fiscal Year 2006*, issued by the Office of the Under Secretary of Defense (Comptroller), April 2005, available at <www.dod. mil/comptroller/defbudget/fy2006/fy2006_greenbook.pdf>.

3.   Alvin Toffler, *Future Shock* (New York: Bantam Books, 1971); and Alvin Toffler, *The Third Wave* (New York: Morrow, 1980).

4.   Alvin and Heidi Toffler, *War and Anti-War: Survival at the Dawn of the Twenty-first Century* (New York: Warner Books, 1993).

5.   Keith Crane, Roger Cliff, Evan Medeiros, James Mulvenon, and William Overholt, *Modernizing China's Military: Opportunities and Constraints* (Santa Monica, CA: RAND, 2005).

6.   Michael E. O'Hanlon, *Neither Star Wars Nor Sanctuary: Constraining the Military Uses of Space* (Washington, DC: Brookings Institution Press, 2004).

7.   Friedman, *The Lexus and the Olive Tree.*

8.   Friedman, *The World Is Flat.*

9.   Ibid., 45.

10.   Peter Ackerman and Jack DuVall, *A Force More Powerful: A Century of Nonviolent Conflict* (New York: St. Martin's Press, 2000).

11.   Kent E. Calder, *Pacific Defense: Arms, Energy, and America's Future in Asia* (New York: William Morrow, 1996).

12.   Jessica Stern, *The Ultimate Terrorists* (Cambridge, MA: Harvard University Press, 1999).

13.   Jessica Stern, *Terror in the Name of God: Why Religious Militants Kill* (New York: Ecco, 2003).

14.   Robert A. Pape, *Dying to Win: The Strategic Logic of Suicide Terrorism* (New York: Random House, 2005).

15.   Ibid., 3.

16.   Ibid., 23.

17.   Ibid., 104.

18.   Stephen Flynn, *America the Vulnerable: How Our Government Is Failing to Protect Us from Terrorism* (New York: HarperCollins, 2004).

19. The United States Commission on National Security/21ˢᵗ Century (Hart-Rudman Commission), *Road Map for National Security: Imperative for Change*, February 2001.

20. Judith Miller, Stephen Engelberg, and William Broad, *Germs: Biological Weapons and America's Secret War* (New York: Simon and Schuster, 2001).

21. See Patricia Coomber and Robert Armstrong, *Coping with an Attack: A Quick Guide to Dealing with Biological, Chemical, and "Dirty Bomb" Attacks* (Washington, DC: Center for Technology and National Security Policy, 2003).

22. Graham T. Allison, *Nuclear Terrorism: The Ultimate Preventable Catastrophe* (New York: Times Books/Henry Holt, 2004).

23. Moisés Naím, *Illicit: How Smugglers, Traffickers, and Copycats Are Hijacking the Global Economy* (New York: Doubleday, 2005).

Chapter Five

1. *A National Security Strategy of Engagement and Enlargement* (Washington DC: The White House, July 1994).

2. William S. Cohen, "New Defense Strategy: Shape, Respond, Prepare," statement to Senate Armed Services Committee, February 3, 1998, available at <www.defenselink.mil/speeches/1998/t19980203-secdef.html. Also see *A National Security Strategy of Engagement and Enlargement* (Washington, DC: The White House, February 1996).

3. *The National Security Strategy of the United States of America* (Washington, DC: The White House, September 2002), available at <www.whitehouse.gov/nsc/nss.pdf>.

4. Henry Kissinger, *Diplomacy* (New York: Simon and Schuster, 1994); Henry Kissinger, *Does America Need a Foreign Policy? Towards a Diplomacy for the 21ˢᵗ Century* (New York: Simon and Schuster, 2001).

5. Henry Kissinger, *A World Restored: Castlereagh, Metternich, and the Restoration of Peace, 1812–1822* (Boston: Houghton Mifflin, 1957).

6. Richard Haass, *The Opportunity: America's Moment to Alter History's Course* (New York: Public Affairs, 2005).

7. Richard Haass, *The Reluctant Sheriff: The United States after the Cold War* (New York: Council on Foreign Relations Press, 1997).

8. Haass, *The Opportunity*, 26.

9. Zbigniew K. Brzezinski, *The Grand Chessboard: American Primacy and Its Geostrategic Imperatives* (New York: Basic Books, 1997).

10. Zbigniew K. Brzezinski, *The Choice: Global Domination or Global Leadership* (New York: Basic Books, 2004).

11. Joseph S. Nye, Jr., *Bound to Lead: The Changing Nature of American Power* (New York: Basic Books, 1990); Paul M. Kennedy, *The Rise and Fall of the Great Powers: Economic Change and Military Conflict from 1500 to 2000* (New York: Vintage Books, 1987).

12. Joseph S. Nye, Jr., *The Paradox of American Power: Why the World's Only Superpower Can't Go It Alone* (New York: Oxford University Press, 2003).

13. Joseph S. Nye, Jr., *Soft Power: The Means to Success in World Politics* (New York: Public Affairs, 2004).

14. Walter Russell Mead, *Power, Terror, Peace, and War: America's Grand Strategy in a World at Risk* (New York: Knopf, 2004).

15. Niall Ferguson, *Colossus: The Price of America's Empire* (New York: Penguin Press, 2004).

16. Ibid., 301.

17. Robert J. Lieber, *The American Era: Power and Strategy for the 21ˢᵗ Century* (New York: Cambridge University Press, 2005).

18. Paul M. Kennedy, *The Rise and Fall of the Great Powers: Economic Change and Military Conflict from 1500 to 2000* (New York: Vintage Books, 1987).

19. See Andrew F. Krepinevich, "Cavalry to Computer: The Pattern of Military Revolutions," *The National Interest* (Fall 1994), 30–42.

20. Kennedy, *The Rise and Fall of the Great Powers*, 515.

21. Paul M. Kennedy quoted in Kwon Ji-Young, "U.S. Faces Challenges on Three Fronts," *The Korea Herald*, October 14, 2005, available at YaleGlobal Online, <yaleglobal.yale.edu/article.print?id=6372>.

22. For budgetary details, see chapter 7, table 7–5 of the *National Defense Budget Estimates for Fiscal Year 2006*, and Congressional Budget Office, *The Long-Term Implication of Current Defense Plans and Alternatives: Detailed Update for Fiscal Year 2006* (Washington, DC: Congressional Budget Office, January 2006). As of September 30, 2004, there were 1,426,836 active-duty personnel, according to the U.S. Department of Defense, Directorate for Information Operations and Reports. See also <www.dior.whs.mil>.

23. Ivo Daalder and James M. Lindsay, *America Unbound: The Bush Revolution in Foreign Policy*, rev. ed. (Washington, DC: The Brookings Institution, 2003, 2005).

24. Ibid., 3.

25. *The 9/11 Commission Report: Final Report of the National Commission on Terrorist Attacks Upon the United States* (Washington, DC: U.S. Government Printing Office, 2004).

26. Samuel P. Huntington, *Who Are We? The Challenges to America's National Identity* (New York: Simon and Schuster, 2004).

27. Robert Kagan, *Of Paradise and Power: America and Europe in the New World Order* (New York: Vintage Books, 2004).

28. Ibid., 3.

29. See David C. Gompert, Richard L. Kugler, and Martin C. Libicki, *Mind the Gap: Promoting a Transatlantic Revolution in Military Affairs* (Washington, DC: National Defense University Press, 1999); also see Daniel S. Hamilton, ed., *Equipping NATO for the 21st Century* (Washington, DC: Center for Transatlantic Relations, 2004).

30. Stephen M. Walt, *Taming American Power: The Global Response to U.S. Primacy* (New York: W.W. Norton, 2005).

31. Ibid., 23.

32. Fareed Zakaria, *The Future of Freedom: Illiberal Democracy at Home and Abroad* (New York: W.W. Norton, 2003).

33. Contributions to this literature include Edward D. Mansfield and Jack Snyder, *Electing to Fight: Why Emerging Democracies Go to War* (Cambridge, MA: The MIT Press, 2005); Samuel P. Huntington, *Political Order in Changing Societies* (New Haven, CT: Yale University Press, 1968); and work by Thomas Carothers, Dankwart Rustow, Robert A. Dahl, Eric Nordlinger, and others.

34. *The National Security Strategy of the United States* (Washington, DC: The White House, 2006).

Chapter Six

1. Budget and workforce data from the 1940s are found in chapter 7 of the *National Defense Budget Estimates for Fiscal Year 2006*.

2. Wesley K. Clark, *Waging Modern War: Bosnia, Kosovo, and the Future of Combat* (New York: Public Affairs, 2001).

3. Benjamin S. Lambeth, *NATO's Air War for Kosovo: A Strategic and Operational Assessment* (Santa Monica, CA: RAND, 2001).

4. Tommy Franks, *American Soldier* (New York: Regan Books, 2004).

5. Data from Secretary of Defense Donald Rumsfeld's news briefings of March 21, 2003, and April 1, 2003. According to the March 2003 news brief, 45 nations were part of the coalition. Notes of the briefings can be found at <www.defenselink.mil/transcripts/2003/t03212003_t0321sd1.html> and <www.defenselink.mil/news/Apr2003/t04012003_t0401sd.html>.

6. Michael R. Gordon and Bernard E. Trainor, *Cobra II: The Inside Story of the Invasion and Occupation of Iraq* (New York: Pantheon Books, 2006), 152–163.

7. Ibid., 163.

8. John Keegan, *The Iraq War* (New York: A.A. Knopf, 2004).

9. Hans Binnendijk, ed., *Transforming America's Military* (Washington, DC: National Defense University Press, 2002).

10. Department of Defense, *Quadrennial Defense Review Report* (Washington, DC: Department of Defense, 2001), available at <www.defenselink.mil/pubs/qdr2001.pdf>.

11. The Joint Chiefs of Staff, *Joint Vision 2020* (Washington, DC: Joint Chiefs of Staff, 2000), available at <www.dtic.mil/jointvision/jv2020.doc>.

12. Department of the Navy, *Naval Transformation Roadmap: Power and Access . . . From the Sea* (Washington, DC: Department of the Navy, 2002), available at <www.oft.osd.mil/library/library_files/document_202_naval_transformation.pdf>; Department of the Army, *Army Transformation Roadmap* (Washington, DC: Department of the Army, 2002), available at <www.oft.osd.mil/library/library_files/document_201_army_transformation.pdf>; Department of the Air Force, *The U.S. Air Force Transformation Flight Plan* (Washington, DC: Department of the Air Force, 2003), available at <www.oft.osd.mil/library/library_files/document_340_AF_TRANS_FLIGHT_PLAN_2003_FINAL_PUBLICLY_RELEASABLE_VERSION.pdf>. The Services' transformation roadmaps are updated annually.

13. See Richard L. Kugler and Hans Binnendijk, "Shaping Future Defense Budgets," *Defense and Technology Paper No. 6* (Washington, DC: Center for Technology and National Security Policy, 2004).

14. Binnendijk, *Transforming America's Military*, xxxi.

15. Hans Binnendijk and Stuart E. Johnson, eds., *Transforming for Stabilization and Reconstruction Operations* (Washington, DC: Center for Technology and National Security Policy, 2004).

16. Douglas A. Macgregor, *Transformation Under Fire: Revolutionizing How America Fights* (Westport, CT: Praeger 2003).

17. Douglas A. Macgregor, *Breaking the Phalanx: A New Design for Landpower in the 21st Century* (Westport, CT: Praeger, 1997).

18. Max Boot, *The Savage Wars of Peace: Small Wars and the Rise of American Power* (New York: Basic Books, 2002).

19. James Dobbins et al., *America's Role in Nation-Building: From Germany to Iraq* (Santa Monica, CA: RAND, 2003).

20. James Dobbins et al., *The UN's Role in Nation-Building: From the Congo to Iraq* (Santa Monica, CA: RAND, 2005).

21. Thomas P.M. Barnett, *The Pentagon's New Map: War and Peace in the Twenty-first Century* (New York: Putnam, 2004).

22. *A National Security Strategy for a New Century* (Washington DC: The White

House, 1997) available at <clinton2.nara.gov/WH/EOP/NSC/html/ documents/nssr.pdf>.

23.   Thomas P.M. Barnett, *Blueprint for Action: A Future Worth Creating* (New York: Putnam, 2005).

24.   See "The Changing Face of War: Into the Fourth Generation," in *Marine Corps Gazette*, 1989.

25.   Michael O'Hanlon, *Defense Strategy for the Post-Saddam Era* (Washington DC: The Brookings Institution, 2005).

26.   Ibid., 72.

27.   Department of Defense, *Quadrennial Defense Review Report 2006* (Washington, DC: Department of Defense, February 6, 2006).

Chapter Seven

1.   Department of Defense, *Directive 3000.05: Military Support for Stability, Security, Transition, and Reconstruction Operations* (Washington, DC: Department of Defense, November 2005), available at <www.dtic.mil/ whs/directives/corres/pdf/d300005_112805/d300005p.pdf>.

Biographies of Authors Reviewed

Peter Ackerman is the founding Chair of the International Center on Nonviolent Conflict. He presently is the Chairman of the Board of Overseers, Fletcher School of Law and Diplomacy, Tufts University, and Chairman of the Board of Freedom House. He also is the founder of Fresh Direct.

Graham Allison is Douglas Dillon Professor of Government and Director of the Belfer Center for Science and International Affairs at Harvard University. In the first Clinton administration, Allison served as Assistant Secretary of Defense for Policy and Plans.

Ronald Asmus is the Executive Director of the Transatlantic Center at the German Marshall Fund for the United States. From 1997 to 2000, Asmus was Deputy Assistant Secretary of State for European Affairs.

Thomas P. M. Barnett is Senior Manager of Enterra Solutions. From 1998 through 2004, Barnett was a Senior Strategic Researcher and Professor in the Warfare Analysis and Research Department at the Center for Naval Warfare Studies at the U.S. Naval War College. From 2001 to 2003, Barnett was the Assistant for Strategic Futures, Office of Force Transformation, at the Office of the Secretary of Defense.

Max Boot is a Senior Fellow in International Security Studies at the Council on Foreign Relations. He is also a contributing editor to the *Weekly Standard* and a weekly columnist for the *Los Angeles Times*.

William Broad writes about science for the *New York Times* and has twice shared the Pulitzer Prize with colleagues there. Covering such topics as outer space, he has worked at the newspaper since 1983 and has written about science for more than two decades, receiving every major journalistic prize in the field.

Zbigniew Brzezinski is a Trustee and Counselor at the Center for Strategic and International Studies and cochairs its Advisory Board with Carla Hills. He is a Professor of American Foreign Policy at the Paul H. Nitze School of Advanced International Studies of the Johns Hopkins University. From 1977 to 1981, Brzezinski was National Security Adviser to President Jimmy Carter.

Kent E. Calder is Edwin O. Reischauer Professor and Director of Japan Studies and the Korea Initiative at the Paul H. Nitze School of Advanced International Studies of the Johns Hopkins University. He is a former Special Adviser to the U.S. Ambassador to Japan.

Wesley K. Clark is a retired General of the U.S. Army and former NATO Supreme Allied Commander. General Clark commanded Operation *Allied Force*, NATO's first major combat action. In 2004, he was a Democratic candidate for President of the United States.

Ivo Daalder is the Sydney Stein, Jr., Chair at the Brookings Institution. He served as the Director for European Affairs at the National Security Council during 1995–1996.

James Dobbins is Director of the International Security and Defense Policy Center at RAND. A career diplomat, he has held senior White House and State Department positions under four Presidents, most recently as the Bush administration's Special Envoy for Afghanistan.

Jack DuVall is the President and founding Director of the International Center on Nonviolent Conflict. His writing includes speeches for Presidential candidates in four national campaigns.

Stephen Engelberg is Managing Editor for Enterprise of *The Oregonian*. He has reported on national security for over a decade and was previously investigations editor for the *New York Times*, where he shared the Pulitzer Prize with colleagues.

Niall Ferguson is Laurence A. Tisch Professor of History at Harvard University. He is also a Senior Research Fellow at Jesus College, Oxford

University, and a Senior Fellow at the Hoover Institution, Stanford University.

Stephen Flynn is the Jeane J. Kirkpatrick Senior Fellow for National Security Studies at the Council on Foreign Relations. During the Clinton administration, he served as Director for Global Issues on the National Security Council.

Tommy Franks is a retired General of the U.S. Army and former Commander of the United States Central Command. He led Operations *Enduring Freedom* and *Iraqi Freedom*.

Thomas L. Friedman is a columnist for the *New York Times*. A three-time Pulitzer Prize winner, he has also served as a financial reporter specializing in news related to the Organization of Petroleum Exporting Countries and oil. He later served as the chief diplomatic correspondent, chief White House correspondent, and international economics correspondent for the *Times*.

Francis Fukuyama is the Bernard L. Schwartz Professor of International Political Economy at the Paul H. Nitze School of Advanced International Studies of the Johns Hopkins University. In 1989, Fukuyama was the Deputy Director of the Policy Planning Staff at the Department of State.

Jeffrey E. Garten is Juan Trippe Professor in the Practice of International Trade, Finance, and Business at the Yale School of Management at Yale University. From 1993 to 1995, Garten was Under Secretary of Commerce for International Trade.

Robert Gilpin is Dwight D. Eisenhower Professor of International Affairs Emeritus at Princeton University. A Fellow of the American Academy of Arts and Sciences, he has been Vice President of the American Political Science Association.

Liah Greenfeld is a Professor in the Political Science Department of Boston University and is coeditor of *Center: Ideas and Institutions*. In the past several years, her research has concentrated on the phenomenon of nationalism and its implications in modern politics, society, and economics.

Richard N. Haass is President of the Council on Foreign Relations. From

2000 to 2003, he was Director of Policy Planning for the Department of State.

Samuel P. Huntington is the Albert J. Weatherhead III University Professor at Harvard University. During 1977 and 1978, he worked at the White House as Coordinator of Security Planning for the National Security Council.

Stuart Johnson is the Deputy Director of the Center for Technology and National Security Policy and Force Transformation Chair of the National Defense University. From 1976 to 1982, he served as principal NATO analyst in the Office of the Secretary of Defense, Program Analysis and Evaluation.

Robert Kagan is senior associate at the Carnegie Endowment for International Peace. He served in the State Department from 1984 to 1988 as a member of the Policy Planning Staff, as principal speechwriter for Secretary of State George P. Shultz, and as Deputy for Policy in the Bureau of Inter-American Affairs.

Robert D. Kaplan is a correspondent to the *Atlantic Monthly*. He has also served as a consultant to the U.S. Army Special Forces Regiment and has been a Senior Fellow at the New America Foundation.

John Keegan is the Defense Editor of the *Daily Telegraph* (London). He spent many years as Senior Lecturer in military history at the Royal Military Academy, Sandhurst, and has been a Fellow at Princeton University and a Professor of History at Vassar College.

Charles W. Kegley, Jr., is the Pearce Professor of International Relations at the University of South Carolina. He has taught at the Georgetown University School of Foreign Service, the University of Texas, Rutgers University (as the Moses and Annuta Back Peace Scholar), and at the People's University of China. He is a member of the Board of Trustees of the Carnegie Council on Ethics and International Affairs.

Paul M. Kennedy is the J. Richardson Dilworth Professor of History at Yale University. He is a former Fellow of the Institute for Advanced Studies at Princeton University and the Alexander von Humboldt-Stiftung, Bonn.

Robert O. Keohane is a Professor of International Affairs at the Woodrow Wilson School, Princeton University. He has served as the Editor of the journal *International Organization* and President of the International Studies Association and the American Political Science Association.

Henry Kissinger is the Founder and Chairman of Kissinger McLarty Associates. He was director of the National Security Council and then Secretary of State during the Nixon presidency. He won the Nobel Peace Prize in 1973.

Bernard Lewis is the Cleveland E. Dodge Professor of Near Eastern Studies, Emeritus, at Princeton University. He was a university teacher until his retirement in 1986; he previously taught at the University of London until 1974.

Robert J. Lieber is Professor of Government and International Affairs at Georgetown University. He has been a consultant to the State Department and for National Intelligence Estimates.

James Lindsay is Vice President and Director of Studies, Maurice R. Greenberg Chair at the Council on Foreign Relations. From 1996 to 1997, he was Director for Global Issues and Multilateral Affairs at the National Security Council.

Charles Lipson is Professor of Political Science and Codirector of the Program on International Politics, Economics, and Security at the University of Chicago. He has also been an officer of the American Political Science Association and editorial board member of *International Organization* and *World Politics.*

Douglas A. Macgregor is an independent defense and foreign policy consultant with Glenside Analysis, Inc. He retired from the U.S. Army as a Colonel in 2004 after 28 years of service, most of which was spent in armor, mechanized infantry, and armored cavalry formations.

Walter Russell Mead is Henry A. Kissinger Senior Fellow for U.S. Foreign Policy at the Council on Foreign Relations. Mead writes regularly on international affairs for the *Los Angeles Times,* where he is a contributing editor.

John J. Mearsheimer is the R. Wendell Harrison Distinguished Service Professor of Political Science and the codirector of the Program on International Security Policy at the University of Chicago. He has been a Research Fellow at the Brookings Institution and a Post-Doctoral Fellow at Harvard University's Center for International Affairs; he is a member of the American Academy of Arts and Sciences.

Judith Miller is an author and a Pulitzer Prize–winning former investigative reporter for the *New York Times*, where she also served as the Washington bureau's news editor and deputy bureau chief. Before joining the *Times*, Ms. Miller was Washington bureau chief of the monthly journal *The Progressive*, contributed regularly to National Public Radio's "All Things Considered," and wrote articles for many publications.

Daniel Patrick Moynihan was a Senator from New York. He held cabinet or sub-cabinet positions under Presidents Kennedy, Johnson, Nixon, and Ford. He also served as Ambassador to India (1973–1975) and as U.S. Permanent Representative to the United Nations (1975–1976).

Moisés Naím is the Editor and Publisher of *Foreign Policy*. He served as Venezuela's Minister of Trade and Industry in the early 1990s.

Joseph S. Nye, Jr., is a University Distinguished Service Professor at Harvard University, where he is also the Sultan of Oman Professor of International Relations and former Dean of Harvard's Kennedy School of Government. He has served as Assistant Secretary of Defense for International Security Affairs, Chair of the National Intelligence Council, and Deputy Assistant Secretary of State for Security Assistance, Science and Technology.

Michael E. O'Hanlon is a Senior Fellow in Foreign Policy Studies at the Brookings Institution. He is a visiting lecturer at Princeton University and a member of the International Institute for Strategic Studies and the Council on Foreign Relations.

Robert A. Pape is Professor of Political Science at the University of Chicago. He has also taught at Dartmouth College and the U.S. Air Force's School of Advanced Airpower Studies.

William Pfaff has written a newspaper column since 1978 for *The International*

Herald Tribune, which is currently published in over 20 countries. From 1972 until 1978, he was Deputy Director of Hudson Research Europe, Ltd., in Paris.

Kenneth M. Pollack is Director of Research, Saban Center for Middle East Policy, and Senior Fellow, Foreign Policy Studies, at the Brookings Institution. During the Clinton administration he was Director for Persian Gulf Affairs, National Security Council.

Samantha Power is a Professor of Practice in Public Policy at Harvard's Kennedy School of Government and a Pulitzer Prize–winning author. She is also Founding Executive Director of the Carr Center for Human Rights Policy at Harvard.

Gregory A. Raymond directs the Honors College at Boise State University. He has been a Pew Faculty Fellow at Harvard University, a consultant to various government agencies, and an Academic Associate of the Atlantic Council.

Anne-Marie Slaughter is Dean of the Woodrow Wilson School of Public and International Affairs and the Bert G. Kerstetter '66 University Professor of Politics and International Affairs at Princeton University. She is a former President of the American Society of International Law and also a Fellow of the American Academy of Arts and Sciences.

Joseph Stanislaw is Cofounder and former Managing Director of Cambridge Energy Research Associates. He was Senior Economist at the Organisation for Economic Cooperation and Development International Energy Agency in Paris and currently serves on the board of the Global Decisions Group and the American University in Paris.

Jessica Stern is a Lecturer in Public Policy and a faculty affiliate at the Belfer Center for Science and International Affairs, Harvard University. From 1994 to 1995, she served as Director for Russian, Ukrainian, and Eurasian Affairs at the National Security Council.

Ross Terrill is an Associate in Research at the Fairbank Center for East Asian Research at Harvard. He has written several books on China, including *Mao: A Biography* (which has been translated into seven languages), *Madame Mao,* and *China in Our Time.*

Alvin Toffler and **Heidi Toffler** cofounded Toffler Associates and serve as cochairs of the firm. Both are Distinguished Adjunct Professors at the National Defense University in Washington and are honorary cochairs of the U.S. Committee for the United Nations Development Fund for Women.

Martin van Creveld is a Professor in the Department of History at the Hebrew University, Jerusalem. He has lectured or taught at almost every strategic institute, military or civilian, in the Western world.

Stephen M. Walt is Academic Dean at the John F. Kennedy School of Government at Harvard University, where he holds the Robert and Renee Belfer Professorship in International Affairs. He has been a consultant for the Institute of Defense Analyses, the Center for Naval Analyses, and the National Defense University.

Daniel Yergin is Cofounder and Chairman of Cambridge Energy Research Associates. He is a member of the U.S. Secretary of Energy's Advisory Board, and he chaired the U.S. Department of Energy's Task Force on Strategic Energy Research and Development.

Fareed Zakaria writes a regular column for *Newsweek* and is a regular member of the roundtable of ABC News' "This Week with George Stephanopoulos" as well as an analyst for ABC News. He serves on the boards of the Trilateral Commission, the International Institute for Strategic Studies, and the Council of Foreign Relations, among others.

Index

About the Authors

Hans Binnendijk is Director of the Center for Technology and National Security Policy and Roosevelt Chair at the National Defense University. He has served on the National Security Council as Senior Director for Defense Policy and Arms Control (1999–2001), as Director of the Institute for National Strategic Studies at the National Defense University (1994–1999), as Principal Deputy Director of the State Department Policy Planning Staff (1993–1994), and as Legislative Director for the Senate Foreign Relations Committee (1981–1985). In academia, he was Director of Georgetown University's Institute for the Study of Diplomacy (1991–1993) and Deputy Director of Studies at the International Institute for Strategic Studies (1988–1991). Dr. Binnendijk received a doctorate in international relations from the Fletcher School of Law and Diplomacy, Tufts University (1972). He is author or coauthor of about 100 publications and reports.

Richard L. Kugler is a Distinguished Research Professor at the Center for Technology and National Security Policy at the National Defense University. A former senior executive in the Office of the Secretary of Defense and Director of the Department of Defense's Strategic Concepts and Development Center in the 1980s, he is a defense planner and strategic analyst with over 30 years of experience in DOD and RAND. His specialties are U.S. defense strategy, global security affairs, and NATO. An operations research analyst and political scientist, he holds a Ph.D. from the Massachusetts Institute of Technology. He is the author of many studies and journal articles and 16 books on defense and security issues.